Russia against the Rest

In this book Richard Sakwa provides a new analysis of the end of the Cold War and the subsequent failure to create a comprehensive and inclusive peace order in Europe. The end of the Cold War did not create a sustainable peace system. Instead, for a quarter of a century a 'cold peace' reflected the tension between cooperative and competitive behaviour. None of the fundamental problems of European security were resolved, and tensions accumulated. In 2014 the crisis exploded in the form of conflict in Ukraine, provoking what some call a 'new Cold War'. *Russia against the Rest* challenges the view that this is a replay of the old conflict, explaining how the tensions between Russia and the Atlantic community reflect a global realignment of the international system. Sakwa provides a balanced and carefully researched analysis of the trajectory of European and global politics since the late 1980s.

Richard Sakwa is Professor of Russian and European Politics at the University of Kent and an Associate Fellow of the Russia and Eurasia Programme at Chatham House. He graduated in History from the London School of Economics and took a PhD from the University of Birmingham. He has published widely on Soviet, Russian and post-communist affairs. Recent books include *Russian Politics and Society* (2008), *Putin: Russia's Choice* (2008), *The Crisis of Russian Democracy: The Dual State, Factionalism, and the Medvedev Succession* (2011), *Putin and the Oligarch: The Khodorkovsky–Yukos Affair* (2014) and *Putin Redux: Power and Contradiction in Contemporary Russia* (2014). His latest book is *Frontline Ukraine: Crisis in the Borderlands*.

D1418748

Russia against the Rest

The Post-Cold War Crisis of World Order

Richard Sakwa

CAMBRIDGE
UNIVERSITY PRESS

CAMBRIDGE
UNIVERSITY PRESS

University Printing House, Cambridge CB2 8BS, United Kingdom

One Liberty Plaza, 20th Floor, New York, NY 10006, USA

477 Williamstown Road, Port Melbourne, VIC 3207, Australia

4843/24, 2nd Floor, Ansari Road, Daryaganj, Delhi – 110002, India

79 Anson Road, #06–04/06, Singapore 079906

Cambridge University Press is part of the University of Cambridge.

It furthers the University's mission by disseminating knowledge in the pursuit of education, learning, and research at the highest international levels of excellence.

www.cambridge.org
Information on this title: www.cambridge.org/9781107160606
DOI: 10.1017/9781316675885

First published 2017

Printed in the United Kingdom by Clays, St Ives plc

A catalogue record for this publication is available from the British Library.

ISBN 978-1-107-16060-6 Hardback
ISBN 978-1-316-61351-1 Paperback

Contents

Acknowledgements

Many people supported and helped me in this project. Elena Chebankova, Andrei Kortunov, Andrej Krickovic, Marlene Laruelle, Maria Lipman, Hugh Miall, or Adrian Pabst, Tatiana Romanova and Elena Shestopal generously shared their time and expertise in reading or talking over part or all of the drafts, and their comments have been invaluable. My colleagues and professional staff at the University of Kent have made the School of Politics and International Relations a congenial and productive place to work, and I am grateful for their support. I am indebted to the academics, specialists and practitioners across the globe who have helped develop the thoughts underlying this work. Conversations and discussions with Russian, Chinese and Western politicians, diplomats, academics and think tank specialists at endless conferences and public events have shaped my thinking. In particular, I would like to thank my friends and colleagues at Chatham House, Carleton University, the Higher School of Economics, Moscow State University, St Petersburg State University, Carnegie Moscow Center, Russian International Affairs Council, East China Normal University, and George Washington University.

I am happy to thank John Haslam at Cambridge University Press for the support and encouragement he has given me in the preparation of this book. It is my pleasure to acknowledge the support of the Research Fund of the Faculty of Social Sciences of the University of Kent, the James Madison Trust, and the European Union's Horizon 2020 research and innovation programme under grant agreement No. 691818. I am grateful to the University of Birmingham for making me an Honorary Senior Research Fellow at what is now called the Centre for Russian, European and Eurasian Studies (CREES), which has provided access to Russian-language electronic materials and a permanent source of comradeship. CREES remains a community of scholars committed to the best practices of 'bourgeois objectivity', and I am proud to be part of that tradition. As an Associate Fellow of the Russian and Eurasian Programme at Chatham House I am part of a continuing debate, which although at times sharp remains (mostly) collegial and scholarly. This also applies to my membership of the Valdai International Discussion Club, which provides an invaluable platform for politicians, practitioners and international scholars to examine common problems and concerns. As always, David Johnson's Russia List (JRL) has been of immeasurable help in keeping up with facts and opinions, and I am indebted to him for his arduous and continuing commitment to covering the contradictions and complexities of Russian life. Russian studies would be immeasurably poorer without his indefatigable work.

I have the good fortune to be part of an international community of scholars dedicated to the study of Russia and global issues, creating a network of colleagues and friends too numerous to list. Naturally, any omissions or mistakes are my sole responsibility. This book is written in the spirit of enquiry, critique and problematisation. Through dialogue, I believe we may achieve something approximating the truth.

Richard Sakwa
Canterbury, March 2017

Abbreviations

AA	Association Agreement (with the EU)
ABM	Anti-Ballistic Missile
AIIB	Asian Infrastructure Investment Bank
APR	Asia-Pacific region
ASEAN	Association of East Asian Nations
BMD	ballistic missile defence
BRI	Belt and Road Initiative
BRICS	Brazil, Russia, India, China and South Africa
CFE	Conventional Forces in Europe (treaty)
CFSP	Common Foreign and Security Policy
CIS	Commonwealth of Independent States
CMEA	Council for Mutual Economic Assistance (Comecon)
CoE	Council of Europe
CSCE	Conference on Security and Cooperation in Europe (now OSCE)
CSDP	Common Security and Defence Policy
CSTO	Collective Security Treaty Organisation
DCFTA	deep and comprehensive free trade area
EaP	Eastern Partnership
EAS	East Asia Summit
ECHR	European Convention on Human Rights
ECtHR	European Court of Human Rights
EDA	European Defence Agency
EEAS	European External Action Service
EEU	Eurasian Economic Union
ENP	European Neighbourhood Policy
ERI	European Reassurance Initiative
EST	European Security Treaty
EU	European Union
GDP	gross domestic product
IMEMO	Institute of the World Economy and International Relations
IMF	International Monetary Fund

INF	Intermediate-Range Nuclear Forces (Treaty)
JCPOA	Joint Comprehensive Plan of Action
MAD	mutually assured destruction
MSR	Maritime Silk Road
NAM	non-aligned movement
NATO	North Atlantic Treaty Organization
NIEO	New International Economic Order
NPT	New Political Thinking
NRC	NATO-Russia Council
OBOR	One Belt One Road
OECD	Organisation for Economic Cooperation and Development
OSCE	Organisation for Security and Cooperation in Europe (previously CSCE)
PACE	Parliamentary Assembly of the Council of Europe
PCA	partnership and cooperation agreement (with the EU)
PfP	Partnership for Peace
PJC	Permanent Joint Council
PPP	purchasing power parity
R2P	responsibility to protect
RCEP	Regional Comprehensive Economic Partnership
SCO	Shanghai Cooperation Organisation
SDI	Strategic Defence Initiative (star wars)
SEEC	Supreme Eurasian Economic Commission
SPIEF	St Petersburg International Economic Forum
SREB	Silk Road Economic Belt
START	Strategic Arms Reduction Treaty (talks)
TPP	Trans-Pacific Partnership
TTIP	Transatlantic Trade and Investment Partnership
UK	United Kingdom
UN	United Nations
UNSC	United Nations Security Council
US	United States
USSR	Union of Soviet Socialist Republics
WTO	World Trade Organization

Introduction

When George Orwell coined the term 'cold war' in an article in *Tribune* in October 1945, he could hardly have imagined that seventy years later we would still be discussing whether the term was the right one to describe the renewed period of confrontation between Russia and the West.[1] The intervening period saw the 'first' Cold War starting soon after the end of the Second World War until the fall of the Berlin Wall in 1989, followed by the twenty-five years of the 'cold peace', which gave way to what some call the new Cold War. The nuclear balance helped prolong indefinitely a 'peace that is no peace', as Orwell put it. In 2014 the European security system established in the wake of the Cold War collapsed in a spectacular manner. It turned out that for a quarter of a century Europe had been living in an extended period of indeterminacy, caught between the continuation of old institutions and practices while new structures and ideas failed to flourish. In those years none of the fundamental problems of European security had been resolved. The failure to create a genuinely inclusive and comprehensive peace order encompassing the whole continent gave way to renewed confrontation and divisions.

Europe once again resumed its apparently interminable 'civil wars'. The conflict in Ukraine exposed the underlying tensions in the European order, and starkly revealed that the security system established at the end of the Cold War was not working. There had long been indications that all was not well, but the collapse of Europe 'whole and free' came as a shock to many. It is easy to blame one side or the other, but instead this book aims to 'problematise' the 'new Cold War', which I will argue is just part of a much larger shift in global politics. The standard definition of 'problematise' is 'Make into or regard as a problem requiring a solution'; in other words, to make something problematic, and that is precisely the aim here. Problematisation was central to Michel Foucault's 'search for truth'; the way that historical developments and their interpretations have

---

[1] George Orwell, 'You and the Atomic Bomb', *Tribune*, 19 October 1945.

1

been reflected upon.[2] I question much of the standard commentary and instead interrogate what too often is regarded as axiological – truths taken as axiomatic and not susceptible to questioning and challenge. This has given rise to a hermetic (closed) style of thinking, which in the end, as René Girard describes so well, leads to an escalation of extremes.

I will examine how various practices come to create a distinctive set of international relations. These practices and the accompanying views were shaped in interaction with each other, but the fundamental dynamic is the enlargement of the apparently victorious Western system, the radicalisation that took place as a result, and Russia's reactions to this expansion and radicalisation. Enlargement meant simply a scaling up of what already existed, whereas successive Moscow leaderships have called for a transformation of global politics. The Cold War ended without a formal peace conference, but by 1989 was clearly over. The last Soviet leader, Mikhail Gorbachev, adopted a genuinely transformative programme of change on coming to power in March 1985. He was inspired by the ideas of Alexander Yakovlev, the Politburo member responsible for ideology during perestroika who is known as the 'godfather of glasnost'.[3] The two understood that the Soviet Union confronted some fundamental challenges, and although it could muddle through, it was faced with declining economic growth, a range of negative social indicators, and the enormous financial burden of confrontation with the West. However, it was not primarily material factors that precipitated the New Political Thinking (NPT) but a reborn idealism that a transformation of international politics was possible. The programme of perestroika (restructuring) became increasingly radical, which by 1989 had effectively dissolved the communist system.

Gorbachev's ambition to transform international politics through the NPT represented a fundamental rethinking of the structural dynamics of international politics.[4] This was a positive politics of transcendence that sought to make the end of the Cold War a common victory, not only of the great powers but for all the countries trapped in between. It drew on the long struggle in Western countries to overcome the 'arms race' and the militarised opposition of the two blocs in Europe and the world.[5]

---

[2] Michel Foucault, 'Polemics, Politics and Problematizations', interview with Paul Rabinow in May 1984, in Paul Rabinow (ed.), *Essential Works of Foucault*, Vol. 1, *Ethics* (New York, The New Press, 1998), pp. 111–20.

[3] Richard Pipes, *Alexander Yakovlev: The Man who Saved Russia from Communism* (DeKalb, Northern Illinois University Press, 2015).

[4] M. S. Gorbachev, *Perestroika: New Thinking for Our Country and the World* (London, Collins, 1987).

[5] Matthew Evangelista, *Unarmed Forces: The Transnational Movement to End the Cold War* (Cornell, Cornell University Press, 2002).

In his speech to the United Nations (UN) on 7 December 1988 Gorbachev effectively declared the Cold War over. He argued that '[f]urther world progress is now possible only through the search for a consensus of all mankind, in movement toward a new world order'.[6] In his speech to the Council of Europe (CoE) in Strasbourg on 6 July 1989 Gorbachev spoke of a 'common European home' stretching from the Atlantic to the Pacific, thus giving voice to the aspiration for pan-European unity that remains to this day in the guise of 'Greater Europe'.[7] The tumultuous events of 1989 were a consequence of this fundamental policy shift. The partially free parliamentary elections of 4 June 1989 in Poland gave the opposition a decisive victory, and in September the country elected its first post-war non-communist prime minister. In the following months the East European communist regimes crumbled one after another, with the Berlin Wall coming down on 9 November. A certain Vladimir Putin, a relatively low level Soviet security (KGB) official, watched these events with alarm from his posting in Dresden.[8] Although he missed the heady excitement of perestroika at home, he nevertheless absorbed the fundamental ideas of the NPT and the principles of perestroika. The fate of the two Germanys was the subject of the Malta summit between the American president George H. W. Bush and Gorbachev in December 1989, followed in later months by controversial discussions over whether a united Germany would join the North Atlantic Treaty Organization (NATO) in whole or in part.[9]

The Malta summit represents the symbolic end of the Cold War.[10] The old order born of the Yalta summit in February 1945 was irrevocably shattered, and the two leaders came together to chart what Bush later called the 'new world order'. The old bloc politics was dissolving and it seemed that everything was possible. Eastern Europe regained its liberty after years of complex servitude, and the Soviet Union embarked on an unprecedented political and social experiment. Gorbachev's urge to transcend the Cold War did not come out of the blue but had been shaped by years of questioning and debate within the Soviet Union, notably in some

---

[6] 'Gorbachev's Speech to the UN', 7 December 1988, https://astro.temple.edu/~rim merma/gorbachev_speech_to_UN.htm, last accessed 26 May 2017.

[7] Mikhail Gorbachev, 'Europe as a Common Home', Address to the Council of Europe, Strasbourg, 6 July 1989, www.cvce.eu/content/publication/2002/9/20/4c021687-98f9-4 727-9e8b-836e0bc1f6fb/publishable_en.pdf, last accessed 26 May 2017.

[8] Vladimir Putin, *First Person: An Astonishingly Frank Self-portrait by Russia's President Vladimir Putin*, with Nataliya Gevorkyan, Natalya Timakova, and Andrei Kolesnikov, translated by Catherine A. Fitzpatrick (London, Hutchinson, 2000).

[9] The period is analysed in detail by Raymond L. Garthoff, *The Great Transition: American-Soviet Relations and the End of the Cold War* (Washington, Brookings Institution Press, 1994).

[10] Robert Service, *The End of the Cold War* (London, Pan, 2016), pp. 416–26.

of its leading research institutions such as the Institute of the World Economy and International Relations (IMEMO).[11] This ferment gave rise to the NPT, the view that the Union of Soviet Socialist Republics (USSR) and the West could not only coexist peacefully, but that ultimately a global order based on cooperative and even amicable geopolitical and ideological pluralism was possible. This was the view that inspired Gorbachev when he launched perestroika, and which shaped his actions at the Malta summit.[12] In the event, rather than registering a positive transcendence of the Cold War, little more than a power shift took place.[13]

The promise of 1989 for Gorbachev and later Russian leaders was an entirely new logic of power in Europe and the world. It appeared that there was a unique opportunity not only to overcome the specific forms of Cold War confrontation but to transcend the logic of ideological conflict that had given rise to it in the first place. This would for the first time allow the unification of the whole continent from Lisbon to Vladivostok as a new political community of free nations, while transforming the quality of global affairs and the character of the international system. Instead, as this book will demonstrate, this new peace order folded in on itself and incorporated so much of the earlier institutional and moral baggage that in the end it reproduced the logic of conflict. That is why the term 'Cold War' has returned. It describes elements of the confrontation in Europe and great power conflict today, although it fails to capture the broader shifts in the international system.

Four key processes shape the discussion in this book. The first is the failure to achieve a transformed and inclusive peace order after 1989. This generated tension long before Putin came to power in 2000. Two contrasting narratives came into conflict. For the West, nothing needed to change. The institutions and ideas of the Atlantic community had effectively won the Cold War, demonstrating the technical and ideological superiority of the Western order. All that was required was for Russia to join the expanded Western community. The door was indeed wide open, but for successive Russian leaders the terms were not right. This was made clear by Boris Yeltsin in the 1990s, in an incoherent and contradictory manner, and by Putin ultimately rather more forcefully. The West invited Russia to join an *expanded* Atlantic community, but Russia sought

---

[11] Nick Bisley, *The End of the Cold War and the Causes of the Soviet Collapse* (Basingstoke, Palgrave, 2004).

[12] For an overview of the evolution in Gorbachev's thinking, see Archie Brown, *The Gorbachev Factor* (Oxford, Oxford University Press, 1996).

[13] Joshua R. Shifrinson, 'The Malta Summit and US–Soviet Relations: Testing the Waters Amidst Stormy Seas. New Insights from American Archives', www.wilson center.org/publication/the-malta-summit-and-us-soviet-relations-testing-the-waters-a midst-stormy-seas, last accessed 26 May 2017.

to join a *transformed* West and a reconfigured Europe, goals which remain active to this day. In other words, Russia was offered membership of the Historic West, but joining would have entailed changing some fundamental elements of its historic identity. Instead, Russia assumed that the prize of Russian membership would have been of such epochal significance that the Historic West would readily transform itself into something else, which in Moscow's view would have become a Greater West. For Gorbachev, who did so much to overcome the division of Europe through the NPT, the end of the Cold War represented a moment when the Soviet Union (and later, the Russian continuer-state) would together with the West create a new political community as equal founding members.

The same idea was at work in Europe. Gorbachev's vision of a common European home was countered by Bush's idea of an enlarged 'Europe whole and free'.[14] The two positions were complementary but not the same, and what began as a difference of emphasis would ultimately turn into a conceptual and practical gulf. Gorbachev and his successors sought to establish a new form of European continentalism, based on unity in diversity and ideational and institutional pluralism. For the Atlantic powers, the issue was unification based on the normative vindication of the anti-communist revolutions of 1989. In value terms, the emphasis was on human rights, democracy and genuine constitutionalism accompanied by Russian integration into the existing Western-led liberal order and its institutions. Both perspectives articulated variations on the same theme, but some sort of overarching reconciliatory framework was required. It is this intangible but essential element that was missing in the cold peace years. The concept of 'Europe whole and free' represented a call to liberate the 'captive nations' of Europe, and this in essence is precisely what Gorbachev achieved through the withdrawal of Soviet power and the dismantling of the Soviet bloc. Even though Russia took the lead in withdrawing from the Soviet Union, precipitating its disintegration in December 1991, Moscow always considered this a rather different process (except for the three Baltic republics, forcibly incorporated into the USSR in 1940 and again in 1944). It would require a long period of state and nation building for the successor states to become established and to create a new model of relations between themselves. Successive Russian leaders, at first mildly and then more forcefully, argued that it would be inappropriate to impose the political solutions devised for another era and in a different set of circumstances onto a wholly different

---

[14] George H. W. Bush, 'A Europe Whole and Free: Remarks to the Citizens in Mainz, Rheingoldhalle, Federal Republic of Germany', 31 May 1989, http://usa.usembassy.de/etexts/ga6-890531.htm, last accessed 26 May 2017.

historical community, the legatees of the Mongol occupation, Muscovy, the Russian Empire and then the Soviet Union.

This gave rise to the second process, a divergence in practices. A difference of intellectual emphasis became a political division, and the gulf between the two positions came to define the new era of confrontation. The Bush formulation inserted an expansionary dynamic (the enlargement of the victorious Atlantic community) into the end of the Cold War; whereas Gorbachev and successive Russian leaders sought to exploit the opening to transcend the conflict in its entirety and to gain some historical space to devise native-grown solutions rather than accepting solutions devised elsewhere. The enlargement agenda came into conflict with the transformative view. Later, the expansive version, in the form of NATO and European Union (EU) enlargement, was radicalised by the newly free countries hedging (some would say over-balancing) against a possible recrudescence of Russian power. However, by denying the logic of transcendence, they precipitated the result that they sought to avert. Europe could not be 'whole and free' if Russia was effectively excluded. It was offered associate membership of an existing enterprise (what I shall call the Historical West), but Russia's enduring aspiration was to become a founder member of a transformed Greater West. An analogous process was at work in Europe, where Russia was offered a 'strategic partnership' with the smaller or core Europe, as institutionalised in the EU, but it always favoured the transformative and pluralistic creation of a Greater Europe, in which it would be at its origins a founder and core member. The idea of Greater Europe displaces the monist idea of the EU as the sole representative of Europe in favour of a more plural model, in which the EU would be part of a broader pan-European community. Both the Greater West and Greater Europe ideas are based on a dialogical approach to politics – the view that engagement transforms both subjects. Instead, the West tried to stay the same and enlarge; while Russia was to change to reflect the assumed new power and normative realities.

The Russian stance had geopolitical connotations, but it was inspired by a normative commitment to a transformed model of international relations, which would ultimately transcend the competitive spatiality inherent in geopolitics. Instead, a different concept of European and global spatiality predominated. The Western insistence on transcendent 'values' rendered them by definition a property of the enlarging Atlantic community. Instead of defining democratisation as a common challenge, it became seen as the ideological arm of an expansive power system. This provoked a range of adverse reactions in Moscow, and in the end Russia reacted by adopting a policy of resistance to what was considered a hegemonic power system that asserted its values not as an autonomous good but as part of the enlarging power system. The assertion of a values-based foreign policy came to be seen as a way of denigrating the interests and the political subjectivity of the entity on which the values are projected. As we shall see, it was not that Russia repudiated the values, but the political order in which they were framed. The expansion of a universal value system denigrated the traditional state-centric model of international relations and was perceived as a threat not only to Russia's status as a great power, but to its security and very existence as an independent subject of international politics.

The problem was compounded by the tension between the proclaimed values of the Atlantic order and its practical manifestations. This can be formulated as the gulf between principles and practices (the problem of 'double standards'). This provoked what this book will call Russia's neo-revisionism – a critique of Western practices in defence of the universal proclaimed principles. Just as Russia had long positioned itself as the defender of the 'true Europe' against the alleged degenerate actual version,[15] Russia today claims to be the exponent of genuine European values that it asserts the West as a whole has lost. Naturally, this presumptuous claim is rejected by the West. For Russia the assertion of some sort of distinctive value system is broader than a return to obscurantist conservatism but part of the larger reassertion of cultural and civilisational pluralism and diversity. Contemporary Russian conservatism is a complex phenomenon, and at its most creative draws on an authentic Russian tradition derived from Vladimir Solovyov's thinking about the unity of the one and the many, with the potential to enrich the liberal tradition globally. The values challenge is also a challenge to the type of hegemony that was established at the end of the Cold War. We shall examine the degree to which Russian complaints and assertions were justified, and the no less important question of whether they are justifiable. While Russian grievances may well have a basis in genuine concerns, this is not the same as arguing that Moscow's responses are justifiable.

This brings us to the third element, the character of the post-Cold War international system. The demise of the Soviet Union ended the bipolar order that predominated in the Cold War, and established America's unipolar hegemony. The unprecedented dominance of the Atlantic system provoked its radicalisation. In the early 2000s the ideology of American leadership and exceptionalism became more sharply delineated as American primacy and global hegemony was consolidated. This was accompanied by the extension of the rule-based system of international order proclaimed by liberal theory, but the tension with hegemonic American leadership was not

[15] Iver B. Neumann, *Russia and the Idea of Europe: A Study in Identity and International Relations* (London, Routledge, 2016).

resolved. From Moscow's perspective, the velvet glove of liberal order was hidden in the mailed fist of the Atlantic power system. In Europe, the EU also consolidated its hegemony, and its normative power became entrenched in a dynamic process of enlargement in the former Soviet bloc countries and the Baltic republics until it came up against resistance in the Balkans and the new Eastern Europe (the former Soviet republics). The various crises besetting the EU brought the long-standing debate about *finalité* back into focus, the question of an ending in terms of physical space and the ideological claim that the EU represented the only 'true' Europe. The expansive claims and practices of the EU in the end provoked confrontation with Russia, an outcome that few had predicted amidst all the talk of 'strategic partnership'. In the cold peace years neither Russia nor any other power was in a position to balance against the dominance of the American-led power system. Russian politicians repeatedly talked of the need to establish a multipolar system, but only after 2012 (when Putin returned to serve his third term as president) did Russia really try to create a more plural international system. Working with China and other allies, the rudiments of an anti-hegemonic 'post-Western' alignment took shape.

The fourth element is developments within Russia itself. Russia's domestic politics are not the focus of this book, but some discussion here and later provides context for foreign policy developments.[16] Liberals argue that foreign policy reflects the character of domestic politics, a claim rejected by most realists. In the Russian case, all leaders irrespective of the degree to which they may be democratic believe that the country is a great power by right.[17] Social reality may well be constructed, but certain themes endure.[18] The chaos and governmental weakness of the 1990s meant that in foreign policy Russia was not able to do much to assert its concerns. The Russian vision of international relations could be safely ignored, but once state capacity and a functioning economy were restored in the 2000s, the inadequacy of the post-Cold War settlement was exposed. In the absence of an overarching peace order in which Russia was a constituent member, Russia became more assertive. This in all likelihood would have been the case even if Russia had become a splendidly functioning democracy; but of course it was not, and this rendered its resistance normatively questionable. The 1990s laid the foundations for democratic capitalism, but of a peculiar

---

[16] For a discussion of domestic developments, see Richard Sakwa, *Putin Redux: Power and Contradiction in Contemporary Russia* (London and New York, Routledge, 2014).

[17] Iver B. Neumann, 'Russia as a Great Power, 1815–2007', *Journal of International Relations and Development*, Vol. 11, 2008, pp. 128–51.

[18] Ted Hopf, *Social Construction of Foreign Policy: Identities and Foreign Policies, Moscow, 1955 and 1999* (Cornell, Cornell University Press, 2002).

sort. A small group of so-called oligarchs appropriated much of the economy, and effectively took over the state. In the regions, democratic elections allowed criminals and bandits to take over swathes of territory. The economy underwent an unprecedented peacetime collapse, shrinking by over 40 per cent. Living standards plummeted and some 40 per cent of the population fell into poverty. Above all, the gulf between an autonomous political regime and the institutions of the constitutional state became apparent from the very beginning.[19] The regime, in the form of the presidency and its allies, suborned the institutions of the constitutional state, above all the independence of the courts, the inviolability of private property and free and fair elections. The gulf between the administrative regime and the constitutional state was already evident in the 1996 presidential election, when Yeltsin was re-elected for a second term with the support of American advisers. Accountability mechanisms were weak, and effective legislative and judicial oversight over the executive was lacking, especially in the absence of effective budgetary powers by the legislature.

In the 2000s accountability mechanisms were further eroded, but in compensation the autonomous power of the oligarchs and wilful regional governors was curbed. Putin took advantage of the commodity boom of the early twenty-first century to consolidate a system that shared part of the windfall energy rents with the population. Standards of living rose and the economy boomed, until brought back to earth by the global financial crisis of 2008. Russia quickly recovered from the 9 per cent fall in gross domestic product (GDP) of 2009, but thereafter growth was at best sluggish. The inadequacies of the bureaucratised state capitalist model were evident well before the multiple crises of 2014, when the oil price fell sharply and sanctions were imposed in response to Russia's intervention in Ukraine. There was a widening gap between the 'system' of constitutional institutions (notably elections, parliament and the judiciary) and the *sistema*, the network of relationships and dependencies within the regime.[20] Nevertheless, the Putin administration now had the resources and will to articulate its frustrations about the post-Cold War order, and to assert more forcefully its narrative about global politics. As will be described later, Russian foreign policy went through four main stages: the enthusiastic *Atlanticism* of the early 1990s; the more sceptical emphasis on

---

[19] Richard Sakwa, 'The Regime System in Russia', *Contemporary Politics*, Vol. 3, No. 1, 1997, pp. 7–25; Richard Sakwa, 'The Dual State in Russia', *Post-Soviet Affairs*, Vol. 26, No. 3, July–September 2010, pp. 185–206; Richard Sakwa, *The Crisis of Russian Democracy: The Dual State, Factionalism and the Medvedev Succession* (Cambridge, Cambridge University Press, 2011).

[20] Alena V. Ledeneva, *Can Russia Modernise?* Sistema, *Power Networks and Informal Governance* (Cambridge, Cambridge University Press, 2013).

multipolarity and the return to a type of *competitive peaceful coexistence* in the late 1990s; Putin's *new realism* of the 2000s, which sought once again to establish an effective relationship with the Atlantic system but became a period of increased alienation; culminating in the fourth phase from 2012, *neo-revisionism*, a sustained pushback against Western hegemonic practices, if not against the values that sustain them.

The fundamental goal of this book is to explain how Europe and the world went full circle, and ended up where it began – in a situation of confrontation and new lines of division. The difference now is that the international system has evolved, and the balance of global power has changed. Russia became relatively isolated in Europe and *vis-à-vis* the Atlantic system, accompanied by elements of the Cold War nuclear confrontation and arms race, the militarisation of politics, harsh rhetoric on all sides, and conflict and competition in regional affairs. However, on a global scale Russia was never so active or important, shaping developments in the Middle East while forging a network of partnerships and strategic alignments with China and other states to create an alternative to the Atlantic power system. But even here, in a harshly competitive international system, Russia still faced a challenging economic and security environment. This is why the book is called *Russia against the Rest*, not to suggest that Russia is alone and without allies, but to highlight Russia's struggle over time to articulate and assert its vision of global politics and its place in the international system.

1   Cold War to Cold Peace

Competing post-Cold War narratives have taken on the character of foundational myths. A political myth is a way of freezing a moment in time and imbuing it with permanent significance. A myth in this context is not a falsehood, but a fiction or constructed narrative that provides a certain interpretation of the evidence. In this case, the various sides cannot agree even on the basic facts, let alone share common interpretive positions on the framework for a sustainable security order. The Russian narrative asserts that at the end of the Cold War the country was not able to join the victor's club on satisfactory terms. By contrast, the Western view stresses that the Atlantic community made strenuous efforts to engage with the much diminished Russia to make it part of an extended security community. If Russia's ambitions exceeded its capacities, and established a set of terms that were incommensurate with its reduced status and power, then that was its problem. Until Russia had completed its systemic transformation into a liberal democracy the country represented a threat to its neighbours and global order, and its membership of transformed institutions threatened to weaken their normative foundations. The Russian response was that systemic transformation was a domestic matter, but in structural terms it had enduring national interests and global concerns that existed independently of any domestic transformation and should be respected by its international partners. Regimes would come and go, but the interests of the state were trans-historical and demanded respect. In other words, the mainstream Russian position distinguishes between systemic issues, the nature of the domestic regime, and structural factors, the interaction of sovereign states in the international system. This view is remarkably consistent and shared in one way or another across the political spectrum, with the exception of radical Western-centric liberals.[1] The

---

[1] On the consistency of Russian narratives and emphasis on the autonomy of the state in international affairs, see Andrei P. Tsygankov, *Russia's Foreign Policy: Change and Continuity in National Identity*, 2nd edn (Lanham, Rowman and Littlefield, 2010), and Andrei P. Tsygankov, *The Strong State in Russia: Development and Crisis* (Oxford, Oxford University Press, 2014).

latter reflected the Atlantic view that domestic systemic transformation should precede international structural change, whereas Russian leaders from Yeltsin to Putin argued that structural change and the removal of perceived or genuine geopolitical threats would facilitate domestic reforms. The impasse was complete.

Myths and Mistakes

Time and again Russia had been unconquerable, but it now proved to be indigestible as well. In conceptual terms, Russia sought to join the 'Historical West', which by the very act of Russia joining would become a 'Greater West'. This would have been a dialogical relationship of the sort outlined by Gorbachev, in which all constituent members of the new community would be transformed by mutual engagement. In this Greater West the existing security institutions would be transformed, and leadership would be shared. This was the prize that Russia considered it had earned by initiating the end of the Cold War, irrespective of any temporary weakness.[2] Gorbachev's political adviser, Andrei Grachev, describes how the radical transformation of Soviet foreign policy was designed to advance domestic political change, but at the same time he demonstrates that the NPT sought to achieve an equally radical transformation of the international system. The NPT was predicated on the view that the Western capitalist powers were not inherently militaristic and aggressive (as standard Soviet Marxist-Leninist thought had postulated), and hence cooperative coexistence between different social systems was possible.[3] Soviet utopianism was replaced by a new ideal, a cooperative framework between states.[4] However, the retreat from Soviet dogma in the cause of a foreign policy free of ideology replaced 'one ideology with another, no longer based, it is true, on Marxist postulates of class struggle or historical determinism, but on "universal democratic values"', which paradoxically were intended to achieve much the same result as the discredited theory of world revolution – a transformation of international politics.[5] The

[2] For a discussion on the end of the Cold War, see William Wohlforth (ed.), *Cold War Endgame: Oral History, Analysis, Debates* (Philadelphia, University of Pennsylvania Press, 2003).

[3] Vendulka Kubálková and A. A. Cruickshank, *Thinking about Soviet 'New Thinking'* (Berkeley, University of California Press, 1989). For the context, see Margot Light, *The Soviet Theory of International Politics* (Brighton, Wheatsheaf, 1987).

[4] This was complemented by Gorbachev's own transformation into a social democrat. See Archie Brown, 'Gorbachev, Lenin, and the Break with Leninism', *Demokratizatsiya*, Vol. 15, No. 2, 2007, pp. 230–44.

[5] Andrei Grachev, *Gorbachev's Gamble: Soviet Foreign Policy and the End of the Cold War* (Cambridge, Polity, 2008), p. 74.

idealistic new thinking 'offered a global mission that would enhance Soviet international status while preserving a distinctive national identity'. This reading of the NPT can be seen as a 'shortcut to greatness': achieving great power status not through economic might and military power but through normative innovation and the transformation of international politics.[6] In the event, Russia was to find that the shortcut led to a dead end.

The new thinking was a type of 'universal ideology' for a global world, with the potential to revive the UN, for so long over-shadowed by Cold War bloc politics.[7] Gorbachev's grand project was to integrate 'the Soviet Union as an equal partner of the Western powers in the world's political family'.[8] Even as he dismantled the Cold War, Gorbachev remained committed to creating a 'humane, democratic socialism' in the Soviet Union. For him, the transcendence of the Cold War did not mean that the Soviet Union would automatically copy the political system of the West.[9] Equally, for him and his successors, Russia would remain an independent sovereign power in international affairs, but now acting in a more cooperative spirit. This would mean joining a new and transformed Greater West. The new peace order would be based on the reunification of the European continent. Gorbachev's common European home speech warned that 'the states of Europe belong to different social systems' and admitted that there was uncertainty about the new 'architecture of our "common home"', but insisted that it would have many rooms.[10] This was a model for an ideationally plural Europe comprised of several sovereign entities. This was a classic Gaullist idea, taken up by François Mitterrand in his plan for a 'European confederation', and by many others and above all the Russian plan for a Greater Europe. On the other side, Bush's 'new world order', first enunciated in his September 1990 address to Congress, stressed enlargement rather than transformation. In practice, both sides in the early post-Cold War years were committed to a middle position, the policy of adaptation of the European political and security architecture to a Russia that itself was committed to adaptation. The Charter of Paris for a New Europe was adopted on 21 November 1990 and heralded 'a new era of democracy, peace and unity',

---

[6] Deborah Welch Larson and Alexei Shevchenko, 'Shortcut to Greatness: The New Thinking and the Revolution in Soviet Foreign Policy', *International Organization*, Vol. 57, No. 1, 2003, pp. 77–109.

[7] Grachev, *Gorbachev's Gamble*, pp. 193–4, quotation at p. 78.

[8] Grachev, *Gorbachev's Gamble*, p. 204.

[9] John Gooding, 'Gorbachev and Democracy', *Soviet Studies*, Vol. 42, No. 2, 1990, pp. 195–231; Neil Robinson, *Ideology and the Collapse of the Soviet System: A Critical History of the Soviet Ideological Discourse* (Aldershot, Edward Elgar, 1995).

[10] Gorbachev, 'Europe as a Common Home'.

stressing that 'Europe is liberating itself from its past'.[11] The focus was on the temporal challenge – overcoming the past; but the contours of the new spatial order were unclear.

Although idealistic, Gorbachev's ideas were responses to real challenges that remain unresolved to this day. Putin's foreign policy later was formulated in more pragmatic terms, but it retained the idealistic streak inherited from the perestroika years. The end of the Cold War was but part of the transformation of the international system. Equally, 1989 was not just about achieving a counter-revolution against the ossified dogmas and social practices of Soviet-style socialism, but the underlying aspiration was to achieve an emancipation from axiological politics in their entirety though 'anti-revolutions'.[12] This represented the positive transcendence of the Cold War through a transformation of international politics. Instead, one form of axiology was replaced by another, and the philosophical closure represented by the 'end of history' (the view that the dissolution of the communist system represented the end of the ideological evolution of humanity) was accompanied by the inadvertent 'end of politics'. Certain issues were considered closed and not susceptible to revision. The end of the Cold War saw no fundamental institutional innovation when it came to European security and development, and instead the Atlantic system (the EU and NATO) enlarged. Institutional enlargement was accompanied by a complex process of norm advancement in which a strengthened monistic system claimed the title to virtue and values.

Russia was offered not a Greater West but membership of the Historical West, and even that apparently on subordinate terms. There was no place for Russia in the triumphant Atlantic system, certainly not as an equal. Given the enormous disparity in power and resources, Russia's effective exclusion from the existing security arrangements did not at first appear to be a problem, but in the end Russia was once again 'lost'.[13] Jack Matlock, the US ambassador to the USSR between 1987 and 1991, notes, 'too many American politicians looked at the end of the Cold

[11] *Charter of Paris for a New Europe* (Paris, CSCE, 1990), www.oscepa.org/documents/all-documents/documents-1/historical-documents-1/673-1990-charter-of-paris-for-a-new-europe/file, last accessed 26 May 2017.

[12] Richard Sakwa, 'Konets epokhi revolyutsii: antirevolyutsionnye revolyutsii 1989–1991 godov' ('The End of the Age of Revolutions: The Anti-revolutions of 1989–1991'), *Politicheskie Issledovaniya – Polis* (Moscow, in Russian), No. 5, 1998, pp. 23–38; Richard Sakwa, 'The Age of Paradox: The Anti-revolutionary Revolutions of 1989–91', in Moira Donald and Tim Rees (eds.), *Reinterpreting Revolution in Twentieth-century Europe* (London, Macmillan, 2001), pp. 159–76.

[13] Peter Conradi, *Who Lost Russia? How the World Entered a New Cold War* (London, Oneworld, 2017).

War as if it were a quasi-military victory rather than a negotiated outcome that benefited both sides'.[14] He notes that 'mythmaking began almost as soon as the Soviet Union fell'; 'Since 1991, these distortions have created a set of beliefs as widespread as they are unfounded'.[15] He argues, as suggested earlier, that the Cold War ended at least two years before the disintegration of the Soviet Union, and that it was Gorbachev's initiatives and not Western military pressure that 'defeated communism'. Above all, Russia was not defeated in the Cold War but it was a common victory.[16] The point is confirmed by Stephen Cohen, who argues that 'the Cold War would have continued unabated, possibly grown worse, had it not been for Gorbachev's initiatives'. He also notes that the Cold War ended well before the disintegration of the Soviet Union, and as Bush had originally argued, it was negotiated so that 'there were no losers, only winners'.[17] Unfortunately, 'the Cold War [had] ended in Moscow, but not in Washington'.[18] This means that the post-Soviet peace was 'lost', and contrary to much Western commentary, 'The new Cold War and the squandering of the post-Soviet peace began not in Moscow but in Washington'.[19] NATO enlargement meant that most of the 'follies' of the (George W.) Bush administration had their roots in the mistakes of the (Bill) Clinton presidency in the 1990s.[20] Cohen believes that the new Cold War is largely the responsibility of the Western powers, who failed to overcome the entrenched patterns of the original conflict.[21]

On the other side, leaders of the Atlantic community feared that premature Russian membership of the Historical West would lead to normative dilution, institutional incoherence and the loss of American leadership. Offensive realists argue that one of the main priorities for a regional hegemon (in this case the US) is not to allow any potential rival to emerge elsewhere.[22] Mearsheimer takes it as a given that Russia is a great power, although one today with a relatively low power capacity. In his view, the cycle of violence will continue, 'because the great powers that shape the international system fear each other and compete for power as a

---

[14] Jack F. Matlock, *Super-Power Illusions: How Myths and False Ideologies Led America Astray – and How to Return to Reality* (New Haven and London, Yale University Press, 2010), p. x.

[15] Matlock, *Super-Power Illusions*, p. 3.   [16] Matlock, *Super-Power Illusions*, pp. 4–6.

[17] Stephen F. Cohen, *Soviet Fates and Lost Alternatives: From Stalinism to the New Cold War* (New York, Columbia University Press, 2009), p. 160.

[18] Cohen, *Soviet Fates and Lost Alternatives*, p. 171.

[19] Cohen, *Soviet Fates and Lost Alternatives*, p. 167.

[20] Cohen, *Soviet Fates and Lost Alternatives*, p.172.

[21] Stephen F. Cohen, *Why Cold War Again? How America Lost Post-Soviet Russia* (London and New York, I. B. Tauris, 2017).

[22] John Mearsheimer, *The Tragedy of Great Power Politics*, updated edn (New York, W. W. Norton, 2014[2001]), pp. 21, 141, 237 and *passim*.

result'.[23] In an anarchic international system (that is, one without some sort of supreme authority), security competition and war between the great powers remain constants, although the intensity of competition varies. States seek to maximise their share of world power, and aim to become the hegemon – 'the only great power in the system'.[24] Regime type has little to do with it, since 'democracies care about security as much as non-democracies do'.[25] The structure of the international system shapes the behaviour of states. This is in sharp contrast to the liberal view, which believes that the domestic characteristics of states shape their foreign policy. Defensive (or structural) realists also believe that states are concerned about the balance of power as they struggle to survive, but unlike offensive realists, states behave defensively to maintain rather than to challenge the balance of power, and form balancing coalitions to counter a potential hegemon.[26] As I shall argue in Chapter 2, drawing on English School thinkers, although the international system remains anarchic, it is tempered by the development of a network of global governance mechanisms (defined as the secondary institutions of international society in English School thinking) that constrain great power competition.

The US leadership did all in its power to avert the Soviet collapse (with the exception of the Baltic republics), concerned above all about the fate of the vast nuclear arsenal.[27] Bush's aspiration for a 'Europe whole and free' tried to avoid a repeat of the harsh peace (*Das Diktat*) imposed on Germany through the Treaty at Versailles in June 1919, which fostered German revanchism and the rise of Hitler, but the absence of adequate institutional innovation to create a larger European security construct meant that Russia remained an outsider. Russian grievances accumulated over the years, but they all stemmed from the Western foundational myth that the particular 'victory' over the Soviet Union had some sort of universal significance that could not be diluted by making compromises with the Soviet continuer-state, the Russian Federation. Equally, Russian mythology stood firmly by the view that the country by its very essence was a great power, and thus worthy not only of the respect accruing from that status, but above all that it was a necessary equal in the management of European and global affairs, and deserved some sort of privileged status as the ender of the Cold War and the largest power on the continent.

[23] Mearsheimer, *Tragedy of Great Power Politics*, p. xv.

[24] Mearsheimer, *Tragedy of Great Power Politics*, p. 2.

[25] Mearsheimer, *Tragedy of Great Power Politics*, p. 4.

[26] Kenneth N. Waltz, *Theory of International Politics* (New York, Random House 1979).

[27] Jack F. Matlock, *Reagan and Gorbachev: How the Cold War Ended* (New York, Random House, 2004).

These incommensurable 'myths' had incalculable consequences for the dynamics of international politics in the post-Cold War years. Ultimately, the division is reducible to the Western view that the institutions, norms and values of the West had in some ways triumphed; and the Russian view, articulated with increasing intensity from the mid-1990s, in favour of geopolitical and ideational pluralism and equality.

The two sides became locked in the narratives of their own making, creating two hermetic discourses with decreasing mutual understanding. The disintegration of the USSR and Russia's weakness undermined the potential for a transformative politics. This left the field clear for the 'enlargers'. Instead of Gorbachev's attempt to achieve a mutual transcendence of the Cold War, it came to an asymmetrical end in which one side could claim victory, thereby condemning the other side to imputed if not actual defeat. In his speech of 25 December 1991 marking Gorbachev's resignation and the disintegration of the Soviet Union, Bush three times described the event as a 'victory' of the American people and values.[28] Shortly afterwards, in his State of the Union address on 27 January 1992, Bush declared that 'by the grace of God, America won the Cold War', insisting that 'the cold war didn't end – it was won'.[29] He announced cuts to the defence budget, and declared the dawning of a new world order of cooperative security, working with Russia and the newly independent states. In the Russian narrative, the world order that emerged represents a negative transcendence of the Cold War, whose very foundational principles are illegitimate – the idea of a Western victory. The view that 'We all lost the Cold War' applies also to the post-Cold War peace.[30] The dissolution of the communist system was conflated with the disintegration of the Soviet Union into a single narrative, even though they were two distinct processes. The US under Bush did all in its power to maintain the integrity of the Soviet state, although welcoming the dissolution of the communist system.[31] The disintegration of the Soviet Union removed one of the poles in the superpower relationship, and Russia to this day aspires to this role, although without the material and ideological resources of its predecessor.

[28] 'Text of Bush's Address to Nation on Gorbachev's Resignation', *New York Times*, 26 December 1991, www.nytimes.com/1991/12/26/world/end-soviet-union-text-bush-s-address-nation-gorbachev-s-resignation.html, last accessed 26 May 2017.

[29] 'Transcript of President Bush's Address on the State of the Union', *New York Times*, 29 January 1992, www.nytimes.com/1992/01/29/us/state-union-transcript-president-bush-s-address-state-union.html?pagewanted=all, last accessed 26 May 2017.

[30] Richard Ned Lebow and Janice Gross Stein, *We All Lost the Cold War* (Princeton, Princeton University Press, 1995).

[31] Described in vivid detail by Serhii Plokhy, *The Last Empire: The Final Days of the Soviet Union* (New York, Oneworld Publications, 2014). For a broad analysis, see Jack F. Matlock, *Autopsy on an Empire: The American Ambassador's Account of the Collapse of the Soviet Union* (New York, Random House, 1995).

The resulting asymmetrical end of the Cold War and incommensurate narratives gave birth to the cold peace.

These are far from abstract debates but shape political outcomes. President Bill Clinton's liberal belief that great power politics was a thing of the past encouraged him to enlarge NATO, even though realists warned him that this would have potentially disastrous consequences. Throughout the cold peace the US acted as offensive realists predicted, hailing liberal nostrums while applying classical methods of containment on Russia – to prevent it from challenging America's hegemonic position. Up to 2014 this containment was 'soft', but nonetheless constrained Russia's strategic options. US policy was governed by realist logic, although couched in benign liberal terms. Through NATO, the US remained an 'onshore balancer', ensuring that the Atlantic system remained pre-eminent on the continent. This 'soft containment' hedged against any potential revival of Russia as an effective great power. Russia's inclusion in the Greater West and its Greater Europe counterpart would have provided a benign security environment to undergo the systemic transformation to make it a worthy member of the transformed West. It would have satisfied Russia's status concerns while enhancing the cumulative economic and security weight of the expanded West at a time when the global balance of power was evidently shifting eastwards. Instead, Russia's post-communist development took place largely outside of the hegemonic structures of the Atlantic system.

Serious attempts were made to mitigate the effects of exclusion (see the section on NATO enlargement in Chapter 3), but ultimately Russia was on its own. Plenty of advice was proffered, and in the 1990s this came with loans and consultants, but the goal was Russia's adaptation to the stringencies of an existing order, not the creation of an expanded community. In the 1990s this was accepted, although not without enormous domestic resistance, while in the 2000s Putin insisted that Russia would devise appropriate solutions to its unique problems. This only accentuated what was always a core feature of Russian international thinking, namely its foreign policy and developmental autonomy. Since joining the European state system in the eighteenth century, Russia strived to remain an independent power.[32] This assumed some sort of community of great powers, and thus the existence of a pluralist international system. At the same time, resistance to Western-sponsored democracy promotion and regime change intensified. Russia became the leading exponent of anti-hegemonic strategies as it tried to break out of its soft containment. Sergei Lavrov, Russia's

---

[32] Andrei Kokoshin, *Real'nyi suverenitet v sovremennoi miropoliticheskoi sistemy*, 3rd edn (Moscow, Evropa, 2006).

foreign minister from 2004, later commented that the rise of the Asia-Pacific region (APR) meant the relative diminution in the influence of the 'so-called "historical West" that was used to seeing itself as the master of the human race's destinies for almost five centuries', intensifying the struggle to shape the world order of the twenty-first century.[33] The Russian *Foreign Policy Concept* of 12 February 2013 argued that the Eurasian Economic Union (EEU) and the BRICS (Brazil, Russia, India, China and South Africa) states would strengthen and ultimately eclipse the Historical West, whose influence was declining.[34] The BRICS alignment seeks a greater role in global economic governance. This anti-hegemonic formulation is no less ambitious than the ideological formulations of the Cold War, but has a far greater chance of being realised. Cold War patterns were reformulated to place Russia at the heart of an alternative model of world order.

The Cold Peace

The attempt to transform the USSR into some sort of union of sovereign states failed, and by the end of 1991 the country no longer existed and fifteen independent republics emerged in its place. Russia was designated the 'continuer-state', assuming responsibility for the international treaties signed by the USSR and inheriting its nuclear weapons and permanent seat on the UN Security Council (UNSC). Russia also in a more intangible sense became the legatee of the USSR's great power status. The USSR had recreated much of the Russian Empire and acted to defend the country's state interests, tempered through the prism of communist internationalist concerns, and now democratic Russia did the same. Russia inherited Soviet institutions, much of the ruling class and many of its attitudes. The price to pay for a bloodless revolution was institutional and elite continuity, which reconstituted itself in a strong neo-Soviet current, reinforced by the reproduction of neo-imperial attitudes. These were balanced by the new spirit of international integration and liberal constitutional adaptation generated by the democratic revolution.

---

[33] Sergey Lavrov, 'Russia's Foreign Policy: Historical Background', *Russia in Global Affairs*, 3 March 2016, www.mid.ru/en/foreign_policy/news/-/asset_publisher/cKNonkJE02Bw/content/id/2124391, last accessed 26 May 2017.

[34] *Kontseptsiya vneshnei politiki Rossiiskoi Federatsii*, MFA, 18 February 2013, www.mid.ru/en/foreign_policy/official_documents/-/asset_publisher/CptICkB6BZ29/content/id/122186?p_p_id=101_INSTANCE_CptICkB6BZ29&_101_INSTANCE_CptICkB6BZ29_languageId=ru_RU, last accessed 26 May 2017. The English version is available as *Concept of the Foreign Policy of the Russian Federation*, www.mid.ru/en/foreign_policy/official_documents/-/asset_publisher/CptICkB6BZ29/content/id/122186, last accessed 26 May 2017.

Contemporary Russia is a combination of several distinct historical orders in permanent tension, and quite often contradiction, with each other.

The Soviet collapse was accompanied by the disintegration of the USSR's major international institutions. After thirty-six years of existence the Warsaw Treaty Organisation (Warsaw Pact) was formally disbanded on 31 March 1991. Created in 1955 in response to the rearmed West Germany joining NATO, the Warsaw Pact was less a defensive alliance than a way of ensuring Soviet dominance over its East European allies. At the same time, the Council for Mutual Economic Assistance (CMEA, or Comecon), created in 1949 in response to the Marshall Plan and the creation of the Organisation for European Economic Co-operation (the forerunner of what became the Organisation for Economic Cooperation and Development (OECD) in 1961), spluttered to an end. The disintegrative impulse even threatened the integrity of the country itself, with a runaway 'war of sovereignties' affecting many of the ethno-federal entities comprising the Russian Federation. The Federation Treaty of 13 March 1992 was initialled by eighteen of Russia's then twenty republics, but Chechnya and Tatarstan refused. In the end a bilateral treaty with Tatarstan and some other 'subjects of the federation' provided a format for the peaceful reconciliation of differences, but it took a devastating war between December 1994 and August 1996 to bring Chechnya back into Moscow's fold. Even that was provisional, and only after a second war from September 1999 to 2004 was the insurgency defeated, and to this day the republic represents a black hole in Russia's constitutional space. Putin's statecraft is designed above all to avert disintegration at home and to assert Russia's position abroad.

There remains a remarkable cultural continuity in Russian ruling elite concerns stretching from the early days of the Russian Empire in the eighteenth century to the Soviet period between 1917 and 1991 and into the post-communist era.[35] The three political regimes – Imperial, Soviet and post-communist – differed fundamentally from each other but were united in the view of Russia's status as an essential power in the European and, later, global system. In the post-Cold War years this view was reinforced by the high degree of elite continuity between the Soviet and post-communist systems. Even Yeltsin's leadership of independent Russia from 1991 to 1999, when the country was most committed to becoming part of the Atlantic system, asserted Russia's status as a great power. The vast, although greatly weakened, security and military-industrial complex had no intention of giving up its power and privileges, while almost all significant politicians were educated in the school of Imperial and Soviet greatness. Most were

---

[35] These are explored by Andrei P. Tsygankov, notably *Russia and the West from Alexander to Putin: Honor in International Relations* (Cambridge, Cambridge University Press, 2012).

ready to cooperate with the West, but only if Russia could retain its freedom of action. Putin made strenuous efforts to find a way of combining adaptation and autonomy, but this attempt broke down from the mid-2000s. Putin's decisions were structured by enduring views about Russia's status in the world, concomitant concerns about domestic order, and a refusal to accept Russia's marginalisation.

Instead of the transformative agenda proposed by Russia, the Historical West pursued the strategy of enlargement. The core institutions of the Atlantic community extended into the old Soviet bloc and into the former Soviet Union itself. Enlargement rather than transformation entailed a specific type of relationship with Russia, whose ambitions to become a founding member of a transformed community were thwarted. Various strategies, short of membership, were devised to mitigate Russia's sense of exclusion. The USSR was a founding member of the Conference on Security and Cooperation in Europe (CSCE), the organisation bringing together all the European states as well as the US and Canada that in December 1994 became the Organisation for Security and Cooperation in Europe (OSCE). The roots of the OSCE lie in the Helsinki process, culminating in the adoption of the Helsinki Final Act in August 1975 encompassing the three 'baskets' of security, economic interaction and the famous 'third basket' of human rights. Since then the Helsinki process has become a Gothic edifice, with the accretion of numerous institutions focusing on conflict regulation, election monitoring and human rights. However, the body, which works by consensus, was not transformed to become the main pillar of security in Europe as Russia hoped. Various plans to establish some sort of European security council, with regional powers equivalent to the UNSC, were scotched. The fifty-seven-member OSCE remains one of the most important European bodies defending human rights and, in particular, monitoring elections through its Office for Democratic Institutions and Human Rights (ODIHR) based in Warsaw, although its focus on the former Soviet states drew Russia's criticism. The OSCE works well as a facilitator but lacks effective agency of its own.

The twenty-five years between 1989 and 2014 quickly assumed the character of a 'cold peace', a period pregnant with the potential for renewed conflict.[36] Instead of a transcendence of the sources of conflict

[36] Janusz Bugajski, *Cold Peace: Russia's New Imperialism* (Westport, Greenwood Press, 2004). Bugajski, as the title of his book suggests, argues that Russia was entirely responsible. Jeffrey E. Garten, *A Cold Peace: America, Japan, Germany, and the Struggle for Supremacy* (New York, The Twentieth Century Fund/Times Books, 1992) applies the concept to what at the time appeared to be America's dawning conflict with Germany and Japan. The term has also been applied to characterise domestic politics: Yoram Gorlizki and Oleg Khlevniuk, *Cold Peace: Stalin and the Soviet Ruling Circle, 1945–1953* (New York, Oxford University Press, 2004).

at the end of the Cold War, a power shift was registered within the framework of a continuation of the structures of conflict. The concept emerged soon after the Soviet collapse, with Cohen already arguing in 1992 that inadequate attention was being devoted to the 'cold peace' with Russia in the American presidential election.[37] The foreign minister, Andrei Kozyrev, as early as 1992 warned against NATO enlargement, and in 1993 Yeltsin complained that various items of Cold War legislation were still on the books in the US. He condemned in particular the Jackson-Vanik amendment of 1974 linking free trade with Jewish emigration, as well as the continuation of 'Captive Nations' discourse, even though most of the states in question had gained their independence.[38] The term was used by Yeltsin at the Budapest OSCE conference in December 1994, when he warned that the American plan to enlarge NATO could plunge Europe 'into a cold peace'.[39] Reminding his audience that the significance of the end of the war half a century earlier was 'the need for a historic reconciliation in Europe', he went on to argue that '[t]here should no longer be enemies, winners or losers, in that Europe. For the first time in history, our continent has a real opportunity to achieve unity.' In his trademark stentorian tone he went on to warn: 'To miss that opportunity means to forget the lessons of the past and to jeopardize our future ... Europe, even before it has managed to shrug off the legacy of the cold war, is at risk of plunging into a cold peace'.[40] In an article the following year, Kozyrev warned that the choice lay between 'cooperation' or a 'cold peace'.[41] An asymmetrical peace order became established, in which one side acted as if it was the victor, while the other refused to 'embrace defeat'.[42] This established the conditions for the cold peace, a mimetic cold war that was unable to understand the sources of its own existence.[43]

The Russian view of world order after the Cold War is that it was boxed into some sort of strategic dead end. The Western ideas and institutions

---

[37] Stephen F. Cohen, 'The Election's Missing Issue: A Cold Peace With Russia?', *The Nation*, Vol. 225, No. 17, 1992, pp. 622–4.

[38] Strobe Talbott, *The Russia Hand: A Memoir of Presidential Diplomacy* (New York, Random House, 2003), p. 63.

[39] Norman Kempster and Dean E. Murphy, 'Broader NATO May Bring "Cold Peace": Yeltsin Warns', *Los Angeles Times*, 6 December 1994, http://articles.latimes.com/1994–12-06/news/mn-5629_1_cold-war, last accessed 26 May 2017.

[40] Talbott, *Russia Hand*, p. 141.

[41] Andrei Kozyrev, 'Partnership or Cold Peace?', *Foreign Policy*, No. 99, Summer 1995, pp. 3–14.

[42] John W. Dower, *Embracing Defeat: Japan in the Wake of World War II* (New York, Norton, 2000).

[43] Richard Sakwa, 'The Cold Peace: Russo-Western Relations as a Mimetic Cold War', *Cambridge Review of International Affairs*, Vol. 26, No. 1, 2013, pp. 203–24.

that had triumphed were considered in some way universal, and certainly contained no inherent sense of *finalité* in Europe or even globally. The only choice for Russia appeared to be to adapt to these ideas and institutions, or face ostracism and isolation. Russia could be a great power but an outsider; or a member of the Historical West, but at the price of renouncing its autonomy as a great power. The liberal democratic and institutional adaptation strategy predominated in the 1990s, but even then it was contested. Yevgeny Primakov, foreign minister from January 1996 to September 1998 and thereafter prime minister to May 1999, promoted a 'multi-vector' policy that sought to balance relations with the Atlantic community with the establishment of a 'strategic partnership' between Russia and China. Nevertheless, this period is defined as a retreat, with Russia giving up positions that it had taken centuries to consolidate. Any attempt to assert a *droit de regard*, let alone what was later called a sphere of 'privileged interests',[44] in its neighbourhood was condemned as a recrudescence of Russian imperialism. The very idea of a 'sphere of influence' for Russia was considered illegitimate, although the scope of 'legitimate' interests and how they could be expressed remained unclear.

In the 1990s Russia was too weak to do anything except to protest against the erosion of its claimed prerogatives as a great power. The poor performance of its military in the first Chechen war exposed just how degraded Russian institutions had become. The Commonwealth of Independent States (CIS) was created in December 1991 to maintain some of the old Soviet links, but it proved to be little more than a way to manage what Leonid Kravchuk, the first president of independent Ukraine, called the 'civilised divorce' of the former Soviet states.[45] But how far should the perceived retreat go? The framing of the question in that way proved anathema to Russian liberals, who looked forward to the creation of sovereign, independent and democratic states in place of what they considered to be the old Russian and Soviet empires. Even statists like Primakov paid little attention to Russia's neighbours, focusing instead on grander geopolitical designs. Primakov favoured what he called a multipolar world order. On a visit to India in 1999 he repeated his call for the creation of a 'strategic triangle' of Russia, India and China (RICs) as a

---

[44] The term was used by Dmitry Medvedev, 'Interv'yu Dmitriya Medvedeva telekanalam "Rossiya", Pervomu, NTV', Sochi, 31 August 2008, www.kremlin.ru/text/appears/2008/08/205991.shtml, last accessed 30 May 2017.

[45] Tatiana Zhurchenko, *Borderlands into Bordered Lands: Geopolitics of Identity in Post-Soviet Ukraine* (Stuttgart, Ibidem-Verlag, 2010), p. 135.

counterbalance to the US.[46] Multipolarity can take a number of different forms, but they all challenge America's predominance and signal Russia's growing resistance.[47]

The cold peace period was shaped by three fundamental processes: first, the institutional consolidation and enlargement of Western bodies created in the Cold War; second, the reinforcement and ultimately the radicalisation of the Western ideational foundations of Cold War discourses and beliefs; and third, the emergence of a politics of resistance in Russia. In terms of institutions, European integration had been one of the conditions of American support for the continent in the post-war years. This does not mean that the establishment of the European Economic Community in 1957 was purely a function of the Cold War; but its development has always been bound up with great power politics, above all as a way of consolidating the European component of the Atlantic system against the Soviet ideological and military threat. With the end of the Cold War, concern about the emergence of a dominant united Germany prompted the transformation of the European Community and its associated bodies into the EU by the Treaty of Maastricht of 7 February 1992. The EU thereafter both deepened and widened to consolidate its position as the pre-eminent institution on the European continent. The enlargement of 2004 brought in eight former communist countries (Czech Republic, Estonia, Hungary, Latvia, Lithuania, Poland, Slovakia and Slovenia) as well as Cyprus and Malta, with Bulgaria and Romania joining in 2007 and Croatia in 2013. In the security sphere, it was flanked by NATO, which also expanded in two main waves – the first in March 1999 brought in Poland, Hungary and the Czech Republic, while the 'big bang' enlargement of March 2004 encompassed seven former communist countries (Bulgaria, Estonia, Latvia, Lithuania, Romania, Slovakia and Slovenia), and with the accession of Albania and Croatia in 2009 NATO membership rose to twenty-eight, the same number as in the EU although with a slightly different composition – twenty-two EU states are also members of NATO. The accession of Montenegro in 2017 brought total NATO membership to twenty-nine, while the UK's departure (Brexit) in 2019 will reduce EU membership to twenty-seven.

These two organisations were buttressed by a range of other organisations, creating a dense network of European international governance.

[46] Amresh Chandra, 'Strategic Triangle among Russia, India and China: Challenges and Prospects', *Journal of Peace Studies*, Vol. 17, No. 2–3, April–September 2010, pp. 40–60.
[47] Thomas Ambrosio, *Challenging America's Global Preeminence: Russia's Quest for Multipolarity* (Farnham, Ashgate, 2005); Martin A. Smith, 'Russia and Multipolarity since the End of the Cold War', *East European Politics*, Vol. 29, No. 1, 2013, pp. 36–51.

The EU was reinforced by the CoE, established in May 1949 and under whose aegis the European Convention on Human Rights (ECHR) and its subsequent Protocols were adopted. The CoE now encompasses forty-seven European states, including Russia but not Belarus or Central Asia. The European Court of Human Rights (ECtHR) acts as the final court of appeal when domestic routes to justice have been exhausted. The Parliamentary Assembly of the Council of Europe (PACE) provides a forum for delegates from national parliaments to engage in discussion and critique. In the security sphere, the OSCE plays an invaluable role as conflict mediator and regulator, but it failed to become the genuinely inclusive and pre-eminent security body in Europe some had anticipated with the end of the Cold War. Nevertheless, the Helsinki Final Act remains one of the foundations of contemporary European order, codifying aspirations for détente and European unification on the basis of trust and human rights. It also represents the ambivalence of that order, with the emphasis on human rights eclipsing the security and economic baskets. Helsinki proved an inadequate foundation for post-Cold War order, since it privileged one aspect (human rights) while failing to devise an adequate framework for negotiated resolution of security and economic commitments. In the absence of a negotiated end to the Cold War, it was assumed that the solutions of the problem of history devised in one historical context could automatically be applied to another.

The absence of any genuinely new structures to institutionalise the post-Cold War order is striking. As Soviet power disintegrated its various multinational institutions in the Eastern part of the continent were dismantled, notably the Warsaw Pact and CMEA, while those of the West flourished. As early as 1992, the American political scientist Ken Jowitt noted the 'inertial policy' of the US, and the Bush administration's 'hypnotic commitment to NATO'. This was presented then and later as 'prudence' (in other words, hedging against renewed threats, primarily from Russia), but this continuity stance, as Jowitt commented, foreclosed a transformative agenda: '[I]n turbulent environments, it is prudent to be imaginative and innovative. There is no evidence of either imagination or innovation in US foreign policy; there is evidence of inertial reaction'.[48] The absence of institutional innovation, let alone a peace conference to hammer out the guiding principles for a radically changed security environment, is a salient feature of the structural asymmetries that marked the post-Cold War system.

---

[48] Ken Jowitt, *New World Disorder: The Leninist Extinction* (Berkeley, University of California Press, 1992), p. 329.

In the ideological sphere the West really had 'won' the Cold War. This was notoriously formulated by Francis Fukuyama as the 'end of history', the exhaustion of systemic alternatives to capitalist democracy.[49] Just as the institutional foundations of the cold peace represented the negative transcendence of the Cold War, reinforcing the structures rather than transforming them, so too in the ideological sphere Marxist historicism was inverted and a liberal historicism about the meaning and purpose of history became the ideational counterpart of the institutional consolidation. This became the intellectual framework for the burgeoning field of 'transitology' and democratisation studies, framed by a new linear teleology. One monological discourse was replaced by another, with profound political repercussions. The opportunity for a genuinely pluralist exploration of new and more inclusive forms of democracy and capitalism was over-shadowed by the appropriation of ready-made solutions. Just as the 'enlargement' agenda predominated in the institutional sphere, the 'application' model prevailed in ideational matters. Capitalism, liberal democracy, human rights, the rule of law and much else were the foundations of the Atlantic community, and these were now extended to the East. The fundamental argument advanced by Russian leaders from the very beginning is that these were now Russian values too, and any proprietary relationship between the Atlantic power system and the normative complex of liberal democracy was illegitimate. In other words, the 'victory' was contingent and situational, and certainly did not mean the triumph of the Western power system. The 'decoupling' argument (as discussed in Chapter 2) became the foundation for Russian neo-revisionism and the anti-hegemonic alignment.

Instead, the ideational and institutional agendas became mutually reinforcing. As far as many in the West and along Russia's borders were concerned, 'Russia was a malignancy in remission: the Yeltsin era was at best a fleeting opportunity to be seized before Russia relapsed into authoritarianism at home and expansionism abroad'.[50] This Cold War view was the driver leading to NATO enlargement, with all of the deleterious consequences for Russo-Western relations, and which in the end provoked the resumption of confrontation. The hedging strategy against the revival of what was taken to be the primordial threat from Russia precluded the possibility of a positive transcendence of the Cold War and stifled institutional and ideational innovation. Not surprisingly, Russia increasingly felt

---

[49] Francis Fukuyama, 'The End of History', *The National Interest*, No. 16, Summer 1989, pp. 3–17; Francis Fukuyama, *The End of History and the Last Man* (New York, Free Press, 1992).

[50] The view of Lennart Meri, president of Estonia, in May 1993, as reported by Talbott, *Russia Hand*, p. 94.

itself to be trapped in a strategic impasse. Nevertheless, Putin tried to find new ways for Russia to become part of an extended West as an equal and sovereign member (the policy of new realism), a balance that in the end eluded him as much as it had done Gorbachev and Yeltsin earlier. Putin's early years continued the retreat. The listening post in Lourdes in Cuba, a vast Soviet facility established in 1962 only ninety-three miles from Key West, was closed in August 2002, and the Russian Navy withdrew from Cam Ranh Bay in Vietnam. Putin sought to transcend the zero-sum logic of Primakov's version of 'peaceful coexistence', which was premised on an irremediably adversarial model of international politics. Putin retained enough of the Gorbachev aspirations of positive transcendence to aspire for a qualitatively better relationship with the Atlantic community. The new realism attempted to achieve a new engagement with the Atlantic community based on a pragmatic balance of interests. Putin's endeavours in this respect, as we shall analyse later, in the end gave way to a situation that was even worse than peaceful coexistence, a confrontation reminiscent of the worst periods of the Cold War. A range of external crises, from Iraq, Libya to Syria, provoked the breakdown.

By the time of his landmark Munich Security Conference speech of February 2007, Putin had clearly decided that the retreat associated with the Soviet collapse was over. His hopes for a pragmatic new realist relationship with the Historical West, based on mutual respect and recognition of the interests, had been disappointed, and he launched a harsh critique of the unipolar hegemonic system. This was accompanied by an assertiveness fuelled by Russia's economic recovery, greater state coherence and the search for an 'anti-hegemonic' alignment. The stage was set for confrontation. The Historical West was reluctant to transform itself into the Greater West, fearing normative dilution and institutional incoherence, but a historic opportunity to move beyond the Cold War in institutional terms was lost. The European security system entered an extended period of rudderless drift. As one of the leading European officials of the period puts it, '[n]o attempt was made by the West to reach out to Russia and discuss what sort of new order we wanted. We had no strategy and did not know what we were looking for.'[51] Russia was subject to soft containment and became trapped in a strategic impasse, and although rather more consistent in its goals, it also lacked a consistent strategy in pursuing them.

[51] Pierre Vimont, ambassador, chef de cabinet to three French prime ministers, including Dominique de Villepin, and from 2010 the inaugural executive secretary-general of the European External Action Service, 'Europe and the Return of Geopolitics', Dahrendorf Forum – LSE Ideas Public Lecture, 22 March 2016.

The quarter-century between 1989 and 2014 turned out to be a fool's paradise in which none of the fundamental problems of European security were resolved. The period can be characterised as a twenty-five years' crisis, repeating patterns of the inter-war years.[52] In a powerful critique of the politicians and policies of the inter-war period, E. H. Carr characterised the years after 1918 as a 'twenty years' crisis' that prepared the way for the Second World War. The combination of the punitive terms of Versailles and the inept idealism of liberal thinkers – whom he calls 'utopians' – of the inter-war years spawned a revisionist Germany bent on revenge. Carr argues that the utopian pursues policies based on 'an ethical standard purporting to be independent of politics and seeking to make politics conform to it', yet the powerful countries advance rules and ethics that promote their own interests but are blind to the way that others can interpret the situation differently. The application of presumed universal standards was highly selective.[53] Just as the roots of the Second World War lie in the way that the First World War ended, so the revival of Cold War conflict today can be explained by the way that the original Cold War ended. Russia today is not another Weimar Germany, let alone another Third Reich, but the structural similarity with the inter-war years is striking, as is the promotion of liberal idealism at the expense of the concerns and interests of others.

Over the Cliff

The way that one conflict ends determines the shape of the next. After the Napoleonic wars, France at the Congress of Vienna was swiftly brought back into the comity of nations, creating a peace order that lasted a century. By contrast, Germany was humiliated and isolated after the First World War, preparing the way for the Second World War. After 1991 no punitive peace was imposed, and instead genuine efforts were made to bring Russia into the expanded political community of liberal democracies and the Atlantic security system. The problem, however, was the mode of integration. Russian leaders, with varying degrees of emphasis but with a striking degree of consistency, insisted on Russia's sovereign equality in those communities. This meant their transformation into something different by mere dint of Russia's membership. The tension between the Historical West power system and Russia's call for

[52] Richard Sakwa, '"New Cold War" or Twenty Years' Crisis?: Russia and International Politics', *International Affairs*, Vol. 84, No. 2, March 2008, pp. 241–67.
[53] E. H. Carr, *The Twenty Years' Crisis, 1919–1939: An Introduction to the Study of International Relations*, reissued with a new introduction and additional material by Michael Cox (London, Palgrave, 2001 [1939]), pp. 19, 43, 69, 71.

its transformation into a Greater West through Russian membership proved irresolvable. The liberal international order demanded the systemic transformation of Russia on the terms of that order; whereas Russia demanded a structural transformation of the power system itself. These contesting demands fuelled the cold peace. Incompatible narratives provoked the breakdown in 2014 and the onset of the new struggle for Europe.

Henry Kissinger, who served as national security adviser (1969–1975) and secretary of state (1973–77), is one of the most important thinkers in the realist tradition to argue that Russia's concerns as a great power required engagement in traditional *Realpolitik* terms. In his Primakov Lecture in February 2016 he noted that many commentators suggested that the US and Russia were entering a new Cold War, but in his view that represented a misreading of the situation and could become a self-fulfilling prophecy. Instead, the fundamental question was: 'How do we reconcile the very different concepts of world order that have evolved in Russia and the United States – and in other major powers – on the basis of historical experience? The goal should be to develop a strategic concept for U.S.–Russian relations within which the points of contention may be managed.' This was a powerful plea for dialogue and engagement: 'In particular, in the emerging multipolar order, Russia should be perceived as an essential element of any new global equilibrium, not primarily as a threat to the United States.' The goal should be 'to merge our futures rather than elaborate our conflicts. This requires respect by both sides of the vital values and interest of the other.'[54]

Kissinger's analysis is confirmed by other American leaders. The former US defence secretary, William Perry, who led the Pentagon between 1994 and 1997, argues that the hostility between Russia and the US was in part provoked by Washington's contemptuous treatment of Russia's security concerns after the Cold War. In particular, NATO enlargement disrupted the work that had been done to convince the Russian military establishment that NATO could be a friend rather than a foe. Perry argued for a slower expansion to avoid alienating Russia, whereas the contrary view was advanced by Richard Holbrooke and supported by the vice president, Al Gore, who believed that 'we could manage the problems this would create with Russia'. Russian views were not considered worthy of discussion and instead were treated with contempt. As Perry puts it, '[i]t wasn't that we listened to their argument and said we don't

[54] Henry A. Kissinger, 'Russia Should be Perceived as an Essential Element of ny New Equilibrium', the Primakov Lecture delivered in Moscow, *The National Interest*, 4 February 2016, http://nationalinterest.org/feature/kissingers-vision-us-russia-relations-15111, last accessed 26 May 2017.

agree with that argument . . . Basically the people I was arguing with when I tried to put the Russian point . . . the response that I got was really; "Who cares what they think? They're a third rate power"'. Such views did not go down well in Moscow. Perry considered resigning over the issue, but feared that this would be interpreted as opposition to NATO enlargement in general, which he favoured. In his view the second major mistake was the Bush administration's decision to deploy a ballistic missile defence (BMD) system in Eastern Europe, with Russian arguments that this threatened their deterrence capabilities dismissed not on the basis of the merits of the argument but again as a case of '[w]ho cares what Russia thinks?'. As for American support for 'colour revolutions', Perry noted the deleterious effect they had on US–Russian relations, with Putin believing that the US actively sought to overthrow his regime.[55]

There was simply no way for Russia to be assimilated into the existing structures of Atlantic security. In part this was because the Atlantic system did not become a more plural 'Euro-Atlantic' system, the long-term Gaullist aspiration of French leaders.[56] In structural terms, Russia was too big, too independent, too proud and ultimately too strong to become part of an expanded 'West'. Its geopolitical concerns and sense of itself as a 'great power' meant that its identity status could not be subsumed into that of the Atlantic West. After 1945 France had faced a similar diminution of its status, and under Charles de Gaulle the continued aspiration for a certain sort of glory provoked tensions with what he called the 'Anglo-Saxon' world.[57] In the Russian case the dilemma was even more intense, since 'abroad' now started in countries that had once been part of home territory. Flanked by thirteen land neighbours (fifteen if Abkhazia and South Ossetia are counted; and even seventeen if we count the Donbass and Lugansk People's Republics in eastern Ukraine) and with limited access to the oceans, and comprising some 185 autochthonous peoples spread across the world's largest country, Russia is a polity in which domestic vulnerabilities and international politics are exceptionally and

[55] Julian Borger, 'Russian Hostility "Partly Caused by West" Claims Former US Defence Head', *Guardian*, 9 March 2016,www.theguardian.com/world/2016/mar/09/russian-hostility-to-west-partly-caused-by-west, last accessed 26 May 2017. Perry develops these points at length in his memoir *My Journey at the Nuclear Brink* (Stanford, Stanford Security Studies, 2015).

[56] The foreign minister between 1997 and 2002 Hubert Védrine argued that 'the entire foreign policy of France is aimed at making the world of tomorrow composed of several poles, not just a single one', quoted by Jeffrey Gedmin, in 'Europe and NATO: Saving the Alliance', in Robert Kagan and William Kristol (eds.), *Present Dangers: Crisis and Opportunity in American Foreign and Defense Policy* (New York and London, Encounter Books, 2000), p. 189.

[57] R. T. Howard, *France's Secret Wars with Britain and America, 1945–2016* (London, Biteback, 2016).

existentially entwined. Russia's perception of itself as a great power and an equal in the management of regional and global affairs nevertheless remains independent of any domestic issues. This narrative was not accepted by the West, a reluctance that later turned into outright hostility as Russia asserted its status of co-manager of international affairs.

Values came to matter as much as interests in relations between European states. From the perspective of the EU, the CoE and other avowedly normative European institutions, this was only right and proper. This was a 'post-modern' style that eschewed great power politics, where state sovereignty was no longer absolute, force was no longer used to resolve disputes, and borders were inviolate while becoming increasingly irrelevant. The goal was to create a zone of peace on the European continent based on human rights, competitive markets, free and fair elections, and liberal institutions in general.[58] The rule of law and in general a bundle of 'good governance' practices were to be advanced to the EU's neighbours as part of the EU's 'external governance' strategy. This was a powerful and attractive vision and transformed much of Eastern Europe. Governance problems have certainly not disappeared, but a framework was established to address them. In the early cold peace years the EU was the single greatest factor in averting the feared 'new world disorder', but in the end, paradoxically, as it pushed deeper into the post-Soviet space it began to generate conflict and its attendant disorder. The EU's conceit that it was post-modern whereas Russia was mired in the toils of modernity based on traditional identities, fixed territory, and a regressive obsession with sovereignty and geopolitics, generated an ontology of conflict that overcame repeated pledges of 'strategic partnership'. As Ian Klinke argues, the EU's presumed post-modern geopolitics remained trapped in a very modern temporality, a representation of time that valorised the present over the past.[59] Robert Cooper is right to note that as long as 'East' and 'West' were constituted as antinomies, then 'the best that could be achieved was a ceasefire and a stalemate . . . Only in the context of a wider vision can a permanent peace be assured.'[60] This 'wider vision' in Russian parlance is Greater Europe. In the end, after a testy relationship that lasted barely two decades, although attended by the usual pledges of undying partnership, Russia and the EU divorced.[61]

[58] Robert Cooper, *The Postmodern State and the World Order* (London, Demos, 1996).
[59] Ian Klinke, 'Postmodern Geopolitics? The European Union Eyes Russia', *Europe-Asia Studies*, Vol. 64, No. 5, 2012, pp. 929–47.
[60] Robert Cooper, *The Breaking of Nations: Order and Chaos in the Twenty-First Century* (New York, Atlantic Monthly Press, 2003), p. 146.
[61] Tatiana Romanova, 'Sanctions and the Future of EU-Russian Economic Relations', *Europe-Asia Studies*, Vol. 68, No. 4, June 2016, pp. 774–96, especially p. 791.

As for NATO, during the cold peace it sought to find a new role while trying to place the relationship with Russia on a stable new footing. This was the period when liberal institutionalism appeared to triumph, constraining the anarchy of a state-centred system through cooperative institutions. Even then, as Waltz noted, although the clouds had lifted a little, 'twenty-five years is a slight base on which to ground optimistic conclusions'. He conceded that realist theory tends to depreciate the importance of institutions, and the 'strange case' of NATO outliving its purpose seemed to confirm the criticism. However, this was mistaken, since it only confirmed the realist postulate that 'international institutions are shaped and limited by the states that found and sustain them and have little independent effect'. Specifically, '[f]ar from invalidating realist theory or casting doubt on it, the recent history of NATO illustrates the subordination of international institutions to national purposes'.[62] The enlargement of the Atlantic system in a perverse manner contributed to the breakdown of European order and the re-emergence of the great power conflict that it was intended to avert.

Russian calls for strategic pluralism were countered by the consolidation of a type of Atlantic monism in which the EU is the predominant political institution, NATO the primary security body, and the normative aspirations of the Atlantic community the prevailing ideational framework. This system is monistic to the degree that it cannot imagine a legitimate alternative framework for European development. This is a type of liberalism that does not encompass a legitimate alternative to itself, and thus subverts the pluralism considered integral to liberalism. By the same token, although the EU claims to be post-modern – in that borders, traditional sovereignty and geopolitics are considered anachronistic – that very claim is couched in the form of a classical modernist meta-narrative of power and hegemony that repudiates the claim itself. The Historical West became monistic, and although ready to engage with others willing to adapt to its ideational and political character, it lacks a language to deal with outsiders such as Russia. The ensuing contradictions provoked the endless tacking between cooperation and conflict of the Atlantic system and Russia in the cold peace years.

Russia did not fit into such a monistic system. Given the failure to find a mode of adaptation that would allow Russia to remain an independent great power, the strategic impasse was confirmed. One of the fundamental mistakes of this period, according to Viktor Kremenyuk, the deputy director of the Russian Academy of Science's (RAN) Institute of the USA

---

[62] Kenneth N. Waltz, 'Structural Realism after the Cold War', *International Security*, Vol. 25, No. 1, Summer 2000, p. 18.

and Canada, was the failure to sign some sort of peace treaty to formalise the discussions at Malta.[63] Above all, this opened the door to endless debates over what was precisely agreed about the enlargement of NATO in the united Germany and beyond. Kremenyuk argues that as long as great powers exist there will always be rivalry between them for spheres of influence, but Russia and the US in the post-Cold War era failed to find a satisfactory balance between rivalry and cooperation.[64] An underlying tension in the bilateral relationship was apparent from the beginning, despite bouts of reconciliatory rhetoric. The first round of NATO enlarge-ment took place under Yeltsin's relatively benign regime, and 'Russia considers its military manoeuvres and other actions to be a defensive response'. Above all, '[r]ejecting any manifestation of spheres of influence is either naïve or supremely arrogant. Russia is hardly the only country to regard the concept as important for its security', and China, Turkey and Saudi Arabia's actions in their respective neighbourhoods behave in a similar manner.[65] The asymmetrical end to the Cold War allowed the institutions and ideas of the West to prevail, inevitably marginalising Russia and its aspirations for some sort of rethinking of the system. These aspirations were articulated by Gorbachev, but were then lost in Russia's rush to join the Western community. What was termed Russia's demo-cratic revolution over-shadowed the late Soviet attempt to reshape the global order on a new basis. Putin returned to a version of Gorbachev's transformative agenda, but in a more assertive manner and in a more hostile international environment.

In his study of what he calls the 'new Cold War' Robert Legvold agrees that 2014 marked a turning point, when 'we went over the cliff' as he puts it, because of Ukraine. He disagrees with those who argue that the new Cold War started with Putin's assumption of power. Legvold's assess-ment is grounded in a sensitive reading of how Russia's international politics evolved during Putin's rule, beginning with serious attempts at engagement which later gave way to disillusionment and estrangement. This view avoids the essentialist position, which argues that the roots of the conflict lie in the nature of the Russian domestic system. Russia's enduring claim to be a great power was already apparent in the Yeltsin years, and in different forms it will undoubtedly be manifested by Putin's

---

[63] Viktor Kremenyuk, *Uroki kholodnoi voiny* (Moscow, Aspekt Press, 2015).

[64] Tamara Zamyatina, 'Russia, US Should Seek Balance of Rivalry and Cooperation to Avoid New Cold War', *TASS*, 19 October 2015, http://tass.ru/en/opinions/830039, last accessed 26 May 2017.

[65] Ted Galen Carpenter, 'The Simple Reason Russia and America Keep Inching towards Crisis', *The National Interest*, 19 January 2017, http://nationalinterest.org/blog/the-skep tics/the-simple-reason-russia-america-keep-inching-towards-crisis-19117, last accessed 26 May 2017.

successor. For Legvold, the roots of the new Cold War lie in the policies of the Bush and Clinton administrations, and were already apparent in the late Kozyrev era. Primakov's espousal of a multipolar world signalled Russia's resistance to America's use of power to constrain Russian interests. Legvold notes that 'neither side ever truly tried to build the comprehensive, integrated European security system that their vaulted rhetoric promised at the end of the Cold War', and '[b]y solving one half of Europe's security problem through NATO enlargement, they accentuated the security problem in Europe's other half and laid waste to the prospect of creating a broader Euro-Atlantic security community'.[66] NATO enlargement, the Kosovo crisis and the endless series of aggravations in the 2000s only reinforced the structural factors precipitating a breakdown in relations.

This was evident in the failure of the 'reset' of Barack Obama's first term. At the Munich Security Conference in February 2009 the US vice president Joseph Biden argued that Russia and the US should press the 'reset button on their relationship'.[67] Obama's reset was, as Angela Stent describes, the fourth attempt to restore relations since the end of the Cold War.[68] The auguries were not good when in Geneva on 6 March 2009 secretary of state Hillary Clinton presented Lavrov with a mistranslated reset button – instead of 'reset' (*perezagruska*), the button was labelled 'overload' (*peregruzka*). There were some achievements. Obama made some concessions on plans to deploy missile defences in Poland and the Czech Republic. New START (Strategic Arms Reduction Treaty, START-3) was signed in Prague on 8 April 2010, committing both sides to significant cuts in nuclear weapons accompanied by verification inspections, and the Northern Distribution Network allowed US forces and material access to Afghanistan through Russia. At the same time, Clinton pursued the cause of 'energy security' by circumventing Russia, and 'teams of US energy experts fanned out across Europe to help countries explore alternatives to Russian gas'.[69] In her memoirs Clinton stressed that even when NATO engaged with Russia, it would retain a 'hedge' capacity 'should a future Russia once again threaten its neighbours'.[70] For Clinton, the reset was based on three elements: 'finding specific areas for cooperation where our interests aligned, standing

[66] Robert Legvold, *Return to Cold War* (Cambridge, Polity, 2016), pp. 99, 100.

[67] Mikhail Zygar, *All the Kremlin's Men: Inside the Court of Vladimir Putin* (New York, Public Affairs, 2016), p. 173.

[68] Angela Stent, *The Limits of Partnership: US–Russian Relations in the Twenty-first Century* (Princeton, Princeton University Press, 2014), p. 212.

[69] Hillary Rodham Clinton, *Hard Choices: A Memoir* (New York, Simon and Schuster, 2014), p. 241.

[70] Clinton, *Hard Choices*, p. 211.

firm where our interests diverged, and engaging consistently with the Russian people themselves'.[71] This was hardly a formula for a successful relationship. The reset was limited in vision and late in arriving, and avoided discussing precisely the contentious issues that were of greatest concern to Moscow, thus reinforcing what could be called a 'discursive block' in international relations. The reset from the Russian perspective offered no prospect of breaking out from its strategic impasse, and was therefore just another variant of the soft containment policy that shaped US policy towards Russia throughout the cold peace.

Both sides were ready to engage in transactional deals, especially on strategic nuclear issues, but the time had passed for anything more unless the framework for the relationship changed, and that was certainly not on offer. There was no genuine dialogue between Moscow and Washington, and instead Michael McFaul, one of the architects of the reset policy, emphasised the alleged values gap between the two sides and declared that he would 'establish a direct relationship with the Russian people' over the Kremlin's head.[72] This was the background to Putin's charge that Clinton 'set the tone for some actors in our country and gave them a signal' at the time of mass protests against electoral fraud in the 4 December 2011 parliamentary ballot.[73] Putin went on to note '[t]hey heard the signal and with the support of the State Department began active work'.[74] This set the agenda for his third presidency, hardening his view that 'the West was inimically opposed to him and his interests, and therefore inimically opposed to Russia itself'.[75] The growing gulf between the two sides reflected the absence of a 'mode of reconciliation' after the Cold War. On the one side, the Atlantic powers were confident in their perceived victory, and genuinely sought to bring Russia into the expanded system as long as the country adapted to the practices of the power system. On the other side, Russia was ready to join but not at the price of transforming fundamental elements of its political identity. NATO is an instrument of collective defence, and its enlargement did not pose a threat to Russia; and Russia was not a neo-imperial power seeking to destroy the sovereignty of its neighbours. The positions were not irreconcilable, but in the absence of a language and the institutions of reconciliation, conflict ensued. The reset's failure, like all previous attempts,

---

[71] Clinton, *Hard Choices*, p. 231.

[72] Nicolai N. Petro, 'Mired in a Yawning Divide', *Moscow Times*, 13 July 2009.

[73] Clinton, *Hard Choices*, p. 235.

[74] Steven Lee Myers, *The New Tsar: The Rise and Reign of Vladimir Putin* (London, Simon and Schuster, 2015), p. 397.

[75] Myers, *New Tsar*, p. 421.

reflected the structural differences in respective understandings of the nature of post-Cold War international order.

The deterioration in relations provoked a rash of books condemning Russia for its recalcitrance and calling for a vigorous response. In 2004 Bugajski talked of a 'cold peace', but by 2008 Edward Lucas, a senior editor at *The Economist*, was already warning of, or more likely calling for, a 'new Cold War'.[76] His tone later became even more apocalyptic, asserting that the former danger of international communism had now given way to the threat posed by the *siloviki* (security officials and their allies), which had established a criminal conspiracy masquerading as a state in the Kremlin.[77] The emphasis now shifted to Russia's attempts to subvert Western order by abusing its institutions and openness.[78] As the crisis in relations intensified, the titles became even more lurid, including one called *Putin's Master Plan: To Destroy Europe, Divide NATO, and Restore Russian Power and Global Influence*.[79] The former chess champion and radical liberal Garry Kasparov was unequivocal in calling on the West to declare 'war' against Putin's regime, insisting that 'the mantra of engagement' was no more than a synonym for appeasement and that '[d]ictators only stop when they are stopped'.[80] In his view, 'Russia's descent back into totalitarianism can be traced to the West doing too much to respect the legacy of the USSR as a great power, not too little'.[81]

The restoration of Russian power and influence was certainly the Kremlin's goal, and NATO had become its bugbear (as realists almost without exception had long warned it would), but what was lacking in such analyses was how Russia's attempts at cooperation until the mid-2000s turned into such bitter enmity. Instead, the focus was on how to counter 'Russian aggression' and 'hybrid warfare'.[82] This genre of litera-ture is profoundly reductionist – reducing Russian foreign policy to the machinations of a diabolic self-seeking clique in the Kremlin, devoid of history, context or national interests. It tells us less about the well-springs

[76] Edward Lucas, *The New Cold War: How the Kremlin Menaces both Russia and the West* (London, Bloomsbury, 2008).

[77] Edward Lucas, *Deception: Spies, Lies and How Russia Dupes the West* (London, Bloomsbury, 2013).

[78] Karen Dawisha, 'Is Russia's Foreign Policy That of a Corporatist-Kleptocratic Regime?', *Post-Soviet Affairs*, Vol. 27, No. 4, 2011, pp. 331–65.

[79] Douglas E. Schoen with Evan Roth Smith, *Putin's Master Plan: To Destroy Europe, Divide NATO, and Restore Russian Power and Global Influence* (New York, Encounter, 2016).

[80] Garry Kasparov with Mig Greengard, *Winter is Coming: Why Vladimir Putin and the Enemies of the Free World Must be Stopped* (London, Atlantic Books, 2015), pp. xix, xxiv, 9, 263.

[81] Kasparov, *Winter is Coming*, p. 29.

[82] For a sceptical view, see Bettina Renz and Hanna Smith, *Russia and Hybrid Warfare: Going beyond the Label* (Helsinki, Aleksanteri Papers No. 1, 2016).

of Russian policy than about the insecurities of the West, for whom the
certainties of the Cold War years appear attractive compared to the
challenges of the new era. Russian foreign policy cannot be reduced to
the way Russia is governed. Foreign policy remains largely the prerogative
of the executive, although it is not insulated from popular and interest
group pressures.[83] The breakdown in relations represented not a new
Cold War (this is discussed in the first section of Chapter 6) but reflected
the dynamics of a putatively post-hegemonic international relations. In
2014, 'Russia broke out of the post-Cold War order and openly challenged the US-led international system'.[84] For Russia, the crisis represented a way out of the strategic impasse.

---

[83] Dmitri Trenin and Bobo Lo, *The Landscape of Russian Foreign Policy Decision-Making*
(Moscow, Moscow Carnegie Centre, 2005).

[84] Dmitri Trenin, *Russia's Breakout from the Post-Cold War System: The Drivers of Putin's
Course*, Carnegie Moscow Centre, 22 December 2014, p. 1, http://carnegieendow
ment.org/files/CP_Trenin_Putin2014_web_Eng.pdf, last accessed 26 May 2017.

2   Order without Hegemony

The Cold War generated conflict but it also provided stability. The removal of bipolar overlay allowed conflicts, as in the Balkans, while the absence of the Soviet threat tempted the Western powers onto the path of regime change in Iraq, Libya and elsewhere. The expansion of the Atlantic security system provoked a classic action-reaction sequence. A security dilemma occurs when attempts to increase the security of one state provokes another to undertake defensive responses, starting an escalation cycle that is hard to break.[1] As Russia perceived itself to be under threat, so it countered by measures that projected an assertive if not outright aggressive image, which in turn exacerbated the threat perceptions of its neighbours and ultimately of the Atlantic alliance as a whole.[2] From a structural realist point of view, this new confrontation was unnecessary. American supremacy and the consolidation of the Atlantic community were not challenged. Although US power in relative terms may be declining, it remains overwhelmingly the most powerful state in the world. Russia has no fundamental opposition to the idea of American leadership as long as it is deployed judiciously and in conformity with international law. The objection in the end was to the way that hegemonic power was exercised, and in particular the strategic dead end which it was perceived to have imposed on Russia. This prompted the creation of an anti-hegemonic alignment with China and some other countries, based ultimately on a pluralist view of a multipolar international system.

The International System and International Society

Kissinger argues that the vitality of an international order depends on the balance it strikes between legitimacy and power, with both subject to evolution and change, but '[w]hen that balance is destroyed, restraints

---

[1] For the classic statement, see Robert Jervis, *Perception and Misperception in International Politics* (Princeton, Princeton University Press, 1976).

[2] Andrej Krickovic, 'Catalyzing Conflict: The Internal Dimension of the Security Dilemma', *Journal of Global Security Studies*, Vol. 1, No. 2, May 2016, pp. 111–26.

disappear, and the field is open to the most expansive claims and most implacable actors; chaos follows until a new system of order is established'.[3] The Versailles settlement in his view placed excessive emphasis on the legitimacy component and appeals to shared principles, and by ignoring the element of power effectively provoked German revisionism.[4] A version of the argument was advanced by Carr, and can be applied with equal force to the end of the Cold War. The influential commentator Sergei Karaganov, Dean of the Faculty of World Economy and International Affairs at the Higher School of Economics in Moscow and Honorary Chairman of the Council on Foreign and Defence Policy (SVOP), argues that a 'Versailles peace' was imposed on Russia,

avoiding direct annexations and contributions but continuously limiting Russia's freedom, spheres of influence and markets and at the same time expanding the area of its own political and military zone of control through NATO enlargement, and its political and economic zone of influence through EU expansion.[5]

Karaganov calls this a 'Weimar policy in velvet gloves', which pushed 'Russia off the political, security and economic stage'. Russia had at first been mainly concerned with NATO enlargement, but later it became clear that

the European Union's enlargement did not benefit Russia either as it was not accompanied, as had been promised and expected, by efforts to create a common and equal human and economic space from Lisbon to Vladivostok. Western geopolitical expansion reduced possible gains for the Russian people from relations with Europe and weakened pro-European feelings in the political class. The logic that eventually prevailed was that the West used Russia's weakness to take away its centuries-old gains and make it even weaker.[6]

This is going too far, since the 'velvet gloves' were real, and there was no intention to punish Russia after 1991. Instead, all sorts of measures were devised to bring Russia into the Atlantic and broader Western community, although recognising the obstacles on the way to Russia's full inclusion. The community was not opposed to Russia joining, but it wanted a different Russia to the one on offer; while Russia wanted to join the community, but on its own terms. The Soviet Union and Russia ended the Cold War in the belief that it would become part of a reconfigured Europe; instead, it was invited to join a Europe that remained embedded

[3] Henry Kissinger, *World Order: Reflections on the Character of Nations and the Course of History* (London, Allen Lane, 2014), p. 66.
[4] Kissinger, *World Order*, p. 83.
[5] Sergei Karaganov, '2014: Predvaritel'nye itogi', *Rossiiskaya gazeta*, 28 November 2014, p. 11.
[6] Sergei Karaganov, 'Novaya ideologicheskaya bor'ba', *Izvestiya*, 21 April 2016, p. 6.

in an Atlantic security system that had largely been devised to keep the Soviet Union at bay. Equally, Russia wanted to join a Historic West that by its membership would be transformed into a Greater West, but the existing members understandably feared that Russian membership would provoke institutional incoherence and normative dilution. This also applied at the continental level, and the historic core Europe of the EU was unwilling to become part of a Greater Europe project. This only intensified Russia's perception that it was trapped into a strategic impasse in which its only choices appeared to be to transform itself in a way that would undermine its historical specificity and geopolitical concerns; or to remain true to a certain vision of itself, and hence remain an outsider to what it considered to be its natural home. To understand why no formula was found to reconcile these positions, we need an understanding of the dynamics of post-Cold War international politics.

Drawing on English School insights, in schematic terms I accentuate the two-level structure to the international system. The English School distinguishes between primary institutions of international society, which are the deep and organic ideas and practices in international relations such as sovereignty, territoriality, balance of power, war, international law, diplomacy and nationalism, and it is these European-generated elements that were expanded to the rest of the world.[7] Russia clearly supports these primary institutions, fearing that the universalist liberal hegemony undermines them. However, no less important are the secondary institutions, such as the UN, which seek to generalise solidarist practices in a plural international system. These secondary institutions are by definition universal, whereas the primary institutions generate practices of exclusion, with the Western core imposing its own 'standards of civilisation' and acting as the gatekeeper, notably in the context of colonialism.[8] The secondary institutions since 1945 have become increasingly ramified. The developing apparatus and processes of global governance have the UN at its apex and latterly complemented by a network of international law and normative expectations. Here also are the institutions of international financial governance, derived initially from the Bretton Woods system comprising the World Bank and the International Monetary Fund (IMF), and the system of global economic governance, notably the World Trade Organisation (WTO), now joined

---

[7] Barry Buzan, *An Introduction to the English School of International Relations* (Cambridge, Polity, 2014), pp. 32–6.

[8] Gerrit W. Gong, *The Standard of 'Civilization' in International Society* (Oxford, Clarendon Press, 1984); Barry Buzan, 'The "Standard of Civilisation" as an English School Concept', *Millennium*, Vol. 42, No. 3, 2014, pp. 576–94.

by some new bodies sponsored by the BRICS states and China, notably the Asian Infrastructure Investment Bank (AIIB).

At the normative level, Tony Blair's speech in Chicago in April 1999 formulated the doctrine of an 'international community' with the duty to intervene in the internal affairs of states to prevent harm.[9] This was then formulated in the responsibility to protect (R2P) UN convention of 2005, which marked an important step in establishing a framework for international intervention in defence of peoples against states. This and other developments erode classical principles of national sovereignty by establishing certain supra-national institutions and norms. The R2P doctrine represented an attempt to 'norm the exception', to provide a legal framework to legitimate over-riding the sovereignty of states. R2P qualitatively changes the nature of humanitarian intervention. This exceptionalist theory transforms the nature of state power, with the protective functions of the state, measured by its ability to provide security, displacing the traditional foundations of representative government and popular sovereignty.[10] Pluralists in the English School tradition are sceptical about this more solidarist version, which effectively renders individual rights sovereign subjects of international law, and argue that states remain the subject of international society and retain moral pre-eminence.[11] This is consonant with the Russian view, which downplays morality in legitimate military interventions, and instead stresses legality, constitutionalism and the protection of its citizens.[12]

Hedley Bull's classic study, *The Anarchical Society*, stresses the elements of cooperation and regulation in relations between states, highlighting the way that transnational ideas generate norms and interests that are institutionalised in the form of international organisations and rules.[13] He explicitly did not 'place major emphasis upon international organisations such as the United Nations', and instead found 'the basic causes of such order as exists in world politics' in the 'institutions of international society that arose before these international organisations were established'.[14] Bull's

---

[9] Speech at the Chicago Economics Club, 23 April 1999, www.tonyblairoffice.org/spee ches/entry/tony-blair-speech-to-chicago-council-on-global-affairs/, last accessed 26 May 2017.

[10] Philip Cunliffe, 'The Doctrine of the "Responsibility to Protect" as a Practice of Political Exceptionalism', *European Journal of International Relations*, Vol. 23, No. 2, 2017, pp. 466–86.

[11] Andrew Linklater and Hidemi Suganami, *The English School of International Relations: A Contemporary Reassessment* (New York, Cambridge University Press, 2006), pp. 59–74.

[12] Roy Allison, *Russia, the West, and Military Intervention* (Oxford, Oxford University Press, 2013), p. 12.

[13] Hedley Bull, *The Anarchical Society: A Study of Order in World Politics* (Oxford, Oxford University Press, 1995[1977]).

[14] Bull, *Anarchical Society*, pp. xvii-xviii.

approach retained much of the traditional thinking about a state-centric world, but this was tempered by the view that states have common interests that can best be advanced through the cooperative institutions of international society.[15] These are the structures of universalism and inter-state cooperation that became increasingly ramified after the Second World War.[16] It is in this sense that I will use the term international society, a broad conceptualisation of the institutions of global governance. After the end of the Cold War they were anticipated to gain greater autonomy and substance. Instead, as Cold War bipolarity gave way to unipolarity, the liberal international order effectively claimed to be synonymous with international society. The US-led liberal international order thus inserted itself into some sort of tutelary relationship with it.[17] In this conception, world order emerges not out of cooperative (solidarist) inter-state practices regulated by international society, but out of American leadership of the liberal international order. The institutions of international society and the liberal international order are effectively fused in this thinking, prompting the 'decoupling' agenda of the anti-hegemonists. A more organic decoupling has always been possible, and relations between the US and the UN have been far from easy, prompting complaints by US legislators about the disproportionate burden.[18] The US contributes 22 per cent of the main UN budget and nearly 29 per cent of peacekeeping costs.[19] There have been various attempts to bypass the UN's authority through 'coalitions of the willing', as in Iraq in 2003, while the idea of a 'League of Democracies' was intended to achieve a similar autonomy from international society in the normative sphere.

The implicit claim of co-terminality was challenged by Russia from the first, supported by other re-emerging or rising powers. The fundamental Russian argument is the traditional state-centric one; that the international system is made up of a plurality of states with their own interests, and that the post-Cold War inversion which claimed a certain universality

---

[15] For the articulation of a less statist ontology of international society than Hedley Bull's, see Adam Watson, *The Evolution of International Society: A Comparative International Analysis*, reissue with a new introduction by Barry Buzan and Richard Little (London, Routledge, 1992).

[16] Anne-Marie Slaughter, *A New World Order* (Princeton, Princeton University Press, 2005) identifies a dense network of 'government networks' that increasingly coordinate cross-border cooperation.

[17] For a discussion, see G. John Ikenberry, *Liberal Order and Imperial Ambition: Essays on American Power and International Order* (Cambridge, Polity, 2004).

[18] For a critique of how the Western powers (above all the US) used the UN to advance their own influence, see Shirley Hazzard, *Defeat of an Ideal: Self-Destruction of the United Nations* (London, Macmillan, 1973).

[19] Ben Quinn, 'US Spending on Foreign Aid and UN Likely to be Biggest Target for Cuts', *Guardian*, 28 February 2017, p. 13.

for the liberal international order (often described in the guise of globalisation) was unacceptable, especially since Russia had been unable to
transform that order into a Greater West. At the same time, Russia's
traditional Westphalian statism is tempered by a commitment to international society, of which it claims (as does China) to have been a founder
member. Their claims are historically justified, and an extensive literature
describes global order before European hegemony.[20] The understanding
of world politics in the modern era has been Eurocentric.[21] For non-
Western powers, international society remains too deeply rooted in the
structure of Western hegemony, and hence for them the goal is to
universalise universalism; in other words, to make international society
work genuinely independently as the highest instance of the common
aspiration of humanity and the nations of which it is composed.[22] More
prosaically, there is now a growing demand for the institutions of global
financial, legal and political governance to work autonomously, resisting
the tutelary claims of the liberal hegemony and the latter's predominance
in the Bretton Woods international financial institutions.[23] The former
Russian foreign minister Igor Ivanov (1998–2004) argues that '[w]e have
entered a very complex and controversial transformation process that
should result in the establishment of a new global order to replace the
one we inherited from the twentieth century'.[24] The struggle for a reba-
lanced globalism by the anti-hegemonic alignment seeks the 'democratisation' of international relations, the 'universalisation' of global
governance, but perhaps above all a cultural change in understanding
world politics.

Critics of liberal internationalist hegemony go further and question
whether this order was ever pluralist. This line of thinking is advanced
in an extensive literature that describes the moment of American unipolar

---

[20] Janet L. Abu-Lughod, *Before European Hegemony: The World System AD 1250–1350* (New York, Oxford University Press, 1991).

[21] John M. Hobson, *The Eurocentric Conception of World Politics: Western International Theory, 1760–2010* (Cambridge, Cambridge University Press, 2012).

[22] For discussion of the issues, see Amitav Acharya, 'Global International Relations (IR) and Regional Worlds: A New Agenda for International Studies', *International Studies Quarterly*, Vol. 58, No. 4, 2014, pp. 647–59; Amitav Acharya, 'Advancing Global IR: Challenges, Contentions, and Contributions', *International Studies Review*, Vol. 18, No. 1, 2016, pp. 4–15.

[23] For a detailed interrogation of English School thinking on international society and how it works in practice, see Andrew Hurrell, *On Global Order: Power, Values, and the Constitution of International Society* (Oxford, Oxford University Press, 2007), including a discussion of regional pluralism (Chapter 10) and 'empire reborn' (Chapter 11).

[24] Igor Ivanov, 'Russia–US Cooperation: If not Today, it will Come Tomorrow', RIAC, 24 March 2017, http://russiancouncil.ru/en/analytics-and-comments/analytics/Igor-Ivano v-Russia-US-Cooperation/, last accessed 30 May 2017.

dominance in terms of 'empire'.[25] In other words, the Wilsonian form of liberal internationalism represented a distinctive form of monist thinking, which, after the asymmetrical end of the Cold War, in the absence of a substantive alternative, was radicalised to become axiological (what Jowitt calls 'absolutist') in its interactions with those outside the hegemonic order. The result was ruinous engagement in futile military expeditions that destabilised whole regions and in the end blew back into Europe in the form of waves of refugees, adding to the swelling tide of economic migrants. The rise of new powers is perceived not as the emergence of an alternative model of global order, but as the destruction of order itself. The putative autonomy of international society constrains the freedom of manoeuvre of dominant powers, provoking a hostile reaction among internationalists in Washington (whether in the neo-conservative or liberal interventionist guise).

The second level is made up of nation states and their various regional combinations, creating what some call a 'multi-order world'.[26] Multipolarity suggests different poles in the framework of a single-level international system, whereas in the binary model presented here the various sub-orders and states interact horizontally with each other in the sphere of international relations, and relate vertically with international society in what could be called the sphere of norms. Neither is exclusive, and norms play an important part in international relations, while in the normative relationship between states and the institutions of international society (like the UN), the power and other considerations of international relations play no small part. This model of the international system is multipolar at the level of horizontal state interactions, but polycentrism is tempered by vertical interactions between the order of states and the order represented by international society. The

---

[25] Indicatively, see Andrew J. Bacevich, *The Imperial Tense: Prospects and Problems of American Empire* (Lanham, Rowman and Littlefield, 2003); Alejandro Colas and Richard Saull, *The War on Terrorism and the American 'Empire' after the Cold War* (London, Routledge, 2005); Gary Dorrien, *Imperial Designs: Neo-Conservatism and the New Pax Americana* (London, Routledge, 2004); Richard Falk, *The Declining World Order: America's Imperial Geopolitics* (London, Routledge, 2004); David Harvey, *The New Imperialism* (Oxford, Oxford University Press, 2005); Chalmers Johnson, *Blowback: The Costs and Consequences of American Empire* (London, Sphere, 2002); Chalmers Johnson, *The Sorrows of Empire: Militarism, Secrecy, and the End of the Republic* (London, Verso, 2004); Ray Kiely, *Empire in the Age of Globalisation: US Hegemony and Neo-Liberal Disorder* (London, Pluto Press, 2005); Charles S. Maier, *Among Empires: American Ascendancy and Its Predecessors* (Cambridge, Harvard University Press, 2006); Michael Mann, *Incoherent Empire* (London, Verso, 2005).

[26] Trine Flockhart, 'The Coming Multi-Order World', *Contemporary Security Policy*, Vol. 37, No. 1, 2016, pp. 3–30. This sophisticated analysis also applies a two-level model, but differs in suggesting several 'orders' or international societies nested within an overall international system. Although I draw on Flockhart's insights, my model is rather different.

universalist normative aspirations of international society are challenged by the particularistic features of competing states and blocs.[27] Flockhart notes that 'a complex network of "inter-order" relationships will determine the character of the coming "multi-order world"', but for her the world orders operate at the single level of states.[28] These interactions in my model are tempered by the vertical relationship with international society, and a different sort of pluralism operates in the international system as a whole. Fu Ying, a former deputy foreign minister and then chair of the Foreign Affairs Committee of the National People's Congress, alluded to this in her speech at the Munich Security Conference on 13 February 2016, when she stressed that 'China supports the current international order. And you may note that the word used is "international order". The Chinese seldom talk about the "world order". What China refers to is the UN-based system including the international institutions and norms.'[29] Chinese officialdom avoids the term 'world order' because of the power assumptions inherent in the term. Fu Ying clarified that China had reservations about the practices of the US-led world order, but rejected the idea that China was creating a parallel order: '[O]f course not, we are part of the international order'.

   The pre-eminent project for world order is the Atlantic community and its broader but increasingly anachronistic appellation of 'the West'. In the original English School formulation, the international society of states devised in Europe expanded in successive waves to encompass the whole world.[30] This really was an 'expansion', enlarging a system into which Russia, with its characteristic ambivalence, was soon incorporated.[31] The assumption that this system was enlarging into an empty field soon provoked resistance, of the sort that the 'enlargement' of the Atlantic

---

[27] English School thinking suggests that the international state system evolved out of institutions like the state, territoriality, the balance of power, diplomacy and sovereignty, which formed in Europe and then expanded through colonialism and then revolutionary nationalists across the world to become truly universal, whereas many of the institutions of international society were created by the Allies during the war and reflected Western values, and were at first relatively exclusive. Without challenging this genealogy, it should be noted that from the first a universalist dynamic was embedded not only in the primary institutions of international society, but also in the top-level secondary institutions, which have since become generalised as the institutions of 'global governance' and have become more delineated and gained in authority.

[28] Flockhart, 'The Coming Multi-Order World', p. 5.

[29] Fu Ying, 'Putting the Order(s) Shift in Perspective', 13 February 2016, www.security conference.de/en/activities/munich-security-conference/msc-2016/speeches/speech-by-f u-ying/, last accessed 26 May 2017.

[30] Hedley Bull and Adam Watson, *The Expansion of International Society* (Oxford, Oxford University Press, 1984).

[31] Iver B. Neumann, 'Entry into International Society Reconceptualised: The Case of Russia', *Review of International Studies*, Vol. 37, No. 2, 2011, pp. 463–84.

system did after the Cold War.[32] The debates raise similar issues and comparable responses, with demands for a pluralistic universalism at the global level.[33] The developing field of global international relations represents a call for the radical pluralisation of the international system. The Russian parlance for this pluralism is multipolarity, or more recently 'polycentrism', a term reflecting the Russian ambition to 'democratise' international relations. The striving for pluralism provides the ideational foundation for the anti-hegemonic alignment encompassing Russia, China and India. Hegemonic power is exercised through institutions that have a 'certain semblance of universality' and an ideology that justifies hegemonic leadership to guarantee that order, whereas counter-hegemony represents an alternative view of the world, typically generated by a coalition of peripheral countries.[34] This is reinforced institutionally by the asynchronic development of the secondary institutions of international society. Although initially most were of Western origin, their development has been governed from the outset less by expansion than by mutual constitution. For example, the establishment of the UN drew on various Western traditions as well as Soviet, Islamic and other ideas. As the secondary institutions strengthen and become more genuinely universal they threaten accustomed patterns of Western hegemony, but at the same time provide the sinews for order after the waning of this hegemony.

The liberal international order has shaped contemporary modernity and retains hegemonic ambitions, although the classical age of Western dominance may well be waning as the unipolar moment gives way to a more multipolar and possibly multi-order world. As argued earlier, at the end of the Cold War Russia aspired to join this Historical West, but at the same time it sought its transformation into a Greater West – an ambition that proved too ambitious for both sides. The collapse of the state socialist alternative model of modernity represented by the Soviet system was not followed by Russia's anticipated seamless return to what Gorbachev-era intellectuals called 'the main highway of history'.[35] It turned out that history has many highways and byways. Russia asserted that it was a senior constitutive component of international society, as a founding

[32] Tim Dunne and Christian Reut-Smith (eds.), *The Globalization of International Society* (Oxford, Oxford University Press, 2017).

[33] See the various publications by Amitav Acharya, indicatively his most recent study: *The End of American World Order* (Cambridge, Polity, 2014).

[34] Robert W. Cox, 'Social Forces, States and World Orders: Beyond International Relations Theory', *Millennium: Journal of International Studies*, Vol. 10, No. 2, 1981, pp. 126–55.

[35] For a classic discussion, see Yurii N. Afanas'ev (ed.), *Inogo ne dano* (Moscow, Progress, 1988).

state of the UN and a permanent member of its Security Council, and sought to lever this to transform the Historical Western order. The self-willed disintegration of the Soviet bloc represented a pledge of Moscow's bona fides as a member of the expanded Western order. What Moscow would not do is enter into some sort of neo-colonial apprenticeship to enter the Historical West.

Russian thinking in the early years tended to mirror the Historical West's own conflation of the liberal international order with international society writ large. Russia viewed itself a founding member of substantial elements of post-war international society, hence it was automatically a constitutive member of the liberal international order. The failure to transform the Historical West into the Greater West in the end reinforced the never-ending domestic debate about Russia's place in the world. In a move earlier signalled by Primakov, Russia after 2012 adopted a politics of resistance, developed the institutions of Eurasian integration, and aligned itself with powers critical of Western hegemony. This was accompanied by longing glances at the West that may have been and the Europe that it may one day become. The evolution in conceptual understanding brought Russia to defend the autonomy of international society against the hegemony of the Historical West. Although reflecting a shift of emphasis in the post-communist era, Russia's defence of the normative order of international law (described as part of the broader order of international society) represents a resumption of Tsarist and Soviet traditions.[36]

This revived appreciation of the multi-layer quality of the international system is reflected in Russia's neo-revisionism: horizontally, critiquing the hegemonic ambitions and double standards of the liberal international order; but vertically, defending the autonomy of international society. Article 15.4 of the Russian constitution proclaims the supremacy of international law over domestic legislation, and although a law of December 2015 allows the Constitutional Court to adjudicate the application of the principle, the constitution has not been amended. The traditional advocacy of multipolarity has now become a more sophisticated defence of multi-level pluralism as well as the pluralism of state-centric international relations. Russia's neo-revisionism does not seek to isolate Russia from international society, but challenges the Historical West's right to define its norms.[37] Russia has reverted to its traditional self-representation as the guardian of international law. As Fu Ying intimated for

---

[36] Lauri Mälksoo, *Russian Approaches to International Law* (Oxford, Oxford University Press, 2015).

[37] Christopher Browning, 'Reassessing Putin's Project: Reflections on IR Theory and the West', *Problems of Post-Communism*, Vol. 55, No. 5, September–October 2008, pp. 3–13.

China, this does not mean the creation of a counter-hegemonic 'world order' or bloc in opposition to the Historical West, but a more profound anti-hegemonic politics.

The tensions and contradictions of the cold peace and Moscow's frustrations generated an anti-hegemonic alignment of states resistant to the hegemonic practices of the Historical West, but defending the autonomy and the universalism of international society. The leading power in this alternative constellation is, of course, China. Russia's relations with China today are better than they have ever been, yet there are points of tension in the bilateral relationship and in the various institutions and networks in which the relationship is embedded. Nevertheless, this alternative alignment shares a common aspiration to share in the management of global affairs, and works together to render the structures of global governance more independent. Russia's so-called 'turn to Asia' can in classic defensive realist terms be seen as part of its long-term attempt to balance against American hegemony; but more substantively, it asserts the normative ambition to create a more plural international system. More practical factors are also at work, including the developmental needs of the Russian Far East, as well as to assert its presence in the dynamically developing East Asian region.[38] The shift represents a partial recasting of Russian self-representation away from the West towards a more Eurasian if not Asian identity. This does not entail the repudiation of Russia's long-term ambition to become part of a transformed Greater West or Greater Europe.

The multilateralism of international society in this model is decoupled from liberal hegemony. This entails the restoration of pluralism to the international system, whose normativity is based on pluralism itself. In other words, cultural diversity, different 'civilisational' paths and pluralist polity construction repudiate the idea that the historical experience of one set of states can act as universal models to all others. This model also achieves Russia's long-term goal of an international security system that transcends military blocs.[39] This is a pluralism founded on the belief that each state has to resolve its own challenges, and that historical experience cannot be transplanted from one context to another (the conceit of much of post-communist democracy promotion). This does not mean that comparative lessons cannot be learned, but it rejects programmatic attempts to transfer models. This is the conceptual basis for the rejection of norm transfer as an appropriate framework for relations between states.

---

[38] Alexander Korolev, 'Russia's Reorientation to Asia: Causes and Strategic Implications', *Pacific Affairs*, Vol. 89, No. 1, March 2016, pp. 53–73.

[39] Enunciated, for example, by Putin in his Victory Day speech, *New York Times*, 9 May 2016.

It does not mean simply the restoration of spheres of influence and the defence of state sovereignty of the Westphalian sort, since resistance to Western hegemony is accompanied by attempts to strengthen the universalism represented by international society.

Pluralism in this interpretation differs from that defined by English School theorists as 'the communitarian disposition towards a state-centric mode of association in which sovereignty and non-intervention serve to contain and sustain cultural and political diversity'. Instead, it shares something with the contrasting English School view of solidarism, defined as 'the disposition either to transcend the states-system with some other mode of association or to develop it beyond the logic of coexistence to one of cooperation on shared projects'.[40] Solidarism promotes the benefits of international community, an inherent feature of the rules-based norms of the secondary institutions of international society, while horizontal relations between states are inherently pluralist, except when combined in various sub-orders. Pluralism is achieved by the recognition of diverse developmental paths to sustain not so much 'multiple modernity' (since modernity by definition can only be singular, although taking a multiplicity of forms), as a number of distinctive security and civilisational complexes, each of which taken together is today conventionally described as a project for world order.[41] Neither is this the pluralism generated, as in the realist paradigm, by the return of great power politics. Instead, the various world orders represent a combination of pluralism and solidarism, with the latter represented by the shared commitment to international society. This is a pluralism of procedure (that world orders can relate to international society autonomously, and not necessarily through alignment with the liberal internationalist order), rather than a pluralism based on substantive normative differences.

This is a substantive invocation of the Grotian position advanced by Bull.[42] He distinguishes between the Hobbesian or realist tradition that sees international relations as a permanent state of conflict between states in a system that is pre-eminently distributive or zero-sum. In this perspective, peace is only a 'period of recuperation' between renewed bouts of war. Contemporary realist thinkers, such as Hans Morgenthau, have developed a complex language to describe

---

[40] Buzan, *An Introduction*, p. 16.

[41] This model in part overlaps with the idea of regional security complexes, in which contiguous states establish a regime of intense security interdependence, Barry Buzan and Ole Waever, *Regions and Powers: The Structure of International Security* (Cambridge, Cambridge University Press, 2003).

[42] The following account is drawn from Bull, *Anarchical Society*, pp. 23–6.

the strategies adopted by states in this endless war for position and status.[43] Dominant states try to get others to bandwagon with them, while weaker powers try to establish counter-balancing coalitions. There is little scope for morality here, and instead the Machiavellian impulse prevails. By contrast, the Kantian or universalist tradition asserts that international politics is capable of generating a 'potential community of mankind'. Various transnational bonds tie nations and peoples together and foster cooperative policies to transcend conflicts, and indeed ultimately to transcend the state system itself. The moral imperative of what we today call human rights, for example, works not only to limit the sovereignty of states but drives towards their replacement by a cosmopolitan society. In between the realist and universalist traditions there is the Grotian idea of a society of states, or international society. Against the Hobbesians, common rules and institutions constrain the bellicosity of states; but by contrast with the Kantians, states remain the fundamental actors in the international system. In the Grotian concept, states are bound not only by the rules of prudence and expediency, but also by the norms of morality and law as generated by the particular international society of the era.

Thus the Christian international society devised in the fifteenth century, in the twentieth gave way to what Bull calls world international society.[44] The League of Nations, the attempt by the Kellogg-Briand Pact of 1928 to renounce war as an instrument to advance state policy, and other idealistic initiatives of the inter-war years proved a false start, and in Carr's view actually impeded rational inter-state diplomacy. Nevertheless, the Grotian impulse returned after the Second World War, and remains embedded in the thickening networks of world international society. The UN represents the highest manifestation of the Grotian or solidarist representation of world order. It seeks to aggregate the concerns of international society while not denying the centrality of sovereign states. The Grotian approach repudiates the ideological homogeneity so deeply embedded in Kantian cosmopolitanism, while rejecting the normative brutality of realist positions. It has no time for the 'end of history' and its concomitant assumption of the 'end of international politics'; but neither does it succumb to the realist imposition of hegemonic order by powerful states. It offers the possibility of combining political realism and normative pluralism.

---

[43] Hans J. Morgenthau, *Politics among Nations: The Struggle for Power and Peace*, 7th edn (New York, McGraw-Hill, 2005).
[44] Bull, *Anarchical Society*, pp. 36–8.

Hegemony and Anti-hegemony

The modern idea of hegemony is drawn from the Gramscian lexicon to denote the combination of coercive and consensual mechanisms by which a ruling order maintains its power. I apply it in that neutral sense here, although in terms of power consolidation and projection the term is anything but neutral. As far as this study of Russian foreign policy and the international system is concerned, in the previous section it was noted that the US-led liberal international order can be called 'hegemonic' on the basis of its expansive claims to global leadership, and the implicit claim of a certain tutelary relationship with the institutions of international society, some of which, like the Bretton Woods institutions, were generated by the liberal order itself. After 1989 this order enlarged to encompass most of the former Soviet bloc and through globalisation shaped a new international political economy. The Soviet collapse represented not only the end of the Cold War but also the exhaustion of a distinctive type of revolutionary socialist challenge to capitalist hegemony. This challenge to what became liberal capitalist modernity had already been signalled at the time of the French Revolution and was later intensified in the guise of Marxist and various workers' movements. The Leninist formulation of this challenge prioritised the vanguard role of the revolutionary party, accompanied by a rather eviscerated understanding of politics and democracy. This was questioned from the outset by such veterans of the workers' movement as Karl Kautsky and Rosa Luxemburg.[45] By contrast, Antonio Gramsci, a leader of the Italian communist party jailed by Benito Mussolini in 1926, in his *Prison Notebooks* outlined a sophisticated understanding of capitalist hegemony and counter-hegemonic strategies based on contestation in the cultural as well as the political terrain.[46]

The hegemonic 'historic bloc' (to use Gramsci's terminology) is more than the contingent 'victor' of the Cold War but represents a power constellation with deep historical roots. The Atlantic system represents not only the apparent triumph of the military-political alliance over a rather moribund state socialist system in the Cold War, but capitalist democracy incorporates traditional Western imperial ambition and the view of the West as the maker of modernity. The liberal international order combines two distinct but entwined elements: the Atlantic power

---

[45] Richard Sakwa, 'The Rise of Leninism: The Death of Political Pluralism in the Post-revolutionary Bolshevik Party', in Tony Brenton (ed.), *Historically Inevitable? Turning Points of the Russian Revolution* (London, Profile Books, 2016), pp. 262–83.

[46] Antonio Gramsci, *Selections from the Prison Notebooks*, edited and translated by Quintin Hoare and Geoffrey Nowell Smith (London, Lawrence and Wishart, 1971).

system encompassing NATO and the EU; and 'the West' as a historical cultural complex, now including many countries far from the Atlantic basin. The dynamism of this historic bloc is generated by its reflexivity, creativity and endless self-doubts; but also in part by awareness that its hegemonic pre-eminence is fragile, torn by contradictions, and increasingly challenged from outside. Nonetheless, the negative transcendence of the Cold War saw not only enlargement but also the radicalisation of the system itself. Hegemonic practices and ideology (the 'end of history') and the consolidation of the primacy of the West were now couched in the universal language of freedom and democracy. This radicalisation represented an inversion, since up to 1989 it had been the Soviet Union that had appealed (at least residually) to the universalism of the workers' movement and international revolution. The inversion challenged Russia's traditional state centrism and undermined the legitimacy of its security concerns, and deprived it of a language in which to express its normative defence of pluralism. American leadership in the unipolar moment was largely unopposed until the rise of challengers, the emergence of multipolarity, and Russia's partial disincorporation from the Western bloc after the hesitant years of adaptation in the 1990s. The loss of expansive self-confidence explains why by the late 2000s the narrative shifted to issues of the 'new world disorder'.[47] This was accompanied by debates about America's relative decline, the multiple crises of the EU, and the challenge of maintaining a rules-based international order based on 'American world order'.[48]

The anti-hegemonic bloc is represented by various subaltern challengers. It is 'anti' rather than counter-hegemonic because it not only challenges the geopolitical dominance of the US-led liberal international order, but above all questions hegemonic leadership itself. This represents a return to the unfinished agenda of 1989, when Gorbachev hoped not only to put an end to the Cold War but also to the conditions that gave rise to it. Although Russian resistance to the Historic West has unique characteristics, it is part of a broader category of attempts by marginal and peripheral actors to revise global power and economic governance. The Soviet Union and, in a different way, China, led the struggle against Western dominance in the Cold War, while the Non-Aligned Movement (NAM), established in Bandung in 1955, sought to find a

---

[47] Bobo Lo, *Russia and the New World Disorder* (Washington, Brookings, 2015); Richard Haas, 'The Unraveling: How to Respond to a Disordered World', *Foreign Affairs*, Vol. 93, No. 6, November–December 2014, pp. 70–9.

[48] G. John Ikenberry, *Liberal Leviathan: The Origins, Crisis, and Transformation of the American World Order* (Princeton, Princeton University Press, 2011); Joseph S. Nye, *Is the American Century Over?* (Cambridge, Polity, 2015).

middle way.[49] In the 1970s the idea of a New International Economic Order (NIEO) challenged the balance of global economic power, while the various peace movements warned of the danger of nuclear catastrophe. After 1991 the anti- and alter-globalisation movements tried to find a new idiom and new agents of resistance, but like their predecessors, these movements soon ran into the sand.[50] Only now, with the re-emergence of China and Russia's alienation from the Atlantic system are serious new players in a position to challenge Western hegemony through what in Russian parlance is called the 'democratisation of international relations', by which is meant the equalisation of power in the system. This is a combination of second world geopolitical challengers (notably, the USSR and then Russia), third world late developers (above all, China and India), and fourth world idealists (various ideas for alt-globalisation, post-industrial environmentalism, and feminist cooperation). Together, they represent a new type of 'historic bloc' based not on ideological contiguity nor on ambitions to replace the dominant power system, but on the idea of pluralism in the international system, Grotian forms of solidarity, and the desire for a more equitable distribution of influence in international society to reflect changed economic and geostrategic realities.

This theme is much discussed in Russian policy documents and speeches. Addressing the Valdai Club on 27 October 2016, Putin reprised the argument. He noted that '[t]he tensions engendered by shifts in distribution of economic and political influence continue to grow. Mutual distrust creates a burden that narrows our possibilities for finding effective responses to the real threats and challenges facing the world today'. The problem arose because of 'mistaken, hasty and to some extent over-confident choices made by some countries' elites a quarter-of-a-century ago. Back then, in the late 1980s–early 1990s, there was a chance not just to accelerate the globalisation process but also to give it a different quality and make it more harmonious and sustainable in nature'. In his view, 'some countries saw themselves as victors in the Cold War, not just saw themselves in this way but said it openly, took the course of simply reshaping the global political and economic order to fit their own interests'. As a result, '[i]n their euphoria, they essentially abandoned substantive and equal dialogue with other actors in international life, chose not to improve or create universal institutions, and attempted instead to bring the entire world under the spread of their own organisations, norms

---

[49] Odd Arne Westad, *The Global Cold War: Third World Interventions and the Making of Our Times* (Cambridge, Cambridge University Press, 2007).

[50] For a study that reflects the inchoate nature of much resistance to first world hegemony, see Michael Hardt and Antonio Negri, *Multitude: War and Democracy in the Age of Empire* (London, Penguin, 2005).

and rules'. The 'rules-based' international order was, from this perspective, applied instrumentally and opportunistically:

Rules and principle, in the economy and politics, are constantly being distorted and we often see what only yesterday was taken as a truth and raised to dogma status reversed completely. If the powers that be today find some standard or norm to their advantage, they force everyone else to comply. But if tomorrow these same standards get in their way, they are swift to throw them in the bin, declare them obsolete, and set or try to set new rules.

He gave the example of the marginalisation of the WTO by closed economic alliances, and the way the OSCE was turned 'into an instrument in the service of someone's foreign policy instruments'. By contrast, Putin praised the institutions of international society, above all the UN, and stressed the importance of sovereignty 'as the central notion of the entire system of international relations'.[51] Putin did not challenge the world order established after the Second World War based on the UN Charter and, we may add, the Helsinki Accords of 1975, but rejected interpretations that justified liberal interventions. This was a classic statement of Putin's grievances and concerns, and was the framework for the development of Russia's 'neo-revisionist' foreign policy after 2012. The critique of the practices of Western hegemony was accompanied by a defence of the impartiality of international society. This was the anti-hegemonic agenda shared by China and other emerging states.

The concept of sovereignty is the cornerstone of the practices of the alternative alignment, but because of the simultaneous commitment to international society, this is not simply a defence of the traditional Westphalian state. The view that Russia has a dual approach to sovereignty, applying a Westphalian model outside post-Soviet Eurasia (where Russia allegedly claims respect for its sovereign statehood); and a post-Soviet model inside it – challenging the US-dominated order while generating a 'non-Western' power identity in the nascent multi-order international system – can be questioned.[52] Russia's defence of the universalism of international society means that Russia is not a consistent Westphalian state. Russia's model of external sovereignty differs little from that of any other major state. Russia's criticism of the international liberal order – that this order is an expression of American hegemony and abuses its privileged relationship with international society (as suggested by Putin in his Valdai

[51] Vladimir Putin, 'Meeting of the Valdai International Discussion Club', 27 October 2016, http://en.kremlin.ru/events/president/news/53151, last accessed 26 May 2017.
[52] Ruth Deyermond, 'The Uses of Sovereignty in Twenty-first Century Russian Foreign Policy', *Europe-Asia Studies*, Vol. 68, No. 6, 2016, pp. 957–84.

speech) – does not represent the repudiation of the underlying principles of that order.

The alleged abuses become particularly acute when the US and its allies invoked the concept of 'humanitarian intervention', as in Kosovo in 1999, without direct UN sanction and against Russia's vociferous objections.[53] Steven Lee Myers notes that NATO's intervention 'infuriated Russia in ways American and European leaders failed to appreciate'.[54] The Iraq war of 2003 was a turning point for Putin, revealing 'the true ambition of the United States ... to dictate its terms to the rest of the world to champion "freedom" and use unilateral means to impose it, to interfere in the internal affairs of other nations'.[55] The Anglo-Saxon intervention in Iraq in 2003 was opposed by the 'old Europe' states of Russia, France and Germany. The invasion was criticised on operational grounds by the 'old Europe' states of France and Germany, but only Russia adopted a consistently normative stance in opposition to such interventions. The erosion of state sovereignty appeared ultimately to be a threat to Russia, in the form of regime change and 'colour revolutions'. This explains the rhetorical escalation in defence of state sovereignty, although Russia in practice continued to pursue a high degree of sovereignty-pooling in numerous international institutions and processes, notably the global governance institutions above and the EEU horizontally. On the other side, the alleged Western shift to post-Westphalian models of sovereignty has been greatly exaggerated. The exception is the EU, but even there the British referendum vote to withdraw (Brexit) of 23 June 2016 exposed the depth of popular opposition to sovereignty-sharing. Even America's hegemonic leadership of the liberal internationalism was threatened by the election of Donald J. Trump as president on 8 November 2016. Just as the unthinkable occurred when Russia withdrew from the Soviet Union in 1991, so the potential American retreat into a form of mercantilist conservative neo-isolationism threatens the foundations of the post-1945 settlement.

In his speech to the 70th anniversary of the UN General Assembly on 23 September 2016, Lavrov neatly encapsulated Russian anti-hegemonic thinking when he condemned 'mentorship, superiority and exceptionalism':

Humankind, in transitioning from a bipolar and unipolar international order to an objectively evolving polycentric, democratic system of international relations, is faced with challenges and threats that are common to all and that can only be

---

[53] James Hughes, 'Russia and the Secession of Kosovo: Power, Norms and the Failure of Multilateralism', *Europe-Asia Studies*, Vol. 65, No. 5, 2013, pp. 992–1016.
[54] Myers, *New Tsar*, p. 143.   [55] Myers, *New Tsar*, pp, 229–30.

overcome by joint efforts ... There is a pressing need to change the philosophy governing relations between states and do away with attempts to interfere in the internal affairs of states and impose development models on countries and nations.

He stressed the need for 'indivisible security' in the Euro-Atlantic region, warned of the dangers of 'double standards' in combating terrorism, and the need to strengthen the 'unifying agenda' of the institutions of international society. There was little mention of freedom and democracy and instead state sovereignty, distinctive paths to modernity and escape from Western tutelage were emphasised.[56] Putin's anniversary address on 28 September 2015 stressed the potential for cooperation: 'Hand in hand with other nations, we will consistently work to strengthen the UN's central, coordinating role. I am convinced that by working together, we will make the world stable and safe, and provide an enabling environment for the development of all nations and peoples'.[57] In other words, this would be partnership on the basis of equality based on the claim that a more pluralist international system would advance public goods such as peace and security.

Neither Russia nor China are classic Westphalian states (if such a category exists), since their commitment to international society (and its regional manifestations) means that they are profoundly engaged in internationalising structures. While 'globalism' is condemned by conservatives as a synonym for state-denying cosmopolitanism and reckless globalisation,[58] Russian 'legal globalists' defend a strong vertical relationship with the secondary institutions of international society.[59] Russia remains a member of the CoE and other institutions of European international society.[60] In economic terms, China has become an integral part of the global division of labour and its purchase of Treasury bonds helps finance the US deficit. Plans to create the land-based Silk Road Economic Belt (SREB) and the Maritime Silk Road (MSR), together creating One Belt One Road (OBOR), now called the Belt and Road Initiative (BRI), are classic moves to overcome

---

[56] 'Foreign Minister Sergey Lavrov's Remarks at the 71st Session of the UN General Assembly', New York, 23 September 2016,www.rusemb.org.uk/fnapr/5782, last accessed 26 May 2017.

[57] Vladimir Putin, '70th Session of the UN General Assembly', 28 September 2015, http://kremlin.ru/events/president/news/50385, last accessed 13 October 2015.

[58] For a classic critique, see Alexander Panarin, *Revansh istorii: Rossiiskaya strategicheskaya initsiava v XXI veke* (Moscow, 1998). An English version was published as *The Revenge of History: Russian Strategic Initiative in the Twenty-first Century* (Moscow, Logos, 1998).

[59] I am grateful to Merlen Camille-Renaud for this point.

[60] Richard Sakwa, 'Russia and Europe: Whose Society?', special issue, Ioannis Stivachtis and Mark Webber (eds.), 'Europe After Enlargement', *The Journal of European Integration*, Vol. 33, No. 2, March 2011, pp. 197–214.

domestic over-accumulation while extending geo-economic influence. The Chinese model of state capitalism, like Russia's, deviates from the classic Anglo-Saxon model to create a dual structure combining statist and market strategies. The Russian version is less developmental, and instead its state corporatist model maintains Russia's peripheral capitalist status while reinforcing the power of the bureaucracy. The Russian model increases opportunities for rent-seeking, systemic corruption and raiding, which undermine property rights, weaken entrepreneurialism and erode the rule of law.[61] The economic basis of Putin's drive to overcome the country's political marginalisation is thereby weakened. A similar argument has been applied to China. Minxin Pei argues that the incomplete reforms since the Tiananmen events in 1989 have allowed a collusive elite to convert power into wealth on a massive and corrupt scale, and China's impressive development rests on a Leninist state in an advanced state of decay.[62]

Russia and China do not challenge US hegemony directly, but both promote parallel structures to complement, and thus transform, the dominant order. This reflects profound shifts in economic power. If in 1990 the G7 countries comprised 64 per cent of global GDP, by 2017 that figure had fallen to 46 per cent. Over the same period the combined GDP of China and India has risen from 5 to 16 per cent of the world total. Russia does not bring much to this party. The gap between Russia's economic power and its foreign policy ambitions is stark. Contemporary Russia has a highly internationalised economy, yet pursues a politics that draws on the repertoire of autarchic states. The country in structural terms is on the semi-periphery of the global economy, and the structure of trade betrays the country's reliance on natural resources. Russia registered one of the steepest GDP falls of all developed economies in the global financial crisis in 2009, with a decline of 9 per cent, exposing vulnerabilities in the Russian economic model. The following year growth was resumed, but the previous average of 6.9 per cent achieved between 2000 and 2008 was not restored. The country registered only 1.3 per cent growth in 2013 and 1.1 per cent in 2014, before stumbling into a 2.8 per cent decline in 2015 as a result of the sharp fall in the price of oil and sanctions. GDP decline in 2016 was 0.2 per cent before growth resumed in 2017. Recessions in 1998 and 2009 were shorter and deeper, allowing faster rebounds. In 2013 Russia ranked fourth in terms of the global inflow of foreign direct investment, and at that time just over half of its trade was conducted with the EU. According to World Bank

---

[61] Stanislav Markus, *Property, Predation, and Protection: Piranha Capitalism in Russia and Ukraine* (Cambridge, Cambridge University Press, 2015).
[62] Minxin Pei, *China's Crony Capitalism: The Dynamics of Regime Decay* (Cambridge, Harvard University Press, 2016).

data, Russia in 2014 in purchasing power parity (PPP) terms was the world's fifth largest economy and Europe's biggest, pushing Germany into sixth place globally.[63] In absolute terms, Russia had the world's eighth largest economy with a GDP of $2.1 billion, representing about 4 per cent of global GDP. Between 2013 and 2015 the Russian economy shrank by 40 per cent in dollar terms, and at $1.3 trillion was relegated to become the world's thirteenth largest economy, comprising only 1.8 per cent of global GDP. In dollar terms, Russia's per capita income of $9,000 is just 28 per cent of the EU average. However, measured in PPP terms, Russia's economy in 2015 (despite the recession) weighed in at $3.4 trillion, making Russia the world's sixth largest economy, and in PPP terms per capita income is $25,000, 65 per cent of the EU average.[64]

Drawing on Immanuel Wallerstein's world-system theory, which focuses on core-periphery relations,[65] Giovanni Arrighi argues that each cycle of accumulation is led by a hegemonic power, accompanied by new ways to organise capital.[66] Sino-American hegemonic competition encourages capital transformation (specifically, away from neo-liberal free markets towards more state-directed investment), and indeed, governance transformation.[67] At the same time, Arrighi notes that the 'endless' accumulation of capital and power culminated in 'the US attempt to create, for the first time in world history, a truly global state'.[68] Both Russia and China became part of this 'state', but at the same time struggle for autonomy – this is the essence of their common anti-hegemonic strategy. In the Russian case this is compounded by the post-Cold War strategic impasse, and for both 'soft containment' provoked resistance. The apparent 'terminal crisis of US hegemony' offered the two countries an opportunity to assert their conception of a more pluralistic international system.[69] However, 'the declining hegemonic power' tried 'to resist

---

[63] World Bank, 'Gross Domestic Product 2014, PPP', shows China at 18.03 trillion international US dollars, the US at 17.42, India at 17.39, Japan at 4.63, Russia at 3.74 and Germany at 3.69, followed by Brazil, Indonesia France and the UK, http://databank.w orldbank.org/data/download/GDP_PPP.pdf, last accessed 26 May 2017.

[64] Richard Connolly, 'Russia Economic Power', in Natasha Kuhrt and Valentina Feklyunina (eds.), *Assessing Russia's Power: A Report* (King's College London and Newcastle University, 2017), p. 21, supplemented by World Bank data.

[65] Immanuel Wallerstein, *World-System Analysis: An Introduction* (Durham, Duke University Press, 2004).

[66] Giovanni Arrighi, *The Long Twentieth Century: Money, Power and the Origins of Our Time* (London, Verso, 2009), p. 231.

[67] This is explored by Zhang Xin, 'Cyclical Changes in the Capitalist World System and China-Russia-EU Competition', Fourteenth Annual Conference (Youth Forum) of the Shanghai Federation of Social Science Associations, 22 September 2016.

[68] Arrighi, *Long Twentieth Century*, pp. 95, 253, analysed at pp. 175–274.

[69] The quotation is from Arrighi, *Long Twentieth Century*, p. 101.

decline by turning itself into a world state'.[70] Inter-state conflict was transformed into a struggle over the operation of the international system. The terms of that struggle were themselves contested. The 'liberal international order' and its associated Atlantic power system presented themselves as universal (the 'global state'), and thus delegitimised resistance. This hermeneutic hegemony is the counterpart of the hegemony itself. Oliver Stuenkel notes that as the industrial power of the West from the nineteenth century eclipsed that of China, 'most intellectuals fell for the notion that the West had found a universal truth and a moral obligation to guide the rest of the world'. He goes on to argue that, '[l]iberalism and empire do not contradict each other but are strongly related'.[71]

Russia's post-Cold War politics of resistance is part of the enduring pattern of anti-colonial resistance. This takes distinctive forms, since Russia had long been an imperial power in its own right, and in its imperial guise had taken advantage of China's 'century of humiliation'. In postcolonial theory a subaltern denotes 'individuals or groups … whose agency is limited and who are deprived by the hegemonic social order of the possibility to make their voices heard'.[72] This certainly describes Russia's strategic impasse, but its status as a subaltern is tempered by its great power ambitions. Morozov argues that this makes Russia both subaltern and imperial, while drawing its model of development from a West that it at the same time condemns. Russia became 'an object of external colonisation that was integrated into the capitalist world-system on unequal terms'.[73] Russia simultaneously belongs to and is excluded from Europe, generating a complex pattern of mutual othering that shapes Russian foreign policy.[74] Russia has a conflicted identity as victim and perpetrator, coloniser and colonised. In the 2000s Russia's resistance to liberal international hegemony was buoyed by growing economic strength and frustration at entrapment in the strategic impasse, contributing to the 'escalating violence that has accompanied the liquidation of the of the Cold War order'.[75]

The contemporary subaltern challenge is an ambivalent phenomenon. Russia and China are not revisionist powers in the classical sense but neo-revisionist: they challenge not the foundations of international society and globalisation, but repudiate the practices of the hegemonic power system.

---

[70] Arrighi, *Long Twentieth Century*, p. 253.
[71] Oliver Stuenkel, *Post-Western World: How Emerging Powers are Remaking Global Order* (Cambridge, Polity, 2016), p. 51.
[72] Viatcheslav Morozov, *Russia's Postcolonial Identity: A Subaltern Empire in a Eurocentric World* (London, Palgrave Macmillan, 2015), p. 1.
[73] Morozov, *Russia's Postcolonial Identity*, p. 31.
[74] Morozov, *Russia's Postcolonial Identity*, pp. 41–2.
[75] Arrighi, *Long Twentieth Century*, p. 389.

Neither Russia nor China wish to create an alternative international system, but they do question the practices of the liberal world order in that system. The Russian strategy to achieve this is inconsistent. Support for the UN and international law is undermined by particularistic interpretations prompted by immediate challenges. Officials argue that Russia was forced to breach the agreed norms of international behaviour (for example, during the Russo-Georgian war in 2008 and in Ukraine in 2014) because of the strategic dead end, leaving it with little choice but to fight back with the 'weapons of the weak', even if it meant repudiating the normative principles enunciated in its foreign, security and defence policy doctrines. Russia sometimes adopts revisionist tactics, but does not pursue a revisionist strategy. This does little to imbue Russian foreign policy with consistency and predictability.

At the same time, the fundamental goal of Russia's anti-hegemonic strategy is not clear. Is it simply to enhance its bargaining power to lever its way into a Greater West? Certainly, some of its associates in the East believe that this is the case, and that Russia's foundational identity as European will ultimately win out, rendering its alignment with eastern powers and engagement in anti-hegemonic strategies instrumental and contingent. The Kremlin leaders are rational enough to understand the dangerous futility of any attempt to defeat, destroy or in any way militarily challenge the power of the Atlantic system. Certainly, the aim is to modify the behaviour of the Historical West, and thus to ensure Russia's greater military and political security, accompanied by a continued transformative impulse. In the absence not only of a mode of reconciliation but even of a basic common language, this modifying strategy assumed the character of normative rivalry, 'soft power' contestation and remilitarised confrontation. The anti-hegemonic bloc is certainly shaped by perceptions of national interest, but at the same time there remains a normative commitment to the transformation of the international system that harks back to the idealism of the late perestroika years. This generates contradictions in Russia's neo-revisionism, but also gains adherents to Russian policy from global sympathisers of what is perceived to be a counter-hegemonic agenda. While Russia may well be against the rest in realist terms, with few genuine allies among even its closest neighbours, in this normative framework Russia is admired by an eclectic mix of traditional sovereigntists, peaceniks, anti-imperialists, critics of globalisation, condemners of hegemonic blundering in international affairs, as well as variegated populists of left and right. The great power alignment with China, India and some other countries has a counter-hegemonic edge, and to that degree it has features of a balancing coalition predicted by realist theory. However, such an interpretation misses the more profound dynamic at work, namely the anti-hegemonic impetus that seeks to ensure that international society genuinely regulates horizontal relations between the great powers.

The challenge of the subalterns is ambivalent and contradictory. Both Russia and China are deeply embedded in the hegemonic structures that they criticise, hence have much to lose if they are undermined. Both states reject American unipolarity and what Ray Silvius calls 'de-territorialised neo-liberal capitalism', and advance multipolarity in the global political economy. The challenge is far from narrowly geopolitical, but encompasses cultural and ideational factors that together make this a civilisational contest.[76] The struggle is between political economies in the broadest traditional sense, and although in part it overlaps with Samuel Huntington's geo-religious conceptualisation of the 'clash of civilisations', what we are describing is an epochal shift away from an Atlantic-centred world.[77] The anti-hegemonic alignment is an intermediate category, and it is too early to talk of a multi-order world, although in time it may arise. Neither is it 'no one's world', since the displacement of hegemonic domination of international society is precisely intended to make it 'everyone's world'.[78] This a pluralistic vision of the international system where no single constellation predominates, representing not a power shift of the type described in realist theory but a transformation of the sort that was anticipated by Russia at the end of the Cold War.

Neither Russia nor China bind themselves into enduring alliance systems, yet have aligned to resist the hermetic features of the hegemonic power system. Conservatives and even non-radical liberals in Russia and China argue that partnership does not mean assimilation, and assert their independent political subjectivity.[79] Lanxin Xiang, the head of the Silk Road research centre in Shanghai, argues that even couching the issue in terms of 'the rise of China' is misleading because it creates a simplified dichotomy: how far China is willing to 'accommodate' to the existing international order by undergoing an internal transformation of its regime; or whether (the theory advanced by neo-conservatives) that China will become a destructive force by 'attempting a global power grab by altering the rules of the game of existing political order to enhance

---

[76] Ray Silvius, *Culture, Political Economy and Civilisation in a Multipolar World Order* (London, Routledge, 2017).

[77] Samuel P. Huntington, 'The Clash of Civilizations?', *Foreign Affairs*, Vol. 72, No. 3, Summer 1993, pp. 23–49; Samuel P. Huntington, *The Clash of Civilizations and the Remaking of World Order* (New York, Simon and Schuster, 1996).

[78] Cf. Charles A. Kupchan, *No One's World: The West, The Rising Rest, and the Coming Global Turn* (New York, Oxford University Press, 2012).

[79] For Russia, see Elena Chebankova, 'Contemporary Russian Conservatism', *Post-Soviet Affairs*, Vol. 32, No. 1, 2016, pp. 28–54.

its political legitimacy'. Instead, like Russia, China has no desire to destroy the current international system, 'but would be certainly prepared to alter some rules of the game according to Chinese tradition, culture, and national interest'. The struggle for transformation will draw on China's civilisational rather than nation state identity. In words that are deeply resonant with the Russian conservative critique of the hegemonic system, Lanxin warns that 'China is prepared for an ideological battle with the West, but unlike a Cold War, it will not be launched as a battle of good versus evil, but as a serious cultural debate'.[80]

The Russian and Chinese alignment in defence of the normative commitment to international society and a pluralistic international relations questions realist arguments. John Mearsheimer, for example, argues that the twenty-first century will be shaped by US–China relations and not US–Russian relations, and that China's increasing strength provokes 'intense security competition with the US'. In his view, there are three possible options. First, Russia aligns with China; second, Russia aligns with the US; and third, Russia remains neutral. Facing US pressure, Russia was aligning with China: the US and its elites 'failed to appreciate Russia's legitimate security concerns by pushing NATO's eastward expansion'.[81] Some Chinese scholars endorse this view, arguing that while relations with Russia will remain stable, the Sino-American relationship will become increasingly turbulent. American leaders were unlikely to renounce their hegemonic ambitions, so the Russo-Chinese partnership will act as a healthy check on Washington's 'unipolar folly'.[82] Neither realist nor liberal internationalist views adequately capture the dynamics of the contemporary international system. In the two-level model, international society centred on the UN, the institutions of global economic and political governance and the structures of international law, temper the sovereignty of states (the liberal view); but at the level of international relations states retain their autonomy and engage in class power plays. International politics in the binary international system is constituted by the constant interplay of the sub-systems. International society in this reading is a common endeavour devised by states in the

---

[80] Lanxin Xiang, 'China and the International "Liberal" (Western) Order', in T. Flockhart et al. (eds.), *Liberal Order in a Post-Western World* (Washington, Transatlantic Academy, May 2014), p. 109.

[81] Alexey Khlebnikov, 'Russian Experts Debate the World of Tomorrow in Valdai', *Russia Direct*, 25 October 2016, www.russia-direct.org/analysis/russian-experts-debate-world-to morrow-valdai, last accessed 26 May 2017. See also an interview, 18 January 2017, http:// valdaiclub.com/multimedia/video/john-mearsheimer-we-are-moving-to-a-multipolar-wor ld-with-three-great-powers/?sphrase_id=42994, last accessed 26 May 2017.

[82] Lanxin Xiang, 'The Peak Moment for China-Russia Ties', *Russia in Global Affairs*, No. 3, July–September 2016, pp. 152–6.

post-war era to temper militarised anarchy and short-sighted economic nationalism; but at the level of inter-state international relations hegemonic and anti-hegemonic struggles continue.

The Possibility of an Alternative

Russia's neo-revisionism does not mean the repudiation of international law and norms.[83] In fact, Russia would argue quite the opposite. The creation of a more pluralistic international system, to balance the unchecked hegemony of the Atlantic system, would allow the secondary institutions of international society to exercise their authority more effectively. In theoretical terms, the struggle for pluralism in the international system represents an attempt to achieve what had been discussed earlier by Robert Keohane in his study *After Hegemony*. Writing in the wake of the 1971 disintegration of core features of the Bretton Woods system, Keohane asked whether the international liberal order could become self-sustaining in the absence of US hegemonic leadership. He argued that cooperation was possible even in the absence of hegemony, despite the pessimism of realists on this issue.[84] The WTO, and in particular its dispute settlement mechanism, is often cited as an example of non-hegemonic cooperation, as is coordination over climate change issues, and of course the UN remains the supreme instance of global solidarism.[85] Realists concede that states cooperate and use international institutions to realise common interests, although they insist that states are the most important actors acting in a self-interested manner in an anarchic environment. For Mearsheimer, 'institutions have minimal influence on state behaviour, and thus hold little promise for promoting stability in the post-Cold War world'.[86] Hegemonic power is thus vital to maintain stability, but what happens when it weakens? In the wake of defeat in the Vietnam War and economic difficulties, the assumption was that American power was in irreversible decline and the US could no longer act as the guardian of global interactions. There was a widespread anticipation that Europe would claim its share of hegemonic responsibility. In the event, American power was far from spent, and although in relative terms was declining from its

---

[83] As asserted mistakenly by Michael McFaul, 'Confronting Putin's Russia', *New York Times*, 23 March 2014, and other liberal ideologues.

[84] Robert Keohane, *After Hegemony: Cooperation and Discord in the World* (Princeton, Princeton University Press, 1984).

[85] Ramesh Thakur, *Governance for a World without World Government*, Valdai Paper No. 35, November 2015, http://valdaiclub.com/a/valdai-papers/governance-for-a-world-without-world-government/, last accessed 26 May 2017.

[86] John Mearsheimer, 'The False Promise of International Institutions', *International Security*, Vol. 19, No. 3, 1994/5, p. 7.

exceptional peak following the destruction of almost everyone else in the early post-war years, it remains by far the most powerful country in the world.[87] In ideological terms, the US was in no mood to relinquish its hegemonic leadership. On this, neo-conservative internationalists, liberal interventionists and conservative neo-isolationists agreed.

The Cold War can be seen as 'a credible but ultimately failed Soviet challenge to US hegemony'.[88] The Soviet collapse did not change the existing hierarchy, with the US at the top, and in fact it was reinforced.[89] Bipolarity allowed the Soviet Union to act as the Eurasian hegemon, but this dissolved after 1991, but realist theory predicted that sooner or later Russia would make a bid to resume the historical pattern: 'This leads to the frankly inductive warning for the West: keep a weather eye on Russia. Russia has often experienced rapid shifts in relative power with dire international consequences ... Russia may be down now, but prudent policymakers should not count it out'.[90] In practice, Russia's resurgence took place in the context of the strengthening of international society. With the end of the Cold War there was a widespread assumption that the UN would come into its own, but unipolarity was no more conducive for 'global governance' than bipolarity. New forms of transnational governance emerged, giving rise to what has been called 'neo-pluralism', but traditional patterns predominate.[91] Russia clearly favours a traditional state-centric view of international relations, although this is tempered by its continued commitment to the institutions of international society. However, the post-Cold War liberal view of global governance represented a revision of traditional international relations, whereas countries such as Russia sought to preserve the classical state-centric approach to global affairs.[92]

The same applies to European security. Contrary to expectations that with the end of the Cold War NATO would be radically scaled down or disbanded, NATO survived its lean years of the cold peace. It looked for a purpose, and went out of area to avoid going out of business. NATO no

[87] Stephen G. Brooks and William C. Wohlforth, *America Abroad: The United States' Global Role in the 21st Century* (New York, Oxford University Press, 2016).

[88] William Wohlforth, 'Realism and the End of the Cold War', *International Security*, Vol. 19, No. 3, 1994/5, p. 97.

[89] Wohlforth, 'Realism and the End of the Cold War', p. 99.

[90] Wohlforth, 'Realism and the End of the Cold War', p. 129.

[91] Philip G. Cerny, 'The Limits of Global Governance: Transnational Neopluralism in a Complex World', in Rafaelle Marchetti (ed.), *Partnerships in International Policymaking: Civil Society and Public Institutions in European and Global Affairs* (Basingstoke and New York, Palgrave Macmillan, 2016), pp. 31–47.

[92] Andrew Hurrell, 'Hegemony, Liberalism and Global Order: What Space for Would-be Great Powers?', *International Affairs*, Vol. 82, No. 1, 2006, pp. 1–19.

longer functioned as 'a treaty of guarantee, because one [could] not answer the fundamental question, guarantee against whom?'.[93] The answer to that question has now been found, and it was the old answer – to guarantee European security against Russia. NATO enlargement may well have been a response to the perceived security needs of the East European states, to fill the alleged security vacuum in the region and to prevent the recrudescence of great power politics, but it entailed a range of negative consequences that only precipitated the eventuality that it sought to avert, namely the emergence of Russia as a perceived security threat. The decision to enlarge NATO remains the single most contested issue of the cold peace years.[94] The 'pull' factor of demand from many of the former communist bloc countries and the 'push' factor from Washington combined to create a security dilemma of the first order. What was actually agreed about NATO enlargement in February 1990 remains controversial, and in later years there was uncertainty in Washington about how to proceed. There was no deliberate plan in the US to take advantage of Russian weakness, and Clinton, the leader who did most to enlarge the alliance, hoped that he could square the circle with Moscow. Discussions in October 1993 advanced earlier ideas and demonstrate the fundamental dilemma:

While desirous of a new relationship with Russia, the United States saw itself as the Cold War victor and had the power to shape the security dynamic across Europe. Yeltsin, meanwhile, believed he had been responsible for the overthrow of communism and wanted his country's place in Europe recognized, but had no power to push back against US initiatives that he believed only served to strengthen his more nationalist opponents within Russia.[95]

Was there an alternative and to what degree was it realistic? The Soviet and Russian leadership at the end of the Cold War and to this day certainly believe that there was a different path, but that for institutional and ideational reasons it was not taken. Drawing on the material already presented, the essence of the 'myth' of an alternative can be summarised as the following, accompanied by critiques. First, that there could have been a positive transcendence of the Cold War in ideational terms, in which all sides repudiated

---

[93] Waltz, 'Structural Realism', p. 19.

[94] For a review of the initial decision, see James M. Goldgeier, 'NATO Expansion: Anatomy of a Decision', *Washington Quarterly*, Vol. 21, No. 1, Winter 1998, pp. 85–102; James M. Goldgeier, *Not Whether but When: The US Decision to Enlarge NATO* (Washington, Brookings, 1999).

[95] James M. Goldgeier, 'Promises Made, Promises Broken? What Yeltsin was Told about NATO in 1993 and Why it Matters', *War on the Rocks*, 12 July 2016, http://warontherocks.com/2016/07/promises-made-promises-broken-what-yeltsin-was-told-about-nato-in-1993-and-why-it-matters/, last accessed 26 May 2017.

not only the immediate structure of conflict but committed themselves to the transformation of the international system itself. This would have effectively meant the self-dissolution of the structures of the Cold War. The Soviet Union under Gorbachev was engaged in just such a process of self-dissolution of the structure of communist power and the Soviet bloc, and dismantling the whole ideological apparatus on which it was based. There was no pressing reason for the West to follow suit. By mere dint of the effective capitulation of the state socialist alternative, Western institutions had demonstrated their resilience, viability and possible superiority. Thus, asymmetry was built into the very foundations of the post-Cold War order.

Second, in security terms, the idea of positive transcendence becomes rather more specific. Although the competitiveness of the Soviet economy was declining, the system in the late 1980s did not face a catastrophic systemic crisis. Ultra-low oil prices did deprive the Soviet economy of vital resources, but there is a general consensus that the Soviet Union could have muddled through indefinitely.[96] In addition, even though bogged down in the war in Afghanistan, it was not Western pressure that forced the Soviet leadership to end the Cold War but a decision of the Soviet leadership in response to domestic considerations. The accelerating pace of domestic reform was accompanied by a NPT in foreign affairs that accepted the possibility of a stable and enduring cooperative relationship with what had previously been categorised as an irredeemably militaristic system of capitalist imperialism.[97] From the Soviet perspective, this was an unforced move which required a reciprocal response from the West. In part, this was forthcoming, and all American presidents, in different ways, tried to establish a supportive relationship with their Soviet and Russian counterparts. But there were limits to this new spirit of partnership, above all grounded on the view that the Atlantic alliance represented a set of values and institutional guarantees that should be neither diluted nor squandered. This is an important argument, but it is two-edged. The Atlantic system was rooted in the Cold War, and its perpetuation meant the survival of Cold War instincts as well. As Goldgeier puts it, '[t]he United States believed it had won the Cold War and sought to ensure the terms of settlement were favourable to American interests. Yeltsin believed he and the Russian people had overthrown communism and wanted the terms of settlement to recognize their interests in being major players in Europe. Given the power disparities, the differences would be hard to reconcile.'[98]

---

[96] For the debate, see Michael Ellman and Vladimir Kontorovich (eds.), *The Destruction of the Soviet Economic System: An Insiders' History* (New York, M. E. Sharpe, 1998).

[97] Bisley, *The End of the Cold War.*   [98] Goldgeier, 'Promises Made, Promises Broken?'.

This brings us to the third point. The relatively hermetic quality to the Atlantic alliance inevitably cast Russia in the role of the outsider. Until 2014 attempts were made to ensure that Russia was not constructed as some sort of Other, against which the alliance could unite; but at the same time, for institutional and ideational reasons, Russia could not become Us, and this meant that the potential division became real when the Ukraine crisis hit. The cold peace could find no solution to the fundamental conundrum: bringing Russia into the West would threaten the transformation of that community into something else; but not doing so created a potential conflict. Liberals posed the question more sharply: how could an illiberal system be integrated into a liberal civilisation? Would this not be a reckless gamble, threatening the security and values of the 830 million citizens of the Atlantic community? These questions are certainly valid, but they deny the possibility of innovation. Would not some sort of strong association between Russia and a reshaped Euro-Atlantic system, based not on the structures of the Cold War but on some reshaped pan-European security alliance, have facilitated Russia's own difficult passage into democratic capitalist modernity? Equally, the development of a more authoritarian order from the mid-2000s was reinforced by the threat perceptions created precisely by Russia's outsider status.

Fourth, there is also the practical aspect. The price to pay for Russia's peaceful transition into the post-communist era was that its elite and security complex was steeped in Cold War attitudes. Yeltsin increasingly relied on security officials, although balanced by a strong liberal contingent, while a large part of Putin's entourage had a security service background. In 1995 Yeltsin protested vociferously against NATO intervention in the Bosnian civil war, opposing military action against the Serbs, although in the end he acquiesced. Although no side in that war was innocent of human rights abuses, the Serbian policy of ethnic cleansing and the three-year siege of Sarajevo required some sort of military intervention. Yeltsin was even more vociferous in protesting against the NATO bombing of Serbia and Kosovo in 1999 without a UN mandate. These cases indicated to the Western leadership that bringing Russia into an expanded Atlantic security system was liable to paralyse its ability to act with resolution. What began as differences of opinion in the 1990s in the later Putin years became a zero-sum view of international politics. The Iraq War of 2003 and the Libyan intervention in 2011 sealed the transformation of the Atlantic alliance into one willing to act without a UN mandate, and ready regardless of Russian views to impose its global perspectives. Despite Russia's claims to be a great power, it was far weaker than the US, and thus the US 'hardly had to worry about fighting against rival great powers' freeing its hand to fight six wars against minor powers since the end of the Cold War.[99] The destabilising consequences of these interventions only added to Russian concerns. The competing myths and interpretations of the end of the Cold War and the tensions of the cold peace years not only reduced the scope for dialogue but also undermined the framework in which such a dialogue could be achieved.

The hegemonic structures of the liberal order were extended, eclipsing hopes that with the end of the Cold War international society would become more truly universal and develop greater autonomy. Instead, the post-Cold War ideology of globalisation posited that it was globalisation itself that was autonomous, transforming sovereignty, nationhood and peoples.[100] The 'empire' of capital accepted no boundaries or limits, transforming transnational corporate governance, the labour process and identities.[101] The neo-liberal penetration of the state by markets in the end generated a series of economic crises, notably the global financial crisis of 2008–09, provoking a backlash in the form of a return to more traditional forms of economic internationalism. The counterpart of globalisation was the idea of 'global governance', which also assumed a depoliticised technocratic dynamic to global affairs, presaged in Gilpin's hegemonic stability theory.[102] Contrary to the view that globalisation and global governance would in some way promote interdependence and strengthen international society, in the absence of a sustainable political settlement, economic relations are susceptible to rupture and even reverses. Relations between Russia and the EU, despite a high level of interdependence, quickly unravelled following the breakdown of European security in 2014. The expansion of the liberal international security and normative order was not a sufficient condition for the expansion of order itself.

[99] Mearsheimer, *Tragedy of Great Power Politics*, pp. 360–1.

[100] Justin Rosenberg, *The Follies of Globalisation Theory: Polemical Essays* (London, Verso Books, 2001); Justin Rosenberg, 'Globalization Theory: A Post-Mortem', *International Politics*, Vol. 42, No. 1, March 2005, pp. 2–74.

[101] Michael Hardt and Antonio Negri, *Empire* (Cambridge, Harvard University Press, 2001).

[102] Robert Gilpin, *War and Change in World Politics* (Cambridge, Cambridge University Press, 1981); Robert Gilpin, 'The Theory of Hegemonic War', *Journal of Interdisciplinary History*, Vol. 18, No. 4, 1988, pp. 591–613.

3   Russian Grievances

The litany of the alleged slights to Russia is a long one, including America's unilateral abrogation of the Anti-Ballistic Missile (ABM) Treaty in June 2002, the war in Iraq, the continued failure to build an inclusive security system in Europe, accompanied by the alleged sponsorship of regime change in Russia's neighbourhood through so-called colour revolutions. The accumulation of Russian grievances began soon after the end of the Cold War, although elements of a new cooperative order were also evident. The Soviet Union supported the West in the First Gulf War of 1991, launched in response to Iraq's seizure of Kuwait in August 1991. The veteran Soviet diplomat and scholar, Primakov, was despatched to Baghdad to broker a settlement. In the event, in an awe-inspiring display of Western military power, Saddam Hussein was expelled from Kuwait, but the allied forces did not move on to Baghdad. Regime change was not yet on the agenda. Equally, the USSR and Russia worked with the West to achieve the peaceful reunification of Germany, and devised collective mechanisms to achieve nuclear non-proliferation in the post-Soviet space. Despite Moscow's willingness to work with the Historical West, no enduring framework for a new peace order was created. As the country disintegrated in late 1991, there were even those in the West, like Dick Cheney (who later served as the junior Bush's vice president, 2001–09), who 'wanted to see the dismantlement not only of the Soviet Union and the Russian empire, but of Russia itself, so it would never again be a threat to the rest of the world'.[1]

A Wounded Power

Instead of a pluralistic order with inherent checks and balances, the West assumed that the expansion of liberal global governance and its security system was equivalent to the new global community in its entirety. All that Russia had to do was to adapt to the new reality. Instead, Russia's growing

[1] Robert Gates, *Duty: Memoirs of a Secretary at War* (London, W. H. Allen, 2014), p. 97.

resistance was defined as anachronistic great power politics. Russia's resistance, as noted, was not to the global governance mechanisms represented by international society, but to the monist international relations practised at the inter-state level. This external dimension intersected with Russia's attempt to grapple with its diminished regional status. The post-imperial syndrome is particularly complex when the empire in question is not across the water but contiguous to a truncated state amidst a divided nation. Russia remains locked in an extended process of identity formation, in which various notions about the character of Russian nationhood and statehood remain contested. The Tsarist system was by its own self-definition an empire, since Peter the Great labelled it so in 1721, but the rejection of 'imperialism' was at the core of Soviet identity. The fifteen post-Soviet republics established sovereign statehood but remain fragile and vulnerable, above all because of the failure to establish a viable framework for interaction between the successor states and the absence of a substantive model of inter-regional relations across the continent. On both sides bonding arrangements predominated over bridging ones. The CIS, now reduced to eleven members following Georgia's defection, remains an important forum, although Russia's main focus is the EEU. Attempts by Russia to advance integrative initiatives are condemned in the West as the recrudescence of empire, while the region as a whole has not yet found an effective model in which functional unity can be achieved while respecting the sovereignty and integrity of neighbours. The question of where Russia's legitimate security and economic interests end and the sovereignty of neighbouring states begin remains one of the great unresolved problems of our day.

The issue lies at the root of Russia's perception of being trapped in a strategic impasse. Soft containment deprived Russia of a legitimate language in which to articulate its interests and frustrations. Instead, the legitimacy of these ostensible interests is questioned, and too often condemned as breaching the rules of the liberal international order or infringing the territorial and political integrity of its neighbours. Equally, within Russia there is a vigorous debate over how to define Russia's national interests. Liberals define these interests in terms of international economic integration and adaptation to the prevalent norms, although even they are not immune to great power temptations. On 25 September 2003 Anatoly Chubais, one of the architects of Russia's liberal economic transformation in the 1990s, drew on American experience of liberal interventions in Afghanistan and elsewhere to describe Russia as the 'natural and unique leader' of some sort of 'liberal empire' in the CIS: 'Liberal imperialism should become Russia's ideology and building up liberal empire

Russia's mission'.[2] A swath of neo-traditionalists called for the restoration of Tsarist or Soviet imperial practices, while Eurasianists insist that there can be no reconciliation between Russia and the West.

There have been five major turning points in European security in the modern era, all following catastrophic wars: the Peace of Westphalia in 1648; the Congress of Vienna (1815) and the subsequent Concert of Europe (1815–54); the end of the First World War and the Paris Peace Conference in 1919, from which Germany (and Soviet Russia) was excluded, resulting in the punitive Versailles Treaty on what was now defined as the defeated power; the end of World War 2, which in 1945 created the UN as a collective security body with the USSR as a permanent member of its Security Council; and the end of the Cold War in 1989. The first, second and the fourth were remarkably successful in establishing post-conflict peace settlements, while the third and the fifth were ultimately disastrous. After 1945, in conditions of Cold War, Germany and Japan were successfully integrated into the expanded liberal order, but only after recognition of defeat and the ensuing fundamental domestic reforms and acceptance of subaltern status. In this sequence, 1989 did not provide a big enough shock to reset the system as in the other 'critical junctures', and it may take another war to do so. Russia engaged in a domestic transformation, but none of its leaders accepted defeat, let alone a subaltern status. Gorbachev sought to compensate domestic weakness by advancing an ideational 'shortcut' alternative to the old structure of international power (the NPT), but Russia's subsequent leaders were forced to come to terms with the old thinking, although couched in the progressive language of liberal hegemony.

The idea of a Russian sphere of influence is anathema to the liberal international order, but in the absence of agreement Russia found itself without a security regime. No existing model seemed to apply. In the classic balance of power relationship, defensive realists argue that even large states tend not to become expansionist once they have a sufficient degree of power; and in turn, once they have adequate security, they do not seek more power.[3] In a balance of power system large nations seek to ensure friendly neighbours, described classically as a 'sphere of influence' which can evolve into an alliance system. When the security arrangements

[2] 'Anatoly Chubais: Russia Should Aim to Create Liberal Empire in CIS', Pravda.ru, 25 September 2003, www.pravdareport.com/news/russia/25-09-2003/52757-0/, last accessed 30 May 2017. For commentary and more of the speech, see Igor Torbakov, 'Russian Policymakers Air Notion of "Liberal Empire" in Caucasus, Central Asia', Eurasianet, 26 October 2003, www.eurasianet.org/departments/insight/articles/ea v102703.shtml, last accessed 26 May 2017.
[3] Waltz, *Theory of International Politics*, Chapter 6.

between the large powers are regulated by an agreed set of rules, a collective security system emerges. The best historical case of such an order is the Concert of Europe in which the five major states (although a defeated power, France became a constitutive member) coordinated external and even domestic security arrangements. This is a vision of a multilateral world order where several powers collectively manage international affairs, but in which no single power is ascendant. A measure of Russia's strategic dead end is that no model appeared to apply after the Cold War. Liberal internationalists (and in particular the Kantians among them) argue that traditional balance of power relationships are redundant in the 'globalised' world, and for them a sphere of influence for Russia is anathema, threatening the sovereignty of its neighbours. However, since no concert of powers was established after the Cold War and the country remained outside the collective security arrangements institutionalised by NATO, Russia was left in limbo. This generated a range of negative reactions, including a sense of alienation and exclusion.[4] It also generated pressure to restore a modernised concert, creating the conditions for great powers to recognise the security interests of others in a manner recognised as legitimate by the smaller powers.[5]

Conflict is inevitably generated when respective spheres are vaguely delineated (and even more so when they are denied), but in the post-Cold War world an additional layer of conflict was provoked by normative contestation over the appropriateness of the very concept. The practical upshot is that the liberal international order was neither prepared to concede that Russia had a zone of 'privileged interests' in its neighbourhood, nor to accept as legitimate the language in which such putative interests could be couched. Inevitably, the fear that its concerns were not being heard prompted the Russian leadership to speak increasingly loudly and forcefully, fostering a rhetorical escalation that in the end spilled-over into violence. As a re-emerging state, Russia sought to ensure that the post-Cold War power shift would be recognised by inclusion in an expanded collective security system. Instead, classic balance of power behaviour predicted by offensive realists came into play, with the rising state trying to gain more power, and the incumbent states formulating a range of measures to constrain the newcomer's challenge – the soft containment described earlier. As Russia recovered some of its erstwhile

---

[4] Vincent Pouliot, *International Security in Practice: The Politics of NATO-Russia Diplomacy* (Cambridge, Cambridge University Press, 2010).

[5] *A Twenty-first Century Concert of Powers: Promoting Great Power Multilateralism for the Post-Atlantic Era*, The 21st Century Concert Study Group, Peace Research Institute Frankfurt, 2014, p. 9.

land-based military power, 'the United States and its European allies [should] start worrying about a new Russian threat'.[6]

Russian realism is tempered by a continued commitment to the institutions of international society. This is complemented by an enduring idealism founded on the belief that ultimately the Historical West could still become a Greater West with Russian participation, and pan-continental initiatives would make Russia a comfortable member of Greater Europe. In other words, despite the withering criticism to which the NPT has been subjected domestically, elements of Gorbachev's idealism endure. Moscow's critics dismiss the normative basis of Moscow's politics of resistance and instead argue that it is based on no more than the traditional Soviet attempt to sow confusion and discord in the Atlantic community, and to drive a wedge between the two wings of the alliance. Russia of course uses all the means at its disposal to break out of the various neo-containment strategies deployed against it, but one of them is the idealist vision of a transformed Greater Europe.

If the viability of a pluralist Greater Europe project is questioned, let alone its potential evolution into a more solidaristic community, then the continent faces three alternatives. First, there is the continued consolidation and enlargement of the Atlantic community, accompanied by conditionality towards its neighbours, and a tutelary relationship with Russia. This is the model from which Moscow, for reasons discussed earlier, felt excluded and provoked the breakdown epitomised by the conflict in and over Ukraine. The second is the 'promise of a continental concert', reprising the Concert of Europe. Many in Russia were attracted to this option, especially since it retained echoes of the Yalta-Potsdam settlement at the end of the Second World War, which legitimated the USSR's status as one of the arbiters of the fate of Europe. The third option is the balance of power, the path that NATO's continued existence was designed to foreclose – since in the end such a system collapsed in 1914.[7]

Gorbachev and Russian leaders sought to transform NATO and supplant it by a pan-European collective security organisation. Failing that, Moscow sought NATO's transformation from a military into a predominantly political organisation.[8] The failure to transform NATO into a cooperative political-security organisation after 1991, and its enlargement to Russia's borders, exacerbated the tensions within the post-Soviet space and

---

[6] Mearsheimer, *Tragedy of Great Power Politics*, p. 85.

[7] For a review of the last two options, see Sten Rynning, 'The False Promise of Continental Concert: Russia, the West and the Necessary Balance of Power', *International Affairs*, Vol. 91, No. 3, 2015, pp. 539–52.

[8] Tom Sauer, 'The Origins of the Ukraine Crisis and the Need for Collective Security between Russia and the West', *Global Policy*, published online, October 2016.

intensified Russia's sense of being trapped in a strategic impasse. It remains a nuclear superpower – in 2016 it had 7,300 nuclear weapons, the US 7,000 and the rest of the world about a 1,000 – but this does not readily translate into diplomatic weight and structural power at the global level. Russia remains the world's largest state, with a permanent seat on the UNSC, and vast natural resources. Yet a sense of grievance was generated by the impasse which prevented the unfurling of its strategic wings. Liberals argue that the very notion of an impasse is misleading. Nothing stopped Russia developing its economy, reinforcing the rule of law and defensible property rights, and allowing a plural and tolerant society to develop. For them, the chimera of great power status undermined political and economic modernisation and the advance towards the liberal international order.[9]

For conservatives of various stripes, however, the West's expansive ideology of universal enlargement represented a threat to Russia's ability to flourish as an autonomous cultural entity and as an independent player in world politics. In Tsygankov's words, '[a]s the West engaged in global expansionist practices, Russia changed its trajectory from being wide open to Western economic and political influences to a selective openness managed by an increasingly strong and nationalistic state'.[10] A values coalition emerged emphasising Russia's distinctiveness and opposed to the West.[11] The cold peace was accompanied by a type of cultural Cold War, in which a swath of Russian intellectuals asserted an alternative cultural identity to that promulgated by the West. This affected the way that they thought about modernisation. Instead of assuming that the West was the model for development, they argued that Russia represented an alternative based above all on statism and distinctiveness (*samobytnost'*). The programme of modernisation outlined by Dmitry Medvedev, who served as president after Putin's constitutionally mandated first two terms came to an end in 2008, was welcomed by liberals, although they were sceptical about his leadership, since Putin over-shadowed him as prime minister. The structural problems were described by Medvedev in his critique 'Forward, Russia!' ('*Rossiya, vperëd!*'), published in September 2009. He identified energy dependency, corruption and the corrosive effects of state paternalism as the three great scourges afflicting the country.[12] The programme

---

[9] For a discussion, see Nick Bisley, *Great Powers in the Changing International Order* (Boulder, Lynne Rienner, 2012).

[10] Andrei P. Tsygankov, 'Crafting the State-Civilization', *Problems of Post-Communism*, Vol. 63, No. 3, 2016, p. 147.

[11] Tsygankov, 'Crafting', p. 152.

[12] Dmitrii Medvedev, 'Rossiya, vperëd!', 10 September 2009, originally published at www.gazeta.ru/comments/2009/09/10_a_3258568.shtml, last accessed 26 May 2017, then placed on the Kremlin's website, http://kremlin.ru/events/president/new s/5413, last accessed 26 May 2017.

repudiated a cultural interpretation of Russian state interests, and was inspired by a globalising developmental agenda. On his return to power in 2012 Putin, characteristically, articulated a developmental strategy that combined both statist and liberal themes, but in the end this only intensified the political stalemate and developmental blockage.[13]

There were plenty of specific grievances. One of the enduring issues was how to combat the terrorist threat. In the period before the attack on the World Trade Center and the Pentagon on 11 September 2001 (9/11) Putin had called on the US for a common front against international terrorist infiltration into the North Caucasus, but 'it soon became clear that the United States was in no hurry to help Russia in its fight against terrorism – failing, for instance, to shut down Islamic organizations accused by Moscow of funding the Chechen underground'.[14] In his call to the White House after the attack, the first foreign leader to do so, Putin argued that 'Russia knows firsthand what terrorism is', and argued that the tragedy was an opportunity to remodel international relations to fight 'the plague of the 21st century'.[15] The organisations were closed immediately after the attack. The pattern continued, and even though personal relations between George W. Bush and Putin were good, 'as soon as the presidents parted company, something went wrong, be it the revolution in Ukraine, Iran's nuclear program, the mess in Iraq, the presence of US intelligence officers in the Caucasus, or US plans to deploy a missile shield in Europe'.[16] Above all, NATO membership for former Soviet republics was a fundamental bone of contention (discussed in the second section of Chapter 3). Russia compensated its perceived strategic vulnerability by creating a values coalition against perceived encroachments on Russia's civilisational space. The emphasis on democracy and civil society promotion in the Freedom Agenda that was applied in Iraq in 2003 generated resistance in many post-Soviet and developing states, taking the form of the imposition of constraints on civil society.[17] Civil society came to be seen as an instrument of a 'newly militaristic, interventionist US geostrategy'.[18] The security dilemma was now complemented by a 'democracy dilemma', in which democratisation was seen as increasing Russian vulnerability and weakening its international positions.

---

[13] Analysed in Sakwa, *Putin Redux*.   [14] Zygar, *All the Kremlin's Men*, p. 34.
[15] Myers, *New Tsar*, p. 204.   [16] Zygar, *All the Kremlin's Men*, p. 173.
[17] Douglas Rutzen, 'Civil Society under Assault', *Journal of Democracy*, Vol. 26, No. 4, 2015, pp. 28–39.
[18] Thomas Carothers and Saskia Brechenmacher, 'Closing Space: Democracy and Human Rights Support under Fire', Carnegie Endowment for International Peace, 20 February 2014, p. 2, http://carnegieendowment.org/2014/02/20/closing-space-democracy-and-h uman-rights-support-under-fire-pub-54503, last accessed 26 May 2017.

The story of the Conventional Forces in Europe (CFE) Treaty is a revealing instance of the strategic impasse and mutual incomprehension between the two sides. The CFE Treaty was signed in Paris on 19 November 1990 by sixteen NATO and six Warsaw Pact members, limiting the number of tanks, armoured vehicles, artillery and military aviation between the Atlantic and the Urals, as well as flank agreements. The CFE came into force on 9 November 1992, but by then the Warsaw Pact had been annulled (1 July 1991) and the USSR had become fifteen independent republics. Separate agreements divided up the various quotas, but the Baltic republics refused to take part. At the OSCE Istanbul summit on 19 November 1999 the CFE Treaty was modified to take into account the various changes, but given Russia's rather limited quota for tanks and other material, this still left NATO with a 3:1 advantage in conventional forces. Nevertheless, NATO countries failed to ratify the CFE Treaty, while Russia fulfilled the conditions in terms of force reductions (but not the extraneous conditions agreed in Istanbul on Russia's withdrawal from Transnistria and Georgia).[19] In a desperate attempt to save the treaty, Moscow convened a conference in Vienna in June 2007, but NATO was intransigent.[20] On 13 July Putin signed an order on the suspension of the CFE Treaty, which came into effect in December 2007, and on 11 March 2015 pulled out altogether. This was yet another item to add to Putin's list of grievances, and '[a]t their next meeting he took the list out of his pocket and put each point to Bush'.[21]

The list also came in handy when Obama was president. Obama supported the reset but his one and only visit to Moscow in mid-2009 was soured when shortly before arriving he stated that Putin had 'one foot in the past'.[22] Obama made it clear that he had come to see Medvedev, and the two had a productive five-hour meeting on 6 July. At a breakfast meeting at Putin's residence in Novo Ogaryevo the next day, Putin lectured him for an hour about Russian concerns. Although Obama has a professorial air, from the Russian perspective he was a poor learner and Putin's arguments left Obama unmoved.[23] Paradoxically, Obama was

[19] Russia, Belarus, Ukraine and some other countries ratified the adapted CFE Treaty, but Estonia, Latvia and Lithuania flatly refused to sign up, which meant that once they joined NATO an uncontrollable grey zone was created in the region.

[20] Artem Kureev, 'The Real Reason why Russia Finally Left the CFE Treaty', *Russia Direct*, 17 March 2015, www.russia-direct.org/opinion/real-reason-why-russia-finally-left-cfe-t reaty, last accessed 26 May 2017.

[21] Zygar, *All the Kremlin's Men*, p. 109.

[22] Chris McGreal and Luke Harding, 'Obama: Putin has One Foot in the Past', *Guardian*, 2 July 2009, www.theguardian.com/world/2009/jul/02/obama-putin-us-russia-relations, last accessed 26 May 2017.

[23] See www.youtube.com/watch?v=5P1q3IDjBaI for the beginning of the meeting. See also www.rt.com/usa/breakfast-at-putin-s/, last accessed 26 May 2017.

one of the few American presidents genuinely committed to the multi-lateralism represented by international society, and thus he was uniquely placed to establish a partnership with Russia. However, his multilateralism was part of the traditional US grand strategy of global leadership, where the 'rule-based international order serves the interests of the United States' better than a closed world 'built around blocs and spheres of influence'.[24] As a result, Obama's leadership offered no way out of the strategic impasse for Russia, intensifying resentment and resistance. It appears that Obama liked neither Putin nor Medvedev, despite Medvedev's efforts to ingratiate himself with the president.[25] Overall, the Obama administration under-estimated Russia's power and resolve, and no basis was found to work on common problems.

NATO Enlargement

With the end of the Cold War, it seemed that NATO had successfully achieved its purpose, above all containing the USSR, and could enter honourable retirement. Instead, the organisation spent the next quarter-century looking for a new role until it returned to fulfil the main function for which it had been created – containing Russia. In the cold peace years NATO survived by going 'out of area' (notably in Kosovo and Afghanistan) and enlarging to encompass a swath of former Soviet bloc countries and even some former Soviet republics. The tension between those who sought a transformation of the power system at the end of the Cold War, and those who emphasised continuity and the consolidation of the power shift in the surviving institutions, was at its sharpest when it came to the fate of the organisation. The struggle between 'regime transformers', who sought to use the full might of American civilian power to change Russia's domestic system, and 'power balancers', who argued that Russia's domestic regime did not shape its foreign policy and, in any case, that the US had a limited ability to shape Russia's internal order, characterised the cold peace years.[26] The enduring tension between these two positions framed Russia's early attempts to join the liberal international order and its security system. NATO faced an existential crisis of purpose, yet in the end the Atlantic security system survived and after 2014 assumed increasingly ramified features as it shifted towards a policy of hard containment.

---

[24] William C. Wohlforth, *The Return of Realpolitik: Stability vs. Change in the US-Led World Order*, Moscow, Valdai Discussion Club, Valdai Paper No. 11, February 2015, p. 7.

[25] Zygar, *All the Kremlin's Men*, p. 173.

[26] James M. Goldgeier and Michael McFaul, *Power and Purpose: US Policy toward Russia after the Cold War* (Washington, Brookings Institution, 2003), p. 5 and *passim*.

Modern Atlanticism was forged during the Second World War to tie the US to the struggle against Nazi Germany. The meeting of 9–12 August 1941 between Winston Churchill and Franklin Roosevelt led to the adoption of the Atlantic Charter. Following America's entry into the war following the Japanese attack on Pearl Harbour on 7 December 1941, the Anglo-American alliance tipped the scales against the continental power of Germany, although the bulk of the fighting took place on the Soviet front. The creation of NATO in 1949 reaffirmed the link between values and security that lay at the core of the Atlantic Charter. The Soviet collapse encouraged the view that containment had been responsible for what was interpreted as a victory of the West. This is hardly surprising, since not only had the opponent collapsed but the continuer-state proclaimed its commitment to the very values that had underpinned the Western alliance. This certainly looked like victory, but it was precisely at this point that the seeds were planted for later conflict. The dominance of the Western security order was consolidated on a selective and exclusive basis, and no new universal security system for Europe was created. From the very beginning Russia chafed at its exclusion, but its weakness in the 1990s allowed only impotent growls over Kosovo, NATO enlargement and other issues. Only in the 2000s, buoyed by rising energy rents, was Russia was able to act on its complaints.

Was the Soviet leadership promised that NATO would not expand to the East? At the time of German unification commitments were given by Western leaders that the eastern part of the united Germany would not become militarised. At a meeting in Moscow on 9 February 1990 secretary of state James Baker promised Gorbachev that if Germany joined the alliance and Russia pulled out its twenty-four divisions, the West would guarantee that NATO would not extend 'the zone of its jurisdiction or military presence in the East by even an inch'.[27] It was clear that this did not refer just to the former German Democratic Republic. Although the question of NATO enlargement to the other Soviet bloc countries was not yet on the agenda, the general idea was very much on the participants' minds.[28] On that day the German foreign minister Hans-Dietrich Genscher told the Soviet foreign minister Eduard Shevardnadze that 'one thing is certain: NATO will not expand

---

[27] Grachev, *Gorbachev's Gamble*, p. 155, and Anatoly Chernyaev's notes of the meeting at p. 250, n. 129.

[28] By contrast, Mark Kramer argues that NATO enlargement simply did not enter anyone's head and was not discussed: Mark Kramer, 'The Myth of a No-NATO-Enlargement Pledge to Russia', *Washington Quarterly*, Vol. 32, No. 2, 2009, pp. 41, 47–8.

to the East'.[29] Although once again it was East Germany that was in question, the commitment reflected an understanding that NATO enlargement was a neuralgic issue for the Soviet Union. Recent studies demonstrate that the commitment not to enlarge NATO covered the whole former Soviet bloc and not just East Germany.[30] Although there was no written commitment, it was clearly understood that NATO enlargement to former Soviet bloc territory would be provocative and divisive. This was a clear moral commitment that carries as much ethical weight as a formal document.[31]

However, times change, and with it the realities on the ground. In December 1991 the USSR disappeared and Russia, as the 'continuer-state', assumed all the treaty obligations, privileges and commitments of the USSR, such as the UNSC seat and external debt. Russia soon entered its 'time of troubles', and its concerns could be ignored. Clinton at first soft-pedalled on NATO enlargement, seeking to provide Yeltsin with a breathing space to deal with his domestic opponents and then to win the 1996 presidential election. In October 1993 Yeltsin came to believe that NATO's Partnership for Peace (PfP) bilateral programme would be extended to all European countries rather than pursuing membership for a select group of nations. In fact, PfP was considered a holding action and not the alternative to NATO enlargement, a misunderstanding that helped shape Russian perceptions of Western bad faith.[32] Russia joined PfP on 22 June 1994, but ultimately this was not enough for East European countries and they pressed to become full members. Clinton began NATO's path of enlargement, reinforcing what Russia perceived to be its strategic impasse with a military dimension. Even the liberals in Russia, notably Chubais, warned that NATO enlargement was a major mistake, provoking a backlash against Yeltsin and the Westernising

---

[29] Josh Cohen, 'Don't let Ukraine into NATO', *Moscow Times*, 19 September 2014; Sten Sauer, 'The False Promise of Continental Concert: Russia, the West and the Necessary Balance of Power', *International Affairs*, Vol. 91, No. 3, 2015, pp. 539–52, makes it clear that commitments not to enlarge NATO covered not just East Germany but all of Eastern Europe.

[30] Mary Elise Sarotte, *1989: The Struggle to Create Post-Cold War Europe* (Princeton, Princeton University Press, 2009); Mary Elise Sarotte, 'Perpetuating US Pre-eminence: The 1990 deals to "Bribe the Soviets Out" and Move Nato In', *International Security*, Vol. 35, No. 1, 2010, pp. 110–37; Mary Elise Sarotte, 'A Broken Promise? What the West Really Told Moscow About NATO Expansion', *Foreign Affairs*, Vol. 93, No. 5, September–October 2014, pp. 90–7.

[31] Joshua R. Shifrinson, 'Put It in Writing: How the West Broke its Promise to Moscow', *Foreign Affairs*, 29 October 2014, www.foreignaffairs.com/articles/142310/joshua-r-itzko witz-shifrinson/put-it-in-writing, last accessed 26 May 2017; Joshua R. Shifrinson, 'Deal or No Deal? The End of the Cold War and US Offer to Limit NATO Expansion', *International Security*, Vol. 40, No. 4, 2016, pp. 7–44.

[32] Goldgeier, 'Promises Made, Promises Broken?'.

reformers as a whole. The enlargers pressed ahead anyway, believing that the window of opportunity should be seized to hedge against a future Russian revival.[33] Existing Russian vulnerabilities were exacerbated, but Russia's weakness meant that Yeltsin could do nothing but complain and acquiesce.

Madeleine Albright, Clinton's second-term secretary of state, made no secret of her distrust of Russia and brought traditional East European concerns – she was born in Prague and only emigrated to the US in 1948 – into the heart of the American administration. Although she 'felt the Central European case for Admission to NATO "in my bones and in my genes"', she nevertheless tried to devise a workable arrangement with Russia.[34] Her views were amplified by Zbigniew Brzezinski, who served as president Jimmy Carter's national security adviser from 1977 to 1981 and returned to advise Obama. Brzezinski was the most forceful advocate of the view that Russia's deimperialisation required what effectively amounted to neo-containment. Already in 1994 he argued '[i]t cannot be stressed strongly enough that without Ukraine, Russia ceases to be an empire, but with Ukraine suborned and then subordinated, Russia automatically becomes an empire'.[35] He repeated the argument three years later:

Ukraine, a new and important space on the Eurasian chessboard, is a geopolitical pivot because its very existence as an independent country helps to transform Russia. Without Ukraine, Russia ceases to be a Eurasian empire. However, if Russia regains control over Ukraine, with its 52 million people and major resources as well as access to the Black Sea, Russia automatically gains the wherewithal to become a major imperial state, spanning Europe and Asia.[36]

He stressed that '[f]or America, the chief geopolitical prize is Eurasia'.[37] What for America was a 'prize' and a piece on the 'grand chessboard', for Russia was its homeland and security concern. As early as June 1998 Brzezinski urged the Ukrainians to prepare to enter NATO by 2010.[38] The strategy of enlargement in the end brought the alliance right up to Russia's borders and provoked the most predictable of conflicts. The risks

[33] Fiona Hill and Clifford Gaddy, *Mr. Putin: Operative in the Kremlin*, new and expanded edn (Washington, Brookings Institution Press, 2015), p. 120.

[34] Talbott, *Russia Hand*, p. 223.

[35] Zbigniew Brzezinski, 'The Premature Partnership', *Foreign Affairs*, Vol. 73, No. 2, March–April 1994, p. 80.

[36] Zbigniew Brzezinski, *The Grand Chessboard: American Primacy and its Geostrategic Imperatives* (New York, Basic Books, 1997), pp. 39, 84–5 and 121–2.

[37] Brzezinski, *Grand Chessboard*, p. 30.

[38] J. L. Black, *Russia Faces NATO Expansion: Bearing Gifts or Bearing Arms?* (Lanham, Rowman and Littlefield, 2000), pp. 5–35, 175–201.

were apparent from the start.[39] In July 1997 an open letter from senior American statesmen to the White House argued that NATO enlargement would be bad for NATO, since it would 'inevitably degrade its ability to carry out its primary mission'; it would be bad for Russia, since it would strengthen the non-democratic opposition; it would be bad for Europe, since it would 'draw a new line of division between the "ins" and "outs" and foster instability'; and it would be bad for America, since it would 'call into question the US commitment to the alliance'.[40] In an interview with Thomas Friedman in 1998, George Kennan, the doyen of international diplomacy and the architect of the original policy of 'containment' of the Soviet Union in the post-war years, was unsparing in his condemnation. Kennan spoke with dismay about the US Senate's ratification of NATO expansion plans:

I think the Russians will react quite adversely and it will affect their policies. I think it is a tragic mistake. There was no reason for this whatsoever. No one was threatening anyone else … This expansion would make the Founding Fathers of this country turn over in their graves. We have signed on to protect a whole series of countries, even though we have neither the resources nor the intention to do so in any serious way.

Not for the first time, the 'superficial and ill-informed' nature of Congressional discussion was condemned. Equally, he adds words that have portent to this day:

I was particularly bothered by the references to Russia as a country dying to attack Western Europe. Don't people understand? Our differences in the cold war were with the Soviet Communist regime. And now we are turning our backs on the very people who mounted the greatest bloodless revolution in history to remove that Soviet regime.[41]

Kennan was not alone in warning that enlargement would be a 'policy error of historic proportions'. As Waltz noted in 2000:

It draws new lines of division in Europe, alienates those left out, and can find no logical stopping place west of Russia. It weakens those Russians most inclined toward liberal democracy and a market economy. It strengthens Russians of the opposite inclination. It pushes Russia toward China instead of drawing Russia toward Europe and America.[42]

---

[39] Powerfully described by Michael MccGwire, 'NATO Expansion: "A Policy Error of Historic Importance"', *Review of International Studies*, Vol. 24, No. 1, 1998, pp. 23–42; reprinted in *International Affairs*, Vol. 84, No. 6, November 2008, pp. 1282–301.

[40] Martin Walker, 'Cold Warrior Foils Warning about NATO', *Moscow Times*, 4 July 1997.

[41] Thomas Friedman, 'Foreign Affairs; Now a Word from X', *New York Times*, 2 May 1998.

[42] Waltz, 'Structural Realism', p. 22.

Kissinger later noted that 'Russia should not be regarded as an incipient NATO country; such a goal would simply move to the Manchurian border the crisis we now face on the Ukrainian one'. In his view, the 'goal should be to find a diplomacy to integrate Russia into a world order which leaves scope for cooperation'.[43]

Liberal internationalists in the Clinton administration dominated the debate and swept aside realist objections. The security concerns of the East European countries became the driving force for enlargement, but these concerns were a function of the larger failure to create a mutually satisfactory and inclusive post-Cold War security order. The idea of Eastern Europe as some sort of 'buffer zone' was clearly unacceptable, and even less the idea of an exclusive Russian 'sphere of interests'. The question posed by the historian Fritz Stern is fundamental: 'What did it say about the options that the Russians might want to keep open tomorrow if they opposed Western security guarantees for the Central Europeans today?'[44] Matlock responds by arguing that '[t]he question should not have been "expand NATO or nothing" but rather to explore how the United States could give adequate assurance to countries in Eastern Europe that their independence would be preserved in the future, and at the same time to create a security system in Europe that would place prime responsibility for the continent's future on Europeans'.[45] Instead, despite the end of the Cold War, the US discouraged a separate European defence identity. More than that, '[t]he Clinton administration, without any provocation, in effect repeated a fundamental mistake made at Versailles in 1919. By excluding Russia from the peace settlement when it was not even a defeated party but actually one of the victors over the Communist Soviet Union, the Clinton administration practically ensured that there would be no new world order in Europe.'[46]

The problem has not been satisfactorily resolved to this day. The conditions for the security of one group resulted in a diminution of security for the other. NATO is clearly a collective defence organisation. However, NATO activism in Bosnia in 1995, Serbia/Kosovo in 1999 and at the head of the International Security Assistance Force (ISAF) force in Afghanistan from December 2001 served as a warning to Moscow of the heavy price that recalcitrant states could pay. NATO enlargement may well have been a 'phantom problem',[47] but in the absence of a

---

[43] Jeffrey Goldberg, 'World Chaos and World Order: Conversations with Henry Kissinger', *The Atlantic*, 10 November 2016, www.theatlantic.com/international/archive/2016/11/kissinger-order-and-chaos/506876/, last accessed 26 May 2017.

[44] Talbott, *Russia Hand*, p. 220.   [45] Matlock, *Super-Power Illusions*, p. 172.

[46] Matlock, *Super-Power Illusions*, p. 173.

[47] The view of Alexander Lebed, as reported by Talbott, *Russia Hand*, p. 221.

comprehensive security framework the fear is that a Russia surrounded by NATO will be constrained and unable to act independently. Enlargement was driven by the view that the former communist states would be transformed by joining the 'civilising institutions and prosperity of the West', just as Germany had been after the war, and that eventually the same would apply to Russia. This not ignoble goal proved self-contradictory. NATO's unilateral enlargement precisely pushed Russia away from the transformative experience that could have been offered by a thoroughly reformed Atlantic community, the Greater West discussed earlier. Russia's ultimate membership of NATO was not officially precluded, although even this postulate proved extremely controversial:

> To traditionalists, bringing an incontinent camel into the tent of the Partnership for Peace was one thing, but bringing an unhousebroken bear into the North Atlantic Alliance was another. They believed a NATO that included Russia was destined to be, at best, just another talk shop like the North Atlantic Cooperation Council (NACC), and even considering such a possibility in the abstract would damage the alliance's effectiveness in the here and now.[48]

Membership would undoubtedly have changed the character of the organisation, and Russia would have tried to assert its influence and power. Certainly, the US saw no reason to share its hegemonic leadership or to dilute the normative basis of the alliance. In the event, enlargement ultimately precipitated conflict of the sort that it was designed to prevent.

The Atlantic powers did seek to sweeten the pill. The North Atlantic Cooperation Council had been established on 20 December 1991 as a forum for dialogue and cooperation with former Warsaw Pact members, providing the framework for Russia's membership of PfP in 1994, and became the Euro-Atlantic Partnership Council in 1997. Aware that none of this provided a substantive framework for engagement, the NATO-Russia Founding Act on Mutual Relations of May 1997 spoke in ringing tones of the onset of a new era:

> NATO and Russia do not consider each other as adversaries. They share the goal of overcoming the vestiges of earlier confrontation and competition and of strengthening mutual trust and cooperation. The present Act reaffirms the determination of NATO and Russia to give concrete substance to their shared commitment to build a stable, peaceful and undivided Europe, whole and free, to the benefit of all its peoples. Making this commitment at the highest political level marks the beginning of a fundamentally new relationship between NATO and Russia. They intend to develop, on the basis of common interest, reciprocity and transparency a strong, stable and enduring partnership.

[48] Talbott, *Russia Hand*, p. 131.

The document outlined nineteen areas for potential cooperation, defined 'the goals and mechanisms of consultation, cooperation, joint decision-making and joint action that will constitute the core of the mutual relations between NATO and Russia', argued that 'NATO has undertaken a historic transformation', and insisted that this was a 'process that will continue'. Above all, NATO promised not to station forces in Eastern Europe on a permanent basis. Cooperation was to be achieved through the creation of a NATO-Russia Permanent Joint Council (PJC). NATO committed itself not to place nuclear weapons on the territory of new members, to work on adapting the CFE Treaty, and above all 'NATO reiterates that in the current and foreseeable security environment, the Alliance will carry out its collective defence and other missions by ensuring the necessary interoperability, integration, and capability for reinforcement rather than by additional permanent stationing of substantial combat forces'.[49] Kissinger denounced the promise not to station nuclear weapons and foreign troops eastward: 'Whoever heard of a military alliance begging with a weakened adversary? NATO should not be turned into an instrument to conciliate Russia or Russia will undermine it.'[50] The Clinton administration worked hard to find ways to blunt the pressure from domestic critics, who tried to get the executive to adopt 'a policy that was coercive in intent, punitive in impact and often counter-productive in consequence'.[51] At the same time, Clinton supported Russia joining the Group of Seven (G7) in 1998, and although Russia was never fully integrated into the financial mechanisms, its membership of the G8 was of enormous symbolic importance.

Despite the lofty rhetoric, the PJC failed to provide an effective platform for engagement at the time of the Kosovo war in 1999, and Russia was once again isolated. Partnership with the US at the best of times could be difficult. As Primakov put it with mock wariness to Albright, 'sometimes I am not sure how much more of your friendship we can stand'.[52] Other Russian leaders were less elegiac in arguing that 'their country's post-cold war settlement with the West was getting harsher as time went on; despite all the rhetoric about win/win, the US was an ungenerous victor'.[53] The open door policy reinforced the hedging strategy of the aspirant nations in Eastern Europe and demonstrated US leadership, while burnishing Clinton's credentials as the leader of the free world.[54]

---

[49] 'Founding Act on Mutual Relations, Cooperation and Security between NATO and the Russian Federation', 27 May 1997, www.nato.int/cps/en/natohq/official_texts_25468.htm, last accessed 26 May 2017.
[50] Talbott, *Russia Hand*, p. 243.   [51] Talbott, *Russia Hand*, p. 253.
[52] Talbott, *Russia Hand*, p. 254.   [53] Talbott, *Russia Hand*, p. 294.
[54] Goldgeier, *Not Whether but When*, p. 218.

His successor, George W. Bush, engineered the 'big bang' enlargement of NATO in 2004. All serious decisions about NATO enlargement were taken in Washington, starting with PfP and all the way through to deciding on which countries would join – until the attempt to accelerate Georgian and Ukrainian membership was blocked by the German chancellor Angela Merkel at the April 2008 Bucharest summit.

NATO ensured the continued American presence in the European security system and stymied attempts by Gaullists and others to develop a separate European Security and Defence Identity (ESDI). The Atlantic order was not transformed into a fully-fledged Euro-Atlantic system. The EU's Common Foreign and Security Policy (CFSP) was launched as part of the Maastricht Treaty to provide more coherence to the EU's foreign relations, while the Common Security and Defence Policy (CSDP) from 2009 sought to strengthen the EU's ability to act externally though enhancing its civilian and military capabilities. The CSDP does not cover the collective defence of the EU but focuses on humanitarian and rescue tasks, crisis management and peacekeeping. Attempts to broaden the Atlantic system into a two-pillar Euro-Atlantic structure were resisted because of fears that an independent European security identity would undermine the cohesion of the alliance as a whole. With the majority also members of NATO, there was the justified fear of duplication. The French attempt in 1996 to bring the West European Union into the EU to create a European Security and Defence Identity was blocked by the British. The Combined Joint Task Force was developed in part to stymie any potential efforts to transform the West European Union into a more active European security force. The British later vetoed the establishment of an operational headquarters for EU forces and blocked greater funding for the European Defence Agency (EDA), an intergovernmental body of the European Council established in 2004, comprising all EU members except Denmark.[55] Instead of doing too much, Europe later was accused of doing too little and of free-riding on the US, condemned by both Obama and rather more forcefully by Trump. Defence spending by the twenty-seven EDA members declined by 10.7 per cent in real terms (€22 billion) between 2005 and 2015.[56] European security remains firmly embedded in the Atlantic security community, although with the emergence of Trump's brand of conservative neo-isolationism it faces unprecedented challenges. Despite revived talk, there is no immediate prospect

[55] For an overview, see Andrew Cottey, *Security in 21st Century Europe*, 2nd edn (Basingstoke, Palgrave Macmillan, 2013).
[56] Sophia Besch, *EU Defence, Brexit and Trump*, Centre for European Reform (CER), December 2016, p. 4.

for the creation of a European army, but there is intense pressure to enhance the European defence contribution.[57]

While the perceived security vacuum in Central and Eastern Europe was plugged by NATO enlargement, this was accompanied by a growing security vacuum across the whole continent. The Strategic Concept adopted by the Washington summit in April 1999 portrayed NATO as 'one of the indispensable foundations for a stable Euro-Atlantic security environment, based on the growth of democratic institutions and commitment to the peaceful resolution of disputes, in which no country would be able to intimidate or coerce any other through the threat or use of force'.[58] The word 'indispensable' is used five times to describe NATO's various functions, including 'the Alliance's commitment to the indispensable transatlantic link'. Absent from this representation was any sense of European continental unity. The repeated invocation of the peaceful order in Europe ignored the way that enlargement generated discord and division. The more NATO enlarged to encompass the former 'captive nations', the harder it became to bring Russia into the expanded community, and the more NATO subverted the peace order which it was committed to defend. Culture and security became entwined, uniting geopolitics and identity in ways that would have explosive consequences.[59]

On coming to power, Putin toyed with the idea of Russia joining not only the EU but also NATO. On a visit to Britain in March 2000, Putin was asked by David Frost about the possibility of Russia joining NATO, to which Putin responded: 'Why not?' The answer was not so much a serious bid for membership as a signal, as Putin put it in the same interview, that 'Russia is part of European culture and I can't imagine my country cut off from Europe or from what we often refer to as the "civilized world" … seeing NATO as an enemy is destructive for Russia'.[60] In the early 2000s Putin seriously engaged with NATO. It appears that informal membership talks were even held in Brussels, until vetoed by Washington.[61] This was the period I identify as the 'new realism' in Russian foreign policy. Coming after the enthusiastic Atlanticism of 1991–96, followed by Primakov's more sceptical policy of competitive coexistence and emphasis on multipolarity, Putin clearly

---

[57] Sophia Besch, *An EU Army? Four Reasons it Will Not Happen*, CER, 12 May 2016.

[58] *The Alliance's Strategic Concept*, 24 April 1999, www.nato.int/cps/en/natohq/official_texts_27433.htm, last accessed 26 May 2017.

[59] Merje Kuus, *Geopolitics Reframed: Security and Identity in Europe's Eastern Enlargement* (Basingstoke, Palgrave Macmillan, 2007).

[60] 'Intervyu V. Putina Devidu Frostu', *Kommersant'*, No. 39, 7 March 2000, p. 2; Alexander Golts, 'Putin Could Aim for Europe Alliance', *Russia Journal*, 20–6 March 2000, p. 8.

[61] I have asked Russian and western officials about these talks, and several have confirmed their existence but refuse to go on record.

resolved that he could do better. The new realism sought to avoid the uncritical Westernism of the early period and the openly competitive character of Primakov's policy, to find a new pattern of cooperative engagement that in the end, Putin believed, could prepare the way for the long-desired creation of a Greater West, with a perspective for deep rapprochement and ultimate Russian membership of NATO and the EU.

Following the 9/11 attack, Putin's offer to help in the struggle against terrorism, including intelligence-sharing and opening up bases in Central Asia to support the war in Afghanistan, opened the door to enhanced cooperation and a more equal partnership. On 28 May 2002 the NATO-Russia Council (NRC) was established at a summit in Rome as 'a mechanism for consultation, consensus-building, cooperation, joint decision and joint action in which the individual NATO member states and Russia work as equal partners on a wide spectrum of security issues of common interest'.[62] Russia's status was enhanced from one against the others to what was intended to be a higher degree of partnership as part of an expanded security community. Nevertheless, the text studiously avoided allowing Russia a 'veto' in any shape or form on NATO security issues.[63] Neither party was pursuing a zero-sum policy, yet in the end without a structural transformation, aspirations for genuine partnership proved nugatory.

Despite repeated warnings that bringing NATO to Russia's borders would be perceived as a strategic threat of the first order, the momentum of NATO enlargement continued. At the Bucharest NATO summit of 2–4 April 2008 Georgia and Ukraine were promised eventual membership. As the Summit Declaration put it, 'NATO welcomes Ukraine's and Georgia's Euro-Atlantic aspirations for membership in NATO. We agreed today that these countries will become members of NATO.' The Declaration once again affirmed the principles on which the community was based:

Recognising the enduring value of the transatlantic link and of NATO as the essential forum for security consultations between Europe and North America, we reaffirmed our solidarity and cohesion and our commitment to the common vision and shared democratic values embodied in the Washington Treaty. The principle of the indivisibility of Allied security is fundamental.[64]

---

[62] This is the description of the NRC on NATO's website, www.nato.int/nrc-website/en/about/index.html, last accessed 26 May 2017.

[63] 'Nato-Russia Council, Rome Declaration, 28 May 2002', www.nato.int/nrc-website/media/59487/2002.05.28_nrc_rome_declaration.pdf, last accessed 26 May 2017.

[64] 'Bucharest Summit Declaration' 3 April 2008, www.nato.int/cps/en/natolive/official_texts_8443.htm, last accessed 26 May 2017.

Membership Action Plans were deferred because of German and French concerns about antagonising Russia, yet the strategic direction had been set for an enlargement of NATO to Russia's borders. Although the Declaration talked of 'indivisibility', it had in mind the security of the Atlantic community itself. The result of enlargement was precisely to enshrine the divisibility of European security, and thus the new partition of Europe. The Bucharest Declaration represents the turning point when differences turned into confrontation.

Both sides tried to prevent an escalation of conflict, but the question of NATO's purpose remained acute. Already in his press conference in July 2001, Putin noted:

We do not consider NATO an enemy organisation or view its existence as a tragedy, although we see no need for it. It was born as the antipode to the Warsaw Pact, as the antipode to the Soviet Union in Eastern Europe. Now there is no Warsaw Pact, no Soviet Union, but NATO exists and is growing.[65]

Both NATO and the EU sought to soften Russia's alienation, but these were mitigation measures rather than the transformation of the European political community. From the Atlantic point of view, this was only natural: Russia represented a much diminished part of the former Soviet Union, and was in certain respects a failed economy and polity, so why should it be treated as an equal in geopolitical terms? At the same time, it was only natural that the perceived security vacuum in Central and Eastern Europe should be filled by a defensive alliance, which by reducing insecurity and risks would in the end enhance even Russia's security. Putin initially was ready to accept the argument and worked hard to improve relations with both the EU and NATO through his policy of new realism, although he, no less than Yeltsin, insisted on Russia's great power status. The puzzle to be explained, then, is why relations with both organisations deteriorated so spectacularly, to the point that outright military conflict is no longer excluded? Ultimately it was the failure to imagine a different future for Europe that created the new dividing lines. From Russia's perspective, there was no security vacuum that needed to be filled; from the West's perspective, who was to deny the 'sovereign choice' of Eastern European states if they wished to enter the world's most successful multilateral security body. The former Warsaw Pact and Baltic states joined NATO to enhance their security; but the very act of doing so created a security dilemma for Russia that undermined the security of all. This fateful geopolitical paradox – that NATO exists to

[65] Andrei Zolotov, 'Putin Answers all But One Question', *Moscow Times*, 19 July 2001, http://old.themoscowtimes.com/sitemap/free/2001/7/article/putin-answers-all-but-one-question/252529.html/, last accessed 26 May 2017.

manage the risks created by its existence – provoked a number of conflicts. The Russo-Georgian War of August 2008 acted as the warning tremor of the major earthquake that engulfed Europe over Ukraine in 2014.

As Simes puts it, '[t]he daring combination of NATO expansion and growing interventionism further accentuated Russia's alienation from the West. Remarkably, NATO failed to consider how its dramatically different conduct would affect relations with Russia or world politics in general'. As the spirit of post-Cold War triumphalism seeped into conventional wisdom, the assumption of the US and its allies was that when they 'wanted to do something in the international arena, they could impose their will without significant costs'. Moscow's concerns were treated 'with either indifference or contemptuous disregard'. The Yeltsin government behaved as an active collaborator in fostering this sense of impunity, with Kozyrev acting 'as if winning favour in Washington and Brussels was a paramount Russian national interest'. In the absence of formal legal guarantees against NATO enlargement, Simes sums up his argument as follows:

The Clinton administration had every legal right to proceed with NATO expansion. What US officials had no right to do was to think that they could move NATO's borders further and further east without changing Russia's perception of the West from friend to adversary.[66]

Simes makes the important point: 'Yet if Russia was not a threat, as Western leaders insisted it was not, why would avoiding the Baltic states' anxiety be a higher priority than stabilizing US and European security relations with Russia, a huge country with almost 150 million population and a massive nuclear arsenal?' The 'unsustainable security architecture' of the inter-war years had contributed to the rise of Nazism and the Second World War, and the mistake was once again repeated: 'While Westerners may believe that NATO's eastward expansion has been peaceful and voluntary, Russians see it as inseparable from NATO's European and global military exploits. How could bringing small new members into NATO and mollifying them outweigh the danger of provoking Russia's anti-Western militarism?'[67]

The absence of a discourse and institutions of reconciliation meant that the geopolitical contestation over space was painted by both sides as a civilisational choice. The axiological dimension reduced the potential for

---

[66] Dmitri K. Simes, 'Russia and America: Destined for Conflict?', *The National Interest*, 26 June 2016, http://nationalinterest.org/feature/russia-america-destined-conflict-16726, last accessed 26 May 2017.

[67] Simes, 'Russia and America'.

diplomatic engagement and compromise. At moments of crisis the NRC turned out to be no more effective than the PJC as a forum for conflict resolution. American vetoed convoking the NRC to discuss the Georgia crisis in August 2008, a move which it later admitted was a mistake. Once again with the onset of the Ukraine crisis, on 1 April 2014 NATO suspended 'all practical civilian and military cooperation between NATO and Russia', although contacts at ambassadorial level were allowed.[68] The suspension of regular political and military dialogue when it was most needed only highlighted the mitigating rather than substantive character of the partnership. The cooperative rhetoric could not reconcile the mismatch in expectations, commitments and perceptions.[69] Above all, no amount of rhetoric could overcome the deep division in conceptions of European security. The institutional architecture of cooperation, despite the aspirations of both sides, was inadequate to meet the structural challenges of European security in the twenty-first century.

Ballistic Missile Defence (BMD)

NATO enlargement was the enduring divisive issue, but it was BMD that Russia considered the greatest strategic threat. The current BMD programme has its roots in the 1980s Strategic Defence Initiative (SDI, known colloquially as 'star wars'). Visiting a nuclear weapons bunker in 1980, Reagan was astonished to discover that the US had no effective defence against a nuclear first strike. This should hardly have come as a surprise. The same applied to the USSR, and the whole theory of deterrence was based on the idea of mutually assured destruction (MAD) in the event of a nuclear exchange. A first strike would be deterred by knowledge that the country launching the attack would be liable to destruction in a second strike. This was the reason for the restrictions placed on anti-ballistic missile systems by treaty in 1972, with each side limited to two ABM complexes (reduced by amendment to one in 1974). If one side could shield themselves from a second strike nuclear attack, they would be tempted to launch a first strike. The 'star wars' programme, announced by Reagan in March 1983, threatened to destabilise the nuclear balance of terror by giving one side first-strike advantage. Vast sums were spent on research on how to shoot down ballistic missiles in the

[68] 'Statement by NATO Foreign Ministers', 1 April 2014, www.nato.int/nrc-website/en/a rticles/20140327-announcement/index.html, last accessed 26 May 2017.
[69] Tuomas Forsberg and Graeme Herd, 'Russia and NATO: From Windows of Opportunities to Closed Doors', *Journal of Contemporary European Studies*, Vol. 23, No. 1, pp. 41–57.

early stages of their flight.[70] The star wars and later BMD programmes were hugely expensive, but became a self-sustaining jobs programme for the military-industrial complex. Star wars was launched in the knowledge that an already over-stretched Soviet economy would be ruined if it sought to replicate the American programme. This was the reason Gorbachev pressed Reagan to abandon SDI at the Reykjavik summit in October 1986, and why both sides seriously discussed the abolition of nuclear weapons in their entirety. Gorbachev repeatedly called on Reagan to abandon SDI, or at least to confine it to laboratory testing, something that Reagan refused to do.[71]

Soon after Putin committed Russia to support the US 'war on terror' after 9/11, on 13 December 2001 Bush announced that America would leave the ABM Treaty after the statutory six-month notice period. This was the first time that the US had withdrawn from a major international arms control treaty. Given the known destabilising effects this would have on the nuclear balance, US withdrawal appeared poor reward for Putin's support, which had been achieved in the face of severe opposition from his own hard-liners. America's unilateral abrogation of the ABM Treaty prepared the way for extended confrontation, in part stoked by Russian fears. A study in 2006 described the degradation of Russia's nuclear arsenal and the weakness of its early warning systems (a problem still not resolved): 'Today, for the first time in almost 50 years, the United States stands on the verge of attaining nuclear primacy',[72] and warned that 'unless they reverse course rapidly, Russia's vulnerability will only increase over time'.[73] The conclusion was stark: 'Washington's pursuit of nuclear primacy helps explain its missile defence strategy'.[74] The missile shield would not defend populations, but would be valuable in an offensive context. A first strike would destroy the bulk of the enemy's (read Russia's) nuclear arsenal, and the shield would mop up any residual retaliatory capacity. This was the challenge to which Russian nuclear planners responded.

The US plan announced in 2007 to install an anti-missile base in Poland and a radar control centre in the Czech Republic is one of the most controversial decisions of our time. It was taken without

---

[70] Gates, *Duty*, pp. 159–67, 398–409, 530–1, provides an informed insider view of US administration thinking about BMD between 2006 and 2010, as well as Russian concerns.

[71] Peter R. Beckman and Paul. W. Crumlish, *The Nuclear Predicament: Nuclear Weapons in the Twenty-First Century*, 3rd edn (London, Pearson, 1999).

[72] Keir A. Lieber and Daryl G. Press, 'The Rise of U.S. Nuclear Primacy', *Foreign Affairs*, Vol. 85, No. 2, March–April 2006, p. 43.

[73] Lieber and Press, 'Rise of U.S. Nuclear Primacy', p. 48.

[74] Lieber and Press, 'Rise of U.S. Nuclear Primacy', p. 52.

consultation with European institutions, thus highlighting the absence of the 'Euro' element in the Atlantic security system. The system was ostensibly to counter the nuclear threat from Iran, although at the time Iran had neither nuclear weapons nor long-range ballistic missiles. The decision has had profound consequences in exacerbating the security dilemma between Russia and the Atlantic alliance. Obama's reset with Russia was accompanied by a change in the missile defence scheme, intended to meet some of Russia's objections. The European Phased Adaptive Approach requires installations in Romania and Poland, and long-range interceptor missiles were replaced by medium-range ones. The modifications did not allay Russian fears that the system as a whole weakened its deterrence capabilities, and Moscow continued vehemently to oppose the project. The BMD issue continued to sour relations between Washington and Moscow.

Obama promised a new era of nuclear sanity, but he left office with the world once again close to nuclear war (see Chapter 7). Even the relatively liberal president of the time Medvedev was brought to despair by BMD plans, warning in 2011 that Russia would have no choice but to upgrade the offensive capabilities of Russian nuclear missiles and to deploy Iskander missiles in Kaliningrad. Russia's leaders pleaded for an end to BMD deployment, fearing that interceptor rockets could easily be replaced with nuclear warheads that could decapitate Russia's top leadership with virtually no warning.[75] The obvious response was to launch at the first sign of an incoming strike, without checking if it was a false alarm.[76] At the Valdai meeting in October 2015, Putin's concerns about BMD came to the surface. In an exchange with Matlock, Putin asked about the drivers of the programme. Matlock was at a loss to answer, but in the end noted the role of the major US arms manufacturers in maintaining the programme. Putin instantly responded that better uses for the money could be found.[77] Putin repeatedly stressed that the ABM Treaty had been 'the cornerstone of the entire international security system', and argued that 'we will have to react somehow, we will need to improve our strike systems in order to defeat these missile defence systems'. He warned that 'we can say confidently that today we are stronger than any potential aggressor. I repeat, any aggressor.'[78] These

[75] Mearsheimer, *Tragedy of Great Power Politics*, pp. 97, 108–9 on the general theory of decapitation.
[76] Jonathan Marshall, 'Summing up Russia's Real Nuclear Fears', Consortiumnews.com, 29 December 2016, https://consortiumnews.com/2016/12/29/summing-up-russias-real-nuclear-fears/, last accessed 26 May 2017.
[77] Personal notes.
[78] 'Vladimir Putin's Annual Press Conference', 23 December 2016, http://en.kremlin.ru/events/president/news/53573, last accessed 26 May 2017.

comments in December 2016 provoked a storm of criticism that Putin was engaging in nuclear sabre rattling, but in fact he was stressing that Russia was modernising its nuclear forces to maintain strategic parity, and that it was strong enough to defeat any attack. Rather than defending peace, the abrogation of the ABM Treaty and BMD development ramped up the nuclear arms race and ultimately made World War III more likely.

Western Interventions

The story of Western interventions in the post-Cold War era is not a happy one. Russia argues that the US and its allies have repeatedly flouted international law in their various interventions, and it is the West rather than Russia that has become revisionist. The post-Cold War sequence begins with Bosnia, which in August 1995 led to the lifting of the siege of Sarajevo. More egregious from Russia's perspective was the seventy-eight-day bombing campaign between March and June 1999, in response to Serbia's brutal policies in Kosovo. The bombing of Serbia in many ways marked a turning point. This is not just because of the long historical ties with Russia, which do exist but were not determinative of Moscow's policy. Pro-Serbianism, and the relics of Pan-Slavism in the rhetoric of which it is couched, was a marginal concern in the 1990s. More important was the use of what Moscow considered excessive force to achieve a questionable goal, namely the separation of Kosovo from Serbia. Russia consistently under-played the human rights atrocities by the Serbian forces under Slobodan Milošević, earlier in Bosnia and now in Kosovo, amidst claims that the latter events were being manipulated by the Kosovo Liberation Army. There was a genuine fear that the attack on Belgrade and Serbian infrastructure was intended as a warning to Moscow. The bombing of a modern European city in pursuit of unclear goals was an event of the first magnitude, and still has a powerful resonance in Russia. In the end Moscow helped broker a deal that allowed the West to call off the campaign with a modicum of dignity. The million Kosovars who had fled at the beginning of the campaign returned to their homes, although Kosovo's status remained in limbo until its unilateral declaration of independence from Serbia on 17 February 2008. At that time Putin warned that the precipitate recognition of Kosovo independence by Western states, notably the US, would have consequences. It was not clear what these consequences would be, but Russia's recognition of the independence of Abkhazia and South Ossetia on 26 August 2008 was probably one of them, and the annexation of Crimea in March 2014 another.

The British involvement in Sierra Leone in 1999 is a classic case of humanitarian intervention, and it quickly achieved its goal of putting an end to the indiscriminate killing of civilians. The NATO-led intervention in Afghanistan from autumn 2001 came in response to the 9/11 attack, and was sanctioned by the UN. The goal was to find Osama bin Laden and the al-Qaeda operatives in Afghanistan and to oust the Taliban regime of Mullah Omar, which had provided a base for the global insurgency. Whether it made strategic sense to engage in a military campaign to achieve these goals is questionable. Mullah Omar had offered to expel Osama bin Laden and his associates, and thus the primary goal could have been achieved without war. It was another matter that the radicalism of the Taliban government, one which had effectively been put in place by earlier Western actions in forcing Russia to stop providing military and financial support for the Soviet-sponsored Mohammed Najibullah government, had become increasingly odious to the West. The destruction of ancient pre-Islamic historical monuments, notably the Bamiyan statues, the public executions, and the exclusion of women from educational and professional opportunities, all suggested that this was a regime ripe for overthrow.

The Anglo-American invasion of Iraq in March 2003 is the classic case of Western powers breaching the international law that they were so keen to defend when it came to others. The invasion was a 'war of choice' and ultimately took place without UN sanction. It was based on the mendacious assertion that Saddam Hussein represented a danger to regional and world peace because of his possession of weapons of mass destruction (WMD). Despite inspectors not having found any evidence, the invasion went ahead anyway. The military operation was extremely effective, but the subsequent dismantling of the institutions of the Iraqi state – the army, the Ba'ath party, and the civil service – opened the door to the chaos from which the country has not yet emerged and which has spread across the region and into Europe in the form of refugees. Putin, with his 'old Europe' allies, France and Germany, from the first opposed military action, arguing that it breached international law and would be destabilising. Putin is a legitimist, deeply opposed to the revolutionary or external overthrow of governments.

A no less fateful Western action took place in Libya, this time driven by supporters of the 'Arab Spring' in Europe, notably president François Hollande of France, and American liberal interventionists.[79] As the 'Arab awakening' rolled across North Africa and the Middle East, long-established leaders were overthrown. The old regime in Tunisia was toppled, and mass rallies in Tahrir Square in Cairo forced President Hosni Mubarak to resign

---

[79] Gates, *Duty*, pp. 510–12, describes the line-up of those in the Obama administration in favour of military intervention.

on 12 February 2011, after thirty years in power. The 'Arab Spring' then spread to Libya. The intervention was partially sanctioned by UNSC Resolution 1973 of 17 March 2011, authorising 'an immediate ceasefire' and imposing a no-fly zone to prevent Colonel Muammar Gaddafi from using air power to attack the insurgency spreading from Benghazi. Medvedev abstained in the UN vote (without consulting Putin). The motion was carried, and two days later in a punishing attack NATO destroyed Libya's entire air defences. With Western support the regime was overthrown, leading to Gaddafi's gruesome murder on 20 October 2011. Once again, regime change was followed by the descent of the country into chaos. Putin was horrified, describing the UN resolution as 'a medieval call for a crusade', and effectively reprimanded Medvedev live on air when he warned that '[w]hat concerns me most is not the armed intervention itself – armed conflicts are nothing new and will likely continue for a long time, unfortunately. My main concern is the light-mindedness with which decisions to use force are taken in international affairs these days.'[80] He was not alone in his criticism, with Algeria's warnings about the likely outcome of the intervention 'treated with contempt' by Paris, London and Washington.[81] The US secretary of defence, Robert Gates, noted that 'I was running out of patience … with people blithely talking about the use of military force as though it were some kind of video game'.[82] By contrast, Putin's erstwhile fellow critic of the Iraq invasion, France, was now urging intervention in Libya. As a result of the chaos in Libya, France was forced to intervene in neighbouring Mali in 2013 to halt the advance of radical Islamic militants. As Putin argued, intervention begets chaos that begets more war that requires yet another intervention.

From the Russian perspective, a pattern was taking shape. International law was fine, but it failed to constrain the Western powers from forcing regime change when they wished. Russia had no particular stake in Libya (apart from oil-related investments), and Putin's main concern was the challenge to legitimate governments. The core of Putin's political identity is legitimism; support for sovereign constituted authorities irrespective of their political character or behaviour – a position he shares with China. The lesson of the Libyan events was not lost on Putin. Gaddafi had come in from the cold, given up his nuclear weapons programme in 2004, signed an

[80] Zygar, *All the Kremlin's Men*, p. 198.

[81] Francis Ghilès, 'With a More Enterprising Russia, Cards are Reshuffled in the Arab World', *The Arab Weekly*, 22 January 2017, www.thearabweekly.com/Opinion/7648/Wi th-a-more-enterprising-Russia,-cards-are-reshuffled-in-the-Arab-world, last accessed 26 May 2017.

[82] Gates, *Duty*, p. 512.

extensive economic modernisation deal with Italy in 2008, and in general put his trust in the West, but 'he was stabbed in the back. When he was a pariah, no one had touched him. But as soon as he opened up, he was not only overthrown but killed in the street like a mangy old cur.'[83] In Egypt, Mubarak's overthrow was followed by a period of uncertainty, which saw the emergence of sectarian conflict on the Iraqi model in which Christian Copts came under attack by Islamic radicals. In the end, a representative of the Muslim Brotherhood, Mohammed Morsi, won the presidential election of June 2012. After a year of increasingly authoritarian and incompetent policies, which saw many of the erstwhile supporters of democratic change turn against him, the military once again intervened, overthrowing Morsi in July 2013 in a violent coup. Harsh repression was unleashed against Morsi's supporters and other resisters, leading to the deaths of at least 10,000. The coup leader, Abdel Fattah el-Sisi, subsequently won the presidential election of May 2014 in a landslide. He soon consolidated his power in a regime that was arguably less tolerant of dissent than Mubarak's.

This was a morality tale of pure Putinism. A popular movement agitating for democracy and human rights overthrows a stagnant and kleptocratic dictatorship, only to find that the alternative is worse: inter-faith and ethnic sectarianism, state disintegration, economic collapse and political chaos, followed in the 'best case' in Egypt by a return of the status quo ante, whereas in Iraq and Libya state collapse continued indefinitely. It was these considerations which shaped Russian policy towards Syria.[84] The modern Syrian state was carved out of the decaying Ottoman Empire by the Sykes-Picot agreement of May 1916, and a tenuous secular developmental state was maintained by the Ba'ath regime after it came to power in a coup in 1963, governed since 1971 by the Alawite Hafez al-Assad. The first two months of demonstrations from March 2011 against the regime of his son, Bashar al-Assad, looked as if they could force reforms from above. Bashar was Western-educated, and on assuming the presidency on the death of his father in 2000, Bashar proposed moderate reforms, encouraged by his long-standing friend, the Turkish leader Recep Tayyip Erdoğan. These ideas were soon stopped by the powerful security establishment, fearing destabilisation in a society made up of Sunnis, Shias, Alawites, Christians, Druze, Yazidis, Kurds and many others. In 2011 intra-systemic reform was again soon exhausted. Heavy-handed repression put an end to hopes of change from above and radicalised the opposition. A devastating civil war ensued, or series of

[83] Zygar, *All the Kremlin's Men*, p. 204.

[84] For a good survey, see Nikolay Kozhanov, *Russia and the Syrian Conflict: Moscow's Domestic, Regional and Strategic Interests* (Berlin and London, Gerlach Press, 2016).

wars. Patrick Cockburn identifies five different conflicts: a popular uprising against Assad; Sunnis against Shias (the Alawites are considered a
heretical Shia sect); Iran (and its Hezbollah allies from Lebanon) against
the US and Saudi Arabia (and its Gulf allies, notably Qatar); and Russia
against the West.[85] The conflict turned into a proxy war between the US
and Russia, with the latter vetoing UN resolutions to stop possible
Western intervention on the Libyan model. By 2017 at least 3 million
Syrians had fled abroad, and some 400,000 had died. The main opposition to the Assad regime turned out to be not moderates supported by the
West but radicals of various stripes, who soon gained control of much of
the north and east of the country. The body which in June 2014 called
itself Islamic State (Daesh) following its capture of Mosul in neighbouring Iraq declared the restoration of the caliphate, and established control
over vast territories in Syria and Iraq. The Syrian Kurds carved out an
autonomous region in the northeast.

Following the use of chemical weapons (sarin gas) in the neighbourhood of Damascus on 21 August 2013, British government attempts to
launch an air campaign were blocked by a vote in the House of Commons.
Obama earlier had asserted that the use of chemical weapons would be a
'red line' that would not be tolerated. The British vote allowed him to
fudge the issue and Congress did not support the use of air power. Putin
seized the opportunity to act as an honest broker, and worked with the US
to negotiate a deal whereby the Syrian regime gave up its chemical
weapons in exchange for non-intervention.[86] The successful *démarche*
reinforced the claim that Russia would act as a constructive power when
treated as an equal, and could use its influence to achieve positive goals in
the international system. For some in the US, this was a case of Russia
meddling in matters that were not its concern, and which left the US
looking marginalised and lacking a coherent strategy.

The practices of humanitarian interventionism gained a more formal
status in the policy of R2P. Although this is not part of international law, it
has gained the force of conventional law since the UN World Summit in
2005. Revulsion against Second World War genocides was reinforced by
the failure to act to prevent mass murder in Rwanda in 1994, as well as the
three-year siege of Sarajevo from 1992 to 1995, and the killings in Kosovo
in the late 1990s. Responsibility to protect is motivated by the desire to
prevent future events of this kind. However, the fundamental critique of

[85] Patrick Cockburn, *Chaos and Caliphate: Jihadis and the West in the Struggle for the Middle
East* (New York and London, OR Books, 2016).
[86] Ray McGovern, 'When Putin Bailed out Obama', Consortium News, 31 August 2016,
https://consortiumnews.com/2016/08/31/when-putin-bailed-out-obama/, last accessed
26 May 2017.

R2P is not so much its challenge to national sovereignty, but the arbitrary manner in which it is applied. Although the normative basis is very different, R2P still smacks to some as too reminiscent of humanitarian intervention, of the sort outlined earlier. Defenders of national sovereignty question the normative basis of the policy, arguing that it opens the door to interventions that may or may not be justified on humanitarian grounds. However, in keeping with Russia's claimed commitment to international society, its critique was more complex than a simple defence of old-fashioned state sovereignty and condemnation of Western-inspired international norms. The assumed great power status 'reinforced a set of assumptions on Russia's part about its role in the world which shape its search for a negotiated international order', which would validate its status in the international system. Its criticisms were thus grounded in rationalist arguments 'based on statist international law'.[87] Russia defends the classic principles of a pluralist international system, above all sovereignty, territorial integrity and non-interference in internal affairs of states unless authorised by the UN. When it came to Kosovo, Libya and above all Syria, Russia drew on the special responsibility of a great power, as asserted by Bull, 'to play a part in determining issues that affect the peace and security of the international system as a whole'.[88]

Democratic Peace and Trans-democracy

The intermeshing of security and normative concerns in a world that remains competitive and anarchic in the post-Cold War era generated two processes. The first is what Glenn Diesen calls 'inter-democracy', the interaction of the EU and NATO in a mutually reinforcing power system.[89] The EU deferred to NATO on security matters, disappointing the aspirations of a diminishing band of Gaullists who favoured the Europeanisation of politics and security. This in the end gave birth to a 'new Atlanticism', envisaging a permanent Atlantic partnership despite the end of the Cold War.[90] The Atlantic security system, moreover, was to be reinforced,

[87] Derek Averre and Lance Davies, 'Russia, Humanitarian Intervention and the Responsibility to Protect: The Case of Syria', *International Affairs*, Vol. 91, No. 4, 2015, pp. 813–34.

[88] Bull, *Anarchical Society*, p. 196, also cited by Averre and Davis, 'Russia, Humanitarian Intervention and the Responsibility to Protect', p. 829.

[89] Glenn Diesen, *EU and NATO Relations with Russia: After the Collapse of the Soviet Union* (Farnham, Ashgate, 2015).

[90] Richard Sakwa, *The New Atlanticism*, Valdai Paper No. 17 (Moscow, Valdai Club, May 2015), www.scribd.com/doc/266515275/The-New-Atlanticism, last accessed 26 May 2017, reprinted as 'The New Atlanticism', *Russia in Global Affairs*, special issue, July–September 2015, pp. 99–109, http://eng.globalaffairs.ru/number/The-New-Atlanticism-17695, last accessed 26 May 2017.

including plans for what came to be called an 'economic NATO', a Transatlantic Trade and Investment Partnership (TTIP). What was 'new' about this Atlanticism was not that it achieved its stated goals of all member countries spending a minimum of 2 per cent of GDP on defence and similar aspirations, but that it provided the framework for the debate over European security and political issues to the exclusion of other possible alternatives. Following the defeat of Nazi Germany, the Atlantic system ensured American predominance in Western Europe as the price to pay to keep the Soviet threat at bay, but after 1989 other possibilities were stymied. Engagement with Russia gave way to the assertion of axiological principles by the inter-democratic Atlantic community. After 2014 all sides understood that attempts to create a transformed cooperative community had failed, and that a new era of confrontation had dawned. The twenty-five years' crisis of the cold peace gave way to a new division of Europe, with the Atlantic community ranged against Russia.

The second process is 'trans-democracy', which describes the elision between security and systemic issues. In the European context, the trans-democratic claim is that security can be advanced by promoting liberal democracy and integration into European institutions. On the global level, this means that the security of the Atlantic power system is best advanced by creating a system of states moulded in the Western image and committed to liberal internationalism, the ideological foundation of post-war American power. The notion of trans-democracy, even though not given that label, has a genealogy starting with Immanuel Kant's article of 1795 called 'Perpetual Peace: A Philosophical Sketch', in which he argued that the republican form of governance would tend to be more pacific than monarchies and empires. Unlike his modern epigones, Kant did not argue that the desired outcome should be facilitated by what is today termed regime change, arguing that '[n]o state shall forcibly interfere in the constitution and government of another state'.[91] Nevertheless, Kantian universalism lies at the very root of the post-Cold War order. The anti-communist revolutions of 1989–91 were neo-Kantian in spirit and intent. The 'third basket' of the Helsinki Final Act made human rights the foundational discourse of the struggle against communist authoritarianism. In the absence of a post-Cold War peace conference, Helsinki became the foundation of the new era, and assumed public form in the 'Paris Charter' of 1990 for a 'Europe whole and free'. The Charter acted as the surrogate peace treaty in the absence of a newly negotiated

---

[91] Immanuel Kant, 'Perpetual Peace: A Philosophical Sketch', in *Kant: Political Writings*, edited by Hans Reiss, 2nd enlarged edn (Cambridge, Cambridge University Press, 1991), p. 96.

document. As Jowitt perceptively noted, this rendered the United States not imperialist but 'inertial and absolutist', unable to extend what he defined as the domestic national characteristic of 'compromise and bargaining' to its international relations.[92] It undermined the conventions of international diplomacy by ensuring that one side claimed the normative high ground, and relegated everyone else to some prehistoric swamp.

Kantian speculations on perpetual peace have generated an extensive literature on the 'democratic peace', the view that democratic states do not go to war with each other.[93] This is intuitively correct for the Atlantic system in the post-war period, since a security community was established that after 1989 expanded to encompass a number of its former adversaries, and it is hardly likely that they will start fighting each other (except possibly in the case of Greece and Turkey). While internal peace reigns, tensions remain with neighbours and external interventions are far from rare.[94] Democratic peace theory has been subjected to withering critique, above all because of the fluidity of definitions of what constitutes a democratic state.[95] Germany in 1914 was in certain respects more democratic (in terms of the breadth of the franchise and scope of social security) than many of the allied states. The argument that democracy and peace are in some way connected is deconstructed by Waltz, who notes that liberals have long sought 'to take the politics out of politics', leaving the state with not much more than managerial functions, assuming that 'the spread of democracy will negate the effects of anarchy'.[96] He insists that '[t]he structure of international politics is not transformed by changes internal to states, however widespread the changes may be'.[97] Pertinent to our study, Waltz notes that undemocratic states are considered bad not so much because of what they do, but because of what they are; hence '[d]emocracies promote war because they at times decide that the way to preserve peace is to defeat nondemocratic states and make them democratic'. With undemocratic states considered a danger to others, '[l]iberal interventionism is again on the march'.[98] It goes without

[92] Jowitt, *New World Disorder*, pp. 279, 330.

[93] For a review of the question, see Michael W. Doyle, *Ways of War and Peace: Realism, Liberalism and Socialism* (New York, W. W. Norton, 1997). See also Michael W. Doyle, *Liberal Peace: Selected Essays* (London, Routledge, 2012).

[94] Drawing on data from the US Congressional Research Service, Brian Toohey calculated that the US used armed force abroad 160 times after 1991, and a grand total of 215 times since 1798, *Australian Financial Review*, 16 February 2017.

[95] Sebastian Rosato, 'The Flawed Logic of Democratic Peace Theory', *American Political Science Review*, Vol. 97, No. 4, November 2003, pp. 585–602.

[96] Waltz, 'Structural Realism', p. 8.   [97] Waltz, 'Structural Realism', p. 10.

[98] Waltz, 'Structural Realism', p. 11.

saying that the object of attack will be labelled undemocratic, as was the case with Wilhelmine Germany in 1914 or Russia today.

The ideology of trans-democracy assumes that if democracy is the best possible form of government and the one that is liable to make allies of the states concerned, then all practicable measures should be employed to achieve the desired end.[99] Liberal international relations theory asserts that there are behavioural differences between liberal democracies and non-liberal states.[100] Democratic peace theory – the view that democratic states do not go to war with each other – is the pre-eminent expression of this ontological distinction between state behaviour based on different domestic political systems and ideologies. If the theory is accurate – and as we saw earlier, it has been heavily criticised for its lack of precision in defining a democratic state and what counts as a war between them – then it does indeed make sense for democracies to make common cause against authoritarian states to enhance their security.[101] This is what has prompted talk of a community or league of democracies, by-passing the UN system in which Russia and China have an equal voice. This would institutionalise a privileged position for self-proclaimed democracies, and would 'dismantle the international law concept of states as sovereign equals', enshrined in the UN Charter.[102]

From the Kremlin's perspective, the main instrument for this trans-democratic approach to the conduct of international politics came to be seen as 'colour' revolutions, mass popular mobilisations against attempts to 'steal' elections. The current cycle began with the overthrow of Milošević in October 2000 in what came to be known as the 'bulldozer revolution', and then progressed through the rose revolution of December 2003 in Georgia, the orange revolution in Ukraine in autumn 2004, and the tulip revolution in Kyrgyzstan in spring 2005, and, in a different way, the Arab Spring from 2011. There is also the 'Twitter revolution' in Moldova in 2009, which brought 'pro-European' forces to power. The Kremlin has consistently questioned the autonomy of these popular movements, and instead argues that they have been manipulated

---

[99] For an excellent theoretical discussion, see Rein Müllerson, *Regime Change: From Democratic Peace Theories to Forcible Regime Change* (Leiden, Martinus Nijhoff, 2013).

[100] Anna Geis, '"The Concert of Democracies": Why Some States are More Equal than Others', *International Politics*, Vol. 50, No. 2, 2013, pp. 257–77.

[101] Note also the argument that *democratising* states tend to be bellicose, E. D. Mansfield and Jack Snyder, *Electing to Fight: Why Emerging Democracies go to War* (Cambridge, Cambridge University Press, 2005). For the original article, see Jack Snyder with Edward D. Mansfield, 'Turbulent Transitions: Why Emerging Democracies go to War', in Jack Snyder, *Power and Progress: International Politics in Transition* (London, Routledge, 2012), pp. 125–43.

[102] Geis, '"Concert of Democracies"', p. 263.

by Western powers. This was evident in Putin's response to the protests against the flawed parliamentary election of 4 December 2011, when he suggested that they had been sponsored by Hillary Clinton. The autonomy of social movements is denied, and instead in the Kremlin view trans-democracy represents the coupling of democracy and human rights with the expansion of the Atlantic community. In a philosophical sense Putin was right: popular democratic revolutions have become a way for the Atlantic ideological and power system to advance. There is plenty of evidence that Western agencies have prepared for, funded and provided ideological support for pro-democracy movements whose ideological orientation is Atlanticist. But in political terms, this means the denial of independent agency to popular demands for free and fair elections, more transparent economies, less corrupt administrative systems and, above all, civic dignity. Although few advocates of democracy promotion openly call for forcible democratisation, the policies of the Clinton and Bush administrations drew on the idea that 'spreading democracy around the world is not only valuable for the people benefiting from liberty and self-determination, but that it was also in the security interests of the United States. The catchy equation was: democracy is freedom is peace.'[103]

One of the foundational principles of Putinism, reinforcing legitimism, is anti-revolutionism. The condemnation of popular revolutions reflects not only concerns about regime survival, which became far more intense from the mid-2000s, but above all a philosophical repudiation of revolution as a method of political renewal.[104] In political terms, the 2000s have seen the emergence of new revolutionary practices, using social media as the primary form of political communication rather than traditional forms of political associations such as parties and trade unions. Speaking in St Petersburg in 2016, Putin talked of the three revolutions experienced by the city (1905 and two in 1917), and urged the press not to facilitate a 'fourth revolution'. He argued that intervention in Syria demonstrated Russia's 'ability to deal with problems not only near our borders but also far from them', and noted how the country's economy had become 'more independent, self-reliant and self-sufficient' and had doubled in size, while Syria had demonstrated how the capabilities of Russia's armed forces had 'increased immeasurably'. Putin went on to warn his audience:

However, what worries our opponents the most is not even this, but the unity and cohesion of the Russian nation, of the multiethnic Russian people. In this connection, attempts are made to weaken us from within, make us more acquiescent,

---

[103] Geis, '"Concert of Democracies"', p. 270.
[104] Richard Sakwa, *Putin: Russia's Choice*, fully revised and updated 2nd edn (London and New York, Routledge, 2008), Chapter 2.

and make us toe their line. What is the easiest way of doing this? It is to spread distrust of the ruling authorities and the bodies of power within society and to set people against each other. This was brilliantly used during the tragic years of World War I, when the country was simply brought to the point of disintegration. Today, this is an exercise in futility.[105]

For Putin the revolutions of 1917 had destroyed the country's future and provoked domestic instability and global chaos. On another occasion he argued that Lenin and the Bolsheviks had placed an 'atomic bomb' under Russia which exploded in 1991.[106] Attempts to undermine the domestic order, he insisted, through revolutionary methods were futile.

While the normative impetus behind these revolutions was inspired by popular revulsion against regimes that sought to perpetuate their power by illegitimate means, in practice these revolutions were swiftly subsumed into the larger geopolitical logic of contestation between Russia and the Atlantic community. The confrontation mimicked Cold War practices. From the Kremlin's perspective, trans-democratic change had become another tool in the Atlantic community's armoury to enhance its security at Russia's expense by recruiting countries that may otherwise have aligned with Moscow. From the West's perspective, these were revolts for democratic freedom against corrupt regimes; for Russia, the overthrow of regimes opened the door to chaos and disorder that in the end blew back to threaten the intervening states themselves.

In a landmark article in 2015 Valerii Gerasimov, the Chief of the Russian General Staff, argued that the lesson of the Arab Spring was that the rules of war had changed, and that viable states could quickly descend into armed conflict and become victims of foreign intervention and sink into an abyss of state collapse, civil conflict and humanitarian catastrophe. The paper was effectively a response to what was perceived to be a new form of Western-inspired 'hybrid warfare'. He noted that 'Frontal engagements of large formations of forces at the strategic and operational level are gradually becoming a thing of the past. Long-distance, contactless actions against the enemy are becoming the main means of achieving combat and operational goals.' He identified eight features of modern hybrid warfare that were applied to subvert states and to gain control of territory without resorting to conventional arms. Regime change could be achieved by the use of civil methods such as propaganda, funding and training of protest groups, and information campaigns aimed at discrediting the opponent.

---

[105] 'Truth and Justice Regional and Local Media Forum', 7 April 2016, http://en.kemlin.ru/events/president/news/51685, last accessed 30 May 2017.

[106] 'Putin Slams Lenin for Laying "Atomic Bomb" Under Russia', *Moscow Times*, 21 January 2016, https://themoscowtimes.com/news/putin-slams-lenin-for-laying-atomic-bomb-under-russia-51544, last accessed 26 May 2017.

He stressed that the 'very rules of war have changed', arguing that non-military means such as the 'use of political, economic and informational, humanitarian, and other non-military measures – applied in coordination with the protest potential of the population', can exceed 'the power of force of weapons in their effectiveness', and 'that the open use of forces – often under the guise of peace-keeping and crisis regulation – is resorted to only at a certain stage, primarily for the achievement of final success in the conflict'.[107] Following the Russian action in Crimea, the term 'hybrid warfare' was applied to Russia's use of mixed methods (propaganda, disinformation, information warfare, and special forces) to achieve what came to be known as a 'non-linear' military victory. What Gerasimov had identified as the Western strategy against Russia, was now interpreted as the blueprint for the Kremlin's attempts to destabilise its neighbours and Western democracies.

[107] Valerii Gerasimov, 'Tsennost' nauki i predvidenii', *Voenno-promyshlennyi kur'er*, No. 8, 27 February 2013, http://vpk-news.ru/articles/14632, last accessed 30 May 2017.

4   Resistance and Neo-revisionism

Russia is commonly charged with having become a revisionist power. The country has apparently repudiated the structure of international politics as it had evolved not only in the post-Cold War years but in the entire post-war era. In particular, the reunification of Crimea was condemned as a clear example of Russia's repudiation of international law to pursue revisionist goals.[1] The unilateral change of a country's borders did indeed run against the practice of international law as it had evolved since 1945. Russia's claim that a precedent had been set with the unilateral secession of Kosovo on 17 February 2008 does not in itself justify Russian actions, since the misbehaviour of one cannot justify emulation by another.[2] In an ambiguous advisory opinion in July 2010, the International Court of Justice concluded that the declaration of independence did not violate international law.[3] The normative and legal basis for self-determination remains as muddled as ever, but usually requires some sort of negotiated process.[4] The fundamental question remains: what provoked Russia to take such an action, which ran counter to everything that it had declared since 1991 and what Putin had tried to do since coming to power in 2000, namely, to establish pragmatic relations with Russia's neighbours? In other words, what brought Russia to a point where it repudiated the substantive legal basis of international politics and its own declared allegiance to those principles?

The argument of this chapter is two-fold. First, that the structural impasse outlined earlier, irrespective of the degree to which it was imagined or real (and it becomes real when absorbed into the social

---

[1] Roy Allison, 'Russian "Deniable" Intervention in Ukraine: How and Why Russia Broke the Rules', *International Affairs*, Vol. 90, No. 6, 2014, pp. 1255–97.

[2] For a critical assessment, see Thomas D. Grant, *Aggression against Ukraine: Territory, Responsibility, and International Law* (New York, Palgrave Macmillan, 2015).

[3] ICJ, 'Accordance with International Law of the Universal Declaration of Independence in Respect of Kosovo', 22 July 2010, www.icj-cij.org/docket/files/141/16010.pdf, last accessed 26 May 2017.

[4] For a recent discussion, see Annemarie Peen Rodt and Stefan Wolff (eds.), *Self-Determination after Kosovo* (London, Routledge, 2015).

imagination), generated increasing frustration in Russia that after 2012 took the form of an increasingly assertive foreign policy. Second, while some events were revisionist acts, they were not part of a sustained revisionist strategy. In Ukraine, Georgia and elsewhere Russia engaged in some selective revisionism, reflecting immediate challenges and changing circumstances, but this was not part of a universal scheme to change the foundations of the international system. Russia was far from being a genuine revisionist power, dedicated to transforming the basis of world order, and instead it became a neo-revisionist power, concerned not with changing the principles of international law but the practices. In other words, Russia continued to endorse the principles of international law and international society, while positioning itself up as their guardian against what were claimed to be the double standards of the Atlantic powers. The Ukraine crisis provoked what the Kremlin considered to be a defensive reaction. However, even though its revisionism may be 'neo', the trend of Russian foreign and domestic policy since the mid-2000s has been towards a reformulated type of conservative traditionalism that challenges the hegemonic constraints of the liberal international order. It also runs up against deeply entrenched practices, which means that the politics of resistance could become just another form of Russia's historic impasse.

The Evolution of Russian Foreign Policy

Russian policy is shaped by the interaction of structural challenges, collective ideas on these challenges, and the preferences of individual leaders.[5] Russia has long been constituted as Europe's 'other', and this has fed back to shape Russia's view of security and sense of itself.[6] Russia's identity remains in flux, although there is a clear evolution away from an initial enthusiasm for all things European and alignment with the West, towards the stronger articulation of Russian national interests and the assertion of a plural and polycentric international system. Russia's great power aspirations have been interpreted as a type of aspirational constructivism directed towards the identity needs of domestic audiences rather than the expression of an aggressive policy towards the Historic West.[7] Every presidential tenure – Yeltsin, Putin and Medvedev (although not Putin's third presidential term) – began with

---

[5] For a perceptive analysis, see Magda Leichtova, *Misunderstanding Russia: Russian Foreign Policy and the West* (Farnham, Ashgate, 2014).

[6] For discussion of security and identity formation, see Alexander Wendt, *Social Theory of International Politics* (Cambridge, Cambridge University Press, 1999).

[7] Anne L. Clunan, *The Social Construction of Russia's Resurgence: Aspirations, Identity, and Security Interests* (Baltimore, Johns Hopkins University Press, 2009).

attempts to establish improved relations between Russia and its Western partners. Medvedev's accession in 2008, despite the Russo-Georgian war, was followed by an explicit 'reset' in relations with the US, but this soon ran into the sands because of its failure to devise a forward-looking agenda. As Trenin comments, '[a]ll these attempts were futile and the other side didn't respond to Russia's initiatives with the same reciprocity' which the Kremlin expected. And 'disappointment came shortly after'.[8] Putin's return to office in 2012, following the Arab Spring, the fall of Gaddafi, and the mass demonstrations against electoral manipulations (in which Putin saw the hand of the West), was notable precisely for recognition that there would be no fresh start. The battle-hardened Putin brought with him a wagon train of resentments, disappointments and recriminations, and pursued a policy of autonomy, neo-revisionism and resistance.

In the early years the Russian leadership accepted realist propositions on the country's relative weakness, and accordingly pursued a policy of cooperation with the Atlantic powers. Disappointed with this strategy and the failure to move towards the associated Greater European ideal, the Russian leadership experimented with a number of strategies, including that of resistance. As Russian power and self-confidence was restored in the 2000s, resistance became more forceful, although the predominant approach remained cooperative. Policy moved from liberal integration in the early 1990s to one shaped by geopolitical realism under Primakov, which in turn between 2000 and 2012 was modified by the pursuit of a policy of pragmatic realism. This new realist turn, prioritising economic development and defence of the status quo, ran into the sands of Iraq, Georgia, Libya and Ukraine. Despite Russia's attempts to become part of the global war on terror following 9/11, soft containment remained and the strategic impasse intensified. The culture of geopolitical realism became predominant, rendering foreign policy more of a zero-sum game. This competitive realism was tempered in the Medvedev years, but intensified with Putin's return to the presidency.[9] After 2012 neo-revisionism predominated, based on the view that there could be no genuine partnership with the Atlantic powers, and hence Russia built up alternatives, above all Eurasian integration and Greater Eurasian

---

[8] *Russia Direct* Interview with Dmitri Trenin, 'Why Russian Society Should Pay More Attention to Kremlin's Foreign Policy', *Russia Direct*, 21 July 2016, www.russia-direct.org/qa/why-russian-society-should-pay-more-attention-kremlins-foreign-policy, last accessed 30 May 2017.

[9] This account draws on Christian Thorun, *Explaining Change in Russian Foreign Policy: The Role of Ideas in Post-Soviet Russia's Conduct towards the West* (Basingstoke, Palgrave Macmillan, 2009).

projects. The enduring theme was maintenance of Russia's status as a great power.[10]

Sergunin traces the various ideas and mechanisms that shaped Russian foreign policy in the post-communist years. He notes the structural flaws in Russian foreign policy that give rise to unpredictability, shaped in large part by the country's search for a national identity. The domestic debate still oscillates between liberalism and conservatism, between the westernising tradition and the more nativist Slavophiles and Eurasianists. Russian foreign policy discourse seeks not only to formulate an international strategy but also to shape a new national identity.[11] Sergunin notes that despite the invasions that Russia has endured, its preferred position is cooperation with the West or parts of it: 'Peter the Great's reforms, the anti-Napoleonic coalition, the "concert of powers" in the Vienna international system, the Entente Cordiale, the anti-Hitler coalition, Gorbachev's New Political Thinking, Yeltsin's early era, Putin's first administration, etc'. In his view, interaction between Western and Russian civil society institutions should take into account the fluid character of the latter, concluding that the two sides should 'refrain from any activities that could be interpreted by the other side as interference in the other's internal affairs. For example, the EU and US should not fund Russian NGOs [non-governmental organisations] that are politically active and try to affect Russia's policymaking'.[12]

Periodisation is a powerful hermeneutic device, and the four stages of Russian foreign policy identified earlier reveal the continuities, ruptures and contradictions.[13] The first period was characterised by a commitment to *Atlanticism*, although in the Russian style whereby the country insisted that it would remain a great power. The gulf between Russia's aspirations and its abilities turned into a yawning chasm. The headlong rush to the market was accompanied by unprecedented economic decline and mass poverty, with budgetary shortfalls made up by IMF loans. Powerful oligarchs bought up large swathes of the Russian economy and claimed political privileges. Nonetheless, the 1990s laid the foundations of a market economy on which Putin would build his model of quasi-corporatist capitalism. Kozyrev was a committed westerniser, but even he recognised that Russia was trapped in a strategic dead end. In a

---

[10] For a study of status in Russian foreign policy, see Andrej Krickovic and Yuval Weber, 'How Can Russia Contribute to our Understanding of Change in World Politics?', paper delivered to the ISA conference, Baltimore, 25 February 2017.

[11] Alexander Sergunin, *Explaining Russian Foreign Policy Behavior: Theory and Practice* (Stuttgart, Ibidem-Verlag, 2016).

[12] 'Decoding the Kremlin's Foreign Policy', interview with Alexander Sergunin by Morgane Fert-Malka, *Russia Direct*, 29 August 2016, www.russia-direct.org/qa/decoding-kremlins-foreign-policy, last accessed 26 May 2017.

[13] For a detailed exposition of these stages, see Sakwa, *Putin's Choice*, pp. 267–98.

wake-up speech to the CSCE in Stockholm in December 1992, he assumed the persona of the next Russian foreign minister, one who pushed Yeltsin and the democratic reformers aside, and warned of the onset of Cold War II. The spoof foreign minister stressed that '[o]ur traditions ... are in Asia and this sets limits to our rapprochement with Europe', and warned that Western forces were 'strengthening their military position in the Baltic states'. Support was pledged for the government of Serbia, and as for Ukraine, '[w]e will firmly insist that former Soviet Republics immediately join a new federation or confederation'.[14] What was intended to be an ironic commentary turned out to be remarkably prescient. Even the liberal Kozyrev sought shared hegemonic leadership in the Atlantic system, something which for institutional and ideational reasons, as we have seen, was not achieved.

The catastrophic social consequences of liberal reforms were reflected at the ballot box.[15] The December 1995 parliamentary elections, as in December 1993, produced a neo-traditionalist majority. Yeltsin dismissed Kozyrev and appointed the veteran Soviet diplomat and academic, Primakov, as foreign minister. Primakov in many ways was the embodiment of the more assertive foreign minister predicted by Kozyrev. As noted, Primakov favoured a multipolar world and an independent global role for Russia. This is a phase characterised by *competitive peaceful coexistence*, reminiscent of Nikita Khrushchev's peaceful coexistence of the 1950s – assuming continued struggle with the West, but falling short of war. Managed competition under Khrushchev, and even more under his successor Leonid Brezhnev, allowed the conventions of the Cold War to be formalised, unlike today's more anarchic confrontation. Primakov sought to tame oligarchic capitalism at home and to reassert Russian interests abroad.[16] The rebalancing of Russian foreign policy was driven as much by shifts in domestic politics as it was by the changing external environment. 'Russian partnership diversification' reflected the 'great identity debate'. Changes in Russian self-perception fostered Russia's

---

[14] William Safire, 'Kozyrev's Wake-Up Slap', *New York Times*, 17 December 1992, www.nyti mes.com/1992/12/17/opinion/essay-kozyrev-s-wake-up-slap.html, last accessed 26 May 2017.

[15] Stephen F. Cohen, *Failed Crusade: America and the Tragedy of Post-Communist Russia* (New York, W. W. Norton, 2000); Peter Reddaway and Dmitri Glinski, *The Tragedy of Russia's Reforms: Market Bolshevism against Democracy* (Washington, The United States Institute of Peace Press, 2001).

[16] Primakov was a prolific author. His important later works include E. M. Primakov, *Mysli vslukh* (Moscow, Rossiiskaya gazeta, 2011); E. M. Primakov, *Vyzovy i alternativy mnogopolyarnogo mira: role Rossii* (Moscow, MGU, 2014); E. M. Primakov, *Mir bez Rossii: k chemu privedet politicheskaya utopiya* (Moscow, Tsentrpoligraf, 2016); E. M. Primakov, *Vstrechi na perekrestakh* (Moscow, Tsentrpoligraf, 2016).

alignment with 'challenger states'.[17] When NATO launched its bombing campaign against Serbia on 24 March 1999, Primakov famously turned his plane back from the US, an act that served to symbolise a larger reorientation in Russian policy.

Between 2000 and 2012 Putin in various formats tried engagement and accommodation with the Historic West, trying to transcend the sterility of competitive coexistence.[18] He was perhaps the most pro-European leader Russia has ever had, and thus sought to join the various institutions of the Atlantic community, notably the EU and NATO. The pragmatic policy of *new realism* was based on classic realist notions of international politics in which states pursue their conception of the national interest without fear or favour. But it also sought to establish a dynamic of mutual advantage through Russia's integration in European and global structures. In other words, Putin sought to finesse the structural stalemate by demonstrating that Russia could be a responsible and cooperative partner, and thus the creation of a Greater West would serve the interests not only of Russia but also of the Atlantic powers. This was evident after 9/11, when Putin offered logistical support and intelligence-sharing, and helped the US-led coalition to remove the Taliban from power. One American official noted that 'Operation Enduring Freedom in Afghanistan in 2001 marked the closest alignment of US and Russian interests, and Russian support was as important as that of any NATO ally'. Russian hopes to turn this into an enduring anti-terrorist coalition were evident throughout the 2000s and during the Syrian crisis. When visiting in November 2001, Putin sought fundamentally to improve relations with the US and NATO: in the words of another US official, 'Putin was ready to deal'. The Bush administration, however, was not willing to offer the deal sought by Putin, and instead within months withdrew from the ABM Treaty and soon after announced that it would bring the Baltic states into NATO by 2004. Even then Putin continued to look for common ground, but he now understood, in the words of an American official, that 'a strategic partnership with the United States means if you accept Washington's agenda, you remain a partner in good standing, but you are not allowed to contribute to developing the agenda jointly; if you object, you will be thrown overboard'. Although it appears Bush was ready to improve relations with Russia, the defence secretary Donald H. Rumsfeld and others in the Bush administration were not. Instead, they prioritised missile defence, enlarging NATO and waging

---

[17] Helen Belopolsky, *Russia and the Challengers: Russian Alignment with China, Iran and Iraq in the Unipolar Era* (Basingstoke, Palgrave Macmillan, 2009), pp. 2, 180 and *passim*.

[18] For a detailed study of his early foreign policy, see J. L. Black, *Vladimir Putin and the New World Order* (Lanham, Rowman and Littlefield, 2004).

war in Iraq: 'Rumsfeld saw Russia as a second-rate power; not worth a hill of beans'.[19]

Europe appeared to offer greater opportunities.[20] In his speech, delivered in German, to the Bundestag on 25 September 2001 Putin argued that Russia's destiny is a European one. Nevertheless, he insisted that the relationship could not be based on hierarchy, identifying the tensions that would later destroy the whole edifice of Russo-EU relations. As Putin put it:

No one calls in question the great value of Europe's relations with the United States. I am just of the opinion that Europe will reinforce its reputation of a strong and truly dependent centre of world politics soundly and for a long time if it succeeds in bringing together its own potential and that of Russia, including its human, territorial and natural resources and its economic, cultural and defence potential.

This was an appeal to create a Greater Europe, separate but not antagonistic to the US. Such statements are typically condemned as part of Russia's alleged primordial strategy to drive a wedge between the two wings of the Atlantic alliance, but Putin's goal was different. By creating a Greater Europe, Putin was in fact arguing that this would be an important step towards the creation of a Greater West, which would unify all. This would be the leitmotif of Putin's leadership. The EU's failure, in Russian eyes, to develop policies of its own doomed the whole endeavour. The wedge argument from Moscow's perspective precisely demonstrated the strategic impasse in which Russia found itself. Putin went on:

We continue to live in the old system of values. We talk about partnership, but in reality we have not yet learned to trust each other. In spite of a plethora of sweet words, we are still surreptitiously opposed to each other. Now we demand loyalty to NATO, now argue about the rationale behind its enlargement. And we are still unable to agree on the problems of a missile defence system.[21]

Putin's attempt to find a third way between naïve Atlanticism and competitive coexistence failed in a spectacular manner, and provoked the breakdown of the European security system.

---

[19] Andrew C. Kuchins, 'That Brief US-Russia Strategic Partnership 15 Years Ago? New Interviews Reveal Why it Derailed', *The Washington Post: Monkey Cage*, 23 September 2016, www.washingtonpost.com/news/monkey-cage/wp/2016/09/23/that-brief-u-s-russia-strategic-partnership-15-years-ago-new-interviews-reveal-why-it-dera iled/, last accessed 26 May 2017. The interviews cited here are part of the larger study by Andrew C. Kuchins, *Elevation and Calibration: A New Russia Policy for America* (Washington, Centre for Global Interests, December 2016).

[20] Analysed in Ted Hopf (ed.), *Russia's European Choice* (Basingstoke, Palgrave Macmillan, 2008).

[21] Vladimir Putin, 'Speech in the Bundestag of the Federal Republic of Germany', 25 September 2001, http://en.kremlin.ru/events/president/transcripts/21340, last accessed 30 May 2017.

The terrorist attack on a school in Beslan, North Ossetia, in September 2004 marked an important turning point in relations. Putin considered that the West effectively supported the Chechen insurgency, taking advantage of Russia's weakness. His emotional speech of 4 September warned that '[s]ome want to tear off a juicy piece of our country. Others help them to do it. They help because they think that Russia, as one of the greatest nuclear powers of the world, is still a threat, and this threat has to be eliminated. And terrorism is only an instrument to achieve these goals.'[22] When it came to the orange revolution in Ukraine a few months later, Putin once again interpreted the events as a Western attempt to separate Ukraine from Russia. Both events encouraged a domestic clamp-down to fight terrorism and avert a colour revolution.[23] Putin's analysis was flawed and partial, yet made sense in the context of Russia's inability to place relations with the West on a stable footing. The response to fears that Western-sponsored trans-democratic regime change was on the agenda only exacerbated the features that encouraged the Western desire for changes to the regime.

Putin's frustrations were vented in his speech at the Munich Security Conference on 10 February 2007. The immediate trigger was Bush's announcement of plans to install the BMD system in Poland and the Czech Republic.[24] Putin's rhetoric revealed deep disappointment that the new realist policy was disintegrating. He stressed the 'universal, indivisible character of security' and warned against the dangers of establishing a 'unipolar world ... in which there is one master, one sovereign. And at the end of the day this is pernicious not only for all those within this system, but also for the sovereign itself because it destroys itself from within.' Putin noted 'those who teach us [about democracy] do not want to learn themselves'. He listed a range of strategic problems, including the marginalisation of the UN, failure to ratify the CFE Treaty, the remilitarisation of Europe through BMD development, NATO enlargement that represented 'a serious provoca-tion that reduces the level of mutual trust', the weakening of the non-proliferation regime and the attempt 'to transform the OSCE into a vulgar instrument to promote the foreign policy interests of one or a group of countries'. He condemned the 'almost uncontained hyper use of force – military force – in international relations, force that is plunging the world into an abyss of permanent conflict'. He warned that '[w]e are

---

[22] 'Putin Tells the Russians "We Shall Be Stronger"', *New York Times*, 5 September 2004, partly retranslated.

[23] Robert Horvath, *Putin's 'Preventative Counter-Revolution': Post-Soviet Authoritarianism and the Spectre of Velvet Revolution* (London and New York, Routledge, 2013).

[24] Myers, *New Tsar*, p. 318.

seeing a greater and greater disdain for the basic principles of international law'. He ended by stressing that Russia 'with a thousand years of history' did not need to be instructed on how to behave in international affairs.[25] The speech reflected the disenchantment of the Russian leader with a Historical West that dismissed Russian concerns as illegitimate and acted with reckless impunity (as in Iraq). Gates spoke after Putin and noted that the speech acted as an 'ice-cold shower', particularly on the European participants, but all that he took from it was that Putin 'was clearly trying to drive a wedge between the Europeans and the United States with his anti-American remarks'.[26]

The Munich speech represented a turning point in Russian foreign policy, but the attempt to achieve the goals of the new realism continued. A further moment of rupture came with Kosovo's unilateral declaration of independence in February 2008, followed by recognition by the US and other leading Atlantic states. At the time Putin warned that this unilateral change in a country's borders without the sanction of that country, in this case Serbia, opened a Pandora's Box of other potential secessions. Putin was unrelenting in his criticism of what he considered to be the high-handed and biased behaviour of the Atlantic states over the issue. Although Putin became increasingly disappointed, he nevertheless still tried to make the new realist programme work. This helps explain why of all possible candidates, Putin chose the most liberal variant of all, Medvedev, to take over after the end of his two mandated terms as president in May 2008. The logic appeared to be that if the West was unable to work with Putin, then perhaps a liberal westerniser like Medvedev could find the magic formula. Medvedev represented not the repudiation of Putinism but an expression of its most liberal and Westernising aspects. It was the perceived failure of this 'experiment' that determined the harder face of Putinism after 2012.

Medvedev's presidency reflected the tensions between the two sides of Russian foreign policy. Policy remained new realist in formulation, combining resistance and cooperation. In response to the Georgian bombardment of Tskhinvali, the capital of South Ossetia, late on 7 August 2008, Russian forces poured through the Roki tunnel and soon routed the Georgian army.[27] In a parallel operation, Russian forces worked with

[25] 'Russian President Vladimir Putin's 'Speech and the Following Discussion at the Munich Conference on Security Policy', 10 February 2007, http://eng.kremlin.ru/transcripts/84 98, last accessed 30 May 2017.
[26] Gates, *Duty*, p. 155.
[27] Richard Sakwa, 'Conspiracy Narratives as a Mode of Engagement in International Politics: The Case of the 2008 Russo-Georgian War', *Russian Review*, Vol. 71, October 2012, pp. 2–30.

local troops to drive the Georgian military out of the last enclaves in Abkhazia, and then drove into Georgia proper, occupying Gori and shelling Poti. The five-day war came to an end in a peace deal brokered by the French president Nicolas Sarkozy on behalf of the EU. An EU fact-finding commission headed by Heidi Tagliavini reported later that Georgian forces started 'full-scale' hostilities, but the conflict had long been brewing.[28] On 26 August 2008 Medvedev recognised the independence of Abkhazia and South Ossetia, marking a sharp break with Russia's hitherto extremely cautious approach to border changes, a shift in part prompted by the partial recognition of Kosovo's independence earlier that year. Recognition that the hot-headed leader of Georgia, Mikheil Saakashvili, bore at least some responsibility for the conflict allowed a swift return to 'business as usual'. Obama's election in November 2008 was followed by the reset of relations between Russia and the US, whose major outcome was New START. Medvedev proved cooperative on a number of issues. In spring 2010 the UNSC adopted resolution 1929, the toughest set of sanctions against Iran, and established the Northern Distribution Network (NDN), a mix of air, rail and lorry routes through Russia to supply allied forces in Afghanistan, by-passing the problematic southern route through Pakistan. The NATO summit in Lisbon on 19 and 20 November 2010, attended by Medvedev, adopted a ten-year Strategic Concept and hosted the first full meeting of the NRC since its establishment in 2002. Medvedev repeated the commitment to a 'strategic partnership' with NATO, and agreed to cooperate on BMD issues and support for the allied effort in Afghanistan. This proved the high point of the reset. Limited in scope and ambition, the reset was limited to the traditional agenda of arms limitation and some transactional issues. It failed to exploit the opportunity offered by the new realism in Russia and a Democratic president in the US. Obama was constrained by the 'bipartisan' model of American global 'leadership' and primacy, and lacked a strategic vision to encompass re-emerging powers like Russia and China.

Medvedev's abstention on UNSC Resolution 1973 of March 2011 was the first time a Russian leader tacitly accepted intervention in another country. As we have seen, the military campaign resulted in the overthrow of the regime and Gaddafi's death. Libya, like Iraq earlier, descended into chaos and destabilised its neighbours, and later allowed Islamic State to establish a hold in the country. It was this above all that ended any uncertainty over Putin's return to the presidency, announced with brutal

---

[28] 'Independent International Fact-Finding Mission on the Conflict in Georgia', September 2009, http://news.bbc.co.uk/1/shared/bsp/hi/pdfs/30_09_09_iiffmgc_re port.pdf, last accessed 26 May 2017.

efficiency on 24 September 2011. The flawed Duma election of 4 December provoked the biggest wave of political protest in the Putin era, but he won a first-round victory in the presidential election of 4 March 2012. The stage was set for a sharp deterioration in relations with the West. Putin's return marks the onset of a new stage in Russian foreign policy, the era of *neo-revisionism*, whose features will be examined in more detail in the final section of Chapter 4. The Ukraine crisis was a symptom of the larger failure to create an inclusive European security order, but more immediately a consequence of the new policy of resistance.

The day before Putin assumed office, on 6 May the demonstration in Bolotnaya Square was brutally disrupted and several dozen participants arrested. A range of repressive legislation was adopted, including tighter controls on civil society and NGOs. A law passed in July 2012 stipulated that those in receipt of external funding had to re-register as 'foreign agents'. The arrival in Moscow of the National Security Agency contractor Edward Snowden on 23 July 2013 was followed a month later by the granting of asylum for a year (later extended to three years). Snowden had planned to continue on to Cuba, but his passport was cancelled and an American interdiction on possible flights meant that he was forced to stay in Russia. Snowden had leaked a mass of classified National Security Agency documents exposing global surveillance programmes and American security agency hacks into the communications of foreign leaders, including Angela Merkel. Obama cancelled the planned state visit to Moscow and instead limited his stay to the G20 summit in St Petersburg on 5 and 6 September. It was at this time that Putin dismissed accusations that the Syrian regime had used chemical weapons against a settlement on the outskirts of Damascus as 'complete claptrap'. Following his cursory talk with Putin at the G20 meeting, the Obama administration made it clear that it had given up on establishing a constructive relationship with him.[29] The feeling was mutual, and although Obama's second-term secretary of state, John Kerry, was indefatigable in negotiations, the absence of a framework for agreement and the lack of trust meant that the 'new normal' was the management of conflict rather than its transformation.

Regime Contradictions and Foreign Policy

Russia's more assertive policy from the mid-2000s is often attributed to the regime's attempt to deflect attention from its own failures and

[29] Zygar, *All the Kremlin's Men*, p. 248.

contradictions.[30] This is in keeping with the thesis that weak states or countries in the throes of democratisation are tempted to engage in diversionary wars to bolster the position of fragile regimes.[31] Is this in fact the case here?[32] There are methodological and conceptual problems with drawing such a conclusion. By assuming that Russian foreign policy is driven by a diversionary logic, the substance of Russian policy is denigrated. I have argued that Russian foreign policy is shaped by its understanding of a two-level international system and a rational appreciation of its position in that system. The Kremlin's view may be contested, but reflects a deep-rooted perspective on international politics that has endured changes of regime and leaders. Instead, the diversionary argument reduces Russia's motives to little more than a strategy of regime survival by distracting attention from domestic failures through external adventures. This is the classic logic enunciated by Vyacheslav Plehve, the interior minister from 1902, regarding the 1904–05 war with Japan. Responding to reproaches that he helped instigate the war, Plehve responded: 'You don't know Russia's internal situation. To avert a revolution, we need a small victorious war.' In the event, Russia was soundly trounced by the rising Asian power, provoking the revolution of 1905. There is a constant interplay between foreign and domestic concerns, but the diversionary explanation of Russian foreign policy fails to engage with the substantive forces generating these policies.

The diversionary view is particularly applied for the period after 2012. The regime's legitimacy had hitherto been based on economic development and appeals to stability, but in the wake of a period of contentious popular mobilisation and declining economic performance, the regime allegedly turned towards patriotic mobilisation and anti-Westernism.[33] Middle class incomes and economic growth were stagnating. On the eve of the annexation of Crimea in March 2014 Putin's approval rating had dropped to 61 per cent, the lowest level since June 2000. Reunification elevated Putin's popularity to the stratospheric levels he had enjoyed in the mid-2000s, rising to 86 per cent in June, just below the peak of 88 per cent in 2008.[34] Critics argue that the foreign adventure was a device to distract attention from faltering economic performance, using the tried and tested (although usually unsuccessful) tactic of a 'short victorious

---

[30] Kathryn Stoner and Michael McFaul, 'Who Lost Russia (This Time)? Vladimir Putin', *The Washington Quarterly*, Vol. 38, No. 2, 2015, pp. 167–87.

[31] Mansfield and Snyder, *Electing to Fight*.

[32] For a sceptical view, see Andrei P. Tsygankov, 'Vladimir Putin's Last Stand: The Sources of Russia's Ukraine Policy', *Post-Soviet Affairs*, Vol. 31, No. 4, 2015, pp. 279–303.

[33] Leon Aron, 'Putinology', *The American Interest*, 30 July 2015, www.aei.org/publication/putinology/, last accessed 26 May 2017.

[34] Levada Centre, www.levada.ru/indeksy, last accessed 30 May 2017.

war'. The drivers of Russian foreign policy had hitherto been primarily external, but after 2014 they allegedly became increasingly domestic: 'Challenging the West turned out to be an effective tool for domestic political consolidation'.[35] The former US ambassador to Russia, Michael McFaul, argued that '[t]he driving force of our current clash with Russia is not American policies, but domestic politics in Russia and Ukraine, specifically Putin's response to popular challenges to his authority . . . To maintain his argument for legitimacy at home, Putin needs perpetual conflict with external enemies . . . Instead of searching for corrections in our past policies, we need to stay the course with our current policies'.[36] McFaul epitomises the degradation of post-Cold War diplomacy, turning it into a bullhorn for regime change, exacerbating conflicts that diplomacy at its best is designed to alleviate.

The Kremlin allegedly was not defending the national interest but the power and privileges of the elite, which came to be dubbed part of 'Putin's kleptocracy'.[37] On this reading, the 'revolution of dignity' in Ukraine from November 2013 was not so much a threat to Russia's strategic security and economic interests as a potential model of a successful democratic alternative that could act as a beacon for disgruntled Russian citizens, who were culturally close to Ukrainians, as well as an alternative model of development for the more liberal part of the Russian elite. As Walter Russell Mead puts it, '[t]he loss of Ukraine to the West would have been intolerable to Putin, and the danger that a Westernizing Ukraine could infect Russians with the belief that their future, too, could be brighter in a Westernizing Russia was a grave threat to his power at home'.[38] Since the orange revolution in 2004, Russian policy towards Ukraine has been interpreted as the attempt to stifle the democratic threat to its authoritarian regime: 'As far as the Kremlin was concerned, Ukraine's rejection of rigged elections and resistance to a corrupt regime was setting an example to Russia's own struggling civil society and had to be stopped at all costs.'[39] Is this really the case? The Putin leadership was certainly intent on containing revolutionary

---

[35] Alexey Arbatov, 'Russian Foreign and Security Policy', Carnegie Moscow Centre, 21 June 2016, http://carnegie.ru/2016/06/21/russian-foreign-and-security-policy/j28d, last accessed 26 May 2017.

[36] 'American Experts on Russia', *Washington Post*, 14 June 2016, in Johnson's Russia List (henceforth JRL) 2016/112, item 1. These are the points he made in testimony to the US House Foreign Affairs Committee hearing on 'US Policy towards Putin's Russia', 14 June 2016.

[37] Karen Dawisha, *Putin's Kleptocracy: Who Owns Russia?* (New York, Simon and Schuster, 2014).

[38] Walter Russell Mead, 'Washington and Brussels: Rethinking Relations with Moscow?', in Aldo Ferrari (ed.), *Putin's Russia: Really Back?* (Milan, Ledi Publishing for ISPI, 2016), p. 52.

[39] Plokhy, *Last Empire*, 'Empire Strikes Back, Foreword to the Paperback Edition', p. xii.

contagion from Ukraine, devising a range of preventative measures to thwart the emergence of a home-grown politicised protest movement.[40] The two explanations are not mutually exclusive, and the regime intensified measures to thwart a Ukraine-style revolution in Moscow. The leading opposition figure, Boris Nemtsov, indeed warned that 'a Russian Maidan is inevitable'.[41] On 15 March 2014 some 30,000 people attended the 'Peace March' ('*Marsh mira*') through the centre of Moscow in protest against the Kremlin's policies in Ukraine. However, in the State Duma vote to ratify the treaty annexing Crimea on 20 March, only one deputy voted against (Ilya Ponomarev), while 445 were in favour. Although concerned to ensure that political activism aligned with regime objectives, the preventative model of Russian actions in Ukraine, or Georgia earlier, is not an adequate explanation of Russian behaviour.

How then should Russian foreign policy be interpreted? In his 'Long Telegram' of 22 February 1946, George Kennan argued that the struggle with the Soviet Union was more cultural than ideological, based on Russia's traditional sense of insecurity. There was the insecurity born of 'a peaceful agricultural people trying to live on vast exposed plain [*sic*] in neighbourhood of fierce nomadic peoples'; but there was also the insecurity spawned by Russia's relative backwardness: 'Russian rulers have invariably sensed that their rule was relatively archaic in form, fragile and artificial in its psychological foundation, unable to stand comparison or contact with political systems of Western countries.' This sense of vulnerability in Kennan's view shaped Moscow's conduct of politics: 'They have learned to seek security only in patient but deadly struggle for total destruction of rival power, never in compacts and compromises with it.'[42] This stark view of Russian behaviour has been revived today. For example, Mead notes that Obama came into office understanding that the West's policy had encouraged 'Russia's development of a new and more confrontational foreign policy', but he nevertheless fell into the trap against which Kennan had warned: 'He assumed that the single source of Russia's hostile behaviour was poor choices by the West, and that a shift in Western policy towards a more conciliatory posture would lead to a reciprocal Russian response.' Hence the conciliatory reset, hoping that a display of good will would change Russian behaviour, but Obama had under-estimated 'Russia's potential to disrupt Western plans and harm

---

[40] Horvath, *Putin's 'Preventative Counter-Revolution'*.

[41] Boris Nemtsov, 'Uroki Maidana', 24 February 2014, www.echo.msk.ru/blog/nemtsov_boris/1264336-echo/, last accessed 30 May 2017.

[42] George Kennan's 'Long Telegram', 22 February 1946, http://nsarchive.gwu.edu/coldwar/documents/episode-1/kennan.htm, last accessed 26 May 2017.

Western interests'.[43] Lacking here is any developed understanding that Russia had interests of its own that were not reducible to the cultural deterministic view of an unremittingly hostile country determined simply to preserve an archaic political regime.[44]

All Kremlin leaders try to insulate foreign policy from domestic social forces, but foreign policy is not practised in a vacuum. Domestic political alignments influence foreign policy. In my view, a factional model helps understand the way that incompatible groups and ideas are kept in permanent balance. The regime draws on these forces but is not dominated by them. Four major ideational-factional blocs shape domestic politics: the liberals (divided in turn between legal constitutionalists, economic liberals, and radicals); statist-*siloviki*, the security bloc (in the broadest terms), who consider themselves part of Russia's long 'guardianship' tradition (*okhraniteli*), but who as a self-identified caste exploit their position for economic advantage; a diverse bloc of neo-traditionalists, ranging from monarchists, neo-Stalinists to Russian nationalists; and Eurasianists, divided into many tendencies but united in their view about a fundamental incompatibility between Russia and the West.[45] Putin's genius as leader is to draw strength from them all but to become dependent on none.

Russia adopted a great power ideology and elements of militarised patriotism,[46] but this was tempered by a pragmatic realism that drew on alternative views. Russian foreign policy under Putin is often characterised as 'imperialist',[47] but this alleged imperialism is at most 'opportunistic and limited'.[48] Putin never allows one group or set of ideas to be applied consistently and across-the-board. This means that no group is able to capture the policy agenda of the system as a whole, but can operate in certain defined spheres and usually in a constrained manner. This reinforces the segmented character of Putinite rule. No single faction – ranging from the hard-line *siloviki*, traditionalist advocates of a mobilisation model of Russian economy and society, conservative statists, to the liberal economists – can push their interests to the extent that they fundamentally

---

[43] Mead, 'Washington and Brussels', p. 41.

[44] For a perceptive analysis, see Aglaya Snetkov, *Russia's Security Policy under Putin: A Critical Perspective* (London, Routledge, 2015).

[45] This meta-factional analysis is examined in my *Putin Redux*, and will be explored further in my *The Putin Phenomenon* (London, I. B. Tauris, forthcoming 2018).

[46] Marlene Laruelle, *Russian Nationalism and the National Reassertion of Russia* (London, Routledge, 2009).

[47] For example, Marcel H. Van Herpen, *Putin's Wars: The Rise of Russia's New Imperialism* (Lanham, Rowman and Littlefield, 2014).

[48] Jardar Østbø, *The New Third Rome: Readings of a Russian Nationalist Myth* (Stuttgart, Ibidem-Verlag, 2016), p. 30.

threaten the prerogatives of other groups. Putin is the supreme faction manager. This provokes incoherence in policy formulation, but the aggregative system means that all groups retain a stake in the system, but none is able to predominate. This is not 'centrism' in the classical sense, since that would suggest that policy becomes amorphous and general. There are certainly elements of this, but the aggregative model suggests, paradoxically, that policy is disaggregated, taking elements from across the spectrum. Policy becomes stochastic, subject to variation generated by the immediate need to maintain regime balance.

This is particularly evident in the economic sphere, where policy is shaped by the intersecting interests of competing factions. Despite his statist preferences, Putin understands perfectly well that a return to Soviet methods would be disastrous. Medvedev replaced Putin as prime minister in May 2012, and his government was dominated by economic liberals. Its economic policy was firmly located in classical liberal macroeconomic orthodoxy. Putin maintains his friendship with the former finance minister, Alexei Kudrin, meeting regularly and listening to his advice. Kudrin was appointed finance minister in May 2000, and in 2011 he called for political reform, including more competitive free elections. He was dismissed by Medvedev in September 2011 following a clash over defence spending. Kudrin identified himself with the protests against the flawed parliamentary election in December 2011, and thereafter set up the Centre for Strategic Research. Putin refused to adopt a consistent policy of state capitalism or a thorough-going mobilisation economic strategy, as advocated by neo-traditionalists.

The factional model takes us only so far, since there remains an underlying ideational unity. Although there are powerful disparate tendencies within as well as between the main ideological blocs, with the partial exception of the radical liberals there is a profound agreement that Russia is a great power, and that by right (as well as its institutional status as a permanent member of the UN Security Council (P5)) it should share responsibility for the management of global affairs. This has been an enduring stance, beginning in the 1990s and is shared across the political spectrum. This is the ocean on which the ship of Russian foreign policy sails. This cannot define the turns a ship will take in stormy times, but it does explain the direction of travel. It also suggests a deeper continuity in foreign policy than the diversionary approach allows. Putin was most comfortable working in the realist-statist paradigm, which draws its ideas from Primakov and earlier Russian statesmen. Notable among these are Prince Alexander Gorchakov, who as foreign minister for a quarter of a century from 1856 healed the wounds inflicted by defeat in the Crimean War, and Pyotr Stolypin, prime minister from 1906 until his assassination in 1911. Gorchakov restored Russia's status as a great power, while Stolypin espoused a form of authoritarian modernisation that has clear resonance with Putin's statism. Gorchakov, moreover, sought to avoid damaging foreign policy engagements to allow the country to modernise, but like Putin, he was not isolationist.[49] Gorchakov's foreign policy in conditions of nineteenth-century multipolarity influences the conduct of Russian international affairs today.[50] Russian foreign policy is reactive and defensive, yet shaped by long-standing ideational commitments.

Rationality and Resistance

Rejection of the diversionary and preventative explanations for Russian policy does not mean that its external behaviour is necessarily rational. Mearsheimer, the leading exponent of 'offensive realism', forcefully argues that Russian actions were a rational defensive response to the unremitting advance of NATO and the Atlantic alliance into a contested region, despite Russia's repeated warnings.[51] Nevertheless, there remains the fundamental question of how rationality in this context can be defined. For liberals, rationality means acceptance of the existing structures of hegemonic power. For them, by resisting the existing global hierarchy, Russia was repeating the mistake of the Soviet Union, which ended in disastrous failure. Even worse, Russia had far fewer resources and is far weaker than the USSR to sustain an oppositional stance. The policy of resistance in their view is not only mistaken but also futile. Radical liberals assert that it is a mistake in normative terms to resist the liberal internationalist global order.

The question then becomes whether the regime's foreign policy priorities are rational and achievable. Let us take as example Russia's long-term advocacy of Greater Europe, a position advanced by Gorbachev from 1988 and one to which Putin remains committed, despite Eurasian and Asian developments. The espousal of a continental vision of unity is clearly a rational goal, offering the possibility of forging a Europe genuinely whole and free, based not on enlargement but on transformation. It is an instrument of institutional and ideational reconciliation, which would put a final end to the Cold War. However, it is irrational to the

[49] F. Splidsboel-Hansen, 'Past and Future Meet: Aleksandr Gorchakov and Russian Foreign Policy', *Europe-Asia Studies*, Vol. 54, No. 3, 2002, pp. 377–96.

[50] Martin A. Smith, 'Russia and Multipolarity'.

[51] John J. Mearsheimer, 'Why the Ukraine Crisis is the West's Fault: The Liberal Delusions that Provoked Putin', *Foreign Affairs*, Vol. 93, No. 5, September–October 2014, pp. 77–89.

degree that it threatens the existing structures of the Atlantic hegemony, and thus from a realist perspective improbable. Why should the existing dominant powers dilute their pre-eminence for a troublesome and importunate rival?[52] It was unrealistic to believe that American and European elites would contemplate the transformation of a system that had delivered so much. Equally, it was not clear how a Greater Europe could be created when Russia lacked the components that could effectively contribute to that broadened order – a functioning and competitive democracy, a dynamic market economy, an independent and active civil society. To be meaningful, the Greater European ideal has to be more than a quasi-alliance of states but a community of nations sharing similar aspirations. From the Atlanticist perspective, the integration of an unreformed system would only disrupt the existing order. In one way or another, radical liberals argue, the Kremlin since 1991 reproduced the '*Russkaya sistema*' of internal despotism, rule *by* law rather than the rule *of* law, imperial forms of internal domination, and external aggression.[53]

This endlessly reproduced '*sistema*', in diverse forms but with an enduring content, is feared by Russia's neighbours, hence the drive to join NATO and the attempt to escape to a mythical 'Europe' that would solve their security and developmental dilemmas. The fears of Russia's neighbours are genuine and serious. But by the same token, Russia's own fears are no less credible. Hence the alternative rationality would suggest that only by creating an inclusive security order would the need for the '*Russkaya sistema*' be obviated. Russia's permanent sense of threat, as noted by Kennan, reinforces despotic internal trends; if the endemic sense of insecurity is removed, then the regime could begin to demobilise. This would allow the transition towards a more competitive market democracy within the enlarged security community. This is the underlying rationale of Russia's espousal of Greater Europe, and the broader aspiration to create a Greater West, a view that was reinforced when it became clear that Russia would remain tangential to the main Atlantic institutions, NATO and the EU. In the event, the failure to find an adequate institutional and ideational mode of reconciliation reinforced the negative features of the *Russkaya sistema*. As far as Russian neo-traditionalists were concerned, Russia remained the Byzantine mirror of

---

[52] Wohlforth, 'Realism and the End of the Cold War'.

[53] Yurii S. Pivovarov, *Russkaya politika v ee istoricheskom i kul'turnom otnosheniyakh* (Moscow, Rosspen, 2006); Yurii S. Pivovarov, 'Russkaya vlast' i publichnaya politika: Zametki istorika o prichinakh neudachi demokraticheskogo tranzita', *Polis*, No. 1, 2006, pp. 12–32; Yurii S. Pivovarov, 'Mezhdu kazachestvom i knutom: K stoletiyu russkoi konstitutsii i russkogo parlamenta', *Polis*, No. 2, 2006, pp. 5–26; Yurii S. Pivovarov and A. I. Fursov, 'Russkaya sistema i reformy', *Pro et Contra*, Vol. 4, No. 4, Autumn 1999, pp. 176–97.

the West. This was reflected in the rich discussion of Russia as the Third Rome. The letter by the monk Filofei of Pskov to Tsar Vasilii III in 1511 asserted that '[t]wo Romes have fallen, a third stands, a fourth there shall not be'. Although used in many different ways, the political myth of Russia as the Third Rome retains extraordinary power over the Russian political imagination.[54] This reinforces neo-Eurasianist philosophies, which after 1991 drew on traditional Slavophile views to reinforce Russian ideas about a special destiny separate from the West to reinforce an imperial and expansive vision of Russian identity.[55]

Just as the invocation of a path dependent and eternally reproduced *Russkaya sistema* fails to convey the innovative elements of constitutionalism and the struggle for defensible property rights, so too in the ideological sphere the Russian elite is profoundly divided on its understanding of Russia's place in Europe and the world.[56] However, Russian elite views have evolved in response to external pressures and domestic constraints. There is broad support for Putin's more assertive foreign policy. Russian elites since 2012 have become more expansionist, in the sense that Russia's interests extend beyond its current borders (doubling from 43.4 per cent in 2012), with 88 per cent believing that the Crimean annexation did not violate internal law or international agreements. Elites have also become more militaristic, with 53 per cent believing that military force is decisive in international relations (up from 35.8%), hence overwhelming support (84.3%) in favour of continuing or even increasing the current relatively high level of military expenditure. Not surprisingly, anti-Americanism is at an unprecedentedly high level, with 80.8 per cent in 2016 agreeing that the US was a threat to Russian security, up from 48.1 per cent four years earlier.[57]

Nationalist assertion of Russian exceptionalism is fanned by the militant ideas in Russian public discourse. For example, the New-Eurasianist Alexander Dugin reprises the argument of the original Eurasianists to assert that Russia is not and cannot be part of Europe and that the

---

[54] Østbø, *New Third Rome*.

[55] Marlene Laruelle, *Russian Eurasianism: An Ideology of Empire*, Translated by Mischa Gabowitsch (Washington, Woodrow Wilson Center Press; Baltimore, The Johns Hopkins University Press, 2008).

[56] For an examination of elite discourses, see Stephen White and Valentina Feklyunina, *Identities and Foreign Policies in Russia, Ukraine and Belarus: The Other Europes* (London, Palgrave Macmillan, 2014), pp. 99–134.

[57] Sharon Rivera, James Bryan, Emma Raynor and Hunter Sobczak, 'Russian Elites are More Militaristic and Anti-American than they have ever Been', *Washington Post*, 22 July 2016, www.washingtonpost.com/news/monkey-cage/wp/2016/07/22/russian-elites-are-more-militaristic-expansionist-and-anti-american-than-theyve-been-in-years-this-new-study-shows/, last accessed 26 May 2017.

relationship between Russia and Europe is inherently conflictual. He draws on an eclectic range of sources to advance his geopolitical theory of immutable conflict between Russia and the West.[58] Although Dugin's influence has been exaggerated, his Eurasianist view that Russia has a special fate to preserve the world from the corrupt values of Western liberal democracy has a deep popular resonance. Polls suggest that Russians hold deeply illiberal views when it comes to homosexuality, with 21 per cent supporting their 'liquidation', and another 37 per cent favour their 'separation from society'. The fastest-growing TV station is Tsargrad TV, a religious-patriotic channel funded by the Kremlin-aligned investment banker Konstantin Malofeev. Appearing on this station, Dugin declared: 'In this epoch of cyborgs, hybrids, mutants, chimeras and virtual reality, mankind will only be saved by tradition.' He argued that 'all modernism – the idea of progress, development, the so-called scientific view of the world, democracy and liberalism [is] a Satanic idea that spells a death sentence for humanity ... the only defence is asserting God, the church, the empire, the congregation of the faithful, the state, and the people's traditions'.[59] Such obscurantist views characterised Putin's third term, undermining attempts to create a more vibrant educational sector and dynamic economy. State-sponsored Puritanism fostered intolerance of diversity and difference, and undermined the legally defended pluralism that is essential for a competitive society.

The influence of such thinking on Putin tends to be greatly exaggerated. Dugin, for example, one of the most enthusiastic supporters of the 'Novorossiya' project in Ukraine, was dismissed from his post at Moscow State University in June 2014. Russian neo-traditionalist thinking has many faces. In terms of commitment to religion and territorial expansion, Vadim Tsymbursky (who died in 2009) is less Orthodox and more 'core-oriented', based on his isolationist notion of 'Island Russia'. Tsymbursky had a varied career, beginning as a philologist and then a researcher at the Institute for US and Canadian Studies. In politics, he began as a 'democrat' in the Gorbachev era, but after 1991 adopted a radically neo-isolationist position with Third Rome Russia represented as an island. Like Nikolai Danilevsky and innumerable other critics of 'Europe', Tsymbursky identified an irreducible tension between the Romano-German civilisation belonging to Western Christianity, whereas Russia belonged to eastern Orthodoxy, culturally opposed to the former. In

---

[58] For his recent thinking on how he would like to see the Putin model, see Aleksandr Dugin, *Novaya formula Putina: osnovy eticheskoi politiki* (Moscow, Algoritm, 2014).

[59] Owen Matthews, 'Revealed: Putin's Covert War on Western Decadence', *The Spectator*, October 2016, www.spectator.co.uk/2016/10/revealed-putins-covert-war-on-western-d ecadence/, last accessed 26 May 2017.

between these two civilisations is the region that Tsymbursky calls the *limitrof*. Here the countries have some elements of both civilisations, accentuating one or the other depending on historical circumstances. Tsymbursky's 'cultural-geographic method' precluded Russia ever becoming part of the West, thus confirming the neo-traditionalist and Eurasianist view that Russia represents not only a self-sufficient civilisation but also an ineluctable rival of the West.[60] Nataliya Narochnitskaya is more Orthodox but equally core-oriented, that is, not imperialist. Narochnitskaya represents the more conservative Orthodox part of the Russian national spectrum, describing herself as a neo-Slavophile. Her most famous work, *Russia and the Russians in World History*, stresses the permanence of conflict between Orthodox Russia and the West. For her, the Third Rome myth has nothing to do with territorial claims. Dugin, on the other hand, is less Orthodox but more imperialist. Egor Kholmgorov is both imperialist and Orthodox. Kholmogorov remains an active participant in the nationalist ferment in Russia, and advances a type of conservative 'pragmatic imperialism'.[61]

In his third term, Putin brought the narrative of 'values' firmly back into the mainstream of political discourse. With the weakening of support for liberal views and the protests in 2011–12 against electoral fraud and his renewed mandate, Putin turned towards what polls suggested would be his core constituency. After over a decade of depoliticised 'pragmatic' rule, Putin sought to shore up his support by espousing the conservative values of the majority. Putin is typically described as a man of tactics and not strategy, and this turn to conservativism had defined limits. It certainly did not mean that he embraced the traditionalist and nationalist agendas – but as the factional model predicts, he did exploit them. Putin was transformed from a pro-European leader to one whose political programme is based on a critique not only of 'the West' in general, but of Europe in particular. Putin's Valdai Club speech of 19 September 2013 was one of his most considered 'ideological' statements, presenting Russia as the keeper of a Western tradition that he argued the West itself had lost.[62] The speech outlined an ideology of conservative traditionalism, but was in danger of making Russia once again the reactionary gendarme of Europe, as it had been during the period of the Holy Alliance after the Congress of Vienna.

Putin was careful not to make himself dependent on Russian nationalism, and it is debatable whether the word is even applicable to him. The ethno-nationalists appealed for solidarity with ethnic Russians abroad, the

---

[60] Østbø, *New Third Rome*, pp. 85–6.   [61] Østbø, *New Third Rome*, pp. 35–6.
[62] Vladimir Putin, 'Meeting of the Valdai International Discussion Club', 19 September 2013, http://eng.news.kremlin.ru/news/6007, last accessed 26 May 2017.

great diaspora of some 25 million people who suddenly found themselves 'abroad' when the Soviet Union disintegrated. In justifying the takeover of Crimea in his 18 March 2014 speech, Putin referred to the need to defend the 'Russian world' (*Russkii mir*).[63] In doing so, he was appealing to a deep-rooted sense that the Russian nation was larger than the contemporary Russian state, encompassing a large but undefined group of *sootechvenniki* (compatriots).[64] The sentiment is shared by other countries which have shrunk as a result of the upheaval and the collapse of empires in the twentieth century. Hungary is a notable case, losing some two-thirds of its territory in the Treaty of Trianon in 1920, leaving large diaspora communities adrift in what are now Serbia, Slovakia and Ukraine. As for Russia, Putin referred to the Russians as a divided people, appealing to national values, but there was no consistent programme to 'reunite' these compatriots by making claims on such areas as northern Kazakhstan or Narva in Estonia. Putin even refused to recognise the entities in eastern Ukraine that appealed to Russia for help. Thus Tsygankov is right to argue that 'Putin is not a nationalist. While appropriating key concepts from the nationalist vocabulary, he alternates them with ideas that nationalists may find objectionable ... By doing so he preserves the flexibility that he needs to preserve the power of the state, which is his true priority.'[65]

Putin's views reflect the deeper changes in Russian society over the last two decades. Bunin and Makarkin describe four long-term trends that underline the increasing alienation between Russia and the West: the strong sense of national self-sufficiency complemented by a commitment to the country's great power status and leading role in the world; the strong sense of historical continuity, despite the numerous ruptures, based on statism and a sense of social justice; the deeply ingrained fear of loss of territory, represented as a spiritual catastrophe; and an emphasis on conspirological readings of public affairs. The idealisation of the West of the perestroika and early post-communist period was gone. Putin's attempts to forge a new relationship with the West through the new realism failed, and his view that the West is not a viable partner is shared by the population.[66] Putinite neo-revisionism and the politics of resistance have a deep social resonance. A VTsIOM (Russia Public Opinion Research Centre) study in mid-2016 found that a quarter of Russians

---

[63] Marlene Laruelle, *The 'Russian World': Russia's Soft Power and Geopolitical Imagination* (Washington, Center on Global Interests, May 2015).

[64] Vladimir Putin, 'Address by the President of the Russian Federation', 18 March 2014, http://en.kremlin.ru/events/president/news/20603, last accessed 26 May 2017.

[65] Andrei Tsygankov, 'Putin is Not a Nationalist', *Moscow Times*, 24 June 2014.

[66] Igor' Bunin and Aleksei Makarkin, 'Rossiya vs. zapad: sotsial'no-politicheskie osnovaniya konflikta', Centre for Political Technologies, December 2014, www.politcom.ru/1 8362.html, last accessed 30 May 2017.

considered Russia a great power, and believed that the country's global influence is significant. Two-fifths placed the goal of becoming one of the world's most successful countries in top place, but reclaiming Russia's status as a superpower came a close second.[67]

Underlying Russia's politics of resistance was a new conservatism that assumed puritan forms. In his Valdai speech in September 2013 Putin warned about the degeneracy of the West. The long-term political challenge was now reinforced by a cultural critique. This was based on a religious-conservative ideology, presenting Russia as a moral bastion against the decadence, sexual licence, porn and gay rights of the West. This was given legislative force in a number of laws from 2012, notably the ban against the propagation of homosexuality among minors and a law criminalising 'offending the feelings of religious believers'. The conservative turn was accompanied by the growing influence of Orthodox fundamentalism. One of the ideologues of this movement was Putin's reputed personal confessor Bishop Tikhon Shevkunov, a leading critic of the decadence of the modern world and the author of the best-selling Russian book of 2012, *Every-Day Saints and Other Stories*.

Militant nationalist views are not typically reflected in official foreign and security policy documents. More precisely, elements of this thinking have been incorporated into official discourse, but only as part of a segmented ideational spectrum of the sort suggested earlier. The 2013 *Foreign Policy Concept* sought to combine universality with Russian specificity. The text describes the world in terms of a 'rivalry of values and development models within the framework of the universal principles of democracy and the market economy'. The *Concept* described Russia as 'an integral and inseparable part of European civilisation', and priority was given to 'relations with the Euro-Atlantic states which, besides geography, economy and history, have common deep-rooted civilisational ties with Russia'.[68] The two-level approach characteristic of Russian foreign policy was maintained. Concepts had earlier been adopted in 2000 and 2008, but both had been quickly superseded by events. The 2000 version had little to say about terrorism, but the 9/11 attacks and the subsequent NATO operation in Afghanistan and the wars in the Middle East brought the issue to the fore. Equally, the 2008 version was overtaken by the Russo-Georgian war and the Atlantic community's neo-containment strategies, although tempered for a time by the reset. The 2013 *Concept* was also soon overtaken by events, and following the crisis

---

[67] RBTH, 'Survey: 1 in 4 Russians Believes Russia is a Great Power', 14 June 2016, https://rbth.com/politics_and_society/2016/06/14/survey-1-in-4-russians-believes-russia-is-a-great-power_602789, last accessed 26 May 2017.

[68] *Kontseptsiya vneshnei politiki Rossiiskoi Federatsii*, MFA, 18 February 2013.

over Ukraine and the sanctions stand-off with the West, the December 2016 version dropped references to 'civilisational' ties with the West, and instead focused on Eurasian integration.

One of the fundamental postulates of the Putin system is to keep social forces and intellectual movements strictly subordinate to the regime. Putin uses these movements as part of his strategy of factional management, and although the genie of irreconcilable Russian nationalism was let out of the bottle in the heat of battle in 2014, since then it has been forced back onto the defensive. There has nevertheless been some spill-over, notably the insertion of the notion of the *katechon*, the Third Rome idea of Russia as the bulwark against the chaos of the apocalypse and the disintegration of world order, into the 2013 *Foreign Policy Concept* of the Russian Federation.[69] Russia is defined as unique to enhance its moral status and global mission. To that degree, Russia is not a mirror of the West but part of that assemblage that we call modernity. A mirror is a glass wall producing a reflection with no depth, inverting left and right and generating a binary logic of Russia and the West. This one-dimensional view stamps the relationship between Russia and the Atlantic community, but it is not an accurate reflection of the way that Russia remains part of a common modernity and reflects its contradictions. The distinctive mix of rational analysis and anti-rational claims shapes a discourse that is tangential to the system in Russia, but which also provides that power with *katechonic* legitimacy. Putin's Russia is not the Third Rome, but it does believe in its unique mission.

Russian Neo-revisionism

Offensive realism suggests that only status quo powers are regional hegemons, which today means the US. All other great powers are inherently revisionist states.[70] This applies to Russia, but revisionism can take many forms. Up to 2012 the goal was to revise the system from within. Only then did Russian foreign policy enter the phase of neo-revisionism. The challenge to American hegemony became overt, but in defence of a pluralistic international relations and the autonomy of international society. Russia's behaviour became more assertive, in part derived from economic recovery bolstered by windfall energy rents, political stabilisation and a growing alienation not so much from the structures of hegemonic power as from its practices. Russia did not challenge the norms of

---

[69] Maria Engström, 'Contemporary Russian Messianism and New Russian Foreign Policy', *Contemporary Security Policy*, Vol. 35, No. 3, 2014, pp. 356–79.
[70] Mearsheimer, *Tragedy of Great Power Politics*, p. 168.

the international system as they had evolved since 1945, although in keeping with the theory of offensive realism, it did challenge the balance of power in that system. However, as far as successive Russian leaders were concerned, Hobbesian anarchy at the international level was tempered by 'the existence of an international society able to moderate the effects of anarchy'.[71] At the heart of Putin's grand strategy was the struggle to defend international society vertically, while challenging the practices of the US-led liberal hegemonic system horizontally. As argued earlier, the underlying normative belief was that there can be order without hegemony. Indeed, Russian neo-revisionism is founded on the belief that hegemonism of the sort practised since 1989 is itself disruptive of order, tempting the dominant powers into ill-considered interventions and the dysfunctional struggle for leadership, foreclosing opportunities for partnership and transformation.

Russia challenged the liberal international order's claim to be the unique upholder of international law, and indeed its inherent claim to be coterminous with international society. Moscow assumed the para-doxical position of challenging the practices of the liberal order while defending the principles of international society. From a status quo power Russia became a distinctive type of neo-revisionist state. It positioned itself as a norm-enforcer, the guardian of international society, but not a norm-innovator. Defence of the principle of the autonomy of interna-tional society and of a pluralist international system is of course a norm, but it is far from new. Thus the struggle is not so much about who gets to set the normative agenda per se, but about the practices associated with implementation. Russia presumed to be able to tell the West how it best could interpret and apply what it claimed to be its unique achievement. Moscow sought to detach liberal democratic values 'from their particu-larist Western roots and to endow them with a somewhat different mean-ing'. For example, by emphasising the principle of sovereignty: '[I]t does not challenge the Western-dominated world order in any radical way; rather, it claims a legitimate voice in the debate about how this world order must evolve'.[72] At the same time, Russia is not so much concerned with changing international hierarchy, but to defend a space for the conduct of international relations for itself, through the universal applica-tion of international law and respect for state sovereignty throughout the international system.

---

[71] Browning, 'Reassessing Putin's Project', p. 7.

[72] Viatcheslav Morozov, 'Subaltern Empire? Towards a Postcolonial Approach to Russian Foreign Policy', *Problems of Post-Communism*, Vol. 60, No. 6, November–December 2013, p. 19.

Lavrov explicitly rejected the charge of 'revisionism' and Russia's 'alleged desire to destroy the established international system', and instead he called for cooperation and dialogue: 'A reliable solution to the problems of the modern world can only be achieved through serious and honest cooperation between the leading states and their associations in order to address common challenges ... such interaction should be based on cultural and civilisational diversity.'[73] This was a pragmatic foreign policy based on a pluralistic international system in which Russia hoped to remain engaged with the West. Lavrov rejected the neo-isolationist and anti-Western policies advocated by parts of the security lobby, neo-traditionalists and above all militant Eurasianists. In this engagement, however, Russia would have to be an 'equal partner', but too often, as Andrei Kortunov notes (especially in relations with the EU), 'the notion of "equality" was nothing but another example of Western double speak', requiring 'unilateral adjustments' to EU norms.[74] The Putinite mainstream did not seek in any substantive sense to become a norm-maker – it was not interested in creating an alternative set of values, but sought adherence to the existing framework of international society centred on the UN while carving out space for its own normative world order at the regional level. As Tatiana Romanova puts it, 'Moscow challenges not values as such but its own inequality in situations where they are applied to specific present-day realities'. This was nothing like the challenge from Islamic State and other rejectionist forces, but 'the reluctance of the West to abandon its exclusive right to interpret values makes Western-Russian collaboration in fighting fundamental threats difficult to achieve'.[75] Putin, moreover, challenged the presumed right of the Atlantic system to judge the democratic development of others, one of the themes of his Munich speech. As he put it in Portugal in May 2007: 'Let's not see the situation as one side being white, clean, and pure, while the other side is some kind of "monster" that has only just crawled out of the forest, with hoofs and horns instead of a normal human appearance.'[76] Neither democracy nor international society more broadly were the property of the Historical West, and in a plural world, historical problems would be resolved in diverse ways. This challenged America's hegemonic position in the global system, and the EU's claim to be a regional hegemon.[77]

---

[73] Lavrov, 'Russia's Foreign Policy'.
[74] Andrey Kortunov, 'How Not to Talk with Russia', RIAC, 15 March 2016, www.ecfr.eu/article/commentary_how_not_to_talk_with_russia_6053, last accessed 30 May 2017.
[75] Tatiana Romanova, *EU's Crises and Its Future*, Valdai Paper No. 54, August 2016, p. 9.
[76] Cited by Browning, 'Reassessing Putin's Project', p. 10.
[77] Hiski Haukkala, 'Russian Reactions to the European Neighbourhood Policy', *Problems of Post-Communism*, Vol. 55, No. 5, September–October 2008, pp. 40–8.

The essence of neo-revisionism is not the attempt to create new rules or to advance an alternative model of international order but to ensure the universal and consistent application of existing norms. It is not the principles of international law and governance that Russia condemns but the practices that accompany their implementation. This reflected Russia's broader perception that it was locked into a strategic stalemate, and that the country was forced into a politics of resistance. As far as Russia is concerned, it was the West that had become revisionist, not Russia. Although the implementation of applicable norms was patchy, Russia did not repudiate them.[78] In its relations with the EU, Russia's neo-revisionist stance means that it was unable to become simply the passive recipient of EU norms, and instead tried to become a co-creator of Europe's destiny.[79] The struggle is not only over contested norms, but also over who has the prerogative to claim their norms as universal.[80] However, it was precisely at the level of practices that there was least room for compromise, and thus Russian neo-revisionism became another form of the impasse, and only intensified tensions between Russia and the Atlantic system.

A revisionist state would seek to challenge the existing balance of power in the system and threaten the foundations of the system itself. This does not apply to contemporary Russia. It is a country that seeks to enhance its status within the existing framework of international society. However, its aspiration to advance its own world order in the two-level international system generates the neo-revisionist impulse. This has been interpreted as spoiler behaviour, characterised by opposition to the initiatives and policies of others without the commensurate advancement of one's own. Elements of this were evident when Russia advanced policies with didactic intent, to teach the West how to obey its own rules. One of Russia's persistent grievances has been the way that the West called for a rule-based

---

[78] James Headley, 'Is Russia Out of Step with European Norms? Assessing Russia's Relationship to European Identity, Values and Norms through the Issue of Self Determination', *Europe-Asia Studies*, Vol. 64, No. 3, 2012, pp. 427–47.

[79] Hiski Haukkala, 'A Norm-Maker or a Norm-Taker? The Changing Normative Parameters of Russia's Place in Europe', in T. Hopf (ed.), *Russia's European Choice*, (Basingstoke, Palgrave Macmillan, 2008), pp. 35–56; Hiski Haukkala, 'The European Union as a Regional Normative Hegemon: The Case of European Neighbourhood Policy', *Europe-Asia Studies*, Vol. 60, No. 9, November 2008, pp. 1601–22; Hiski Haukkala, 'Lost in Translation? Why the EU has Failed to Influence Russia's Development', *Europe-Asia Studies*, Vol. 61, No. 10, December 2009, pp. 1757–75; Hiski Haukkala, *The EU-Russia Strategic Partnership: The Limits of Post-Sovereignty in International Relations* (London and New York, Routledge, 2010).

[80] Hiski Haukkala, 'From Cooperative to Contested Europe? The Conflict in Ukraine as a Culmination of a Long-Term Crisis in EU-Russia Relations', *Journal of Contemporary European Studies*, Vol. 23, No. 1, 2015, pp. 25–40.

international society, but when these rules were at cross-purposes with Western intent (as in Iraq in 2003), the rulebook was abandoned. Nevertheless, Russia remains a profoundly status quo power, since it has nothing to gain from the collapse of the international system. Elements of revisionism do creep in when it comes to creating a cultural alternative non-Western order. It is this combination of conservatism and challenges to contemporary practices that generates neo-revisionism, which can be defined as an unstable combination of attempts to modify the structures and practices of the hegemonic global order while remaining firmly ensconced in that order.

Russian neo-revisionism is profoundly ambiguous. On the one side, its critique of Western behaviour in the post-Cold War era has wide resonance in the West itself. Atlantic interventions in the Yugoslav wars in the 1990s were contested but ultimately can be justified in normative terms. However, in the 2000s liberal interventions metastasised into trans-democratic crusades for democracy and regime change. Bush's 'freedom agenda' represented a radicalisation of Reagan's move in the early 1980s to go onto the attack against the Soviet Union, a memory that remains painful in certain circles in Russia even today. The invasion of Iraq in 2003 remains the symbol of irresponsible interventionism. At the same time, the adoption of R2P represented a step towards the reassertion of the sovereignty of peoples rather than states. If Putin was the crude defender of sovereignty as so often presented, Russia would have resisted R2P far more, but in the event the country adapted to the stipulations of the policy as well as any other.[81] The invocation of R2P in August 2008 to avert 'genocide' in South Ossetia was inappropriate,[82] and the danger was exaggerated (although not entirely absent) in 2014 during the takeover of Crimea. Above all, Russian advocacy of a plural international system is attractive to many. Old-style Gaullists, for example, had always aspired to render the EU into an authority on a par with the US, even though lacking its hard power. China of course was Russia's natural ally in its anti-hegemonic aspirations. Many in what had formerly been known as the 'third world', particularly participants of the NAM, also had sympathy with attempts to balance US primacy with alternative sources of authority. This ultimately is the significance of the BRICS association.

One of the key aspects of Putin's multi-faceted political identity analysed by Hill and Gaddy is as 'the history man'.[83] Putin was good enough

---

[81] Averre and Davies, 'Russia, Humanitarian Intervention and the Responsibility to Protect'.

[82] Roy Allison, 'Russia Resurgent? Moscow's Campaign to "Coerce Georgia to Peace"', *International Affairs*, Vol. 84, No. 6, November 2008, pp. 1145–71.

[83] Hill and Gaddy, *Mr. Putin*, pp. 63–75.

a historian to understand that both the Tsarist Empire and the Soviet Union had collapsed because of 'imperial over-stretch', engagement in futile conflicts that they could not ultimately win.[84] The yawning gap between Russian pretensions and its capacities has re-emerged. For this reason Russia's politics of resistance under Putin is carefully managed, seeking to avoid isolation and over-extension. Nevertheless, when the Kremlin considers that existential questions of Russian security are at stake, Putin's style is to strike forcefully and resolutely. This was the case when he launched the second Chechen war in September 1999, and again when Russia seized the Crimea in spring 2014. Moscow's view is that if the security concerns of the Central and East European states were taken so seriously as to prompt NATO enlargement, then by the same token Russian concerns about its security, including the perceived consequences of NATO enlargement, are no less legitimate. None of the actors in the cold peace era were able to find a formula that would satisfy the security concerns of both. In other words, the absence of an institutional or conceptual mode of reconciliation in the end drove the sides apart.

Russian commentators tend to exaggerate the extent of American and European relative decline to justify behaviour that would be appropriate for a world that is indeed post-hegemonic. In fact, as argued earlier, American leadership remains intact and has powerful resources to direct against challengers.[85] Susan Strange and others have long argued that the issue is not so much the decline of American power, but that the US itself has become the victim of the market forces it has unleashed through financial deregulation and the international drive to low-cost labour, as well as its abuse of reserve currency privileges to run an almost permanent balance of payments deficit.[86] This is what gave rise to the Trump phenomenon, and fed the illusion of radicals in Russia that the West would collapse under the weight of its own contradictions. Such views tempt Russia onto the path of outright revisionism, which so far Putin has resisted. Instead, Putin's foreign policy has been 'reactionary', in both senses of the word. Russia has reacted to every significant event in world politics, asserting its point of view even when, typically, its view was not welcomed. More than that, the reaction was characteristically one of outrage and condemnation of Western policy. This was at its sharpest

---

[84] Paul Kennedy, *The Rise and Fall of the Great Powers: Economic Change and Military Conflict from 1500 and 2000* (London, Unwin Hyman, 1988).

[85] As argued by Joseph S. Nye, to counter the 'declinism' prevalent at the time, in *Bound to Lead: The Changing Nature of American Power* (New York, Basic Books, 1991). The argument was restated later in Nye, *Is the American Century Over?*.

[86] Susan Strange, *The Retreat of the State: The Diffusion of Power in the World Economy* (Cambridge, Cambridge University Press, 1996).

in the post-Soviet region, where the absence of any agreed rules of engagement provoked endless skirmishes and conflicts, most notably in the South Caucasus and ultimately over Ukraine. Russia was unable to articulate a non-reactionary perspective on world politics, and even its advocacy of state-centric pluralism and international society tends to be defined in opposition to US hegemony rather than as a positive good in itself.

In the second sense, as George L. Mosse argues in his studies of fascism, reactionary politics feeds off normative threats.[87] Although impatient of the constraints of competitive democracy and genuine constitutionalism, Putin's 'reactionary' politics lacks the substantive communitarian impulse that lies at the heart of the fascist syndrome.[88] Russian politics remains intensely pluralist (although lacking effective formal institutional articulation), and rejects the crude majoritarianism typical even of some of the new-born illiberal democracies in Europe. Putin has at times strategically deployed the power of Russian nationalism, notably in 2014, but soon after fought to tame the rampant bear, understanding that Russia's pluricultural and multi-confessional society would be torn apart if culturally defined majoritarian politics were allowed free rein. Russia's cultural critique of alleged Western degeneration, voiced with strident fervour by the outriders of Putinite reaction in parliament and some regions, gave rise to some repressive legislation at home, notably the ban on homosexual propaganda among minors, but abroad gained traction initially only among some marginal right-wing groups. The critique of the multicultural loss of national identities was voiced by leaders as disparate as Merkel and David Cameron, but none repudiated the fundamental principles of tolerance and cultural pluralism. Russia's cultural critique of the West tended only to intensify the country's isolation from Western elite groups, but resonated with domestic critiques of neo-liberal economic policies and social liberalism.

Russia has become a symbol of resistance to the liberal hegemonic order. This resistance is tempered by Russia's aspirations to become part of a transformed power system, and by the weakness, both material and ideational, of the foundations of its opposition. Nevertheless, the failure, in Moscow's view, to create an inclusive and equitable peace

---

[87] George L. Mosse, *The Fascist Revolution: Towards a General Theory of Fascism* (New York, Howard Fertig, 2000).

[88] Olga Oliker, 'Putinism, Populism and the Defence of Liberal Democracy', *Survival*, Vol. 59, No. 1, 2017, pp. 7–24. See also Steffen Kailitz and Andreas Umland, 'Why Fascists Took Over the Reichstag but Have Not Captured the Kremlin: A Comparison of Weimar Germany and Post-Soviet Russia', *Nationalities Papers*, Vol. 45, No. 2, 2017, pp. 206–21.

order after 1989 propelled Russia into the ranks of the outsiders. Naturally, an outsider will seek to find common cause with others who also feel aggrieved by the existing balance of power, and this Russia has done with China and some other countries. It also encouraged foreign dissidents, although this tactic is fraught with perils. In supporting an eclectic mix of left and right populists in the established democracies, Russia became associated with positions that it did not necessarily share, although most of them (notably Marine Le Pen at the head of the Front National in France) sought improved relations with Russia. The ultimate paradox is that elements of the insurgency against old-style globalisation were ultimately absorbed by Trump's White House. Given the dualism of Russia's strategy – to challenge the Atlantic system horizontally, but to defend the principles of international society vertically – Russia (along with China) ended up defending the UN system and the liberal trading order at a time when its core state, the US, began to defect from the order that it had created. For Russia, the process was less a defection than frustration over the terms on which it had to join.

5   Europe, Eurasia and Heartland Conflicts

There are certain enduring themes in Russian foreign policy, notably great power aspirations, status concerns, as well as a certain transformative quality, which when stymied provokes neo-revisionism. In later years the theme of resistance became more prominent in response to what was perceived to be entrapment in a form of soft containment. No viable formula could be found to place Russia's relations with its Atlantic partners on a sustainable long-term basis, and Russia entered a phase of neo-revisionism and resistance. The debate over the shape of the greater European community and its relationship with the Atlantic system shaped political relations. Russia refused to accept that the EU was the primary body speaking for 'Europe', and instead advanced a more plural understanding of European space. Russia became the centre of plans for deeper Eurasian integration, while the EU advanced more ambitious projects for alignment with the countries in between, turning the 'common neighbourhood' into a zone of contestation. The contrasting models ultimately provoked a breakdown. The struggle over Ukraine was a symptom and not the cause of the deterioration in relations. Elements of Cold War contestation were restored. Instead of a Greater Europe, Europe is once again divided.

Visions of Europe

Contemporary Europe is shaped by the long shadow cast by the Cold War. American power guaranteed European security against the Soviet Union, and it remains the regional hegemon, blocking the emergence of a challenger.[1] Brooks and Wohlforth dismiss talk of America's decline or retrenchment, and instead argue that US predominance will last long into the twenty-first century, although they concede that the rise of China will

---

[1] Stephen G. Brooks and William C. Wohlforth, *World Out of Balance: International Relations and the Challenge of American Primacy* (Princeton and Oxford, Princeton University Press, 2008).

necessitate some adjustments to American grand strategy.[2] The predicate
of such a strategy is the soft containment of Russia, which took harder
forms after 2014. Arguably, Western Europe has also long been
embroiled in a form of soft containment, preventing the transformation
of Atlanticism into fully fledged Euro-Atlanticism (in which Europe
would have a more articulated defence and security identity), let alone a
new form of Gaullist continentalism. David Calleo describes the tension
between three macro-historical projects shaped by the Cold War that
competed to define the future: the Europe-Atlantic alliance, the EU,
and the global economy.[3] He argued that a new confrontation could be
avoided only if Russia was integrated into pan-European institutions of a
new type, ones which reflected the new realities of the post-Cold War
era.[4] Some years later he warned that the American elite's commitment to
a unipolar vision was dangerous not only for the world but also for
America itself, unbalancing its domestic constitution and tempting the
US into ill-fated foreign adventures. He notes that '[a] world system
dominated by one superpower is a bold and radical program. If successful, it would mean for the first time in modern history a world without a
general balance of power.'[5] He called for greater friendly balancing from
Europe and a shift from glorying in past triumphs to recognition of the
plural character of world order. This was precisely Russia's agenda.

   This pluralism is evident in Europe itself. Contemporary Europe is
characterised by three models – the smaller, wider and greater. The
smaller, or core, Europe is represented by the EU, and although buffeted
by various challenges, including the euro-zone crisis, Britain's departure
(Brexit), illicit migration and refugee flows, and a crisis of identity and
purpose, the community remains the world's largest trading bloc and an
influential normative actor. The EU is the world's most successful integration project and retains the capacity for adaptation. The EU also
represents a distinctive 'post-modern' style of politics. As Mead puts it,
'[t]he European Union is a daring and imaginative political construct;
essentially, it seeks to replace diplomacy and power politics among
European states with judicial, political and administrative tools'. He
notes that Russia remains wedded to classical geopolitical thinking, and
thus for it 'the EU is less about eliminating diplomacy in Europe than it is

[2] Brooks and Wohlforth, *America Abroad*.
[3] David P. Calleo, *Rethinking Europe's Future* (Princeton, Princeton University Press,
   2003).
[4] Calleo, *Rethinking Europe's Future*, pp. 348–53.
[5] David P. Calleo, *Follies of Power: America's Unipolar Fantasy* (Cambridge, Cambridge
   University Press, 2009), p. 4.

about excluding Russia from Europe'.[6] This is not entirely accurate. Although the Russian elite was schooled in the traditional practices of power politics, this is tempered by an understanding of post-sovereignty trends in international politics, with Russia a supporter of the global governance institutions of international society at the global level and, with rather less enthusiasm, the CoE at the regional level. The problem from the Kremlin's perspective is that post-sovereign practices have tended to dispense with mechanisms to manage contrasting national interests and to depoliticise the whole process. It is inaccurate to call Russia a nineteenth-century power, as so many did during the Ukraine crisis, but twenty-first-century practices have tended only to intensify the strategic impasse in which Russian elites consider themselves trapped. In other words, *mutatis mutandis*, the EU is a microcosm of the international system outlined earlier: a combination of supra-national institutions (the equivalent of international society), and member states (the sovereign states in the international system), regulated by classic practices of inter-governmentalism. This two-level EU system changes the character of the participating states, just as recognition of the autonomy of international society tempers the sovereignty of states in the international system.[7]

At the continental level, the EU effectively claimed to be the only serious integration project. It would deal with other states bilaterally, notably Russia and Turkey, but treated alternative integration projects as illegitimate. This gave rise to the 'wider Europe', which substantively encompassed all states that were not in or becoming part of the EU. By the early 2000s, the question of how the EU would relate to its neighbours became urgent. Romano Prodi, the president of the European Commission, introduced the 'wider Europe' agenda, which later became the European Neighbourhood Policy (ENP), in Brussels on 5 and 6 December 2002 with the words: 'I want to see a "ring of friends" surrounding the Union and its closest European neighbours, from Morocco to Russia and the Black Sea'.[8] 'Wider Europe' became the term used to describe the EU's policy towards the larger region.[9] The EU Neighbourhood Info Centre later described the ENP as aiming to bring 'Europe and its neighbours

---

[6] Mead, 'Washington and Brussels', p. 40.

[7] For the EU, see Christopher Bickerton, *European Integration: From Nation States to Member States* (Oxford, Oxford University Press, 2012).

[8] Romano Prodi, 'A Wider Europe: A Proximity Policy as the Key to Stability', Brussels, 5–6 December 2002, http://europa.eu/rapid/press-release_SPEECH-02–619_en.htm, last accessed 30 May 2017.

[9] 'Wider Europe – Neighbourhood: A New Framework for Relations with Our Eastern and Southern Neighbours', Communication from the Commission to the Council and the European Parliament, Brussels, 11 March 2003, http://eeas.europa.eu/enp/pdf/pdf/com03_104_en.pdf, last accessed 26 May 2017.

closer, to their mutual benefit and interest. It was conceived after the 2004 enlargement of the EU with 10 new member countries, in order to avoid creating new borders in Europe.'[10]

The three major attempts to institutionalise a 'strategic partnership' with Russia – the Partnership and Cooperation Agreement (PCA), signed in 1994 but only coming into effect in 1997 because of the first Chechen war, the four common spaces of the mid-2000s, and the Partnership for Modernisation of the Medvedev years – registered a declining belief that partnership could become genuine interdependent cooperation (see Chapter 9). Instead, when the ENP took the form of the Eastern Partnership (EaP) it stoked conflict in the neighbourhood. The EaP was mooted in May 2008 by the Polish foreign minister Radosław (Radek) Sikorksi and supported by the prime minister, Donald Tusk. They subsequently drafted in the Swedish foreign minister, Carl Bildt, to give the idea greater heft in intra-EU negotiations. Tusk later wrote that 'I never doubted that the geopolitical game between Russia and Europe, and between Russia and Poland, was about Ukraine'.[11] Instead of finding ways to transcend the deepening confrontation, the EaP gave continental division institutional form. The geopolitical colouration of the EaP repudiated fundamental elements of the value system of the original core Europe. The EU ultimately incorporated the language of competition and the rhetoric of exclusion that reinforced European monism and betrayed aspirations for pan-European unification. Throughout the region politicians were dubbed 'pro-European' or 'pro-Russian', simplifying complex choices and disregarding historical affiliations.

The initial idea of the EaP was to reinforce the eastern dimension of the ENP, with the ultimate aim of bringing countries like Ukraine and Moldova into the EU. The strategy later changed: 'Indeed, without the Russian intervention in Georgia in 2008, in the opinion of one Commission official, the Eastern Partnership might have amounted to rather less in the way of substance.'[12] The EaP was formally launched in Prague in May 2009 and targeted the six former Soviet states on the EU's borders: Belarus, Moldova and Ukraine, and Azerbaijan, Armenia and Georgia in the South Caucasus. The EaP was not considered a step towards EU membership but sought to create a zone of friends along

---

[10] EU Neighbourhood Info Centre, 'The European Neighbourhood Policy (ENP)', www.en pi-info.eu/main.php?id=344&id_type=2, last accessed 26 May 2017.

[11] Henry Foy, 'Donald Tusk: "Russia is our strategic problem"', *Financial Times*, 29 November 2014, p. 3.

[12] Nathaniel Copsey and Karolina Pomorska, 'The Influence of Newer Member States in the European Union: The Case of Poland and the Eastern Partnership', *Europe-Asia Studies*, Vol. 66, No. 3, May 2014, p. 430.

the EU's borders by drawing these countries into a Western orientation. The previous pattern of bilateral relations was retained but deepened, with Association Agreements (AAs) to be signed with individual countries, which were then to be reinforced by the intensification of bilateral economic relations through the establishment of a 'deep and comprehensive free trade area' (DCFTA). The EaP was criticised on a number of grounds, notably the lack of an articulated perspective for ultimate EU membership and its relatively limited funding. The EaP represented a return of bloc politics to Europe, although formally Russia was called on to join. A US cable in 2008 revealed by WikiLeaks acknowledged that the initiative was to 'counter Russia's influence in Eastern Europe'. The cable talked of the 'Sikorski doctrine' to push back against Russia, but warned that 'Poland's eastern policies could elicit a sharp Russian reaction', but nevertheless concluded that 'Poland can be a reliable ally as we [the US government] look for ways to enhance western influence beyond NATO's eastern borders'.[13]

The EaP represented a qualitative change in the character of European politics.[14] While opposed to NATO expansion, Russia initially considered EU enlargement a benign process, but the entry of a number of former Soviet bloc countries in 2004 changed perceptions. The EaP represented a further qualitative change, introducing an explicit element of geopolitical contestation into relations. The high level of interaction, moreover, effectively precluded EaP members (once they had signed the AAs and DCFTAs) from engaging in Eurasian integration projects. The security dynamic was reinforced by the Lisbon Treaty, which came into force in December 2009, requiring associated countries to align their defence and security policies with the EU. The extension of the EU's sphere of influence came to be seen as the harbinger of NATO enlargement. The EU's advance would certainly set back 'Putin's Eurasian dream', the ambition to create a Russian-dominated sphere in Eurasia that would be able to hold its own in the global geopolitical struggle with America and China.[15] Russia's various proposals for the trilateral regulation of neighbourhood matters were rebuffed, typically by deployment of the usual 'wedge' argument. At the time of the Prague summit in May 2009 launching the EaP, Putin suggested creating a tripartite structure to modernise the Ukrainian gas pipeline system, but this was brusquely

[13] 'Poland: A Natural U.S. Ally on Eastern Policy', 12 December 2008, https://wikileaks.org/plusd/cables/08WARSAW1409_a.html, last accessed 30 May 2017.

[14] Dominik Tolksdorf, *The EU, Russia and the Eastern Partnership: What Dynamics under the New German Government?*, Russie.Nei.Visions No. 74 (Paris, IFRI, February 2014).

[15] Christopher Marsh and Nikolas K. Gvosdev, *Russian Foreign Policy: Interests, Vectors and Sectors* (New York, CQ Press, 2013).

dismissed, as were all Russia's later tripartite and pan-continental initiatives. From the benign intentions outlined by Prodi, wider Europe was transformed into a struggle for influence.

The third model is Greater Europe, the continental vision in which Europe would emerge from the superpower overlay of the Cold War to become an independent pole in world politics.[16] With its roots in various inter-war plans for 'pan-Europa', and then in Gaullist aspirations for a more autonomous voice for Europe in the post-war Atlantic system, the idea was reinvigorated by Gorbachev's plans for a common European home. In the 1990s the idea was eclipsed by more immediate concerns, but even convinced Atlanticists such as Kozyrev argued that Russia would become part not only of the Atlantic security system but also that its great power ambitions would be fulfilled in the larger European context. The president at the time, Yeltsin, never failed to argue that 'Europe without Russia is not Europe at all. Only with Russia can it be a Greater Europe, with no possible equal anywhere on the globe.'[17] The two complemented each other: Russia was a vast and relatively under-developed country rich in natural endowments, while Western Europe had advanced technologies but needed energy and other resources. This is a theme repeated by Lavrov, who argued that the end of the Cold War

offered a unique opportunity to change the European architecture on the principles of indivisible and equal security and broad co-operation without dividing lines. We had a practical chance to mend Europe's divide and implement the dream of a common European home, which many European thinkers and politicians, including President Charles de Gaulle of France, wholeheartedly embraced. Russia was fully open to this option and advanced many proposals and initiatives in this connection.[18]

Russia favoured strengthening the military and political components of the OSCE, but instead NATO became the pre-eminent security organisation. No political form could be found to encompass the two halves of the continent.

The Russian leadership expended considerable effort to devise a new 'architecture' for a united Europe to give organisational form to Russia's continental aspirations. A major initiative in this respect was Medvedev's call, in a speech in Berlin on 5 June 2008, for a new European Security

---

[16] Alexei A. Gromyko and V. P. Fëdorova (eds.), *Bol'shaya Evropa: Idei, real'nost', perspektivy* (Moscow, Ves' mir, 2014); Alexei A. Gromyko, 'Smaller or Greater Europe?', *Revista di Studi Politici Internazionali*, Vol. 81, Issue 324, October–December 2014, pp. 517–26.

[17] Cited by Leonid Bershidsky, 'No Illusions Left, I'm Leaving Russia', *Moscow Times*, 19 June 2014.

[18] Lavrov, 'Russia's Foreign Policy'.

Treaty (EST). Medvedev argued for the creation of a genuinely inclusive security system to avoid new dividing lines. The initiative reflected the long-standing tension between two models of European security noted earlier. The strictly Atlanticist view focused on US security guarantees for its NATO allies, a view staunchly supported by the UK, the Netherlands, Denmark and Norway. The Euro-Atlantic approach recognised US leadership but sought to complement it with continental security initiatives, a view traditionally supported by France and Germany.[19] Medvedev's initiative was not intended to drive a wedge between the US and its European NATO allies, but to strengthen the Euro-Atlanticist perspective, primarily through the OSCE. Medvedev argued for 'the necessity of ensuring the unity of the entire Euro-Atlantic space'. It reiterated Moscow's long-standing concern about 'NATO-centrism' in Europe and sought to 'transform the OSCE into a fully-fledged regional organisation'. By November 2009 a draft EST was published, calling on signatories to 'cooperate with each other on the basis of the principles of indivisible, equal and undiminished security. Any security measures taken by a Party to the Treaty individually or together with other Parties, including in the framework of any international organization military alliance [read NATO] or coalition, shall be implemented with due regard to security interests of all other Parties.' Apart from this fundamental assertion, allowing Russia to block further NATO enlargement, the draft was rather thin.[20] The OSCE launched the 'Corfu process' in June 2009 'to restore confidence and take forward dialogue on wider European security', but in the end nothing was achieved.[21] The Euro-Atlantic Security Initiative of 2011, a commission seeking to lay the 'intellectual foundations for an inclusive Euro-Atlantic security system for the twenty-first century',[22] was yet another attempt to reform the system of European security, but ultimately it too was unable to prevail against hermetic Atlanticism.

Lavrov reflected on the dilemmas of building Greater Europe in an important speech at the PACE in April 2010. He stressed the importance of the CoE as a soft security structure and the OSCE as the framework for legally binding agreements, but insisted that the EST was essential to compensate for the failure to create a 'European architecture that would unite each and every state without exception in the Euro-Atlantic region

---

[19] Alexey Fenenko, 'The Myth of a "Hybrid War" in Ukraine', *Russia Direct*, 16 June 2015.
[20] 'The Draft of the European Security Treaty', 29 November 2009, http://en.kremlin.ru/events/president/news/6152, last accessed 26 May 2017.
[21] OSCE, 'Restoring Trust: The Corfu Process', 1 December 2010, www.osce.org/mc/87193, last accessed 30 May 2017.
[22] The Euro-Atlantic Security Initiative, www.nti.org/about/projects/euro-atlantic-security-initiative-easi/, last accessed 26 May 2017.

into a single organization based on clear and legally binding principles and providing equal security for all'. The main problem for him was that 'the principle of indivisible security proclaimed in the Euro-Atlantic area at the highest level in the 1990s was not embodied in international law'.[23] In keeping with his original strong European leanings, in a speech in Berlin on 26 November 2010 Putin called for the geopolitical unification of 'Greater Europe' from Lisbon to Vladivostok to create a genuine 'strategic partnership'.[24] Europe and Russia were to be united into a common strategic and economic area in which resources were pooled. A shared developmental strategy would allow the industrial and military-strategic potential of the region from the Atlantic to the Pacific to be exploited to the maximum. This continental project would lay the foundations for Europe to emerge as a distinctive pole, comparable to China and the United States. Medvedev reprised some of these themes at NATO's summit in Lisbon in November 2010.[25] It was in this spirit that Karaganov argued that the EU and Russia should establish not only a partnership but a strategic union or alliance, which would counteract the relative decline of Europe's global status and economic weight. He acknowledged that this would be hard to achieve because of the 'unfinished character of the "Cold War" in both institutional and intellectual terms'. In his view, the roots of the Cold War were not removed, hence 'some re-growth appeared, because no Europe-wide peace agreement was made to end the Cold War'.[26] This 'unfinished character' in the end allowed Cold War-style politics to return. Rather surprisingly, given the crisis in Ukraine and the souring of relations, Putin returned to the idea of creating a free trade zone from the Atlantic to the Pacific at the Russo-EU summit in Brussels on 28 January 2014 (the last to be held in

---

[23] 'Transcript of Address of Sergey V. Lavrov', Council of Europe, Strasbourg, 29 April 2010, http://en.interaffairs.ru/exclusive/14-transcript-of-address-by-sergey-lavrov-minis ter-for-foreign-affairs-of-the-russian-federation-at-the-spring-part-of-the-61st-parlia mentary-assembly-session-strasbourg-29-april-2010.html, last accessed 26 May 2017.

[24] Speech delivered to the Fourth Berlin Economic Leadership meeting organised by the *Süddeutsche Zeitung*, which the day before was presented as an article in that paper. A summary of the speech is at http://premier.gov.ru/events/news/13120/, last accessed 30 May 2017; the article is Wladimir Putin 'Von Lissabon bis Wladiwostok. Handelspakt zwischen Russland und Europa: Moskau will als Lehre aus der größten Krise der Weltwirtschaft seit acht Jahrzehnten wesentlich enger mit der Europäischen Union zusammenarbeiten', *Süddeutsche Zeitung*, 25 November 2010, www.sueddeutsche.de, last accessed 14 December 2010.

[25] Dmitry Medvedev, 'Press-konferentsiya po itogam zasedaniya Soveta Rossiya-NATO', Lisbon, 20 November 2010, http://kremlin.ru/transcripts/9570, last accessed 26 May 2017.

[26] Sergei Karaganov, 'To Conclude the Unfinished War', in Sergei Karaganov et al., *Rossiya vs Evropa: Protivostoyanie ili Soyuz* (Moscow, Astrel', 2009), p. 13.

that format).[27] Despite the breakdown in relations, Russia refused to relinquish the Greater European cooperative path of development.[28]

Russia's Greater European initiatives were typically seen in the West as being little more than a cover for the establishment of a 'greater Russia' by stealth. The Atlantic community's intense vigilance against attempts to drive a wedge between its two wings has been mentioned several times, and it has been so since various Soviet plans for European security were advanced by Khrushchev in the 1950s. This Cold War hermetic view prevails to this day, accompanied by the enduring fear that any idea emanating outside of the NATO system is potentially divisive and dangerous. Russia's proposals to resolve the numerous conflicts in Europe were treated with scepticism when not dismissed as self-serving and partisan. This was the case throughout the various Balkan crises in the 1990s, and with Russian proposals to resolve the frozen conflict in Transnistria, notably with the Kozak Memorandum in 2003. William Hill, who served two spells as head of the OSCE Mission to Moldova between 1999 and 2006, reveals how Russia was systemically shut out from the resolution of the Transnistria issue.[29] Russia's effective exclusion from such processes generated neo-revisionism. From Moscow perspective, it was the Atlantic alliance that was driving a wedge between Russia and Europe, isolating it from the larger process of continental unification.

Eurasian Integration

The pan-continental 'institutional deficit' left Europe divided. In the new geopolitical reality, 'Russia is no longer the eastern flank of the failed Greater Europe and is becoming the western flank of the emerging Greater Eurasia'.[30] Russia's grand strategy remained what it had been since the end of the Cold War – to break out of the strategic impasse in Eurasia and Europe by forcing the Atlantic system to recognise Russia's

[27] Vladimir Putin, 'Russia-EU Summit', 28 January 2014, http://eng.kremlin.ru/tran scripts/6575, last accessed 26 May 2017.
[28] Alexei Gromyko, 'Russia, the US, and Smaller Europe (the EU): Competition for Leadership in a Polycentric World', Institute of Europe, Russian Academy of Sciences, Working Paper No. 14, 2015. The Russian version is published as Aleksei Gromyko, 'Rossiya, SShA, Malaya Evropa (ES): Konkurentsiya za liderstvo v mire politsentrichnosti', *Sovremennaya Evropa*, No. 4, 2015, pp. 5–14.
[29] William H. Hill, *Russia, the Near Abroad and the West: Lessons from the Moldova-Transdniestria Conflict* (Washington, Woodrow Wilson Center Press and Baltimore, The Johns Hopkins University Press, 2012), and personal discussion.
[30] Igor Ivanov, 'Russia, Ukraine and the Future of Europe', RIAC, 19 March 2016, http://russiancouncil.ru/en/analytics-and-comments/analytics/russia-ukraine-and-the-future-of-europe/, last accessed 30 May 2017.

security concerns, to confirm Russia's status as a great power, and to advance the cause of a plural international system by deepening alignment with like-minded states.

Classical geopolitical thinking is a constitutive part of Russian public discourse, but the country's defence of the autonomy of international society moderates classic Westphalian and geopolitical practices. Russia's centrality was outlined in Halford Mackinder's 'Heartland Theory' in 1904. Originating in the context of Anglo-Russian rivalry over India, Mackinder argued that Russia could become a global hegemon by dominating Eurasia. Russia was the successor of the vast Mongol Empire, and in the late nineteenth century took advantage of Chinese weakness in its 'century of humiliation'. Russia grabbed 1.5 million square kilometres in two 'unequal treaties', opening up an extensive new coastline from Vladivostok to Nikolaevsk. In Mackinder's view, Russia's dominance of the heartland would diminish the reach of the maritime nations led by Britain, and undermine the balance between land and maritime powers.[31] In the event, Russia's defeat by Japan in 1905 demonstrated the flexibility of maritime nations, and although the Pax Britannica did decline, it was replaced by the Pax Americana. This was theorised by the American geopolitical thinker Nicholas Spykman, who stressed the mobility and other advantages of maritime powers such as Britain and the US, and called on them to engage in off-shore balancing to contain any emerging Eurasian hegemon.[32] Commentators from Brzezinski onwards in the post-communist era have warned against Russia dominating the Eurasian landmass, as it had done in the Imperial and Soviet periods – even though the demise of these two systems demonstrates that control of space does not guarantee survival in the absence of modernisation. Leading realist theorists today argue that the US should renounce the policy of intervention for one of off-shore balancing to contain Russia and China. What Russia should do as the subject of such 'balancing' is unclear. The scope of its 'legitimate' interests in post-Soviet Eurasia remains contested.

Alienation from the West encouraged alternative strategies, above all a concerted strategy to shape Russia as a bi-continental power.[33] Russia was in danger of being ground between the new giant millstones of our

---

[31] Halford. J. Mackinder, 'The Geographical Pivot of History', *The Geographical Journal*, Vol. 170, No. 4, 1904, pp. 421–44.

[32] Nicholas J. Spykman, *The Geography of the Peace* (New York, Harcourt and Brace, 1942).

[33] Richard Sakwa, 'Dualism at Home and Abroad: Russian Foreign Policy Neo-Revisionism and Bicontinentalism', in David Cadier and Margot Light (eds.), *Russia's Foreign Policy* (London, Palgrave Macmillan, 2015), pp. 65–79, from which this section draws.

era – enduring Atlanticism and the rising Greater Asia. In domestic politics the regime balances between the meta-factions, so Russia's bi-continentalism balances between East and West to restore the centrality of Eurasia. Russia never accepted peripherality in the Historical West, but as the geopolitical situation changed, Putin tried to avoid peripherality in Asia. This was an ambitious agenda, and Russia's economic weakness and the under-development of its Far Eastern regions limited its fulfilment. At the same time, although estranged from the West, Russia certainly had no intention of turning its back on Europe. The greater intensity of engagement with Asia, and in particular with China, did not entail a shift from 'strategic partnership' to an exclusive 'strategic alliance' (see Chapter 10). As in domestic politics, so in international relations, Putin sought to achieve decisional autonomy and strategic flexibility. The Russian response to the security dilemma at the heart of the cold peace included increases in defence spending and the strengthening of the Collective Security Treaty Organisation (CSTO), a Moscow-led collective security alliance comprised of Armenia, Belarus, Kazakhstan, Kyrgyzstan, Russia and Tajikistan, with Afghanistan and Serbia observer states. Another way to achieve strategic autonomy was the creation of the EEU.

The CIS had been an ambitious attempt to maintain the unity of the post-Soviet space, but its launch in December 1991 was chaotic and unprepared, and characterised by the divergent ambitions of its members. Turkmenistan and Ukraine never signed its Charter, and thus remained 'participants' rather than 'members'. As an international organisation the CIS has had few achievements, although it facilitated the 'civilised divorce' of the former fraternal republics and acted as a forum for the leaders to coordinate policies.[34] With the breach in relations with the West, Russia turned to intensified forms of Eurasian integration. The initiative was certainly not Russia's alone, and as early as 29 March 1994 in a speech at Moscow State University the president of Kazakhstan, Nursultan Nazarbaev, talked of creating a Eurasian Union, an idea to which he returned in October 2011.[35] With little prospect of a Greater West or Greater Europe, Russia sought to create its own Greater Eurasia. The Eurasian Economic Community was established in October 2000, and on its basis in 2007 Russia, Belarus and Kazakhstan created a

---

[34] Muratbek Imanaliev, 'The Commonwealth of Independent States: Not Subject to Reform', *Valdai Discussion Club*, 4 July 2016, http://valdaiclub.com/news/common wealth-of-independent-states-not-subject-to-reform/, last accessed 26 May 2017.

[35] Nursultan Nazarbaev, 'Evraziiskii soyuz: ot idei k istorii budushchego', *Izvestiya*, 25 October 2011, p. 1, http://izvestia.ru/news/504908, last accessed 30 May 2017. For a broader discussion, see Bulat Sultanov, 'Kazakhstan and Eurasian Integration', in Piotr Dutkiewicz and Richard Sakwa (eds.), *Eurasian Integration: The View from Within* (London and New York, Routledge, 2015), pp. 97–110.

customs union, formalised on 25 January 2008 with the signing of nine trade agreements covering tariffs, anti-dumping, statistics and taxation. In June 2009 further steps were taken with the creation of the Eurasian Customs Union, which was formally launched on 1 January 2010 and by 1 July 2011 trade barriers had been removed. The Eurasian Customs Union developed an institutional and political identity that far surpassed any other post-Soviet integration project, and even challenged the EU for hegemony in the region.[36] In a complementary process, the three countries on 1 January 2012 created the Common Economic Space (CES) within the framework of the CIS, an institution that satisfied Ukraine's desire for the advantages of a free trade area without the obligations of a customs union. The Common Economic Space covered standardised legislation and the free movement of capital, services and labour.

The cornerstone of Putin's renewed presidency was Eurasian integration. Putin's keynote article, published in October 2011 as one of a series of programmatic texts for his third term, outlined plans to enlarge the existing customs union and its evolution into the EEU and eventually a Eurasian Union. Putin argued that Eurasian integration was prompted by the global economic crisis but also reflected the needs and traditions of the region. The distinguishing feature of the envisaged new phase of Eurasian integration was the creation of supra-national structures, including a Eurasian Commission. Putin noted that it had taken forty years to travel from the European Coal and Steel Community to the fully-fledged EU, a path that he suggested would be traversed far more quickly in Eurasia. He denied that this in any way represented the recreation of the Soviet Union, since it would be open to new members and would be based on maximally liberalised trade regulations. The EEU was to complement rather than to compete with the EU. The idea was not to 'fence ourselves off from anyone', but the EEU would be founded on 'universal integrative principles as an inalienable part of Greater Europe, united by mutual values of freedom, democracy and market rules'. At the same time, Eurasian integration would allow Russia to maintain its status as a great power and lay the foundations for a future 'multipolar world order'.[37]

The EEU Treaty was signed on 29 May 2014 and systematised the provisions already contained in the Eurasian Customs Union and the Common Economic Space, including free movement of goods, capital

[36] For detailed analysis, see Rilka Dragneva and Kataryna Wolczuk (eds.), *Eurasian Economic Integration: Law, Policy and Politics* (Cheltenham, Edward Elgar, 2013).

[37] Vladimir Putin, 'Novyi integratsionnyi proekt dlya Evrazii: budushchee, kotoroe rozhdaetsya segodnya', *Izvestiya*, 3 October 2011, p. 1. An English version can be found at http://premier.gov.ru/events/news/16622, last accessed 30 May 2017.

and labour and regulatory harmonisation in nineteen areas. The main innovation was a common market for services, starting with less important sectors and gradually expanding to cover sectors like telecommunications, transport and financial services. By the mid-2020s the EEU planned to establish a common financial and banking regulatory and monitoring authority located in Kazakhstan. The most ambitious proposals were postponed, notably the liberalisation of markets in a number of sensitive goods, including pharmaceuticals, and the creation of a common oil, gas and electricity market.[38] The EEU Treaty in effect unified the existing legal-regulatory framework of the Common Economic Space and the customs union, consisting of over one hundred international treaties signed between 1995 and 2012, into one document. Codification was anticipated to improve compliance across the whole spectrum of issues, including finance, trade and investment, transport, energy, industry, and agro-industry, while facilitating macro-economic coordination. The ultimate goal was to create a fully-fledged Eurasian Union with its own *acquis* covering technical, labour, mobility and other norms that would, like the EU, improve economic governance throughout the region.

On 1 January 2015 the Eurasian Customs Union and the Common Economic Space combined to create the EEU. Its birth could hardly have been less auspicious, with conflict in Ukraine, tensions with the West, and a deep economic recession. As the DCFTA between Ukraine and the EU came into effect (see the third section of Chapter 5), on 1 December 2015 Putin suspended the free trade area between Russia and Ukraine. The five-member EEU (Armenia, Belarus, Kazakhstan, Kyrgyzstan and Russia), covers three-quarters of the post-Soviet space with a population of 183 million and a total GDP of around $2.7 trillion. Compared to the EU's combined GDP of $16.6 trillion, this is rather small, yet it marked an important step towards deep Eurasian integration. The brute GDP figures may not be impressive, but the EEU contains 20 per cent of global gas and 15 per cent of oil reserves. The Supreme Eurasian Economic Commission (SEEC) became the supra-national regulatory body, whose presidency rotates annually between the deputy prime ministers of the EEU member states.[39] Each Member State, irrespective of size, has two

---

[38] Ekaterina Furman and Alexander Libman, 'Europeanisation and the Eurasian Economic Union', in Piotr Dutkiewicz and Richard Sakwa (eds.), *Eurasian Integration: The View from Within* (London and New York, Routledge, 2015), pp. 173–92.

[39] A compendium of useful information can be found in Eurasian Economic Commission, *Eurasian Economic Integration: Facts and Figures* (Moscow, 2014), http://eurasiancommis sion.org/ru/Documents/broshura26Body_ENGL_final2013_2.pdf, last accessed 26 May 2017.

representatives with equal rights, and the body works through consensus. At the inauguration meeting of the SEEC in the Kremlin on 23 December 2014, Putin promised to build a comprehensive space with integrated regulation of energy and financial markets by 2015.[40]

Eurasian integration has a dual character. The first is the functional intensification of the long-standing goal of creating some sort of post-Soviet political and economic community. The earliest iteration of this was the CIS, but it achieved few of its positive ambitions and instead presided over the separation of the Soviet states, and in the end this gave rise to the creation of the EEU. The second aim is rather more ambitious, namely to use Eurasian integration instrumentally to create a building block for the future pan-continental edifice of Greater Europe. Eurasian integration offers a model for the autochthonous development of a significant proportion of the globe, a potential partner for the EU in creating a continental union, as well as acting as a counter-weight to growing Chinese influence in Central Asia while helping to manage that influence. As we shall see, in due course the character of duality changed, and instead of becoming part of Greater Europe, the EEU became a foundational institution of what from mid-2016 became known as the Greater Eurasia Project.

Eurasian integration remains a controversial project, not least in Russia. There are many models of regional integration, and in its liberal forms is usually considered a progressive phenomenon, reducing barriers to inter-state trade, allowing labour mobility and in general improving competitiveness. But as so often when it comes to Russia, the project was subject to radical critique. The American secretary of state, Hillary Clinton, at an OSCE foreign ministers' meeting in Dublin on 6 December 2012, condemned Russia's alleged attempt to 'rebuild the Soviet empire' and to 're-sovietise' countries that had emerged from the ruins of the USSR: 'We know what the goal is and we are trying to figure out ways to slow down or prevent it.'[41] This was an astonishing statement by any measure, but reflected the long-term hostility of the Historical West, and in particular the US, to the revival of any unified political space in the heart of Eurasia. This reinforced the Kremlin's sense of strategic impasse, with the Atlantic powers opposing Russia's attempts to rebuild an economic and political community with its neighbours. One of the conditions for good relations with the West appeared to be a ban on the re-establishment of any Eurasian economic and political community.

---

[40] Vladimir Putin, 'Zayavleniya dlya pressy po itogam zasedaniya VEES', 23 December 2014, www.kremlin.ru/transcripts/47318, last accessed 30 May 2017.

[41] 'Clinton Calls Eurasian Integration an Effort to Re-Sovietize', RFE/RL, *Russia Report*, 9 December 2012.

This is not to suggest that the process was not controversial. While regional economic integration is part of the response to challenges of globalisation, allowing a group of states to engage in more intense economic engagement while enhancing their bargaining power in the global system, the Eurasian model of regional integration is unique in several respects. First, it focuses not on the *creation* of closer economic and social ties, but above all entails *reconstitution*, the rebuilding of links ruptured at the time of the Soviet collapse. This entails an appeal to the past as well as traditional cultural and personal ties, and thus rather than presenting itself as a progressive phenomenon, it assumes some archaic characteristics. Second, the re-establishment of some sort of supra-national community inevitably prompts fears that the Moscow-centred power relations of the Tsarist and Soviet orders would be re-established. Coercive pressure was brought to bear on Armenia to force it to announce on 3 September 2013 that it would join the EEU, and thus not sign the AA with the EU. This is also the case with the trade war with Ukraine in summer 2013, intended to dissuade the country from signing its AA with the EU at the Vilnius summit (see the third section of Chapter 5). Third, it was not clear what the problem was to which Eurasian integration was the response. The former Soviet states had diversified their trading patterns, and there were few barriers to the development of economic relations and labour mobility, especially with the creation of the CIS free trade area in 2012. Fourth, the enormous disparities in size and economic weight between the smallest and the largest member of the new community is greater than in any other comparable union. It is hard to envisage a union of equals where the power disparities are so enormous, although balancing mechanism operate in the SEEC to ensure that the interests of the smaller states are represented.[42]

There were other concerns. Eurasian integration worried liberal economists, fearing that the loss of economic sovereignty to the new Commission would reduce manageability and raise the spectre of separation from Europe and the West, as advocated by radical Eurasian ideologists such as Dugin. These, in turn, were not enthused by commitment to liberal economic institutionalism embedded in the EEU's founding documents, which sought to act in compliance with WTO rules and broader patterns of globalisation. Russian nationalists in the Alexander Solzhenitsyn tradition had always wanted Russia to focus on its own national development, casting aside the burden of empire and responsibility for neighbours, and from this

---

[42] For a discussion of the dilemmas and benefits of Eurasian integration, see Rilka Dragneva and Kataryna Wolczuk, *The Eurasian Economic Union: Deals, Rules and the Exercise of Power* (London, Chatham House, REP Research Paper, May 2017).

perspective Eurasian integration was a step backwards, once again assuming responsibility for the development of neighbouring states. These concerns were compounded by Russia's dominance of the CSTO. On the other side, the geographical proximity and historical connections between the countries means that they faced common challenges.[43] Russia's predominance inevitably endows it with hegemonic ambitions, and over the years it has veered between hard and soft manifestations of this. Up to 2014 economic and other instruments were used to maintain soft hegemony, but in Ukraine in 2014 harder forms were employed. In terms of developing regional integration, this had disastrous consequences, with Ukraine vigorously distancing itself not only from any form of Eurasian integration, but even from maintaining existing economic and other links with Russia. The shift to hard power in 2014 was not a manifestation of traditional Russian imperialism or the alleged primeval urge for territorial aggrandisement, or even as an act of diversionary warfare, but reflected 'the dearth of soft and economic power resources to pursue the larger goal of regional integration', which was considered essential to maintain Russia's status as a great power.[44] Russian policy was torn between contesting forms of hegemony, while the path to a non-hegemonic strategy was obscured by the intense geopolitical completion within and for the region.[45] Rather than pursuing what some consider is coercive integration, Russia could present itself as a regional security provider.[46]

Eurasian integration is thus a fundamentally contested project. Even Putin's enthusiasm began to wane when confronted by the reality of the loss of sovereignty, the difficulties of ensuring foreign policy coordination with Belarus and Kazakhstan, and the prospects of a long-term rift with the West. Regional integration remained an important part of his policy agenda, but, characteristically, he sought to keep his policy options open. The strategic alignment with China was accompanied by macro-regional alliance-building in the format of the Shanghai Cooperation Organisation and BRICS. Nonetheless, Putin refused to accept that Russia would become an outcast from Europe, and his turn to Asia and the world was accompanied by attempts to rebuild the relationship with the Atlantic community. The EEU was initially considered a stepping stone in that

---

[43] David Lane and Vsevolod Samokhvalov (eds.), 'Eurasia in a Global Context', special issue of *European Politics and Society*, Vol. 17, No. S1, 2016.

[44] Andrej Krickovic and Maxim Bratersky, 'Benevolent Hegemon, Neighbourhood Bully, or Regional Security Provider? Russia's Efforts to Promote Regional Integration after the 2013–2014 Ukraine Crisis', *Eurasian Geography and Economics*, Vol. 57, No. 2, 2016, p. 181.

[45] Michael O. Slobodchikoff, *Building Hegemonic Order Russia's Way: Order, Stability, and Predictability in the Post-Soviet Space* (Lanham, Lexington Books, 2014).

[46] Krickovic and Bratersky, 'Benevolent Hegemon'.

direction, by creating a pillar with which the EU would engage on terms approaching equality. It remains uncertain whether Russia today has the quality of 'geo-centrism', the regional attractive power with which other countries seek to identify. Eurasian integration does respond to certain needs of its members, but a coercive dynamic is also present. Resistance to regional integration may leave the EEU little more than a customs union. The character of Russia's regional hegemony has not yet been resolved.

Ukraine and the Breakdown of the Cold Peace

The crisis from 2014 was an extreme symptom of the failure to create a sustainable post-Cold War European security order.[47] Russia and the Atlantic powers entered into an intense security competition in the Caucasus and Ukraine.[48] It is still hard to understand how what was in essence not much more than a technical agreement between Ukraine and the EU escalated into a crisis that brought the world to the verge of great power conflict, profoundly damaging the country and reviving the institutions and ideological confrontation of the Cold War.[49] Ukraine had been negotiating an AA with the EU since 2007, and it had been initialled by both parties on 30 March 2012 and was due to be signed (along with its associated DCFTA) at the second summit of the EaP in Vilnius on 28 and 29 November 2013.[50] The 1,000-page AA was far more than an economic and technical agreement, but also covered 'military security issues', and in the short-term offered little in the way of economic support. On 21 November 2013 the Ukrainian president, Viktor Yanukovych, announced that he would postpone signing. A protest movement gathered on the *Maidan Nezalehnosti* (Independence Square) in the centre of Kiev. The increasingly polarised confrontation ended with Yanukovych's flight from Kiev on 22 February 2014 and the coming to power of a radical nationalist government committed to the 'European choice' and a turn away from Russia.

Yanukovych had been elected president in February 2010 with the support of Russophone forces, but the Kremlin had also been open to working constructively with his main opponent, Yulia Tymoshenko.

[47] Richard Sakwa, *Frontline Ukraine: Crisis in the Borderlands*, extended edn with new Afterword (London, I. B. Tauris, 2016).

[48] Gerard Toal, *Near Abroad: Putin, the West and the Contest over Ukraine and the Caucasus* (Oxford, Oxford University Press, 2017).

[49] J. L. Black, *The Return of the Cold War: Ukraine, the West and Russia* (London, Routledge, 2016).

[50] For details, see Rilka Dragneva and Kataryna Wolczuk, *Ukraine between the EU and Russia: The Integration Challenge* (London, Palgrave Macmillan, 2015).

Putin's personal relations with Yanukovych were never warm, and relations with Moscow during his presidency remained strained. Certain Russian strategic goals were conceded, notably the extension of the lease of the Sevastopol base in Crimea, the home of Russia's Black Sea Fleet, to 2042 and the declaration of Ukraine's non-bloc status (in other words, repudiating NATO membership). The Black Sea region has long been a fracture zone where competing imperial projects clashed. It is the meeting point of the Balkans, the Caucasus, Eurasia, the Middle East and inner Asia, and although a major site of cultural development it has also been the cauldron of civilisational conflict.[51] Huntington, in his 'clash of civilisations', described Ukraine as a 'cleft' society. The conflicts in the region reflect the broader failure to find a mode of reconciliation in the post-Cold War years. Here the EU, Russia, and the US jostle for influence, while Turkey remains a regional power with a range of concerns that render it an increasingly uncomfortable member of NATO and an unlikely entrant to the EU, despite the launching of membership negotiations in October 2005. Above all, it is here – in Georgia and Ukraine – that Russia drew a line in the sand to resist what was perceived to be the further encroachment of the Atlantic community into its traditional sphere of influence.[52] Initially taking the form of an ambiguous contest over values and influence, in which competition was tempered by narratives of partnership and cooperation, this gave way to harsh geopolitical contestation.

NATO's Bucharest summit in April 2007 offered Georgia and Ukraine the long-term prospect of membership, but the immediate option of a Membership Action Plan was vetoed by Germany and France. The Russo-Georgian conflict of August 2008 was the first war to stop NATO enlargement; Ukraine was the second. In practice, under Obama the drive for NATO enlargement was moderated and limited to preparatory moves. This was in keeping with Obama's focus on overcoming the global financial crisis, disentanglement from the wars in Iraq and Afghanistan, and the pursuit of global objectives in East Asia. It was the EU that now made the running in advancing to the East, with democratic conditionality at the heart of its eastern engagement strategy. However, as Frank Schimmelfennig notes, the EU 'again loosened its democratic conditionality and focused on drawing the post-Soviet countries out of the Russian orbit. The EU-Russian competition for influence has thus become more intense over time – but apparently less

[51] Charles King, *The Black Sea: A History* (Oxford, Oxford University Press, 2004).
[52] Carol Weaver, *The Politics of the Black Sea Region: EU Neighbourhood, Conflict Zone or Future Security Community?* (Basingstoke, Ashgate, 2013).

about democracy as such.'[53] Narrow representations of Europe found natural allies among nationalists in Ukraine, provoking the greatest threat to European peace since 1945.

Realists tend to look at the structural features of the breakdown, accompanied by the transfer of Crimea and the armed hostilities in the Donbass, but the no less important aspect is Ukraine's internal evolution. Two models of Ukrainian state development compete.[54] The monist view suggests that Ukraine is in a postcolonial situation, and that its state and national development is predicated on separation from Russia. This means the primacy of the Ukrainian language, and an ideology of cultural and national difference. This monist view can be generous, tolerant and capacious, as evidenced by the granting of citizenship to all those living in Ukraine in 1991, irrespective of nationality and background, and later in the widespread use of Russian in the media and cultural life, although not formally in education and increasingly less in public administration (all official documents, for example, until the 2012 language law allowed some regional exceptions, were only in Ukrainian). The monist view has a darker side, drawing on the inter-war militant nationalist tradition of the Organisation of Ukrainian Nationalists and the cult of Stepan Bandera. In other words, while monist nationalism could take civic forms, it was susceptible to exclusivist pressures. On the other side, the pluralist view of Ukrainian national development stresses Ukraine's multiple identities and traditions, and wants them to be given constitutional expression, possibly in some form of consociationalism. The corollary is greater openness to links with Russia and Eurasia as a whole, and less of an obsession with the ideology of 'Europeanism'. This view draws on the tradition of pluralist national development advocated by the 'national Bolshevik' Alexander Shumsky, the Ukrainian Commissar of Enlightenment (1924–27) at the time of *korenizatsiya* (indigenisation) in the early Soviet years, and Vyacheslav Chornovil, one of the founders of the Rukh independence movement in 1989, who died in suspicious circumstances in March 1999 as he prepared to launch his presidential campaign.

Yanukovych was thus heir to a divided society, which he exploited to maintain power. Following his decision not to sign the AA, Russia offered a loan of $15 billion. Moscow insisted that the AA was incompatible with the existing free trade agreement, fearing that EU goods would undermine the Russian market – in conditions where the regulatory regime

---

[53] Frank Schimmelfennig, review of Jakob Tolstrup, *Russia vs. the EU: The Competition for Influence in Post-Soviet States* (Boulder, First Forum Press, 2014), in *Slavic Review*, Vol. 74, No. 1, Spring 2015, p. 220.
[54] Sakwa, *Frontline Ukraine*.

governing rules of origin were susceptible to corruption. Although it was Yanukovych's turn away from the EU that precipitated the crisis, it was his authoritarianism and corruption that ultimately brought about his downfall. The Ukrainian revolution was the first in the post-communist area not provoked by the theft of an election. Indeed, it was one of the first not to be labelled a 'colour revolution' – it was, quite simply, a revolution; signalling that revolution had returned as a mode of political change. A deal on pre-term elections agreed with EU negotiators on 21 February 2014 would have allowed Yanukovych to stay in power in the interim, and Putin was furious at the perceived bad faith of the West in not upholding the deal. It appeared once again to be a case of foreign-sponsored 'regime change'. Like all revolutions, it had multiple layers and divergent inter-pretations. For the Atlantic powers, this was a 'revolution of dignity' against a corrupt authoritarian regime;[55] for Moscow, this was an illegal seizure of power by an insurgent group backed by the West. What is incontrovertible is that Russia and the Atlantic system stumbled into geopolitical competition.[56] The EU suffered an extraordinary inversion: instead of overcoming the logic of conflict, it became the instrument for its reproduction.

The change of power in Kiev in 2014 was attended by a militant nationalist rhetoric, accompanied by plans to abolish the language law of 2012. The status of the Sevastopol base was immediately raised. Crimea had long been a disputed territory, having only been transferred into Ukrainian jurisdiction in 1954. The 2001 census revealed that 58 per cent of the population were Russians, 24 per cent Ukrainians, and 12 per cent Tatars. Already in 2008 the Razumkov polling agency found that 63.8 per cent of Crimeans wished to secede from Ukraine to join Russia.[57] Such sentiments were later tempered, and before 2014 there was little in the way of active separatism. Nevertheless, the Sevastopol question never entirely disappeared, particularly in the mind of Moscow mayor Yuri Luzhkov. In November 2008 he argued that 'Sevastopol has never belonged to Ukraine . . . Crimea was given to Ukraine by the stroke of a pen . . . and it pains the heart of every Russian'. More consequentially,

[55] Andrew Wilson, *Ukraine Crisis: What It Means for the West* (London and New Haven, Yale University Press, 2014).

[56] Marvin Kalb, *Imperial Gamble: Putin, Ukraine, and the New Cold War* (Washington, Brookings Institution Press, 2015).

[57] Razumkov Centre, *National Security and Defence*, No. 10, 2008, pp. 19–22, annex 1, 'Prospects of Crimea: Regional Status', www.razumkov.org.ua/eng/files/category_jour nal/NSD104_eng_2.pdf, last accessed 10 May 2016; Razumkov Centre, *National Security and Defence*, No. 5 (109), 2009, 'Crimean Society: Dividing Lines and Prospects of Consolidation', p. 23 for comparable data, http://old.razumkov.org.ua/en g/files/category_journal/NSD109_eng.pdf, last accessed 30 May 2017.

the cause was taken up by Igor Sechin, the leading figure in the conservative-security bloc.[58] Moscow's response, as in 2008, turned into offensive action, including the takeover of Crimea and the probing of Ukrainian weakness in the Donbas, 'Novorossiya' and beyond. The 'hybrid' military campaign in Crimea was complemented by a referendum on 16 March 2014 which asked the Crimean people whether they wanted to join Russia as a federal subject, or whether they wanted to restore the 1992 constitution and thus remain as part of Ukraine under new terms. Maintaining the status quo was not on offer. The official figure of 83.1 per cent turnout is disputed by observers, and the more realistic figure is around 66 per cent.[59] The official result states that 96.77 per cent voted to join Russia, while 2.51 per cent voted for restoration of the 1992 constitution. Even if exaggerated, the overwhelming majority of the population was undoubtedly in favour of joining Russia. On 18 March Putin delivered a triumphal speech in the Kremlin, and documents were signed bringing Crimea into the Russian Federation as two subjects: the city of Sevastopol and the Republic of Crimea.

The crisis saw a shift in Russian identity discourse away from the state to the nation, and the Russian state was presented as the champion of Russians abroad. The boundaries between Russia and Ukraine were blurred as Putin repeatedly insisted that the two were essentially one people. The high point of this ethnicised discourse, which served to justify irredentist claims to Crimea, was Putin's 18 March speech, in which the word '*Russkii*' was mentioned twenty-nine times.[60] He described the Russian people as 'the largest divided people in the world', and talked of Russia being 'robbed' of Crimea when the Soviet Union disintegrated. He portrayed the coming together of Russia and Crimea as similar to German reunification in 1990.[61] The 'Russian world' (*Russki Mir*) identity discourse, based on a common language, culture and shared past, encountered resistance in Ukraine since it was incompatible not only with monist representations of Ukrainian identity, but even with pluralist interpretations.[62] At the same time, the attempt to apply international law to justify Russia's actions is questionable.[63] Nevertheless, Crimea's

[58] Zygar, *All the Kremlin's Men*, p. 186.

[59] Interview in October 2015 with a leading pollster, the head of one of the polling agencies contracted to gauge the mood in Crimea before the referendum.

[60] Yuri Teper, 'Official Russian Identity Discourse in Light of the Annexation of Crimea: National or Imperial?', *Post-Soviet Affairs*, Vol. 32, No. 4, 2015, p. 385.

[61] Putin, 'Address', 18 March 2014.

[62] Cf. Valentina Feklyunina, 'Soft Power and Identity: Russia, Ukraine and the "Russian World(s)"', *European Journal of International Relations*, Vol. 22, No. 4, 2016, pp. 773–96.

[63] Allison, 'Russian "Deniable" Intervention'.

return can legitimately be considered a 'democratic secession', since the overwhelming majority of the population (as later independent opinion polls confirmed) favoured being part of Russia; although the view that it represents an 'imperial annexation' is justified to the degree that it lacked agreement with the country from which the territory seceded.

Russia's goals were straightforward but only partially achieved. First, Crimea was forced out of Ukrainian jurisdiction, thus satisfying the aspirations of a large proportion (although by far not all) of the peninsula's population, as well as a powerful strand of Russian patriotic opinion. Russian language, culture and identity would now be preserved on the territory, free of the threat of the Ukrainian nationalising state. This pressure had been mitigated by extensive Crimean autonomy since the 1990s, but the monist nationalism and its militarised forms triumphant in the Maidan was certainly perceived as a threat, hence the rapid sealing off of the territory and the precipitate referendum and secession/annexation. Russian, Ukrainian and Tatar were immediately granted the status of official languages, but elements of the Ukrainian and Tatar populations remain disgruntled. Their concerns can only be allayed by ensuring that their rights are fully protected. Second, the goal of Sevastopol remaining the home port for the Black Sea Fleet was achieved in its entirety. This was followed by the modernisation of its composition, something prohibited by the previous leasing arrangements. The revitalised Black Sea Fleet now allows Russia to project its power not only in the Black Sea but in the Mediterranean as a whole.

Russia's other actions met with far less success. From April 2014 attention focused on the Donbas (Donetsk and Lugansk regions), where an insurgency gathered pace. The idea of creating some sort of pro-Russian entity called Novorossiya was always fanciful, overestimating the degree of separatist sentiment in the eastern part of Ukraine. The protest movement against the new Kiev authorities had solid local backing, but the initial aim was autonomy rather than separation. Russia endorsed this goal, but its advocacy of federalisation did not help the cause of the constitutional devolution and sharing of power. When the idea of federalisation in the Donbas turned into separatist slogans, followed soon after by an armed insurgency, covertly assisted by activists and some state bodies in Russia, then the new Kiev authorities not only resisted such moves but also launched what they called an 'Anti-Terrorist Operation', targeting its disgruntled citizens in the region. Genuine federalisation would automatically represent the triumph of the pluralist representation of Ukrainian statehood, and by that measure it was inevitably opposed by monists, who would have to share power with a newly embedded pluralism and modify narrow nationalist aspirations. This was not something that the monists were ready to do, especially when they felt empowered by their triumph in the Maidan and by the victory of an oligarch, Petro Poroshenko, sympathetic to their cause in the 25 May presidential election. In June the new administration finally signed the AA with the EU, although its implementation was phased.

Putin acted decisively in Crimea, but he was less resolute in the Donbas. He tried to stop the referendums on the independence of Donetsk and Lugansk in May, and then refused to accept the result. Russian military support for the insurgents was always far less than they sought, except at times when they were in danger of suffering military defeats, and he did not subscribe to the exaggerated nationalist discourse on the issue.[64] The Kremlin proffered support at critical moments, but otherwise Russian policy was subordinate to political considerations and the larger problem of Russia's relations with the international community.[65] The inadvertent shooting down of Malaysia Airlines flight MH17 on 17 July on its way from Amsterdam to Kuala Lumpur, with the loss of all 298 on board (193 of whom were Dutch, forty-three Malaysian and twenty-seven Australian), proved a rupture point for relations with the Atlantic powers. Following the tragedy the idea was mooted to send up to 9,000 combat troops to eastern Ukraine, but the plan was aborted when Germany refused to participate either directly or indirectly.[66] Instead, a range of sanctions was imposed on Russia. The war peaked in August 2014, when the insurgent forces were on the brink of defeat. Russian support led to a crushing Ukrainian defeat at the battle of Ilovaisk towards the end of the month, followed by the Minsk-1 peace deal. Russia later supported the assault on Debaltsevo, leading to the Minsk-2 peace deal of 15 February 2015. The Normandy Four (Russia, Ukraine, France and Germany) framework, established in June 2014, remains in place to manage the crisis.

From an early point, Russia sought to find a way to extricate itself from the imbroglio with minimum damage to its reputation as a loyal patron and without appearing to capitulate to Western demands. Nationalists were disappointed by Putin's refusal to endorse their ideological view of Russian policy.[67] Although Putin was allegedly pursuing a nationalistic

---

[64] Marlene Laruelle, 'The Three Colors of Novorossiya, or the Russian Nationalist Mythmaking of the Ukrainian Crisis', *Post-Soviet Affairs*, Vol. 32, No. 1, 2015, pp. 55–74.

[65] Teper, 'Official Russian Identity Discourse'.

[66] John Helmer, 'The Obama Shoe-Banging Moment on the Ukraine Front: Dutch and Australian Troops were Planning to Start War with Russia after MH17 was Shot Down', 15 June 2016, https://newcoldwar.org/obama-shoe-banging-moment-ukrainian-front-dutch-australian-troops-planning-start-war-russia-mh17-shot/, last accessed 26 May 2017.

[67] Pål Kolstø, 'Crimea vs. Donbas: How Putin Won Russian Nationalist Support – and Lost it Again', *Slavic Review*, Vol. 75, No. 3, Fall, 2016, pp. 702–25. See also Pål Kolstø and Helge Blakkisrud (eds.), *The New Russian Nationalism: Imperialism, Ethnicity and Authoritarianism 2000–2015* (Edinburgh, Edinburgh University Press, 2016).

foreign policy, his concern to maintain regime autonomy meant that he could not allow Russian nationalists to take ownership of it. The Putinite style of governance allowed the Kremlin to exploit the power of Russian nationalism, and this was reflected in Putin's sky-high popularity ratings following the annexation of Crimea, but could not allow nationalists a place in the power system. By 2016 the genie of Russian nationalism was firmly back in the bottle, and the regime regained its autonomy from social forces.

A further Russian goal was to assert a set of institutional choices, above all to prevent NATO membership. Here the result was mixed. Although it is unlikely that Ukraine will be joining the alliance any time soon, the crisis galvanised the organisation and thus increased the threat potential and military capacity of the organisation (see Chapter 7). Equally, the signing of the AA brought Ukraine into the Atlantic security system and definitively foreclosed membership of the EEU. Finally, Russia's long-standing ambition to be treated as an equal in the world system exposed the flaws in the system itself. America quickly mobilised against Russia, and convinced the EU to maintain solidarity in imposing sanctions. Russia was excluded from the G8, and the planned summit in Sochi was cancelled and instead a smaller G7 meeting took place in London. The Russian delegation in PACE was suspended, and the country's quest for membership of the OECD was indefinitely delayed. Talks on a new Russian-EU visa regime as well as on the new Basic Agreement to replace the PCA, which had made little progress since 2007, were frozen.

From Russia's perspective, the reunification of Crimea and intervention in eastern Ukraine were forced moves provoked by the overthrow of a legitimately elected government.[68] Yanukovych had never been a particular friend of Russia, although he represented a tendency in Ukrainian politics that sought to accommodate Russian interests. His ouster not only threatened Putin's concept of legitimism in the post-Soviet space, opposing so-called 'colour revolutions' and supporting incumbent leaders, but also had a strategic aspect, above all Sevastopol. This is why Mearsheimer argues that the West was responsible for the crisis, with EU enlargement acting as the stalking horse for future NATO expansion.[69] Trenin notes that '[t]he EU failed to appreciate the geopolitical, economic and even psychological importance of Ukraine to the Russian leadership', and had been negligent in failing to take into account the wider consideration of its EaP. At the crucial moment the EU 'failed to

---

[68] For a discussion of Russian motives, see Elizabeth A. Wood, William E. Pomeranz, E. Wayne Merry and Maxim Trudolyubov, *Roots of Russia's War in Ukraine* (Washington, Woodrow Wilson Center Press with Columbia University Press, 2015).

[69] Mearsheimer, 'Why the Ukraine Crisis is the West's Fault'.

manage a soft landing for the Yanukovych regime and the ensuing power transfer, and thus the EU was exposed as an irrelevant and – in the Kremlin's view – an untrustworthy actor'.[70] Yanukovych's ouster exacerbated internal divisions and in the end destroyed the crucial economic and social relationship between Russia and Ukraine.[71] This was a tragedy for Europe, for Russia, and above all Ukraine, provoked by the 'zero-sum policies pursued by Russia, the US and the EU'.[72]

[70] Dmitri Trenin, *Should We Fear Russia?* (Cambridge, Polity, 2016), pp. 70–1.
[71] For an early study of the tensions, see Anatol Lieven, *Ukraine and Russia: A Fraternal Rivalry* (Washington, US Institute of Peace Press, 1999).
[72] Sam Charap and Timothy Colton, *Everyone Loses: The Ukraine Crisis and the Ruinous Contest for Post-Soviet Eurasia* (London, Routledge/Adelphi, 2016), p. 23 and *passim*.

6   After the Cold Peace

The quarter-century of the cold peace after 1989 had resolved none of the fundamental issues of European security and global affairs. As far as the 'victors' were concerned, there was not a problem. The despotic system of European communism had dissolved and its associated geopolitical power system had disintegrated, allowing the former 'captive nations' to exercise their sovereign choice to align with the Atlantic community, while extending the sphere of freedom and democracy. If Russia did not like this, then that was its problem, and reflected its failure to complete its democratic transformation. Russia's ill-founded and intemperate claims to be a 'great power', a status warranted neither by its economic weight nor its social power, fostered the illusion of co-responsibility for the management of world affairs and challenged American primacy. Russia's economic and political system did not deserve recognition as equivalent to those of the Historic West, and it would be morally wrong to grant Russia a status which threatened to undermine the achievements of the post-war liberal order. On the other side, Russian attempts to expand the post-Cold War security and political community to create a 'Greater West' and a transformed Greater Europe were stymied. The Kremlin's perception that the country's strategic space for independent development was blocked generated a rhetoric in favour of multipolarity and pluralism that by the mid-2000s was translated into a more assertive policy of resistance. It is clear that 'Russia has not only broken out of the post-Cold War order in its former neighbourhood but challenged that order elsewhere'.[1] Incommensurate views of European order meant that the continent entered a twenty-five years' crisis, which after 2014 turned from a cold peace into something akin to a 'new Cold War'. Incompatible narratives gave way to competing views of global order, and Europe and the world entered a new period of confrontation.

[1] Trenin, *Should We Fear Russia?*, p. vi.

Global Shifts and Not a New Cold War

The roots of the crisis lie in the structure of international politics established in the 1990s. Unlike the rapid political rehabilitation of France after the Napoleonic wars and the reconstruction of Germany after 1945, the former enemy after 1989 was not adequately integrated into the post-conflict order. The brute fact of this failure was recognised from the very beginning, and remains a nagging sore in Europe, with deleterious global implications. The enlargement of NATO to fill a perceived security vacuum in Central and Eastern Europe created the security threat that it was designed to avert. Bill Clinton's presidency assumed that Russia would remain weak; and if not weak then reformed in such a way that it would assent to American hegemony. Instead, Russia under Putin became both strong and unwilling to subordinate itself to American geostrategic imperatives. Russia challenged US geopolitical ambitions in the post-Soviet space and chafed at what it perceived to be the silken threads of soft containment, while the US refused to accept that Russia had any inalienable rights in its neighbourhood and stymied any Russian moves to become a regional power, all the while insisting that spheres of influence were 'anachronistic and unconscionable'.[2] On that basis, Western leaders 'steadfastly refused to concede Moscow even a limited sphere of influence or security zone along its borders'. This was a bipartisan policy in the US, accompanied by talk of 'Russian aggression'; countered by the view that 'geography matters': 'Smart great powers show a decent respect for the security zones and spheres of influence of other great powers.'[3] From this perspective, the idea of spheres of influence is not simply a great power instrument to denigrate the sovereignty of others, but (as the English School would argue) has a normative core that helps regulate inter-state relations.[4]

In practice, the 'Russian sphere of influence' concerned mostly symbolic rather than actual influence. Given Russia's severe 'post-imperial trauma', symbolism was important. Chinese penetration of Central Asia should have worried Russia more than the EU's advance into the east European borderlands, but because Chinese policies were embedded in a substantive multilateral framework, its actions were communicated to ensure that Moscow was not subject to nasty surprises. Chinese sensitivity to Russian cultural, diplomatic and security concerns encouraged Moscow to view

---

[2] Lo, *Russia and the New World Disorder*, p. 178.

[3] Ted Galen Carpenter, 'NATO Must Stop Crowding Russia', *The National Interest*, 15 June 2016, http://nationalinterest.org/blog/the-skeptics/nato-must-stop-crowding-russia-16607, last accessed 26 May 2017.

[4] Susanna Hast, *Spheres of Influence in International Relations: History, Theory and Politics* (Farnham, Ashgate, 2014).

Chinese activities as benign.[5] Faced by two very contrasting cultures of international power, the Chinese and the Atlantic, Moscow firmly plumped for the former. After 1989 the Atlantic security system worked to prevent the resurgence of great power politics, with the endless shifting alliances and balancing that brought the world to war in 1914. However, the unintended consequence was that the Cold War system was perpetuated. Unable to transcend the logic of the Cold War or to establish an inclusive multilateral framework (such as a beefed up OSCE or some sort of 'union of Europe'), the continent once again became the victim of 'great power' bloc rivalry, with NATO and its allies ranged against Russia and its anti-hegemonic allies.[6]

Russia hankered after the system established after the Napoleonic wars. As the Valdai Club put it in its briefing document for the 12th session in 2015, '[t]he Congress of Vienna remained in session for many months ... seeking a new order for the continent's development. Heads of state and diplomats sought to create a system of international relations, which could manage the conflicts that arise inevitably between major states, while avoiding head-on collisions and minimising damage'.[7] By contrast, after 1989 the aim was to protect the states and their sovereignty from outside forces while establishing a mechanism for conflict resolution within the system. Instead of which, the interests of certain countries were negated leading to a 'Hobbesian moment': 'Attempts to build relations on ideological, rather than pragmatic foundations invariably lead to a dead end of violent escalation. Foreign policy loses its way and wars are the result.'[8] The claim of Western double standards underlies Russia's shift towards a neo-revisionist stance. The US acted as both the cornerstone of the liberal trading order and the institutions of liberal internationalism that together represent the 'globalisation' that triumphed after 1989; but at the same time the US is at the centre of a vast geopolitical power system and military-industrial complex whose power is unprecedented in world history. The tension between the two gives rise, in the Russian view, to an endless chain of 'double standards'. This is the America that, according to Russian critics, subverts its own defence of liberal institutionalism and the rules-based world order. The exercise of

---

[5] Kortunov, 'How Not to Talk with Russia'.
[6] Mearsheimer, *Tragedy of Great Power Politics*.
[7] *War and Peace in the 21st Century: A New International Balance as the Guarantee of Stability*, Materials for Discussion at the 12th Annual Meeting of the Valdai Discussion Club, Sochi, 19–22 October 2015, p. 1. The final report was published as *War and Peace in the 21st Century: International Stability and Balance of the New Type*, Valdai Discussion Club Report, January 2016, http://valdaiclub.com/publications/reports/international-stability-and-balance-of-the-new-type/, last accessed 26 May 2017.
[8] *War and Peace in the 21st Century*, Valdai Discussion Club Report, p. 2.

realist power strategies undermines the values of economic globalisation and liberal universalism.

The ideology of globalisation suggested that intensified economic and technological interdependence would render old-fashioned inter-state warfare redundant. This revived the idea advanced by Norman Angell in 1909 in his *The Great Illusion* that war between the industrial powers would be futile and economically disruptive, although he did not argue that such conflict was impossible. Following the end of the Cold War, the highly contested idea of the 'democratic peace' went further to argue that *democratic* states do not go to war with each other; an argument as we have seen that hinges on what one defines as a democratic state. A range of theories argue that in one way or another classical geopolitics and the realist appreciation of world politics as the endless struggle for power, status and recognition has given way to a liberal international order in which institutions mediate conflict and trade tempers national rivalries. In this scheme, the geopolitical argument that the international system is driven by the hard-headed power-maximisation strategies of sovereign states is anachronistic and dangerous. The idea of interdependence posits that as the economic links intensify, a new political community is forged. This idea of complex interdependence did not appear to apply to Russia's relationship with the EU, or even to integration into the global economy.

The post-Cold War peace order in Europe was fragile, exclusive and unsustainable. Perversely, this generated incentives to reinforce the Atlantic system. Russia's complaints served only to demonstrate the country's failure to transform, justifying the policies that aroused Russia's complaints. This axiological escalation served only to add a political dimension to the mounting security dilemma. The more the Historical West advanced towards Russia and its neighbourhood, the more the Russian leadership feared 'regime change', and responded with repressive and manipulative political strategies that only reinforced the pathologies that required political reform in the first place. Transdemocratic pressure for political change inhibited evolutionary political reform. The crisis of the inter-war years, in which the peace and normative agendas were accompanied by the punitive dynamic of the Treaty of Versailles had lasted twenty years, but the cold peace after 1989 lasted twenty-five.[9] As early as 2000 Gorbachev noted, '[a]pparently, the West is incapable of dealing in a reasonable way with the results of the new thinking that freed the world from bloc politics and total confrontation'.[10]

---

[9] Sakwa, '"New Cold War"'.

[10] Mikhail Gorbachev and Daisaku Ikeda, *Moral Lessons of the Twentieth Century: Gorbachev and Ikeda on Buddhism and Communism* (London: I. B. Tauris, 2005), p. 147.

This prompted him to endorse President Vladimir Putin's policies in 2014, including 'reunification' with Crimea, signalling the end of the era of optimism born of perestroika in the late 1980s. The Atlantic institutions enlarged to encompass the in-between countries eager to join, but this reinstated a bloc dynamic in which a frontier was restored. Europe 'whole and free' was built without Russia, which meant that the continent was neither whole nor free.

Relations between Russia and the Atlantic community had long been deteriorating, but in 2014 the gloves came off and the two sides squared up against each in a manner reminiscent of the worst periods in their history of mutual estrangement. Russia once again, as in the Cold War years, came to represent a type of universal Klingon Empire, the embodiment of all evil but lacking defined characteristics other than evil itself. The evil was generic and universal, and thus not susceptible to rational examination.[11] By contrast, the Historical West presented itself as the United Federation of Planets, exuding a benign rationalism and defence of international order, where its expansive ambitions were portrayed as progressive and rule-bound. In other words, two existential ontologies confronted each other, and in the absence of a common language and mutual rationalities, the gulf widened.

The Ukrainian crisis exposed the tensions in the post-Cold War international system. As Fyodor Lukyanov notes, 'Russian-American relations have actually passed into the confrontation mode. Moscow and Washington again perceive each other as straight-out opponents, and do not hide this fact'.[12] Russia was no longer regarded as a partner for NATO but its potential enemy. Trenin argues that '[t]he Ukraine crisis has ended the era of post-Cold War engagement, which failed to culminate in integration between the West and Russia. In a stunning reversal, the crisis has opened up a period of intense geopolitical competition, rivalry, and even confrontation between Moscow and Washington, but also between Moscow and Brussels.' The site of the 'intensifying competition' was the countries in between, with '[t]he revolutionary coup in Kiev, supported by Washington, ... interpreted in Moscow as a prelude to Ukraine's eventual accession to NATO', to which Putin 'responded with his own coup in Crimea'. He noted that '[t]he "gray" buffer zone between Europe and Russia, which has existed ever since the breakup of

---

[11] Cf. Stefan Rossbach, *Gnostic Wars: The Cold War in the Context of a History of Western Spirituality* (Edinburgh, Edinburgh University Press, 1999).

[12] Fedor Luk'yanov, 'Nepovtorimyi ustoichivyi dukh', *Rossiiskaya gazeta*, 14 May 2014, www.globalaffairs.ru/redcol/Nepovtorimyi-ustoichivyi-dukh-16635, last accessed 30 May 2017.

the Soviet Union, is unravelling'.[13] The struggle was, he noted, the first open great power clash since the end of the Cold War. In this, Europe was both an actor as well as America's ally; and it was also the site of a conflict that was peripheral to America's core interests. Europe's inability to prevent and regulate conflicts on its territory brought America back at the time when it had been 'pivoting' to Asia.

At the 2016 Munich Security Conference the Russian prime minister, Medvedev, was stark in his assessment: 'Speaking bluntly, we are rapidly sliding into a new Cold War. Russia is presented as well-nigh the biggest threat to NATO, Europe, America and other countries ... They show frightening films about Russia provoking a nuclear war. I am confused: is this 2016 or 1962?'[14] Russian intervention in Syria from September 2015 demonstrated military muscle to reinforce the Russian argument that it was a great power that should be recognised by the West and consulted by the US in dealing with global issues. Interpreted by some in the West as a threat, Medvedev's comment was in keeping with Moscow's long-standing appeal for cooperation and negotiation. Critics, however, like Stefan Meister argue that 'discussion of the possibility of a new Cold War with Russia is not only misleading, but also dangerous. It gives the impression – both to Western "realists" and Russian leaders – that Moscow and the West could cooperate in a transactional way now as they did then; in other words: that a deal with Moscow is possible.' Instead, Meister stresses that Putin's regime was incomparably weaker than its Soviet predecessor, and argued that '[i]t is a crony regime, lacking any long-term strategy except staying in power'. He stressed the high costs for Russia of imitating global power, which only weakened the country, and 'the weaker Russia becomes, the more aggressively its leadership will act to distract from its failures'. He repeated the argument of Russia's liberal opposition that no deal was possible with the regime, since '[f]or Putin there are no rules except the power of the strongest'. Meister insisted that no balance of power is possible in the current international order, especially since Russia had 'learned to use Western vulnerabilities to undermine the credibility of Western media, politics, and governance'. In short, '[t]o accept the paradigm of the Cold War would mean giving Russia a role in international politics that it cannot fill and assuming it is possible to negotiate

---

[13] Dmitri Trenin, 'Get Ready World: The US-Russian Rivalry is Back', 28 May 2014, www .carnegie.ru/2014/05/28/get-ready-world-u.s.-russian-rivalry-is-back/hbvg, last accessed 26 May 2017.

[14] 'Vystuplenie Dmitriya Medvedeva na panel'noi diskussi', Munich Security Conference, 13 February 2016, http://government.ru/news/21784/, last accessed 30 May 2017.

with this Russian leadership'. The policy response was for the West to strengthen its resilience in domestic policy and military terms.[15]

Such arguments reflect mainstream Atlanticist positions. The terms used to describe the new era of confrontation are as contentious as its character. In a sober analysis from a very different perspective, Andrew Monaghan argues that the use of the term 'New Cold War' is anachronistic and perverse, and limits discussion to the functioning of the previous era rather than providing an adequate analysis of the factors provoking the failures of the present.[16] The differences between the present confrontation and the Cold War are clear: there are no massive armies confronting each other across a fortified 'iron curtain'; there is no ideological confrontation on a global scale; and on certain issues, such as the war on terror, there are elements of cooperation. Yet, the Cold War system has been reproduced: nuclear forces operating the MAD deterrence strategy; escalating military budgets, notably in Russia and the US; proxy conflicts in the Middle East and elsewhere; and a virulent propaganda war. The institutional and ideational framework of the Cold War were never dismantled and now sprang back into life, including new dividing lines across Europe, the remilitarisation of relations, a renewed logic of nuclear escalation, as well as the coarsening of public discourse and mutual demonisation.

Nonetheless, all this does not amount to a new Cold War. The term is anachronistic and misleading, imposing an outdated pattern on contemporary international politics that fails to incorporate new actors and new dynamics. Looked at from a parochial European angle and in the frame of US–Russian relations, then undoubtedly many of the elements of the old Cold War have been revived, but the term does not reflect the character of the international system today. The emphasis on arms control, as witnessed in the reset, was certainly reminiscent of traditional issues, and the confrontation between NATO and Russia along a line dividing Europe is taken from the Cold War handbook. In other words, elements of a new Cold War have been revived, but are no longer determinative but part of a changed dynamic of contestation between different representations of world order. At the vertical level, the struggle to strengthen the institutions of international society remains part of the agenda. At the end of the Cold War there was a widespread belief that the UN would finally be able to function as a type of global parliament based on dialogue and

---

[15] Stefan Meister, 'In Search of Lost Time: Moscow's Warnings of a "New Cold War" Are Out of Sync with Today's Realities', *Berlin Policy Journal*, 11 March 2016, http://berlin policyjournal.com/in-search-of-lost-time/, last accessed 30 May 2017.
[16] Andrew Monaghan, *A 'New Cold War'? Abusing History, Misunderstanding Russia* (London, Chatham House Research Paper, May 2015).

consensus. However, unipolarity was no more conducive than bipolarity to granting autonomy to supra-national bodies. The great powers stubbornly defended their prerogatives, and the greatest power most of all.

Chapter 2 argued that the international system today is a two-level system, in which antagonism between the US-led liberal international order and the nascent anti-hegemonic bloc of Russia, China and allies challenges the practices but not the principles of the first world order, while remaining committed to the secondary institutions of international society. The struggle between hegemons and subalterns creates a complex and shifting landscape in international politics, with no front lines and no clear ideological divisions. Russia and China aspire to be part of the hegemonic coalition, but on conditions of equality, but today are increasingly creating parallel non-Western institutions. Looked at from the perspective of Asia, talk of a new Cold War appears tragically inappropriate, and reflects Western hegemony over the discourse of international politics reminiscent of the classic era of colonialism.[17] Looked at from a global perspective, the old bipolar structure of the Cold War has not been restored and instead a polycentric system has emerged, with points of concentration such as the old-established Atlantic system and its allies and a rising constellation of anti-hegemonic powers, united as much in their distaste for hegemony itself as by opposition to the hegemony of the liberal international order. In this framework, elements of a new Cold War have emerged in Europe and in US–Russian relations, but only as part of the larger struggle between representations of global order.

In this struggle, Russia is far from isolated and at the heart of alternative strategies and organisations. The potential for reconciliation with the Historic West at the end of the Cold War had been missed. This was not the first time. Following the death of Stalin on 5 March 1953, the new collective leadership of Khrushchev, Grigory Malenkov and Lavrenty Beria (before he was liquidated by his colleagues), very quickly changed direction, calling off the anti-Jewish campaign, releasing a million

---

[17] This came out clearly in the keynote address of Ambassador Zhang Deguang, secretary-general of the SCO, to the 7th East Asian Conference on Slavic-Eurasian Studies in Shanghai on 24 September 2016, personal notes. Zhang was scathing in his criticism of the hegemonic powers, arguing that globalisation has led to the emergence of new poles and that power relationships in Asia have changed. In his view, the US was the world's last hegemon and there would not be another, not China nor Russia, and instead a new type of international relations would emerge. He argued that in Europe the US's primary aim was to constrain Russia and to limit its power and at the same time to disrupt relations between the former Soviet states. It was NATO's advance that provoked the Ukraine crisis, leading to a Russian response. On Crimea, the Chinese position was clear: 'We look at the issue in a comprehensive and historical manner.' US policy was 'to contain and reduce Russia', which was not a sustainable policy and provoked Russia's revolt.

prisoners, curtailing the powers of the security apparatus, and, above all, signalling to the West that the Soviet Union wanted to improve relations. Winston Churchill, in the dying days of his leadership, wrote to the newly installed US president, Dwight Eisenhower, urging the convocation of a summit with the new Soviet leadership. The secretary of state, John Foster Dulles, living up to his hard-line reputation, was categorically opposed, considering the Soviet Union the embodiment of evil and the greatest threat to Western civilisation in a thousand years. In the few months between Stalin's death and the Berlin uprising of June 1953 the opportunity of moving beyond the Cold War was missed, and for over three decades a generation suffered in its toils.[18]

The mismanaged Iraq invasion of 2003 will loom large in any discussion of post-Cold War international politics. Mearsheimer argues that while the Iraq disaster 'killed hundreds of thousands, has cost trillions of dollars and has unleashed serious problems for the Mideast region in general while allowing the rise of ISIS', in 'realistic foreign policy terms' it was not a catastrophic event for the US, which was hardly damaged by the fiasco apart from in financial and reputational terms. In his opinion there was a far greater disaster in the making, 'that is, the total mismanagement of the relationship with Russia ever since the downfall of communism'. He considered the drive by Washington democracy promoters to push Ukraine into the Western economic and political sphere a major miscalculation, since they failed to realise or did not care that whatever happens in Kiev is a vital interest to Moscow.[19] In response, sanctions were imposed on Russia, but from the offensive realist perspective, this only exacerbated the problem to which they were posited as the solution.

Russia adjusted to the harder containment measures. From the Kremlin's perspective, it was responding to attempts to tie it down and box it in. From the West's perspective, Russia had become a 'rogue' state, flouting international law by intervening in a neighbouring state and seizing its territory, and supporting a proxy war. The Russian view is that it was acting defensively against Western states, which had launched an illegal war in Iraq, recognised Kosovo, and then intervened in Syria without the permission of the legitimate government. It appeared perverse for Western leaders to become apoplectic when the sovereignty of Ukraine was threatened, whereas they acted with supreme disregard for international law when it came to the Middle East. Israel's annexation of the Golan Heights in 1981 and its settlements in the occupied West Bank

[18] Joshua Rubenstein, *The Last Days of Stalin* (London and New Haven, Yale University Press, 2016).
[19] Reported by Philip Giraldi, 'How the World Ends', *The Unz Review*, 24 May 2016, www.unz.com/article/how-the-world-ends/, last accessed 26 May 2017.

flouted numerous UN resolutions, yet no sanctions were imposed on the country. Kosovo's unilateral declaration of independence took place without even the pretence of a referendum but was nevertheless supported by the US, even though it ran against the established practices defending the territorial integrity of states. There may well be good historical and humanitarian reasons to support Israel and Kosovo, but in terms of international law, the policies are questionable.

An important part of the current clash is the power to decide what is legal and illegal, and in that struggle Russia has few instruments. The subaltern combination of Russia and China is precisely an attempt to challenge the prerogatives of the hegemonic power system to decide. In Schmittean terms, they wish to wrest the power of determining the exception from the dominant powers. The struggle also takes place in the cultural realm. Russia's media offensive, including the use of RT (formerly Russia Today) and other 'soft power' tools, could at most be of marginal benefit in an international system in which power is distributed so unevenly. Already in 2007 Moscow established the *Russkii Mir* (Russian World) foundation, similar to the British Council or China's Confucius Institutes, to advance Russia's language and culture, and it now has some 100 branches globally. Equally, the Rossotrudnichestvo agency focuses on public diplomacy in the spheres of science and culture, and its various offices across the world work closely with local Russian embassies, news agencies and cultural centres. These 'soft power' agencies are useful in cultural terms, but only Russia's permanent membership of the UNSC gives it veto powers in managing international politics. Not surprisingly, critics began to question Russia's eligibility, even though the US had long been critical of the UN as one of the few international society institutions that can hold it to account.

For Karaganov, America launched its policy of containing Russia in 2012 when it realised 'that Russia would not, as they had hoped, join the mainstream of general Western policy'. This subsequently became clear in the high level of symbolic violence directed against Russia: 'The flow of misinformation and at times outright slander that dominated the Western media in the run-up to the Winter Olympic Games in Sochi [in February 2014] was able to convince even the very last of the doubters that such a turn-round existed. So to some extent it seems to me that Russia's actions, including during the Ukrainian events, were a pre-emptive strike.' Russia prepared for a new confrontation, since it had become 'obvious that the policy of appeasement or simple co-operation had not borne any positive fruits. The West had continued its expansion into the zones of Russian interests, and had expanded its zone of influence and control.' The policy, in Karaganov's view, was not so much driven by Obama personally, whose main concern was the modernisation of

America, but 'the traditional foreign policy establishment, in which people from the 1990s predominate, who are used to seeing Russia on its knees and begging. They perceive the existence of another Russia as a personal humiliation and insult.' For them the 'task was not simply containing Russia but seems to be aimed at regime change'.[20]

For European politicians the challenge was rather different, 'to demonstrate that the European project was developing and not degenerating', in other words, that after the long economic crisis, Europe was 'alive and still useful to someone'. For both the Americans and the Europeans the Ukrainian crisis was an opportunity to punish Russia for its successful foreign policy activism in 2013, notably in brokering the chemical weapons deal in Syria. Russia's 'tough, skilful and determined foreign policy' allowed 'Russia's weight in the world to exceed its real capacities, particularly in the economic sphere, many times over. We had already to some extent started almost to compete with America.' Thus the Ukraine events exposed a more profound rupture: 'It is that Russia no longer wants to play by the rules previously suggested to it, which I call a "Versailles policy in velvet gloves"', the policy that had humiliated Germany after the First World War and prepared the way for the second. 'The same policy, albeit in a milder form, has unfortunately been conducted in relation to Russia'. Karaganov looked forward to the signing of the long-delayed treaty with the EU that would ultimately allow the world to gain a third pillar: 'A two-pillar system based on the China-America axis is by definition unstable.'[21] This is the Greater European vision to unify the EU and the other lands in between. This is the continentalism that had originally inspired European integration, and the project's collapse precipitated the new confrontation.

The Ukraine crisis ushered in a new period of Russo-American rivalry, even confrontation. Although superficially reminiscent of the Cold War, there are important differences. As Trenin notes,

Today's situation has a values component to it but is not nearly as focused on ideology as the conflict between communism and liberal democracy was. It has a traditional military dimension too, but this aspect is not – as yet – dominant. The current crisis has global implications, but, in and of itself, it is not central to the global system. Most importantly, unlike the Cold war, the present crisis is not the organizing principle of either world politics or even the foreign policies of the conflict's main contestants, particularly that of the United States.[22]

---

[20] In Evgenii Shestakov, 'Mir stanovitsya vse menee prozapadnym', *Rossiiskaya gazeta*, No. 93, 24 April 2014, p. 10.

[21] Shestakov, 'Mir stanovitsya'.

[22] Dmitri Trenin, 'The Ukraine Crisis and the Resumption of Great-Power Rivalry', Carnegie Moscow Centre, 9 July 2014, http://carnegie.ru/2014/07/09/ukraine-crisis-and-resumption-of-great-power-rivalry/hfgs, last accessed 26 May 2017.

The closest historical analogy in his view was the 'Great Game' rivalry between the British Empire and Russia in the nineteenth century; rumbling away in the background but mostly not at the centre of the foreign policy of either state. As for the new European crisis, its severity came as a surprise to all the main actors. Ukraine's precipitate movement towards 'Europe' meant that both the country and the continent lost balance. America's support for regime change in Ukraine was interpreted as a direct challenge, and Putin's dramatic moves surprised the world. Russia's response was precipitated by events in Ukraine, but was the culmination of decades of frustration at its strategic impasse and soft containment.

Russia's actions ended the indeterminacy of the cold peace. Everything was now clear, and the illusions were over. There would be no expanded and inclusive new West, and neither would there be a Greater Europe. Russia had harboured hopes that the EU offered a way of mediating differences with the Historical West. Negotiations to renew the ten-year PCA were inconclusive and exposed the weak foundations on which the Russo-EU partnership was based. Talks over the new Basic Agreement had long stalled, including the establishment of a visa-free regime and energy partnership. The militancy of many of the post-2004 new member states of the EU further narrowed the scope for cooperation, and ruled out trilateral mechanisms. Russia's response to the AA between the EU and Ukraine appears exaggerated, but for Russia it was an unacceptable symptom of a deeper malaise. Russia had never objected to good relations between the EU and EaP countries, but it argued that these should be mediated within the framework of some sort of Greater European framework to ensure that no country was forced to choose between Europe and Eurasia. It was just such a choice, posed in the sharpest manner possible, that precipitated the crisis of 2014.

For the West, Russia was now a 'spoiler' and its policies 'obstructive'. Russia had worked with its P5 + 1 partners (France, Germany, Russia, the UK and the US plus the EU) to achieve the Joint Comprehensive Plan of Action (JCPOA) to halt Iran's nuclear weapons programme, which was signed in July 2015. Following the nuclear deal, Russian–Iranian relations intensified. Russia finally agreed to deliver the S-300 air-defence missile systems, originally contracted in 2007 and then cancelled in 2010 by Medvedev. Economic and investment ties between the two countries deepened, but a residue of mistrust remained. In the early nineteenth century Persia had lost territory to Tsarist Russia, and the Soviet Union occupied half the country in the Second World War. Soviet support for Baghdad in the 1980–88 Iran–Iraq war, the long delay in completing the Bushehr nuclear reactor, and Russia's development of relations with

Iran's arch-enemies Israel and Saudi Arabia did not help matters.[23] Nevertheless, the two countries were effectively allied in the Syrian conflict, and Iran emerged as one of Russia's key partners.

Russia's diplomacy was less welcome when it came to Syria, since its actions were pursued independently and at cross-purposes with Western plans. Walter Mead admits that 'Westerners ... fundamentally misread what the collapse of the Soviet Union meant: the ideological triumph of liberal capitalist democracy over communism, not the obsolescence of hard power', although he accepts that 'China, Iran and Russia never bought into the geopolitical settlement that followed the Cold War'.[24] He labels Russia a 'revisionist' power, which as I have argued earlier is a category mistake. It is not that Russia rejects the 'liberal world order' in favour of geopolitics; but that the West's own geopolitics is couched in liberal language yet threatens countries seeking autonomy in the international system. As Tony Brenton, the British ambassador to Russia from 2004 to 2008, argued, Western policy was built on two false premises. The first was that 'we have to stop a revanchist Russia', on the rampage from Crimea, eastern Ukraine and then on to the Baltic republics and Poland. Instead, Russia wants 'influence, not territory', and 'the "we must stand up to Putin as we did to Hitler" line is pure schoolboy politics'. The second false premise was 'that economic sanctions can stop Russia'. He noted that sanctions had been deployed against Russia six times since the Second World War, and they never worked. Ukraine agreed to a ceasefire when it started losing the war, not because Russia changed its strategy.[25] This is not a new Cold War but something more momentous and potentially more dangerous. There are no guidelines for international behaviour in an international system in which new players and concerns are shaping the agenda.

Sanctions and Neo-containment

Sanctions have become a distinctive form of contemporary international politics. A commentary notes that '[e]conomic sanctions have become the "silver bullet" of American foreign policy over the past decade, because they're cheaper and more effective in compelling adversaries

---

[23] Mark N. Katz, 'Can Russia and Iran Still be Friends after the Nuclear Deal?, *The National Interest*, 7 July 2016, http://nationalinterest.org/feature/can-russia-iran-still-be-friends-after-the-nuclear-deal-16880, last accessed 26 May 2017.

[24] Walter Russell Mead, 'The Return of Geopolitics: The Revenge of the Revisionist Powers', *Foreign Affairs*, Vol. 93, No. 3, May–June 2014, p. 69.

[25] Tony Brenton, 'It's Time to Back away from the Russian Wolf', *Daily Telegraph*, 10 September 2014.

than traditional military power'.[26] In other words, sanctions have emerged as 'the indispensable tool of American statecraft'.[27] This represents a distinct type of 'hybrid warfare'. By 2016, sixteen UN-mandated sanctions regimes were in place, and numerous bilateral ones, including those imposed on Russia by the EU, the US and its allies. Russia had long imposed discretionary and mostly short-term sanctions on its neighbours, notably against Belarus, Georgia, Moldova and Ukraine. Western sanctions merged into a broader policy designed to constrain Russia. Ivo Daalder, the former US permanent representative to NATO, was blunt in his assessment that attempts to 'bring Russia around to a more constructive attitude' through 'political and economic engagement' was not a short-term policy: 'Now, as then, containment must be a long-term strategy, best sustained by emphasising western strengths and Russian weakness.'[28] The perverse effects have also been marked, encouraging Russia to make itself 'sanctions-proof' by insulating itself from Western financial and credit agencies, encouraging Russia and China to create alternatives, all the while damaging the European economies while not modifying Russian behaviour in the least, and indeed 'enabling Putin to further consolidate his power'.[29]

Sanctions against Russia were imposed in four waves, beginning with targeted sanctions against individuals close to Putin and those involved in the transfer of Crimea, through to a range of sectoral sanctions imposed after the downing of flight MH70 in July 2014.[30] The EU sanctions prevented Russian state banks from raising long-term loans in the EU, banned the use of dual-use technology that could be used for military purposes, prohibited future EU-Russia arms sales, and limited the sale of a wide range of oil industry equipment. In addition, access to capital markets was limited for three major state oil firms (Rosneft, Transneft and Gazprom Neft) as well as Gazprom. The EU sanctions were subject to six-monthly renewal requiring the unanimous agreement of all twenty-eight members. By spring 2016, 146 Russian, Ukrainian and Crimean citizens as well as thirty-seven organisations were on the list. They were

---

[26] David Ignatius, in the *Washington Post*, 29 March 2016, quoted by Alastair Crook, 'Silver Bullets and Neutron Bombs', *The Spokesman*, No. 132, 2016, pp. 43–8, at p. 45.

[27] F. Joseph Dresen, 'Sanctions Emerge as the Indispensable Tool of American Statecraft', Washington, Kennan Cable No. 9, 1 June 2015.

[28] Ivo Daalder, 'The Best Answer to Russian Aggression is Containment', *Financial Times*, 16 October 2016.

[29] Emma Ashford, 'Not-So-Smart Sanctions', *Foreign Affairs*, Vol. 95, No. 1, January–February 2016, p. 120.

[30] The precise timing and scope of western sanctions are listed in Sergey Aleksashenko, *Evaluating Western Sanctions on Russia* (Washington, Atlantic Council, December 2016), Appendix, pp. 20–3.

charged with undermining the territorial integrity of Ukraine, and the individuals were subject to asset freezes and travel bans. The US imposed its first round of sectoral sanctions on 16 July 2014, imposing restrictions on two banks and two energy companies, and the list was gradually extended. Overall, sectoral sanctions can be divided into three groups: financial sanctions including a ban on trading bonds and equity and a ban on loans with maturity periods over thirty days for some of Russia's largest state-controlled banks and companies; defence industry embargoes stopping arms sales and a ban on the export of dual-use technologies; and sanctions on the energy sector, including bans on exporting equipment and some services for Arctic and deep-water oil exploration or production, and for shale oil exploration.[31] By early 2017 the US had placed sanctions on 172 Russian citizens and 350 different entities.

Putin's annual presidential address to the Federal Assembly on 4 December 2014 outlined the key challenges facing Russia. It was delivered in his trademark confident manner, but could not disguise the feeling that his vaunted good luck could be running out. He forcefully asserted Russia's sovereignty and right to pursue its own path, and defended Russian policy in Ukraine. The key issue was 'inter-regionalism': how to find an adequate way for Russia and its allies to interact with the EU and the Atlantic alliance. Despite external pressures, Russia would not isolate itself, although it would have to rely more on its own resources. In a rather surprising move, he indicated that rather than intensifying state controls, the crisis would force Russia to liberalise and to develop a more dynamic small and medium business sector by removing the deadweight of the bureaucracy. He insisted that Russia would not turn back to the past for models of its future.[32]

Medvedev at this time admitted that 'the sanctions have cost our economy tens of billions of dollars', but observed that 'the European economy has lost €40 billion by terminating contracts with Russia and approving restrictive measures, and next year it will lose €50 billion. This is the price they have to pay. In other words, the sanctions don't benefit anyone ... No one needs the sanctions, and they almost never lead to a desired goal.' He warned that Russia had not yet recovered from the great recession of 2008–09, admitting that 'negative trends have been adding up in our economy for the past few years ... There were signs of crisis in the economy all along.' Medvedev described how Russia, in its Soviet

---

[31] Aleksashenko, *Evaluating Western Sanctions*, p. 4.

[32] Vladimir Putin, 'Presidential Address to the Federal Assembly', 4 December 2014, http://eng.kremlin.ru/transcripts/23341, last accessed 30 May 2017; in Russian: 'Poslanie Prezidenta Federal'nomu Sobraniyu', 4 December 2014, http://kremlin.ru/transcripts/471 73, last accessed 30 May 2017.

guise, had lived most of the twentieth century under some sort of sanctions regime. In 1925, the Soviet Union had been prohibited from making payments in gold, and in 1932 import from the USSR was banned. In the late 1940s the so-called COCOM (Coordinating Committee for Multilateral Export Controls) restrictions were imposed on the export of certain types of goods, primarily technical equipment and technology. In 1974, 'the notorious Jackson-Vanik amendment', as he termed it, was adopted, imposing trade restrictions in connection with Jewish emigration, and remained in force until 2012, long after travel freedoms had been introduced. In the 1980s and early 1990s the US pressured its European allies not to sell advanced engineering technologies to build the Urengoi-Pomary-Uzhgorod gas pipeline: 'That project simply became a target of sanctions. So, we lived the entire 20th century under periodic, constant sanctions.' He noted that since 1989 China has also been subject to a sanctions regime, but nevertheless that country, like Russia, continued to implement its developmental plans.[33]

Russia's counter-sanctions in August 2014 banned certain food imports from the EU and its allies. EU food exports to Russia at the time were worth some $13 billion annually, around 10 per cent of the value of the EU's total exports to Russia. Russian producers were encouraged to fill the gap as import substitution plans were accelerated, and alternative suppliers were sought in Latin America and elsewhere. Medvedev had long stressed the need for economic diversification, but noted 'Let's face it: the dependence on oil in our country didn't happen yesterday. It dates back to the 1970s. It was back then that we got hooked on oil exports and took advantage of high oil prices.'[34] Once again, economic diversification and reduced dependency on high commodity prices were emphasised. The overall effect of the sanctions was to reinforce the existing trends towards the securitisation of Russian political economy.[35] Sanctions intensified what was already a deteriorating economic situation. In 2015 the Russian economy declined by 3.7 per cent, industrial production shrank by 3.4 per cent, inflation remained high at 12.9 per cent, and real incomes fell for the first time in fifteen years, by 4.7 per cent, while wages fell by 9.3 per cent.[36] The thirty-day credit limit to Russian banks provoked a shortage of liquidity. Limited access to

---

[33] 'In Conversation with Dmitry Medvedev: Interview with Five Television Channels', 10 December 2014, http://government.ru/news/16036/, last accessed 30 May 2017.

[34] 'In Conversation with Dmitry Medvedev: Interview with Five Television Channels'.

[35] Richard Connolly, 'The Empire Strikes Back: Economic Statecraft and the Securitisation of Political Economy in Russia', *Europe-Asia Studies*, Vol. 68, No. 4, June 2016, pp. 750–73.

[36] Data from Rosstat, *Rossiiskaya gazeta*, 11 March 2016.

Western financial markets forced Russian companies to reduce their debt burden. According to research conducted by Citigroup, sanctions accounted for only 10 per cent of the output decline up to late 2015.[37]

At the same time, Russia's leaders travelled the globe looking for opportunities to diversify markets, particularly in the energy sphere, including Argentina and Venezuela in Latin America, and the energy-poor nations of India and Pakistan in South Asia. There were various plans to build oil and gas pipelines to the two countries. A barter programme with Iran was agreed in April 2015 for Russia to buy up to 500,000 barrels of Iranian crude per day in exchange for Russian grain, steel, construction and other equipment. In September 2016 it looked as if the relationship could assume a military dimension, with Russian warplanes using an Iranian base to attack Islamic State in Syria, but the arrangement was swiftly terminated amidst popular resentment in Iran. Iran insisted that it was an equal partner with Russia in Middle Eastern affairs, and national pride ruled out the creation of a foreign base. 'Mutual mistrust, ambitions, and fears are natural constraints that make it impossible to enter into a full-fledged alliance, but Tehran and Moscow are willing to cooperate and support each other's efforts on an ad hoc basis.'[38] Diversification in economic and political terms would not be easy.

The dramatic fall in oil prices caused the Russian economy most harm. In July 2014 oil hit a high of $115 per barrel, but by December prices collapsed to $60, and thereafter fell to a low of $30 a barrel in January 2016 before stabilising at around $55. In 2014 oil and gas revenues contributed 53 per cent to the budget, but by 2015 this had already fallen to 43 per cent. The Russian budget for 2014 required a barrel price of $100 to remain in balance, and the 2015 budget assumed an average price of $80, whereas by 2017 the budget assumed $40. The rouble's value against foreign currencies fell precipitously. Instead of burning through foreign currency reserves to keep the rouble within the permitted 9 per cent band against foreign currencies, on 10 November the Central Bank of Russia (CBR) accelerated plans to allow the rouble to float freely. The CBR had learned at least one lesson from the 2008–09 crisis, when it spent over $200 billion in an attempt to maintain the rouble's value. Nevertheless, by then the CBR had already spent $80 billion in

---

[37] Leonid Bershidsky, 'Putin Doesn't Mind Oil's Fall', Bloomberg, 26 November 2015, www.bloomberg.com/view/articles/2015–11-26/putin-doesn-t-mind-oil-s-fall, last accessed 30 May 2017.

[38] Nikolay Kozhanov, 'Russia's Foothold in Iran: Why Tehran Changed its Mind', Carnegie Moscow Centre, 5 September 2016, http://carnegie.ru/commentary/2016/09/05/russia-s-foothold-in-iran-why-tehran-changed-its-mind/j4yf, last accessed 26 May 2017.

interventions to prop up the currency. A one-point interest rate rise in early December did little to stop the decline, and on 15 December interest rates were hiked up by 6.5 percentage points from 10.5 to 17 per cent, but even this was not enough to halt the slide. The fall continued, and the rouble lost 50 per cent of its value against the dollar in 2014. As Larry Elliott put it, 'Russia has spent the past nine months fighting an economic war against the west – and Tuesday 16 December was the day the war was lost'.[39]

Trade flows decreased sharply in the areas directly affected by sanctions, although the slowdown in EU-Russia trade had begun in 2013. By 2015 agricultural exports from the EU to Russia fell by half compared to 2013, while hydrocarbon exports to the EU had fallen by 42 per cent compared to the 2012 peak. Since 2013 Russia had been importing fewer engineering goods and this now intensified, threatening long-term productivity. Investment fell sharply, with EU foreign direct investment in Russia's economy falling by 44 per cent in 2014, and Russian foreign direct investment in the EU by 21 per cent. The South Stream gas pipeline project was cancelled in December 2014, the Total-Lukoil joint venture for the development of the Bazhenov shale formation put on hold, and Arctic shelf energy development reduced. Other sectors were hardly affected, including mechanical engineering, nuclear power, chemicals and retail. There were even some benefits, since the falling rouble exchange rate provided a boost for Russian exports. Russia's total foreign debt for 2014–15 fell by over $200 billion or 30 per cent, with the net foreign debt of the Russian banking sector decreasing by $56.6 billion in 2015 compared to 2013. Sovereign debt was relatively low, and 90 per cent of Russian foreign debt was owned by corporations, suggesting a significant weakening of the investment position of Russian big business.[40]

The sanctioning countries lost $60.2 billion in export revenues from December 2013 to June 2015, with 82.2 per cent of the losses derived from items not affected by Russian counter-sanctions. The EU accounted for 76.7 per cent of the lost trade. Individually, Norway and Australia were damaged the most, losing 45 per cent of anticipated export volumes (mostly in agricultural products, hit by Russian counter-sanctions). Germany lost the most in value terms, losing over $832 million per month or 27 per cent of the total lost trade (mostly in non-embargoed

[39] Larry Elliott, 'The Day that Russia lost its Economic War against the West', *Guardian*, 17 December 2014, p. 15.
[40] Anastasia Nevskaya, 'Russia-EU Economic Relations: Assessing Two Years of Sanctions', *Russia Direct*, 16 June 2016, www.russia-direct.org/analysis/russia-eu-eco nomic-relations-assessing-two-years-sanctions, last accessed 26 May 2017.

goods), while the US accounted for just 0.4 per cent of the total trade losses.[41] The currency depreciation by the end of 2014 meant that in dollar terms Russian GDP halved, driving it down, as noted, from eighth to thirteenth place, roughly equal to Mexico and Indonesia. With the Russian economy reeling from the 'perfect storm' of drastically falling oil prices, sanctions and currency depreciation, the Obama administration threatened a fifth wave of punitive measures. The US Senate on 11 December passed the 'Ukraine Freedom Support Act 2014', which stipulated further sanctions and recognised Ukraine, alongside Georgia and Moldova, as Washington's main allies outside NATO.

Russia responded by trying to become more self-reliant through a programme of import substitution. By 2016 the economic situation had stabilised, with inflation falling below 5 per cent for the first time since 1991, and growth once again in prospect. As Waltz notes, '[i]nterdependence, like integration, depends on other conditions', and even before the sanctions Russia had behaved as realist theory predicted: 'States, if they can afford to, shy away from becoming excessively dependent on goods and resources that may be denied them in crises and wars.'[42] This became state policy after 2014, notably in defence procurement and agriculture. It also applied to the EU, which now even more than after the Ukrainian energy cut-offs in 2006 and 2009 sought to reduce dependency on Russian gas supplies. Mutual estrangement gathered pace. In 2013 Russia imported about a third of its food, mostly from the EU, but by late 2016 imports had fallen to a fifth and shelves were filled with high-quality Russian goods. Russian spending on food imports fell from $60 billion to $20 billion.

The fundamental question remains: to what degree are sanctions effective? The classic study by Hufbauer and Schott suggests that when sanctions have limited objectives, such as the release of political prisoners, they worked in only 34 per cent of cases, and when they sought more ambitious goals, such as changing a political system, they were effective in 30 per cent of cases.[43] UN sanctions were even less effective, achieving their goals only about a fifth of the time. Sanctions always hit the weak and innocent, and are thus more effective against democratic regimes than authoritarian ones. In the Russian case, the aim was not explicitly to

---

[41] Matthieu Crozet and Julian Hinz, *Collateral Damage: The Impact of the Russia Sanctions on Sanctioning Countries' Exports*, Paris, Centre d'Etudes Prospectives et d'Informations Internationales (CEPII) Working Paper, No. 16, June 2016, www.cepii.fr/CEPII/en/publications/wp/abstract.asp?NoDoc=9213, last accessed 26 May 2017.

[42] Waltz, 'Structural Realism', p. 15.

[43] Gary Clyde Hufbauer and Jeffrey J. Schott, *Economic Sanctions Reconsidered*, 3rd revised edn (Washington, Peterson Institute, 2009).

achieve regime change but to modify its policy on Ukraine. There was no evidence that the sanctions had the desired effect, although it is unknowable what actions Russia might have taken in their absence. In economic terms, the sanctions tended to strengthen the sectors that were more internationally integrated, while the corporatist enterprises at home were shielded by state support. The distorted pattern of the economy was accentuated. However, even at the height of the sanctions a consortium of energy companies announced plans to build Nord Stream 2, a second pair of gas lines under the Baltic to Griefswald in Germany. Even the government of Bavaria, run by the Christian Social Union (CSU), warned that sanctions were pointless.

For some commentators sanctions signalled a welcome shift towards the primacy of politics over economics, and thus implicitly of principle over pragmatism.[44] This is an important point, but misleading. It assumes that critics of sanctions are 'appeasers', devoid of principle and recognising only profit and not values. This may well apply to certain business interests, who naturally seek market opportunities unimpeded by political distortions, which in itself is not a bad principle. This after all is what engagement theory (and the idea of interdependence) tried to teach – that economic and other relations (for example, between West and East Germany) would moderate behaviour and create a community of interests, the fundamental principle of *Ostpolitik*. More substantively, opponents of sanctions also defend principles, which are no less normatively grounded than its advocates. First, if the crisis of 2014 indeed exposed an underlying crisis, then, as the veteran Russian expert Angus Roxburgh puts it: 'It has long been my contention that we should deal with the causes of Putin's aggressive behaviour, not the symptoms.'[45] Indeed, Western sanctions only confirmed the Kremlin's view that the West sought Russia's long-term strategic isolation. Instead of dealing with the structural conditions that led to the breakdown, sanctions reinforced the negative features of Russian behaviour that they sought to change. It was in this context that ideas for some sort of Helsinki-2 or other 'grand bargain' or Congress of Vienna-style conference were advanced.

Second, and building on the first point, critics argue that proponents of sanctions fundamentally misread the situation in Russia. Enduring strategic interests and not systemic governance failings or regime preservation determined the country's foreign policy. The failure of outside powers to recognise Russia's concerns provoked the breakdown. These

[44] For example, Hannes Adomeit, 'Germany's Russia Policy: From Sanctions to Nord Stream 2?', Transatlantic Academy 2015–16 Paper Series, No. 3, March 2016, p. 1.

[45] Angus Roxburgh, 'To Wreck Russia's Economy would be Disaster for the West', *Guardian*, 17 December 2014, p. 30.

interests in certain cases coincided with those of the West, as in the fight against the Taliban in Afghanistan and preventing Iran becoming a nuclear weapons state. Thus a wise policy, it could be argued, would be to separate critique of Russia's systemic failings (which were no more egregious than those of many of the West's close allies) from engagement at the structural level, focusing on transactional matters of mutual concern. Third, and more profoundly, opponents of sanctions defend the fundamental principle of ideational and geopolitical pluralism. Sanctions, and the associated claims of universal jurisdiction, are intended to advance the idea of international law and the rule-based international order. But this defence of fine principles misses the power factor – that principles are applied selectively and in a distorted manner to the advantage of the power holders. The practices, and not the normative principles on which they are based, precipitated Russia's neo-revisionism and are challenged by the nascent post-West. Opposition to sanctions does not denote the absence of principle, but the defence of a set of principles that are no less coherent than their proponents. Russia's defiant reaction only exacerbated the problems of which sanctions were a response. In his speech celebrating the repatriation of Crimea, Putin warned:

We have all the reasons to believe that the infamous policy of containment of Russia which was happening in the 18th, 19th and 20th century is still going on. They are constantly trying to drive us into a corner because we have an independent position, because we maintain it and because we call things as they are and do not engage in hypocrisy ... If you press the spring, it will release at some point. Something you should remember.[46]

The warning was ignored.

A Change of Epochs

The year 2014 marked the tipping point from one era to another. Up to then, although with decreasing conviction, Russia still believed that some sort of transformation of relations with the US and the EU was possible. These hopes had been disappointed because of the inability of the Historical West to adapt after the end of the Cold War and Russia remaining mired in 'history', failing to transform into a democracy on the Western model. In 2014 illusions died, and the Russian–US confrontation 'is set to last long because its roots are systemic rather than situational'. The US will fight to preserve its 'global leadership', even though this ran counter to long-term historic trends, while Russia would 'not

---

[46] Putin, 'Address', 18 March 2014.

renounce a strategy whereby it seeks to become an independent power centre with its own regional projects and an equal role in global decision-making'.[47] Both saw each other as declining powers, creating a dynamic of incompatible purpose and perceptions.

The new era of confrontation is rooted in the asymmetrical end of the Cold War and the policy of enlarging the Atlantic community without negotiating an inclusive framework for European inter-regionalism. For Roxburgh, 'it is time to recognise that George W. Bush's disastrous foreign policy legacy encompasses far more than just Iraq, torture and the fanning of terrorism'. Specifically,

> It was the Bush administration that created the sense of insecurity that has caused Russia to react, and overreact, to every perceived threat – including, most recently, the perception that Ukraine was being forcibly dragged out of Russia's orbit and into the west's. Bush unilaterally abandoned the anti-ballistic missile treaty, seen by Russia as the cornerstone of strategic balance; he began building a missile shield on Russia's doorstep; he expanded Nato to Russia's frontiers, blithely granting the east Europeans 'security' while causing Russia to feel threatened. The solution is clear. Abandon the missile shield. End the expansion of Nato. And think boldly about a new security arrangement for the whole of Europe – one that will bring Russia in rather than leaving it outside feeling vulnerable.

Above all, he exhorted a return to the Greater European agenda that was outlined at the very beginning of the era in which it was intended by the architect of perestroika to be foundational: 'Let us return to the ideals of 1989, when Mikhail Gorbachev sought a new "common European home". That is what every Russian leader since him has wanted – while the west, it seems, never did.'[48]

In his year-end interview in 2014 Lavrov struck a defiant note. He denounced the EU for holding Russia responsible for the conflict in Ukraine, and insisted that its imposition of 'unilateral sanctions on Moscow' was 'illegal, condemned by the UN General Assembly and runs contrary to WTO standards'. He went on to warn that 'attempts to speak to Russia using the language of ultimatums is totally unacceptable and will yield no results'. Russia had no choice but to limit food imports from the EU, since '[b]y restricting the access of Russian financial institutions to European financial instruments, Brussels has de facto created more favourable conditions for European goods in our market'. He stressed that '[w]e are not going to discuss any criteria for lifting sanctions. Lifting sanctions is the responsibility of those who imposed them.

---

[47] Dmitry Suslov, 'Russia–US: How to Overcome the New Confrontation', Valdai Club, 6 October 2016, http://valdaiclub.com/a/highlights/russia-us-how-to-overcome-new-con frontation/, last accessed 26 May 2017.

[48] Roxburgh, 'To Wreck Russia's Economy'.

Surely, if the European Union shows common sense, Russia will be ready for constructive dialogue on the issue.' He described how the US had wound down bilateral dialogue in spring 2014 on matters of common concern, such as the fight against terrorism and drugs. Sanctions had been accompanied by 'Washington's aggressive utterances including labelling Russia, along with ISIL [Islamic State] and Ebola virus, as a primary global threat'. He warned 'the times when international relations were defined by one or several superpowers have passed. In the modern world, where several independent centres of power operate, attempts to isolate some of the leaders or impose one's own unilateral recipes from a position of "exceptionalism", which the US has taken, is futile'.[49] In his interview with the France 24 television station on 16 December, Lavrov argued that the sanctions were intended to put an end to Putin's regime. He observed that Russia's military doctrine stated that NATO's expansion and the deployment of its military infrastructure closer to Russia's borders represented a security risk, but 'it never mentions that NATO is an enemy'. As a result of the Ukraine crisis, NATO had cut all ties with Russia, including 'practical cooperative mechanisms, including on Afghanistan', counter-terrorism and other issues.[50] Addressing participants at the Gorchakov Public Diplomacy Foundation on 16 December 2014, Lavrov outlined how Russia saw the big picture: '[W]hat we believe is happening is nothing less than a change of historical epochs, the formation of a new, more democratic and fair polycentric world order.' The process was not going smoothly, with existing conflicts being 'compounded by new ones'. He listed some of the outstanding problems: 'We have yet to find a solution to the internal Ukrainian crisis, which broke out as a result of external pressure on Kiev to choose in favour of the Western vector, while ignoring the Eastern vector.' Along with the crisis in the Middle East and North Africa and the threat of terrorism and extremism, he warned that '[a] serious destabilising factor is the practice of the export of democracy in various parts of the world and regime change through "colour revolutions" or the use of other methods to impose development recipes on sovereign nations from the outside, without taking into account their traditions and national specifics'. But he took a positive

[49] 'Lavrov's Big Interview: Russia-NATO Relations, Arms Race and Ukraine', *Sputnik*/Ria Novosti, 9 December 2014, in JRL, No. 259, 2014, item 8.
[50] 'Foreign Minister of the Russian Federation Sergey Lavrov's Interview with TV Channel France 24', Moscow, 16 December 2014, www.mid.ru/en/press_service/minister_spee ches/-/asset_publisher/7OvQR5KJWVmR/content/id/848819, last accessed 30 May 2017. Lavrov condemned the 'bloc discipline' in the Atlantic community, which he argued was 'stricter than the discipline that existed within the Warsaw Treaty Organisation', 'Russia's Lavrov Gives Interview to State TV', 25 December 2014, ministry transcript of 30 December 2014.

view: 'We are confident that this negative trend can and must be reversed.'[51]

George Friedman, the head of the analytical agency Stratfor, provides the broader strategic picture, noting

The United States has spent the past century pursuing a single objective: avoiding the rise of any single hegemon that might be able to exploit Western European technology and capital and Russian resources and manpower. The United States intervened in World War I in 1917 to block German hegemony, and again in World War II. In the Cold War the goal was to prevent Russian hegemony. US strategic policy has been consistent for a century.

The US would interdict the rise of a potential alternative centre of hegemonic power, and thus Friedman argues that 'the United States has a legitimate fear of Russia in Ukraine. If Russia manages to reassert its power in Ukraine, then what will come next? Russia has military and political power that could begin to impinge on Europe. Therefore it is not irrational for the United States, and at least some European countries to want to assert their power in Ukraine.'[52]

In a meeting with the Federal Security Service (FSB) on 26 March 2015, Putin stressed the range of challenges, including NATO developing 'its rapid response forces and ... boosting its infrastructure near our borders', but above all Putin warned that Russia had to oppose attempts to undermine its political system: 'They are using a whole range of means for the so-called containment of Russia – from attempts at political isolation and economic pressure to a full-scale information war and tools used by special services.' He warned that Western special services would not give up attempts to 'use non-government groups and politicised unions to discredit Russian authorities and destabilise the internal situation in Russia. They are already planning actions for the period of the forthcoming elections in 2016 and 2018.' Putin said that the authorities would maintain their dialogue with the opposition and Russian civil society, but warned that 'it makes no sense to argue with those who work on order from outside, who serve the interests not of their nation but an alien nation or nations'.[53] This was a harshly conspiratorial view of

[51] 'Foreign Minister Sergey Lavrov's address at a meeting with participants in the "Dialogue for the Future: Russia and the World Around" annual research and education programme of the Gorchakov Public Diplomacy Fund, Moscow', 12 December 2014, www.mid.ru/en/press_service/minister_speeches/-/asset_publisher/7OvQR5KJWVmR/c ontent/id/826793, last accessed 30 May 2017.

[52] George Friedman, 'Viewing Russia from the Inside', Stratfor.com, 16 December 2014, www.stratfor.com/weekly/viewing-russia-inside#axzz3MdaSkTug, last accessed 26 May 2017.

[53] 'Zasedanie kollegii FSB', 26 March 2015, http://kremlin.ru/transcripts/47963, last accessed 30 May 2017.

the world that denied autonomy and agency to those struggling for the rule of law, genuinely competitive elections and secure property rights within Russia. It was both a symptom and a cause of the strategic impasse in which Russia had found itself for a quarter of a century.

At the St Petersburg International Economic Forum in June 2016 Putin shocked many with his statement:

America is a great power. Today, probably, the only superpower. We accept that. We want to and are ready to work with the United States. Elections are going to take place, there will be a head of state with huge powers. There are complex domestic political and economic processes going on in the USA. The world needs strong nations, like the US. But we don't need them constantly getting mixed up in our affairs, telling us how to live, preventing Europe from building a relationship with us.[54]

Putin accepted the fact of US pre-eminence, but he criticised its overweening ambition to instruct the world. He repeated his long-standing view that without the US poisoning relations, the EU and Russia would have been able to reset relations. This failed to take into account the EU's internal sources of criticism of Russian behaviour. In looking forward to the American presidential elections, he could hardly have anticipated that Russia would become the salient issue. Russia was endowed with super-agency, accused of hacking, attempting to undermine American democracy, and even of exerting some sort of hold over the 'Siberian candidate'. Trump did indeed represent a threat to the established order, but this was generated from within.

---

[54] 'Plenarnoe zasedanie Peterburgskogo mezhdunarodnogo ekonomicheskogo foruma', 17 June 2016, http://kremlin.ru/events/president/transcripts/52178, last accessed 30 May 2017.

Friedrich Nietzsche observed in his *Will to Power* that 'Necessity is not an established fact, but rather an interpretation'. Never was this truer than of the twenty-first-century confrontation between Russia and the West. The breakdown of the cold peace marked the culmination of trends that had been apparent from the first days of Russian independence. Even the liberal foreign minister Andrei Kozyrev warned that 'NATO's advance toward Russia's borders cannot but be seen as a continuation, though by inertia, of a policy aimed at containment of Russia'.[1] The crisis exposed the failures of a security system and allowed Europe's apparently endless civil war to resume. During the cold peace, relations between Russia and the Historical West were torn between conflict and cooperation. Differences had been particularly acute over the Balkan wars and NATO enlargement, but even on these issues there were elements of cooperation, especially after 9/11 when Russia agreed to share intelligence and open up bases in Central Asia. In April 2008 the Northern Distribution Network for American supplies for Afghanistan opened. Russia was a constructive partner in the nuclear weapon limitation talks with Iran, leading to the JCPOA of July 2015. Nevertheless, following the Georgian and Ukraine wars, the country was perceived as threatening and hostile. The European security order disintegrated, and Russia was presented as a threat to its neighbours, the law-based liberal international order, and to the leadership of the Historical West. On the other side, the consolidation and expansion of the Atlantic system came to be seen as a threat to Russia's security and its ability to forge close relations with neighbours, with institutional and ideological soft containment driving Russia into a strategic dead end. From 2012 Russia advanced an ideology of difference, asserted a strategy of resistance, and constructed anti-hegemonic alliances. The failure to create a new political and security community in Europe set the stage for a renewed era of global confrontation.

[1] Kozyrev, 'Partnership or Cold Peace?' p. 13.

Rhetorical Violence and Insecurity

In his speech to the British parliament in December 1984, Gorbachev argued that 'Europe is our common home. A home, and not a "theatre of military operations"'. In the same speech he introduced the concept of 'new political thinking', which served as the framework for the end of the Cold War. Three decades later the cycle was complete, and Europe once again became a 'theatre of military operations'. The Ukraine crisis was a 'game changer',[2] and thereafter Russia was touted as the enemy of the West. There had been earlier crises, notably in 2008, but from 2014 the break was definitive and the NATO alliance was resecuritised in opposition to Russia.[3] The language of partnership was abandoned. The NATO summit in Newport, Wales, on 4 and 5 September 2014 adopted a 'Readiness Action Plan' to establish 'spearhead' military bases in the frontline East European states and established a rapid-reaction force headquartered in Poland. Military bases were established in Poland and the Baltic republics, with a fixed although not permanent deployment of brigade-strength forces. NATO mobilisation against the perceived Russian threat technically remained within the NATO-Russia Founding Act, but its spirit was violated. NATO returned to its original mission of the hard containment of Russia. Once again an 'iron curtain' divided Europe, no longer from 'Trieste in the Adriatic to Stettin on the Baltic', as Winston Churchill put it in his Fulton, Missouri, speech in February 1946, but from Narva on the Baltic to Mariupol on the Sea of Azov. Just as in the original Cold War, a situation of neither war nor peace prevailed, and as Gerasimov, the Chief of the Russian General Staff argued, it became increasingly difficult to tell the difference between the two.[4]

The trend towards confrontation was reflected in Hillary Clinton's memoirs, *Hard Choices*, published before her 2016 presidential campaign. She had always been a hardliner on Russian issues, and was sceptical about the reset but had been convinced by Obama to give it a try. With the younger and more outward looking Medvedev installed as president, there appeared to be a window of opportunity, but as we have seen, the reset had a limited vision, and following the Libyan events and the disputed parliamentary election of December 2011, relations once again soured. Soon after Putin's return to the presidency, in June 2012 Clinton

---

[2] As noted by Robert Bell, the US secretary of defence's representative in Europe, Ewen MacAskill, 'US Urges Nato States to Raise Defence Spending to Counter Russia', *Guardian*, 24 June 2014, p. 19.

[3] James Sperling and Mark Webber, 'NATO and the Ukraine Crisis: Collective Securitisation', *European Journal of International Security*, Vol. 2, No. 1, 2016, pp. 19–46.

[4] Valerii Gerasimov, 'Mir na granyakh voiny', *Voenno-promyshlennyi kur'er*, No. 10, 15 March 2017, http://vpk-news.ru/articles/35591, last accessed 9 June 2017.

warned Obama to be ready to take a harder line, arguing that Putin was 'deeply resentful of the US and suspicious of our actions', and sought to reclaim lost influence in the neighbourhood. She argued that although the project was called 'regional integration' it was in fact 'code for rebuilding a lost empire'.[5] In her final memo about Russia in January 2013 Clinton noted that the 'reset' had in the end turned into a setback, and she urged Obama to set a 'new course' by taking a harder line against Putin. She argued that the relationship between Washington and Moscow would 'likely get worse before it got better', and Obama had to be 'realistic' about the danger that Putin posed to his neighbours and the world order.[6] She argued '[w]e should hit the pause button on new efforts. Don't appear too eager to work together. Don't flatter Putin with high-level attention.' Russian intransigence would not prevent the US pursuing its goals in Syria and elsewhere. 'Strength and resolve were the only language Putin would understand.'[7] She insisted that the US remained 'the indispensable nation', and as secretary of state she supported Gaddafi's overthrow and advocated US intervention in Syria. As a reviewer notes, 'Clinton's exceptionalism promotes an implicit double standard that separates the US from the rest of the world'. Her Asia pivot asserted that America was back in its 'traditional leadership role in Asia', which, naturally enough, the Chinese perceived as an attempt to block its rise: 'Why China shouldn't claim a "leadership role" in its own part of the world, and the US should, is one of the mysteries of the exceptionalist faith'.[8] Obama followed Clinton's advice, although rather less militantly. He agreed to a summit with Putin in September 2013, but it was cancelled when Snowden was granted sanctuary.

On the other side, Russia's politics of resistance was accompanied by a harsher and more conservative tone. In his address to the Federal Assembly in December 2012, Putin talked of Russia as a 'state-civilisation', a formulation that shifted the emphasis from the democratic state as a civic community towards a more traditional representation of the state as the defender of cultural traditions and national virtue.[9] Putin's revival of Alexander III's phrase that 'Russia has only two allies: its army and navy' confirmed the trend.[10] This was accompanied by a harsh media campaign.

---

[5] Clinton, *Hard Choices*, p. 236.   [6] Clinton, *Hard Choices*, p. 244.
[7] Joby Warrick and Karen De Young, 'From "Reset" to "Pause": The Real Story behind Hillary Clinton's Feud with Vladimir Putin', *Washington Post*, 3 November 2016.
[8] Jackson Lears, 'We Came, We Saw, He Died', *London Review of Books*, 5 February 2015, pp. 8–11, at p. 9.
[9] Vladimir Putin, 'Address to the Federal Assembly', 12 December 2012, http://eng.kremlin.ru/news/4739, last accessed 30 May 2017.
[10] Yury Smityuk, 'Putin Agrees with Emperor that Russia's only Allies are Army and Navy', *TASS*, 16 April 2015, http://tass.ru/en/russia/789866, last accessed 30 May 2017.

Under the leadership of Svetlana Mironyuk the RIA Novosti news and project agency had been thoroughly modernised and gained a deserved reputation for journalistic integrity and relative openness. In a characteristic *coup de main* in December 2013, as the Maidan revolution gathered force, Mironyuk was dismissed and RIA Novosti was brought under the control of a new mega-news agency called Rossiya Segodnya (Russia Today), which also controlled the RT television station, and the revived Sputnik and TASS agencies. These were all led by Dmitry Kisilev, a fire-raising television talk-show host. The main state-controlled television channels poured out a stream of bile, conspiracy theories, and opprobrium against the Historical West in general and the US in particular. Although Putin in formal exchanges was always careful to talk of Russia's Western 'partners', the word 'partner' quickly became a synonym for opponent.

An equivalent process was at work in the West. A BBC2 film in February 2016 acted out the scenario of a Russian attack on Latvia escalating into a nuclear exchange.[11] The Rand Corporation estimated that 'Russia could overrun Eastern Europe in just three days because NATO has not been bolstering its fleet since Vladimir Putin took Crimea', and it would take 'just 36 to 60 hours to occupy the Baltic states'. Compromise was presented as appeasement and a betrayal of the West's values and principles, while for Russia the perceived threat from the West required social consolidation and political discipline.[12] A powerful patriotic surge after the return of Crimea saw Putin's popularity reach new heights. In the West Putin was demonised and caricatured as the epitome of evil, manipulating populist challengers and shaping electoral outcomes – even to the point that it was alleged that Trump's election was in some way the outcome of fiendish Kremlin interventions. On the one side, there was the view that Russia had conclusively broken with the Western-centric system, while on the other the view prevailed that the Historical West had lost its sense of balance and proportion. The West's failure to solve its problems and contradictions prompted the search for scapegoats – and who better than Russia to fulfil this now traditional role.

These are caricatures, but the fundamental dilemma was clear: although long over, Cold War institutional and ideational structures remained. Although after 2012 Russia's tone and posture changed, there were profound continuities in the Kremlin's underlying grand strategy. The

---

[11] BBC2, 'World War Three: Inside the War Room', 3 February 2016.
[12] Pavel Koshkin, 'Buzz about World War III only Fuels Russia's Confrontation with the West', *Russia Direct*, 4 February 2016, www.russia-direct.org/analysis/buzz-about-worl d-war-iii-only-fuels-russias-confrontation-west, last accessed 30 May 2017.

National Security Strategy of 31 December 2015 revealed Moscow's increased sense of insecurity. The document starkly warned of the threats:

Expanding the force potential of NATO and endowing it with global functions that are implemented in violation of international legal norms, the bloc's heightened military activity, its continued expansion and the approach of its military infrastructure to Russia's borders, all create a threat to national security.[13]

The *Strategy* portrayed Russia as a global player with legitimate regional concerns, and noted the containment strategy facing the country. Despite the shift towards conflict, the *Strategy* was consistent with previous iterations.[14] The geopolitical confrontation with the West was now defined as a threat, accompanied by a new emphasis on the 'hybrid' wars conducted against Russia. Although self-reliance and self-sufficiency was stressed, there was no major shift towards the 'securitisation' of new policy areas. Securitisation is not the same as militarisation, and indicates the way that 'normal' politics gives way to the priority of national security discourses, which then shape policy.[15] On the other side, the crisis of 2014 prompted more classic securitisation moves as NATO shifted from the language of cooperation to defence cooperation against Russia. The US and UK focused on the threats to the international liberal order, while Germany and the EU were more concerned about threats to European peace and the deterioration in EU-Russian relations.[16]

Revisions to the *Foreign Policy Concept* reflected Moscow's evaluation of the changes in international affairs, including the deterioration in relations with the West, turmoil in the Middle East and North Africa and the associated rise in terrorism. Lavrov argued that the new document would 'reiterate the key principles of the Russian foreign policy, including its self-sufficiency, its multi-vector nature and openness to equal cooperation with everyone expressing mutual interest with the aim of effective settlement of numerous present-day challenges'. He noted that international politics were going through a turbulent period associated with 'the formation of a new polycentric system of the global order': 'We see a growing competition on the issue [of] what shape the future international

---

[13] 'Strategiya natsional'noi bezopasnosti Rossiiskoi Federatsii', *Rossiiskaya gazeta*, 31 December 2015, http://rg.ru/2015/12/31/nac-bezopasnost-site-dok.html, last accessed 9 June 2017.

[14] For earlier analysis, see Marcel DeHaas, *Russian Security Policy under Putin* (London, Routledge, 2010).

[15] Edwin Bacon and Bettina Renz with Julian Cooper, *Securitising Russia: The Domestic Politics of Putin* (Manchester, Manchester University Press, 2006).

[16] Bernhard Stahl, Robin Lucke and Anne Felfeli, 'Comeback of the Transatlantic Security Community? Comparative Securitisation in the Crimea Crisis', *East European Politics*, Vol. 32, No. 4, 2016, p. 539.

system would assume'.[17] The new *Concept* was issued on 30 November 2016, and in the circumstances was remarkably emollient. There was little sense of a condition of 'war' between Russia and the Atlantic community, and the document reaffirmed many of the points of the February 2013 version, although there was less emphasis on Russia's Western vocation and more on Eurasian integration.

The new *Concept* stressed Russia's desire for good relations with all its 'partners', the continued commitment to multilateral organisations and international economic integration, the supremacy of international law, the central role of the UN, the importance of democracy, and Russia's contribution to peace and security in Europe. The overall theoretical model remained the same: 'The contemporary world is going through a period of profound changes, the essence of which is the formation of a polycentric international system.' The West's attempt to impede this natural shift generated instability in the international system. Russia would 'resist the attempts of individual states or groups of states to revise the generally recognised principles of international order', for instance, using the principle of R2P to intervene in the internal affairs of other countries. Above all, the document affirmed Russia's status as an independent player in international affairs, the refusal to be drawn into any alliances or putative blocs, and the strengthening of news media 'to convey the Russian viewpoint to broad circles of the world community'. Even though at the time Russia was embroiled in the Syrian conflict, the Middle East was still ranked behind the post-Soviet space, Europe, the US and Asia-Pacific in its regional priorities.

Rather than enunciating an alternative ideological project or the creation of some sort of Eurasian civilisation, the *Concept* reiterated Russia's support for 'universal democratic values'. Regional integration would be in conformity with WTO rules, and there was no suggestion that Russia would turn its back on globalisation. Instead, the document stressed Russia's ambition to enjoy good relations with the EU and to establish 'constructive, stable and predictable cooperation with the countries of the EU'. The Greater Europe ambition was retained in the form of Russia's wish 'to create a common economic and humanitarian space from the Atlantic to the Pacific Ocean on the basis of the harmonisation of the processes of European and Eurasian integration'. Even NATO was spared some of the harshest criticism, although the *Concept* registered 'a negative attitude towards NATO's expansion and the alliance's military structure approaching Russia's borders'. Instead, Russia sought 'an equal partnership' while establishing 'mutually beneficial relations with the United States'. The *Concept* accused the US and its allies of undermining 'global stability' by trying to 'contain' Russia, and reserved the right to 'react harshly to any unfriendly' moves. Cooperation was only possible on the basis of 'equality, mutual respect of interests, and non-interference in one another's internal affairs'. Russia's goal was good relations with all states based on 'mutual respect', and there was no enunciation of a counter-hegemonic strategy, although 'polycentrism' was defended and 'full-scale' partnership and cooperation with China was stressed. The tone overall was defensive, although pronounced in a confident tone that suggested a belief that the tide of history was turning in Moscow's favour. There was little sense of 'Russia against the rest', and instead the document stressed commitment to the universal principles embedded in international society, as long as these were not abused to justify interference in the internal affairs of states.[18]

The *Concept* represented an important restatement of Russian concerns. The confident tone was reflected in Putin's annual address to the Federal Assembly on 1 December 2016. The focus was on reform in domestic policy, although there were no substantive ideas on how to tackle economic stagnation, and the foreign policy passages were conciliatory in tone. He noted that '[u]nlike some of our colleagues abroad, who consider Russia an adversary, we do not seek and never have sought enemies. We need friends. But we will not allow our interests to be infringed upon or ignored. We want to and will decide our destiny ourselves and build our present and future without others' unasked for advice and prompting.'[19] Moscow sought to repair relations with the US following Trump's election in the framework of multipolarity and recognition of Russia's interests. The sticking point remained the tension between a 'values-based foreign policy', which in the Historical West was code for the enlargement of the hegemonic liberal world order without what was condemned as 'spheres of interest', or a more interest-driven recognition of a pluralist international system in which powers have divergent concerns but use the traditional instruments of statecraft to resolve them.

Military Modernisation

Russian neo-revisionism was buttressed by increasing military power.[20] Following the Russo-Georgian war, in October 2008 Russia launched one of the most far-reaching and comprehensive military reforms in its history.

---

[18] *Kontsepsiya vneshnei politiki Rossiiskoi Federatsii*, 30 November 2016, www.scrf.gov.ru/security/international/document25/, last accessed 9 June 2017.

[19] Vladimir Putin, 'Presidential Address to the Federal Assembly', 1 December 2016, http://en.kremlin.ru/events/president/news/53379, last accessed 30 May 2017.

[20] Bettina Renz and Hanna Smith, *Russia's Military Revival* (Cambridge, Polity, 2017).

Under the direction of defence minister Anatoly Serdyukov, the traditional mass-mobilisation army was transformed into combat-ready armed forces, accompanied by the radical modernisation of command and control structures, improved training, strengthened elite units, and above all the upgrading of weapons and equipment. Russia's military potential was transformed. The force structure shifted from the old army divisions, designed to fight frontal warfare against conventional armies, to more agile all-purpose brigades of some five to six thousand people suitable for guerrilla and other forms of unconventional warfare. Russian pilots began to train for more than twenty hours a year, whereas for NATO pilots, failure to complete thirty hours a month requires a re-examination. Nevertheless, the Crimean and Syrian conflicts demonstrated that Russia could mount effective expeditionary campaigns, while providing useful field training. Russia was once again by far the pre-eminent military power in Eurasia, and could credibly assert itself as a great power. This inevitably challenged the post-Cold War security system, effectively the one created after the Second World War to contain the USSR.

By 2014 the armed forces had signed up 295,000 professional soldiers (*kontraktniki*), with plans to recruit 55,000 annually thereafter. In November 2012 Sergei Shoigu was appointed defence minister, and he partially returned to army groups and divisions from what was initially planned to be an entirely brigade-based army. Problems remained, including the ability not only to recruit but to keep *kontraktniki* and the supply of sufficient high quality and competitive modern weapons from the Russian defence industry. In December 2011 Dmitry Rogozin was appointed deputy prime minister in charge of the defence and space industry. The 2020 state armament programme envisaged spending $300 billion to replace 70 per cent of military hardware, with new generations of domestically produced equipment, including fighter planes, air-defence systems, cruise missiles and tanks. The 2025 programme was far less ambitious, and its launch was delayed by two years to 2018. In late 2014 a third modernised submarine-launched ballistic missile (SLBM) carrier was added to the Russian navy. Each holds sixteen Bulava missiles with six independently targetable warheads apiece, totalling 288 in highly mobile and tested vessels. In 2014 Russia surpassed all other countries in the number (thirty-eight) of space launches, and it also successfully tested the heavy Angara-A-5 rocket with a dummy payload.[21] Russia made enormous strides in restoring its military power, and was at pains to stress, in word and deed, that it was not a Serbia, Afghanistan, Iraq or Libya, and was in a position to resist Atlantic *force majeure*.

---

[21] Patrick Armstrong, 'Military etc', *Russian Federation Sitrep*, 8 January 2015.

After 1989 European military budgets and force personnel had fallen dramatically. By 2014 the US had only 33,000 land forces stationed permanently on the continent, down from some 200,000 during the Cold War. By contrast, Russian military expenditure rose sharply. Defence spending rose, both in absolute terms and as a percentage of GDP. Russia tripled its spending on defence between 2000 and 2015, rising from $28.8 billion to $91 billion (in constant 2014 US dollars).[22] Russian defence spending reached 3.8 per cent of GDP in 2010, a record 5.4 per cent in 2015, and thereafter declined to 3.18 per cent in 2016 and was planned to fall a further 7 per cent in 2017. In 2010, military expenditure represented 15.9 per cent of federal government spending, but by 2015 it peaked at 25.8 per cent.[23] By comparison, in 2016 the US defence budget was $573 billion, while China's was $135 billion. In his State of the Union speech on 13 January 2016, Obama justifiably countered 'talk of American economic decline' and rhetoric about 'our enemies getting stronger and America getting weaker'. He boasted that '[t]he United States of America is the most powerful nation on Earth. Period. It's not even close. We spend more on our military than the next eight nations [including Russia and China] combined.' To rub in the message, he stressed 'when it comes to every important international issue, people of the world do not look to Beijing or Moscow to lead – they call us'.[24] The US provides 70 per cent of NATO's budget, and although the rate of decline has fallen, only Poland and Estonia increased their defence spending to exceed the 2 per cent threshold agreed at the Wales summit. NATO's twenty-eight members are responsible for about 70 per cent of the world's staggering $1.7 trillion annual military expenditure. Despite the end of the Cold War, global military spending has increased annually since 1996. In 2015 the US alone was responsible for 36 per cent of military spending ($596 billion), China for 13 per cent (132 billion), and Russia 4 per cent (66.4 billion).[25] Russia's defence spending in 2015 was only 8 per cent of NATO's combined total. The disparity in economic power was no less stark, with the combined NATO GDP running at some

[22] SIPRI Military Expenditure Database, www.sipri.org/databases/milex, last accessed 30 May 2017.

[23] Richard Connolly, 'Hard Times? Defence Spending and the Russian Economy', *Russian Analytical Digest*, No. 196, 23 December 2016, p. 2; 'Raskhody prorvali liniyu oborony', *Vedomosti*, 9 September 2016, p. 5.

[24] The White House, 'Remarks of President Barack Obama: State of the Union Address as Delivered', 13 January 2016, www.whitehouse.gov/the-press-office/2016/01/12/remarks-president-barack-obama-%E2%80%93-prepared-delivery-state-union-address, last accessed 30 May 2017.

[25] SIPRI, 'Trends in World Military Expenditure, 2015', April 2016, http://books.sipri.org/files/FS/SIPRIFS1604.pdf, last accessed 30 May 2017.

$40 trillion with 900 million citizens, dwarfing Russia's $1.5 trillion GDP and 146 million people. Russia was far from being a peer competitor of the US and its allies.

Not only were the odds in military and economic terms firmly stacked against Russia, but its relative position had declined sharply compared to that of the Soviet Union. Warsaw Pact military expenditures represented some 80 per cent of NATO's in the final stages of the Cold War, whereas today they are less than a tenth of what they had been earlier.[26] Russian military expenditure is 8 per cent of NATO's, and 11 per cent that of the US. The US maintains around 800 bases in 74 countries, whereas Russia has military bases in Tajikistan (7,500 service personnel), Belarus, Armenia, Kyrgyzstan (400), Abkhazia (4,000), and Transnistria, and shares a military facility in Vietnam. Russia also has peacekeepers in South Ossetia and Transnistria. Since 1977 the country has used the naval supply facility in the Syrian port of Tartus, and it now has a 49-year lease on the base. In October 2016 the Russian Navy announced plans to build piers capable of berthing up to eleven ships simultaneously. The Russian airbase at Khmeimim (part of the Bassel Al-Assad civilian airport) was pressed into service in September 2015, and Russia now has a 49-year lease on the facility. It is covered by the Latakia signals intelligence (SIGINT) base, with all three facilities defended by powerful interlocking anti-aircraft missile systems. There are discussions to re-establish the powerful SIGINT facility at Lourdes in Cuba, closed by Putin as a goodwill gesture in August 2002. In 2016 there was also talk of Russia returning to the Cam Ranh Bay naval base in Vietnam, from which it had finally sailed in May 2002.

In December 2014, amendments to Russia's 2010 *Military Doctrine* were approved by the Russian Security Council, painting a grim picture of Russia's security environment. It warned that NATO expansion, the 'strengthening of its military potential' and 'its assumption of global tasks and attempts to solve them in violation of international law', represented a risk or danger (*opasnost*), although not formulated as a threat (*ugroza*).[27] This was not new, but it now made Russia's stance explicit. For the first time there was a section on 'internal military risks', warning of externally sponsored regime change in Russia's neighbourhood to constrain Russia's influence. Reprising Gerasimov's earlier observations, the *Doctrine* stated that modern military conflicts are characterised by 'a complex mixture of

---

[26] Jan Oberg, 'Why is NATO so Irrational Today?', Counterpunch.org, 30 June 2016, www.counterpunch.org/2016/06/30/why-is-nato-so-irrational-today/, last accessed 30 May 2017.

[27] *Voennaya doktrina Rossiiskoi Federatsii*, 25 December 2014, Article 12, www.scrf.gov.ru/security/military/document129/, last accessed 9 June 2017.

military force with political, economic, information and other non-military means, implemented with the extensive use of the protest potential of the population and special operation forces'.[28] Although the *Doctrine* had Western strategies of 'regime change' in mind, this describes the 'hybrid warfare' practised by Russia in Ukraine. Gerasimov had argued that 'the role of non-military means of achieving political and strategic goals has grown, and in many cases they exceed the power of force of weapons in their effectiveness'. To ensure coordination between military and ideational forms of struggle, a Centre for National Defence was established combining representatives from the military and the government, including the media regulator and food hygiene inspectorate. It was clear that Russia considered itself to be engaged in a multi-layered confrontation with the Historical West, in which military force was only one dimension.[29] The security services also stepped up their activities. Addressing the FSB board on 26 February 2016, Putin warned that foreign intelligence agencies had intensified their activities in Russia. In the previous year he noted that 'we put a stop to the activity of more than 400 foreign intelligence officers and agents, with criminal charges brought against 23 of these people'.[30]

The arms race of the Cold War era was revived. The rising tide of arms exports by the US and Russia went in particular to the Middle East and Southeast Asia. Tensions in Ukraine and elsewhere meant that countries ramped up defence spending. In 2015 alone sales rose by $6.6 billion to take the value of the global arms market to $65 billion (US sales were $22.9 billion, with Russia in second place at $7.4 billion).[31] In the period 2012–16 the US accounted for 33 per cent of global arms exports, and Russia 23 per cent, with 70 per cent of Russian exports going to four countries: India, Vietnam, China and Algeria.[32] The defence industry plays an important part in the Russian economy, benefiting from increased defence procurement after 2011 and buoyant arms sales abroad.[33] Institutional changes also followed. Speaking at Chatham House on 19 June 2014, NATO

---

[28] *Voennaya doktrina.*

[29] Margarete Klein, *Russia's Military: On the Rise?*, Washington, Transatlantic Academy, 2015–16 Paper Series, No. 2.

[30] 'Meeting of the Federal Security Service Board', 26 February 2016, http://en.kremlin.ru/events/president/news/51397, last accessed 30 May 2017.

[31] IHS Jane's, *Global Defence Trade Report*, 13 June 2016, http://press.ihs.com/press-release/aerospace-defense-security/record-breaking-65-billion-global-defence-trade-2015-fueled, last accessed 9 June 2017.

[32] 'Increase in Arms Transfers Driven by Demand in the Middle East and Asia, Says SIPRI', 20 February 2017, www.sipri.org/media/press-release/2017/increase-arms-transfers-driven-demand-middle-east-and-asia-says-sipri, last accessed 30 May 2017.

[33] For analysis, including weaknesses of the sector, see Richard Connolly and Cecilie Sendstad, *Russia's Role as an Arms Exporter* (London, Chatham House Research Paper, March 2017).

secretary general Anders Fogh Rasmussen stressed that NATO would change its force posture to give it capability in case of unexpected threats, but warned that this could not be done on the cheap. He noted that Russia had increased its defence spending by some 50 per cent since 2008, while NATO had decreased its spending by 20 per cent. He claimed that the disproportionate US share was unsustainable, and he urged Europe to pick up more of the bill and meet the 2 per cent NATO defence benchmark (at that time median European defence spending was 1.6 per cent). He insisted that the Transatlantic partnership was the foundation of world order, 'the bedrock of our shared security . . . an essential source of stability in an unpredictable world . . . we are more than a military alliance but a community of values'.[34]

NATO now entered a period of expanding defence budgets, extensive military exercises along Russia's border, and frequent naval incursions into the Black Sea. Even some traditionally neutral countries considered joining. Finnish public opinion remains firmly opposed, but the Finnish defence minister, Carl Haglund, in June 2014 argued that 'I think the grounds for Nato membership are stronger than ever'.[35] Visiting Finland at that time, Lavrov noted that 'Anti-Semitism started World War II, Russsophobia could start the third'.[36] The Baltic republics feared that Russia would use the stealth tactics employed in Crimea. The concern was sharpest in Estonia and Latvia, where there were sizeable Russian minorities deprived of automatic citizenship rights. As far as Russian analysts were concerned, 'in spite of Crimea, Russia poses no threat to the West, its forces heavily outnumbered by Nato'.[37] NATO was reinvigorated with a new sense of purpose, until Trump's election once again sowed doubts and discord.

In response to planned NATO deployments, in early 2016 Shoigu announced the creation of three divisions in western and southwestern Russia. The First Guards Tank Army would be recreated with two to three tank divisions, motorised rifle divisions and artillery and extensive engineering support. It would be the first to receive the new Armata range of Armoured Fighting Vehicles (AFVs). The new army would be based in Russia's Western Military District to defend against a possible NATO

---

[34] Anders Fogh Rasmussen, 'The Future of NATO: A Strong Alliance in an Unpredictable World', 19 June 2014, www.chathamhouse.org/event/future-nato-strong-alliance-unpre dictable-world?dm_i=1TYB,2KAXB,BIUSVI,9CS08,1, last accessed 30 May 2017.

[35] MacAskill, 'US Urges Nato States to Raise Defence Spending to Counter Russia'.

[36] Pavel Koshkin, 'Will the Ukraine Crisis Bring Finland into NATO?', *Russia Direct*, 17 June 2014, www.russia-direct.org/debates/will-ukraine-crisis-bring-finland-nato, last accessed 9 June 2017.

[37] MacAskill, 'US Urges Nato States to Raise Defence Spending to Counter Russia'.

attack.[38] In other words, the possibility of frontal warfare was restored. NATO focused on a possible threat to the Baltic republics and the so-called 'Suwalki Gap' (like the Fulda Gap of old) between Kaliningrad and Belarus, but the main focus of Russian deployments was further south. Russia had long threatened to deploy the Iskander-M missile system to Kaliningrad, but this took place on a permanent basis only in 2016. The air forces there up to that time comprised of only a few old SU-27s and SU-24Ms, while the air defences still used the old Tochka-U missile system. In other words, 'Moscow is essentially demonstratively ignoring all the NATO hysteria surrounding the Baltic republics, making it clear that it has no intention of threatening Baltic and Scandinavian countries or Poland and is not seeking conflict there'. By contrast, the creation of three army groupings on the border with Ukraine, where there had been no troops at all in 2013, made possible a rapid strike if an attempt was made to seize the Donbas by force. For Russia, the main security threat was now perceived to come from Ukraine.[39] This revealed the gulf between Russian and NATO views of European security. For NATO, enlarging the alliance and moving forces up to Russia's borders would make Europe safer; for Russia, these moves were seen as threatening and confrontational.

All of this should be kept in context. As noted, the Atlantic alliance is overwhelmingly more powerful than Russia. The population of the NATO alliance is six times that of Russia, its combined defence expenditure at least twenty times greater, and its GDP surpasses Russia's at least twenty-fold. Russian military expenditure is only 8 per cent of the combined NATO total. The US accounts for 36 per cent of global military expenditure, while Russia's represents 4 per cent. In addition, NATO's advance to within 500 miles of Moscow gives it strategic depth that has commensurately been lost by Russia. In 2016, moreover, defence spending started to fall as pressure on the budget mounted because of sluggish economic activity and low oil prices.[40] For the first time since the 1990s Russia was not one of the top five defence spenders, with the US still in first place, followed by China, the UK, India and Saudi Arabia, with Russia only sixth.[41] Nevertheless, the gap was closing; in 1992 the US defence budget was seventy-seven times greater than Russia's, but in 2015 it was only ten times larger. Russia was a regional power with global

---

[38] Patrick Armstrong, 'First Guards Tank Army', *Russian Federation Sitrep*, 25 February 2016.

[39] Ruslan Pukhov, 'Nashakarta Afriki', *Vedomosti*, 15 July 2016, p. 7.

[40] 'Russian Defence Spending Going Down after Record Growth in 2015', *Sputnik*, 13 October 2016.

[41] Peggy Hollinger, 'India Moves into Top Five Global Defence Spenders', *Financial Times*, 12 December 2016.

ambitions and responsibilities. The gap between capacities and ambitions had narrowed, but had not disappeared.

Dialogue and Deterrence

NATO policy tends to change at a glacial pace, but once set in motion, it is hard to modify. The European Reassurance Initiative (ERI) was launched by Obama in June 2014 with a $1 billion budget for training and force rotation, but already by 2017 the Pentagon envisaged a near-fourfold funding increase to $3.4 billion. US operations for NATO in Europe come under the umbrella of Operation Atlantic Resolve, including the deployment of rotating battalion groups and enhanced exercises for the 100,000 US troops (in all services) deployed on the continent. Counter-insurgency strategies gave way to planning for great power conflict. After 9/11 terrorism issues predominated, but now military planners prepared for what they call a 'big war', large-scale and high-level conflict with a major adversary such as Russia or China. Planning focused on a potential conflict taking place on NATO's eastern flank between the Baltic and the Black seas. This was prompted by 'Russian aggression in Ukraine and Chinese adventurism in the South China Sea', but it also reflected deeper concerns: 'Probe more deeply into the thinking of senior leaders and a different picture emerges. Running throughout this discussion is a pervasive anxiety that the strategic advantages once possessed by the West are slipping away as other powers gain increased military and geopolitical leverage.' The organisational and material capacities on display in Crimea and Syria, compared to the ragtag forces in Chechnya and South Ossetia earlier, demonstrated that Russian military investment was paying off. Equally, the Chinese military had gained new capacities and challenged the American view of the South China Sea as an American lake. All this was accompanied by the 'militarisation of international relations', with a shift away from the negotiating table towards sabre rattling.[42] This was reminiscent of the early 1900s. Christopher Clark's *The Sleepwalkers* describes how military officers in 1914 convinced European leaders to engage in armed rather than diplomatic responses to threats and affronts.[43]

By February 2016 US Air Force General Philip M. Breedlove, the head of NATO's armed forces, argued that the era of trying to work with Russia

---

[42] Michael T. Klare, 'Sleepwalking into a Major War', *Le Monde Diplomatique*, September 2016, www.1913intel.com/2016/09/07/sleepwalking-into-a-big-war-by-michael-t-klare-le-monde-diplomatique-english-edition-september-2016-2/, last accessed 30 May 2017.

[43] Christopher Clark, *The Sleepwalkers: How Europe Went to War in 1914* (London, Penguin, 2013).

was over, asserting that 'Russia does not want to challenge the agreed rules of international order. It wants to rewrite them.' Breedlove supported the Pentagon's request for increased funding for the ERI, and noted that long-term work would focus on five areas: building infrastructure such as ports, rail yards and training areas; prepositioning equipment; increasing rotational forces; building the capacities of NATO allies; and conducting training and exercises with allies. Although he noted that '[t]his is not the Cold War', he nevertheless warned that Russia was 'weaponising' the Syrian refugee crisis, with Russian airstrikes hitting civilians, causing them to flee and overwhelm Europe.[44] He voiced the view of many in America when he argued that '[t]he foundation of any strategy in Europe must be the recognition that Russia poses an enduring existential threat to the United States, its allies, and the international order. Russia is determined to once again become a global power.'[45] Although he accepted there was some scope to work with Russia on common challenges, such as Iranian nuclear issues, he insisted that '[t]he Kremlin respects only strength and sees opportunity in the weakness and inattention of others'.[46] Secret emails exposed in mid-2016 revealed 'a clandestine network of Western agitators around the NATO military chief, whose presence fuelled the conflict in Ukraine'. The questionable sources of Breedlove's alarmist pronouncements, based in conservative think tanks in Washington, sought to get offensive weapons delivered to Kiev, and Merkel and Obama were condemned for their restraint.[47]

The Warsaw summit of NATO leaders on 8 and 9 July 2016 confirmed the dual track strategy of 'deterrence and dialogue'. This returned the alliance to the position of the Harmel Report of 1967, which institutionalised a dual track approach of defence and dialogue. The post-Cold War promise off dismantling military confrontation in Europe was sharply reversed. The summit met in the wake of the Brexit vote and NATO's largest exercises since the Cold War. The Anaconda-2016 exercise involved 31,000 troops from twenty-four countries, responding to what had become a classic-post-Ukraine scenario of Russia provoking a crisis on

[44] Rebecca Kheel, 'Top US Commander: Russia Wants to "Rewrite" International Order', *The Hill*, 25 February 2016, http://thehill.com/policy/defense/270796-top-us-comman der-russia-wants-to-rewrite-international-order, last accessed 30 May 2017.

[45] Philip M. Breedlove, 'NATO's Next Act: How to Handle Russia and Other Threats', *Foreign Affairs*, Vol. 95, No. 4, July–August 2016, p. 102.

[46] Breedlove, 'NATO's Next Act', p. 103.

[47] Christopher Schult and Klaus Wiegrefe, 'Dangerous Propaganda', *Der Spiegel*, 28 July 2016, reproduced in DC Leaks, 'Breedlove Conspired to Lie about Russian Aggression in Ukraine, Get More Weapons Delivered to Kiev', www.sott.net/article/324462-DC-Leaks-Breedlove-conspired-to-lie-about-Russian-aggression-in-Ukraine-get-more-wea pons-deliveries-for-Kiev, last accessed 30 May 2017.

the border with Estonia that escalates into war. The BALTOPS multi-national naval exercise in July 2016 was one of the largest since they began in 1971, demonstrating the prowess of detachments of the US fleet of 274 ships (expected to rise to over 300 by 2020). The US-led Operation Sabre Strike was the largest since they had been launched in 2010, bringing together over 10,000 troops from thirteen countries. The remilitarisation of European security rolled back the gains of the early post-communist years. The increased frequency and scale of exercises and the rotation of forces in the three Baltic republics and Poland demonstrated how the conflict was becoming increasingly entrenched. The 'reassurance' of NATO's eastern members forced 'deterrence' measures against Russia.

On the eve of the Warsaw summit the foreign minister, Frank-Walter Steinmeier (who in March 2017 became president of Germany), criticised NATO, noting that '[w]hoever believes that a symbolic tank parade on the alliance's eastern border will bring security is mistaken'. He warned '[w]hat we should not do now is to inflame the situation by loud sabre-rattling and war-mongering', and called for dialogue with Moscow: 'We are well-advised not to create pretexts to renew an old confrontation', stressing it would be 'fatal to search only for military solutions and a policy of deterrence'.[48] The next day General Peter Pavel, chair of NATO's military committee, was equally dismissive of alarmist talk and unequivocally stated that Russia was not a threat to the West: 'It is not the aim of NATO to create a military barrier against broad-scale Russian aggression, because such aggression is not on the agenda and no intelligence assessment suggests such a thing.'[49] In his pre-summit press conference Jens Stoltenberg, the NATO secretary general, insisted that 'NATO does not seek confrontation. We don't want a new cold war, what we do is proportionate [and] defensive'.[50] Nevertheless, the Warsaw summit confirmed a range of military responses to what was essentially a political conflict.

The Warsaw communiqué noted that since the Wales summit in 2014 the alliance had 'taken a range of steps to reinforce our collective defence,

---

[48] Justin Huggler, 'German Foreign Minister Accuses NATO of "Warmongering" Against Russia', *The Telegraph*, 18 June 2016, www.telegraph.co.uk/news/2016/06/18/german-f oreign-minister-accuses-nato-of-warmongering-against-rus/, last accessed 30 May 2017.

[49] Tyler Durden, 'NATO General Admits that Russia is not a Threat to the Region', *Zero Hedge*, 22 June 2016, www.zerohedge.com/news/2016-06-22/nato-general-admits-rus sia-not-threat-region, last accessed 30 May 2017; for Pavel's comments, see also Joe Lauria, 'Europeans Contest US Anti-Russian Hype', Consortiumnews.com, 27 June 2016, https://consortiumnews.com/2016/06/27/europeans-contest-us-anti-russian-hyp e/, last accessed 30 May 2017, and 'NATO Commander sees no Imminent Threat to Baltics', 20 June 2016, www.reuters.com/article/us-nato-russia-pavel-idUSKCN0Z616 T, last accessed 30 May 2017.

[50] 'Pre-Summit Press Conference by NATO Secretary General Jens Stoltenberg', 4 July 2016, www.nato.int/cps/en/natohq/opinions_133053.htm, last accessed 30 May 2017.

enhance our capabilities, and strengthen our resilience', including the creation of the Very High Readiness Joint Task Force (VJTF), also known as the Spearhead Force, with the capacity to deploy within two to three days. This was part of America's ERI, intended to improve deterrence readiness from the Baltic to the Black Sea. The document noted:

There is an arc of insecurity and instability along NATO's periphery and beyond. The Alliance faces a range of security challenges and threats that originate both from the east and from the south; from state and non-state actors; from military forces and from terrorist, cyber, or hybrid attacks. Russia's aggressive actions, including provocative military activities in the periphery of NATO territory and its demonstrated willingness to attain political goals by the threat and use of force, are a source of regional instability, fundamentally challenge the Alliance, have damaged Euro-Atlantic security, and threaten our long-standing goal of a Europe whole, free, and at peace.

Russian policy on a broad range of issues was excoriated:

Russia's destabilising actions and policies include: the ongoing illegal and illegitimate annexation of Crimea, which we do not and will not recognise and which we call on Russia to reverse; the violation of sovereign borders by force; the deliberate destabilisation of eastern Ukraine; large-scale snap exercises contrary to the spirit of the Vienna Document, and provocative military activities near NATO borders, including in the Baltic and Black Sea regions and the Eastern Mediterranean; its irresponsible and aggressive nuclear rhetoric, military concept and underlying posture; and its repeated violations of NATO Allied airspace. In addition, Russia's military intervention, significant military presence and support for the regime in Syria, and its use of its military presence in the Black Sea to project power into the Eastern Mediterranean have posed further risks and challenges for the security of Allies and others.

Dialogue was defined in minimalist terms: 'Talking to Russia allows us to communicate clearly our positions, with the crisis in and around Ukraine being, in current circumstances, the first topic on our agenda.' The deployment of rotational military forces to the Baltic states and Poland to 'deter' Russia was confirmed, although there would not be permanent bases. Four battalions totalling around 4,000 troops from sixteen countries would be deployed, led by the US in Poland, Britain in Estonia, Canada in Latvia and Germany in Lithuania. NATO took over the US-built missile shield in Europe, and the alliance reaffirmed its commitment to a mix of conventional and nuclear forces, a classic Cold War stance that recognised Russia's predominance in conventional forces in Europe. NATO also agreed to support the Afghan security forces and the EU's military mission off the Libyan coast, and NATO and the EU signed a cooperation pact for joint maritime patrols and work on preventing Russian cyber-attacks.[51] Stoltenberg denied that Russia presented 'any imminent threat to any Nato ally', and argued that strong defence should be accompanied by 'constructive dialogue'. 'The cold war', he insisted, 'is history and should remain history.'[52] In his post-summit press conference he reasserted: 'NATO poses no threat to any country. We do not want a new Cold War. We do not want a new arms race. And we do not seek confrontation.'[53] Nevertheless, twenty-four of the 139 paragraphs of the final communiqué dealt with the containment of Russia. At the same time, there was no dramatic shift in nuclear posture, such as redirecting the BMD systems against Russia, and the new force deployments were largely of symbolic 'reassurance' significance. Equally, the hopes of countries such as Georgia, even Ukraine, that the crisis would accelerate their membership were disappointed.[54] NATO was not preparing for a full-scale Cold War against Russia. Nevertheless, its moves to stabilise the security situation in Europe failed to address the root causes of the crisis, which in part lay in NATO's own expansionary dynamic.

The Kremlin responded calmly to the summit's animadversions, although insisted that NATO was countering a 'non-existent' threat. Russia maintained some 330,000 troops in the western part of the country, now extensively reformed and re-equipped. Karaganov noted how 'NATO quantitatively exceeds Russia in all components of military power except nuclear capabilities', so the idea that Russia would attack a NATO country was fanciful. Even though Russia was the target of a propaganda campaign, he argued:

There is no need to repeat the folly of the late Soviet and early Russian periods when we wanted to please the West and hoped for an equitable and stable security system in Europe. An analogue of that policy today would be an attempt to resume relations with NATO in the old format. Russia's weakness and attempts at appeasement helped turn the alliance from a predominantly defensive bloc, as it was during the Cold War, into an offensive one and the main factor of military and political instability in Europe.

[51] 'Warsaw Summit Communiqué', 9 July 2016, www.nato.int/cps/en/natohq/official_texts_133169.htm, last accessed 30 May 2017.

[52] Mary Dejevsky, 'Will Nato's Warmer Words Prevent a New Cold War?', *Guardian*, 11 July 2016, p. 23.

[53] 'Press Conference by NATO Secretary General Jens Stoltenberg following the meetings of the North Atlantic Council at the level of Heads of State and Government', 8 July 2016, www.nato.int/cps/en/natohq/opinions_133276.htm?selectedLocale=en, last accessed 30 May 2017.

[54] 'Gruziya na beskonechnom puti v NATO', *Kommersant*, 6 September 2016, reproduced in https://news.rambler.ru/caucasus/34652503-gruziya-na-beskonechnom-puti-v-nato/, last accessed 9 June 2017.

In his view, security dialogue could no longer be limited to the old European framework, stressing that '[a]s long as we remain within it, and the West does not want to give up the old system, this framework reproduces confrontation'. A 'Eurasian cooperation, development and development dialogue' was required, encompassing the region from Shannon to Shanghai.[55]

In his eighth biennial meeting with Russian ambassadors on 30 June 2016 Putin maintained the relatively emollient tone evident at that time. Only the previous autumn he had referred to Western countries as 'our geopolitical adversaries', but in St Petersburg he referred to the US at the world's 'only superpower' and insisted 'we want to work with the United States and we are prepared to'. Nevertheless, at the ambassadors' meeting he condemned the way that 'partners continue stubborn attempts to retain their monopoly on geopolitical domination ... By this, I mean, for example, the practice of intervening in other countries' internal affairs, provoking regional conflicts, exporting so-called "colour revolutions" and so on.' Putin noted Russia's success in arranging ceasefires and facilitating peace talks in Syria, in cooperation with 'the United States and other partners'. He went on to emphasise 'that we are interested in close cooperation with the United States on international affairs'. He made it clear that he sought a deal over Ukraine, but only as long as Russian concerns were satisfied. These include that Ukraine remained a neutral state and unaligned with the West: 'We want to see a Ukraine that is a good neighbour and a predictable and civilized partner living in peace at home and in the world.' He considered it unacceptable to continue the Ukrainian crisis and to blame Russia for it: 'This only aggravates the consequences of the great mistake that was NATO's decision to expand eastwards rather than to start building, with Russia as a full-fledged partner, a new architecture for equal and indivisible security from the Atlantic to the Pacific'. Despite the evident setbacks, Putin remained committed to the Greater European idea: 'Let me stress that not only has Russia not abandoned the idea of establishing a common economic and humanitarian space from the Atlantic to the Pacific together with the European Union, but we also think this would be the most promising policy in terms of guaranteeing the entire Eurasian continent's long-term sustainable development.'[56]

Despite the militancy of the rhetoric, opinion polls revealed that majorities in most European countries opposed their countries going to war

[55] Sergei Karaganov, 'Missiles in Europe: Back to the Future?', *Russia in Global Affairs*, July–August 2016, http://eng.globalaffairs.ru/pubcol/Missiles-in-Europe-Back-to-the-Future-18267, last accessed 30 May 2017.

[56] Vladimir Putin, 'Meeting of Russian Federation Ambassadors and Permanent Envoys', 30 June 2016, http://en.kremlin.ru/events/president/news/52298, last accessed 30 May 2017.

with Russia to defend their NATO partners. In Germany, the pivot state of the new Atlanticism, the majority against was as high as 57 per cent.[57] It was not even certain that America would be prepared to incinerate its cities to defend the peripheral European states. NATO committed itself to the defence of the Baltic states, but in a great power conflict they would be indefensible. This was unlikely to be tested, since most traditional European powers did not really believe that armed confrontation was imminent. A report by the Atlantic Council on 4 March 2016 argued that NATO's European members would be unable to fight a war against Russia. The report warned that many of the key members of the alliance were weakened by 'chronic underfunding', and 'critical deficiencies' in what they termed 'hollowed out' armed forces. The report noted that Germany had only ten working Tiger helicopters out of a fleet of thirty-one, and just 280 of its 406 Marder armoured infantry vehicles were active. The UK would be challenged to deploy a brigade, let alone a division, at credible levels of combat readiness.[58] This contrasts with the view advanced by Breedlove. In April 2015 he argued that '[o]ur top concern is a revanchist Russia. Russia is blatantly challenging the rules and principles that have been the bedrock of European security for decades. The challenge is global, not regional, and enduring, not temporary.'[59] He warned that the '[t]he Security challenges around Europe are only growing sharper and more complicated', with the threat from Russia at the top of his list, although he warned that more resources and greater commitment were needed. He insisted that 'these challenges means our own US efforts in Europe remain utterly essential: more important now than any time in recent history', and stressed that '[t]here is simply no substitute for our forward presence in Europe', but warned that '[r]otational presence is no substitute as permanent forward presence in building relationships for signalling our commitment'.[60]

A year later he was confident that American troops would easily beat Russia in any conflict. He argued that '[t]o counter Russia, EUCOM [US

[57] Alexander Mercouris, 'NATO Wants to End Russia's Independence – Not Just Prolong its Own Existence', *The Duran*, 12 May 2016, http://theduran.com/nato-wants-to-end-russia-independence-not-just-prolong-own-existence/, last accessed 30 May 2017.

[58] The report was prepared by six senior defence experts, including the former NATO Secretary General Jaap de Hoop Scheffer, and deputy supreme commander Sir Richard Shirreff, Atlantic Council, 4 March 2016.

[59] Senate Armed Services Committee, 'Opening Statement by General Phil Breedlove, Commander, US European Command', 30 April 2015, http://eucom.mil/media-librar y/article/33031/senate-armed-services-committee-opening-statement-by-general-phil-b reedlove-commander-u-s-european, last accessed 9 June 2017.

[60] 'Department of Defense Press Briefing by General Breedlove in the Pentagon Briefing Room', 25 February 2015, www.defense.gov/News/News-Transcripts/Transcript-View/ Article/607020, last accessed 30 May 2017.

European Command], working with allies and partners, is deterring Russia now and preparing to fight and win if necessary'.[61] In what he considered to be a salutary warning, NATO's former deputy supreme allied commander in Europe, General Sir Richard Shirreff, warned of war between Russia and NATO in 2017. Modelled on NATO experience of war-gaming future conflicts, the book argued that Russia's 'invasion and seizure' of Georgia (in 2008) was the 'Rhineland moment', which was ignored by the West as it continued 'business as usual', while the seizure of Crimea was the 'Sudetenland moment', and the Baltic republics would be next. The book urged Western countries to prepare for and increase their defence spending.[62] The book described a classic diversionary war, in which the fictional leader, known mysteriously as Vladimir Vladimirovich, launches an unprovoked war (by abducting some American soldiers in Kharkov, followed in short order by an invasion of the Baltic republics) in response to falling poll ratings, anticipating that a 'small victorious war' would restore his fortunes.

Shirreff was no Churchill, Putin was not Hitler, and twenty-first-century Europe is not replaying the 1900s or the 1930s. Yet the structural tensions are reminiscent of the earlier periods. The new militarism is driven by genuine contradictions in the European security order and in global politics more broadly. The flames of conflict are fanned by military leaders, defence industries, think tanks, the media, and parliamentarians. Peripheral issues can easily turn into a conflagration, as in Sarajevo in June 1914. Nevertheless, there is a natural reluctance to believe that Europe is once again threatened with the devastation of 1945, hence the mixed enthusiasm in Europe for neo-containment policies. By contrast, the American mainland had been spared the bombing and destruction, and had created a formidable military machine to fight the Cold War. This became an independent force swelled by that war. In his resignation speech on 17 January 1961, Dwight D. Eisenhower warned of the dire threat to democratic government posed by what he called the 'military-industrial complex', the union of defence contractors and the arms industry. BMD is an example of the expensive pursuit of technological solutions to political problems. In the post-Cold War years the scissors widened between continued American militarism and Europe's cashing in of the peace dividend. The new Atlanticism sought to close the gap.[63] The

---

[61] Quoted in 'NATO Can't Fight Russians in Europe, Says Leading US Think Tank', www.rt.com, 26 February 2016.

[62] Richard Shirreff, *2017 War with Russia: An Urgent Warning from Senior Military Command* (London, Coronet, 2016).

[63] A whole slew of publications warned that old threats such as Russia were joined by new threats like Islamic State as the West's will as well as capacity to shape the world were declining. For example, Mark Urban, *The Edge: Is the Military Dominance of the West Coming to an End?* (Boston, Little, Brown, 2015).

task was facilitated by the emergence of a recalcitrant Russia as the enemy 'other' against which the Western alliance could mobilise.

Strategic Instability and Nuclear Insecurity

The architecture of nuclear security built up over the post-war decades is unravelling. The global stock of nuclear weapons peaked in the mid-1980s at nearly 70,000, with the US deploying over 30,000, with 400 targeted on Moscow alone. The stock of nuclear weapons was greatly reduced in the post-Cold War years, primarily as a result of cuts by Russia and the US. At the start of 2016 the total of nuclear weapons was 15,395, including 4,120 deployed operationally. At that time Russia had 7,290 nuclear warheads, including tactical, and the US 7,000, accounting for 93 per cent of the world total. The post-Cold War decline in nuclear arms has now slowed and could soon be reversed. Russia and the US have extensive nuclear modernisation plans, while India, Pakistan and North Korea are planning to expand their arsenals.[64] The US 2015 *National Military Strategy* outlined a trillion dollar nuclear modernisation programme, including $355 billion on twelve new nuclear-armed strategic submarines, up to 100 new strategic bombers, new land-based intercontinental ballistic missiles (ICBMs) deployable on mobile launchers, and over 1,000 nuclear-capable cruise missiles. The latter were considered especially destabilising since there is no way for the intended target to know whether they are armed with conventional or nuclear variants, widening the scope for miscalculation and unintended escalation.[65] Soon after the announcement, Putin declared that Russia would add forty new ICBMs to its nuclear arsenal. This signalled that Russia would respond robustly to the implicit threat in the *Strategy*. Russia was right to be concerned, since US nuclear force modernisation undermines strategic stability. The new burst-height compensating super-fuse technology means that Russia's entire land-based nuclear arsenal is susceptible to a first-strike attack.[66]

---

[64] SIPRI annual report, 'Global Nuclear Weapons: Downsizing but Modernizing', 13 June 2016, www.sipri.org/media/press-release/2016/global-nuclear-weapons-downsizing-mo dernizing, last accessed 30 May 2017.
[65] Borger, 'Threat of Nuclear Disaster Returns'.
[66] Hans M. Kristensen, Matthew McKinzie and Theodore A. Postol, 'How US Nuclear Force Modernization is Undermining Strategic Stability: The Burst-Height Compensating Super-Fuze', *Bulletin of the Atomic Scientists*, 1 March 2017, http://thebulletin.org/how-us-nuclear-force-modernization-undermining-strategic-stability-burst-height-compensating-supe r10578, last accessed 30 May 2017. For an illuminating discussion, see Aleksei Arbatov, 'Opasnaya modernizatsiya amerikanskikh yadernykh boegolovok?', RIAC, 17 March 2017, http://russiancouncil.ru/analytics-and-comments/analytics/opasnaya-modernizatsiya-ameri kanskikh-yadernykh-boegolovok/, last accessed 9 June 2017.

Alexei Arbatov, a leading expert in the field, warns that the whole system of arms control, which began with the 1963 Partial Test Ban Treaty, is breaking down. He warned that 'today marks the first time in a half century that there is a real prospect of losing the legal regime for managing the most horrific instrument of devastation ever created'. He noted that although the two key treaties – the 1987 Intermediate-Range Nuclear Forces (INF) Treaty and New START – remained in force (the latter until 2021), the agreements were under severe pressure. The issues dividing Russia and the US were many. Lavrov stressed that the global US missile defence system posed a threat 'not only to Russia's security, but also to the entire world, because of a possible imbalance in strategic forces' and warned that Russia would respond with 'adequate measures', although it had 'no intention to drift into a costly arms race', and dismissed US accusations that Russia was in breach of the INF Treaty.[67] Since July 2014 the US had indeed accused Moscow of violating the 1987 treaty, which prohibits all launchers and ground-launched missiles with a range of 500 to 5,500 km, assumedly by testing the R-500 intermediate-range missile. This was only part of a broader breakdown. As we have seen, the US unilaterally left the ABM Treaty in June 2002, and had no plans to ratify the 1996 Comprehensive Nuclear Test Ban Treaty. On the Russian side, there are plenty of voices calling for the country to leave the whole system, including even the keystone in the nuclear control architecture, the Nuclear Non-Proliferation Treaty, which came into force in 1970. As Arbatov writes: 'Although arms control has faced difficulties in the past, never before have virtually all negotiating tracks been simultaneously stalled, existing treaties been eroded by political and technological developments, and the planning for next steps been so in doubt.'[68]

Igor Ivanov warns that '[t]he risk of confrontation with the use of nuclear weapons in Europe is higher than in the 1980s'. He argued that the missile defence shield being installed by the US raised the stakes, with the sites in Poland becoming operational in 2018, bringing US capabilities right to the Russian border. Ivanov warned that '[i]t can be assured that once the US deploys its missile defence system in Poland, Russia would respond by deploying its own missile defence systems in Kaliningrad'.[69] No mutually understood strategic framework replaced

[67] 'Lavrov's Big Interview'.

[68] Alexei Arbatov, 'An Unnoticed Crisis: The End of History for Nuclear Arms Control?', Carnegie Moscow Centre, 16 March 2015, http://carnegie.ru/2015/03/16/unnoticed-cr isis-end-of-history-for-nuclear-arms-control, last accessed 30 May 2017.

[69] Robin Emmott, 'Risk of Nuclear War in Europe Growing, Warns Russian Ex-Minister', Reuters, 19 March 2016, www.reuters.com/article/us-ukraine-crisis-russia-idUSKCN0 WL0EV, last accessed 30 May 2017.

the Cold War paradigm. New START limited Russia and the US each to no more than 700 deployed delivery vehicles and 1,550 warheads. It requires eighteen annual on-site inspections of land, sea and air nuclear bases, and the exchange of up to forty-two annual notifications of changes at strategic nuclear arms sites. A five-year extension beyond 2021 was envisaged, but needs to be agreed by both sides. The US abrogation of the ABM Treaty remained an intense bone of contention. Russia sought negotiations for a new BMD Treaty, involving other nuclear states and not just Russia and the US, to limit the number and capability of such systems, and a prohibition on their deployment abroad.[70] With the stalemate in Russo-US relations, the prospects for the nuclear arms control agenda look bleak.[71]

In 2012 Russia pulled out of the Nunn-Lugar Cooperative Threat Reduction Programme, under which it had received considerable US assistance to manage its superfluous nuclear arsenal. In summer 2013 strategic stability talks between Moscow and Washington came to an end, and for the first time in decades there were no great power talks on nuclear issues. Instead, both sides alleged that the other was violating existing agreements, including the INF Treaty. There was even talk of Russia abrogating the INF Treaty, on the grounds that the Soviet Union had eliminated its land-based intermediate missiles while leaving US air and sea launched missiles in place. Another gripe was that Russia was the only state in its neighbourhood prohibited from deploying these weapons, whereas shielded by two great oceans the US was safe on its island-continent.[72] On 3 October 2016, Putin suspended the agreement on the destruction of part of the enormous stockpile of weapons-grade plutonium. Putin cited 'the emergence of a threat to strategic stability' and unfriendly actions by the US. The litany of grievances included NATO actions in Europe and alleged US support for right-wing groups in Ukraine. He imposed an improbable list of conditions, calling on America to compensate Moscow for the damage caused by sanctions, as well as for Russia's 'forced counter-sanctions'. The statement also called for the repeal of the December 2012 Magnitsky Act that sanctioned eighteen Russians allegedly involved in a massive tax fraud scheme and the death of the whistle-blowing Russian lawyer and auditor, Sergei Magnitsky. The

---

[70] Vladimir Kozin, 'Anti-Ballistic Missile Defence: The US Provocation that Threatens World Peace', *The Duran*, 23 May 2016, http://theduran.com/anti-ballistic-missle-defe nce-us-provocation-threatens-world-peace/, last accessed 30 May 2017.

[71] Vladimir Dvorkin, 'A New Russian-US Nuclear Treaty or an Extension of New START', Carnegie Moscow Centre, 1 August 2016, http://carnegie.ru/publications/?f a=64435, last accessed 30 May 2017.

[72] For a full discussion, see Ulrich Kühn and Anna Péczeli, 'Russia, NATO, and the INF Treaty', *Strategic Studies Quarterly*, Spring 2017, pp. 66–99.

Kremlin had responded by imposing a ban on Americans adopting Russian children. Putin's message then and in the new bill was clear: 'Russia will start acting as an equal, whether or not the US wants to treat it as one'.[73]

These were all issues that Moscow considered obstacles to the normalisation of relations with Washington. The plutonium agreement had been signed in 2000 (one of the achievements of Putin's early years), to make arms reductions irreversible by destroying 34 tons each, enough for 17,000 nuclear weapons combined. In 2016 the US is estimated to have had around 95 tons and Russia 128 tons of weapons-grade plutonium. The deal stipulated that the plutonium would be blended with uranium to make a mixed-oxide fuel (MOX) for use in power stations. Cost over-runs prompted Obama to cancel plans to build a MOX plant in South Carolina, and instead sought to use dilution and disposal technologies, which could theoretically (although with great difficulty) allow the plutonium to be extracted at some later point.[74] The revised American strategy probably made sense in the circumstances, although the Russian side could hardly believe that the world's greatest power was incapable of building a MOX plant, whereas Russia's had long been in operation. The repudiation of this deal was another sign of the breakdown in trust and, ominously, the end of cooperation between Russia and the US in ensuring the safety of nuclear arsenals. Hitherto Moscow had kept strategic issues separate from other aspects of bilateral relations, but now it became dependent on a long list of unachievable demands. Even common interests could not overcome the growing hostility between the two powers.

In May 2016 the ground missile complex 'Aegis Ashore' was commissioned in Deveselu in Romania as part of NATO's BMD system. The site houses twenty-four SM-3 missile interceptors capable of hitting intermediate-range ballistic missiles warheads as well as a SPY-1D radar system. The next day ground was broken for a second SM-3 installation in Redzikowo in Poland for commissioning in 2018. Although the JCPOA had stopped Iran's nuclear weapons programme, it continued with its ballistic missile programme, and thus the US argued that the missile shield was still required. The Polish site offered little extra capability against Iran, and thus expenditure on it – the Romanian site had cost $800 million – was largely a political investment to 'reassure' its Polish

---

[73] Leonid Bershidsky, 'Putin's Ultimatum to the Next US President', Bloomberg, 4 October 2016, www.bloomberg.com/view/articles/2016-10-04/putin-s-ultimatum-to-the-next-u-s-p resident, last accessed 30 May 2017.

[74] Mike Eckel, 'Putin Suspends US-Russia Plutonium Deal, Blaming NATO, Sanctions, Magnitsky Act', RFE/RL, *Russia Report*, 3 October 2016.

ally. Missile defence had become a sacred shibboleth in the US Congress, irrespective of its capacities and political implications. The European Phased Adaptive Approach poses at most a limited threat to Russia's strategic nuclear arsenal, since the SM-3 interceptors lack the velocity to engage with ICBM warheads. Nevertheless, in the event of conflict, the bases are well placed to attack major Russian cities in the western part of the country. Above all, Moscow was concerned that advances in ballistic missile technology posed a long-term threat, especially when considered in conjunction with other technological developments that could provide the US with a devastating first-strike capability.

Moscow's position was determined by a deep sense of vulnerability in terms of conventional Prompt Global Strike capabilities, nuclear weapons, cyber-weapons, and now missile defence systems. Visiting Finland in July 2016, Putin warned that the BMD system was 'being deployed under the far-fetched pretext of countering the Iranian nuclear threat after this threat has been eliminated', and he warned that the Aegis system could be rapidly converted to launch mid-range cruise missiles of over two thousands kilometres: 'And this can be done absolutely covertly, secretly within a few hours, all you need is to change the computer software.'[75] As for future challenges, the emergence of hypersonic missiles accompanied by increasingly precise ballistic missiles and a reliable ABM network could allow the US to launch a decapitation strike.[76] This would destroy Russia's leadership and nuclear arsenal, and any surviving Russian retaliatory missile strike would be intercepted and destroyed by the new advanced ABM systems. From the Kremlin's perspective, the US seemed to be pursuing the strategy outlined in the notorious *Foreign Affairs* article of 2006, discussed earlier, which talked of 'the rise of nuclear primacy'.[77] Although US policy-makers sometimes defended BMD as a step towards a more defensive nuclear strategy, 'the truth is that they wanted defences in order to facilitate winning a nuclear war at reasonable cost'.[78]

Russia deployed Iskander missiles to Kaliningrad, accompanied by S-400 missiles. Moscow also devoted considerable resources to modernising its nuclear forces, including the introduction of a new generation of ICBMs. After years of troubled development, the Bulava submarine-launched ballistic missiles is now deployed. The new SS-X-30 Sarmat

---

[75] Vladimir Putin, 'Press Statements and Answers to Journalists' Questions Following Russian-Finnish Talks', 1 July 2016, http://en.kremlin.ru/events/president/transcripts/5 2312, last accessed 30 May 2017.
[76] Vladimir Dvorkin, 'Hypersonic Threats: The Need for a Realistic Assessment', Carnegie Moscow Centre, 9 August 2016, http://carnegie.ru/2016/08/09/hypersonic-threats-nee d-for-realistic-assessment/j3is, last accessed 30 May 2017.
[77] Lieber and Press, 'The Rise of US Nuclear Primacy'.
[78] Mearsheimer, *Tragedy of Great Power Politics*, p. 228.

missile is also being tested. This is accompanied by concern that Russia has lowered its threshold for the use of nuclear weapons. This was dismissed by Olga Oliker, one of the leading experts in the field. She notes that 'de-escalation strategies' had been much discussed in the 1990s, when Russia's conventional forces were catastrophically weak, but as Russia's conventional forces demonstrated greater capabilities, there was little evidence that Russia employed an 'escalate to de-escalate strategy' or contemplated the use of tactical nuclear weapons. The Russian leadership repeatedly stressed its nuclear resources, but this was more a sign of weakness than bellicosity. The 2010 *Military Doctrine*, contrary to expectations, did not provide for 'preventive' nuclear strikes to deter conventional attacks, and in fact the threshold went up rather than down, and this was confirmed in 2014. Russia, like the US, continues to modernise its nuclear forces, but this has nothing to do with a reduction in the threshold for their use. The introduction of new dual-capable systems, such as the Iskander missile, is potentially destabilising, but so are the American equivalents. Oliker notes that there is a lot to be worried about, including Russia's reliance on silo-based ICBMs that are hard to protect. At a time when Russia's early warning systems lack adequate satellites, the fear of an American first strike could provoke a pre-emptive attack. It is not always easy to distinguish a flock of geese from incoming ICBMs. Oliker stresses that Russian officials and military personnel take nuclear weapons seriously, but the ambiguities surrounding new dual-use missiles keep potential adversaries off-balance, reducing transparency and increasing the risk of miscalculation.[79]

In 2015 the Doomsday Clock, run by the Bulletin of the Atomic Scientists, was advanced to three minutes to midnight, a setting seen only twice before at the worst times of the Cold War – in 1984, following the Able Archer scare of autumn 1983, and 1949, when the Soviet Union tested its first nuclear weapon. Only once was it worse, at two minutes to midnight, in 1953 when the US decided to pursue the hydrogen bomb. With the continued deterioration in the strategic environment, in early 2017 the clock was pushed forward to two-and-a-half minutes to midnight.[80] William Perry feared the breakdown in strategic arms control. Speaking shortly before North Korea's fourth nuclear test on 6 January 2016, he warned: 'The probability of a nuclear calamity is higher today, I believe, than it was during the cold war . . . A new danger has been

[79] Olga Oliker, 'No, Russia Isn't Trying to Make Nuclear War Easier', *The National Interest*, 23 May 2016, http://nationalinterest.org/feature/no-russia-isnt-trying-make-nuclear-war-easier-16310, last accessed 30 May 2017.

[80] Bulletin of the Atomic Scientists, 'Timeline', http://thebulletin.org/timeline, last accessed 30 May 2017.

rising in the past three years and that is the possibility there might be a nuclear exchange between the United States and Russia . . . brought about by a substantial miscalculation, a false alarm'.[81] The Russian leadership is terrified of a 'decapitation strike', of the sort launched against Gaddafi and Hussein earlier. Although these two cases failed, Russia's opposition to the American missile defence system in Europe 'is driven by fear of the role it could play in a surprise attack'.[82] Over 1,000 ICBMs in the US and Russia remain on hair trigger alert, operating a policy of 'launch-on-warning', giving the respective leaders less than half an hour to respond to radar data showing incoming missiles. Russia's strategic activism in Ukraine and Syria and the assertive posture of its air and sea patrols along the borders with NATO risked provoking a confrontation. To reassure its Eastern European allies, Washington also stepped up its flights. In 2015 it despatched a formation of strategic bombers across the Arctic for the first time since the Cold War. For Moscow, its patrols were no more than a response to the threat posed by NATO advancing to its borders.

Despite the Cold War becoming an increasingly distant memory, neither the US nor Russia repudiated the first-strike doctrine. With both sides fearing the erosion of second strike capabilities, the incentive is to launch first and ask questions later. With a combined total of 1,800 nuclear weapons on immediate alert, the US president would have some thirty minutes to decide whether early warning satellite data showing an attack were credible, while the Russian leader has about half that time since it lacks working early warning satellites. Communication channels between NATO and Russia have now been reduced far below those of the 1970s and 1980s. Even then, the Able Archer NATO exercise in autumn 1983 took the world to the brink of the apocalypse, a position to which we have now returned. Matters are aggravated by the new threats of cyber-warfare and the danger of nuclear command systems succumbing to attack. The former head of the US Strategic Command, General Robert Kehler, in a Rumsfeldian manner, admitted ignorance of the level of strategic vulnerability: 'We don't know what we don't know.'[83]

There were three occasions during the Cold War when there was the immediate danger of nuclear weapons being used – the Korean War of 1950–53, the Cuban missile crisis of October 1962, and autumn 1983 – but today we are effectively in a permanent condition of danger,

---

[81] Julian Borger, 'Threat of Nuclear Disaster Returns – and This Time Risks Could be Higher Than in Cold War', *Guardian*, 8 January 2016, p. 24.

[82] Eric Schlosser, 'World War Three, by Mistake', *New Yorker*, 23 December 2016, www.newyorker.com/news/news-desk/world-war-three-by-mistake, last accessed 30 May 2017.

[83] Borger, 'Threat of Nuclear Disaster Returns'.

with few of the restraining mechanisms. The Iranian nuclear deal in 2015 was a significant achievement, but resolved none of the issues that prompted Iran to aspire to nuclear weapons in the first place. The Libyan lesson of a country voluntarily giving up its nuclear weapons programme and then being attacked continues to resonate. Fears for its security prompted Pyongyang to leave the Nuclear Non-Proliferation Treaty and to accelerate its nuclear weapons programme. Similar fears prompted Moscow to make increasing references to its nuclear arsenal in public discourse. Even on the operational level, trust between the former superpowers has evaporated. This is yet another reason why the idea of a new Cold War is anachronistic. The dangers today are much greater in conditions where the wars of alternative reality are even more intense. The columnist Simon Jenkins notes that '[h]istorians such as Richard Rhodes and Andrew Alexander have catalogued the Nato mendacity and fear-mongering that was the cold war arms race with Russia. Rhodes's *Arsenals of Folly* showed such recklessness raised rather than lowered the risk of nuclear miscalculation.'[84] Rhodes demonstrates how Reagan's arms build-up in the early 1980s convinced the Soviet Union that the US was preparing for war, until the Nuclear Non-Proliferation Treaty achieved a dramatic reversal, allowing Reagan and Gorbachev to begin the de-escalation process at Reykjavik in 1986.[85] Andrew Alexander argues that America's global power since 1945 has been accompanied by a shocking incomprehension of the outside world, provoking a series of catastrophic foreign policy failures in which war was not the last resort of policy but the first. These blunders in his view began with the Cold War, countering a threat of Soviet expansionism that did not exist.[86]

Soon after the promulgation of the 2015 US *Military Strategy*, Putin addressed an expanded meeting of the Security Council in the Kremlin on 3 July 2015. He departed from his customary usage of the term 'partners' to argue: 'We cannot hope that some of our geopolitical opponents will change their hostile course anytime in the foreseeable future.' He noted: 'We know the reasons for the pressure being put on Russia. We follow an independent domestic and foreign policy and our sovereignty is not up for sale. This does not go down well in some quarters, but this is inevitable.' This was the first time that he had acknowledged so openly

---

[84] Simon Jenkins, 'Renew Trident? It'd Make More Sense to Put Dad's Army Back in Uniform', *Guardian*, 14 January 2016, p. 33.

[85] Richard Rhodes, *Arsenals of Folly: The Making of the Nuclear Arms Race* (London, Simon and Schuster, 2009).

[86] Andrew Alexander, *America and the Imperialism of Ignorance: US Foreign Policy since 1945* (London, Biteback, 2012).

that Russia was under attack. Nevertheless, he retained his customary confidence: 'It is clear today that attempts to split and divide our society, play on our problems, and seek out our vulnerable spots and weak links have not produced the results hoped for by those who imposed these restrictive measures on our country and continue to support them.'[87] The structural imbalances of the post-1989 order provoked resistance, which has the potential to become overt conflict.

[87] 'Security Council Meeting', 3 July 2015, http://en.kremlin.ru/events/president/news/49 862, last accessed 30 May 2017.

8   America and Global Leadership

Realist theory suggests that American policy is designed to 'keep a new balance of power from forming' in Asia and elsewhere, by maintaining a global network of military bases and enlarging NATO, but the same theory holds that '[t]he American aspiration to freeze historical development by working to keep the world unipolar is doomed'.[1] In practice, American troop levels in Europe declined as they were deployed to fight America's various wars in Afghanistan and Iraq. Under Obama there was a policy shift towards Asia and other regions, where the challenges were considered to be most immediate. Yet the fundamental structure of European security remained unresolved. The failure to create an inclusive security system in which all powers felt equally secure reinforced the unipolar (monist) interpretation of the new global order. Russia was faced by the choice of acquiescence or resistance. In the end, the balance tilted towards the latter, but this was not the option that Moscow considered optimal, and thus appeals were made for the terms of acquiescence to be made more palatable. This was the basis for Russia's neo-revisionism – to challenge the practices rather than the principles of the Atlantic power system, and to foster multipolarity in the international system. As far as the US was concerned, it bore the greatest responsibility for the maintenance of international law and a rules-based world order. Russian and American views were not incommensurate at the normative level, since the basis of Russia's critique of US hegemony appealed to the universal principles of international society. But it was precisely at the level of practices that the US power system was least prepared to share leadership. The neo-revisionist strategy became just another form of Russia's strategic impasse. Instead of a negotiated end to the Cold War to create a Greater West, it appeared that the shift in the balance of relative power to the East would allow the emergence of a post-Western alignment.

---

[1] Waltz, 'Structural Realism', p. 36.

Reality Wars and American Power

In a telephone call to Obama on 2 March 2014, Merkel apparently stated that 'after speaking with Mr. Putin she was not sure he was in touch with reality, people briefed on the call said. "In another world", she said'.[2] Merkel's alleged view that Putin creates his own reality has been much quoted and much misunderstood. She was referring specifically to Putin's comments at the time of the Russian takeover of Crimea, when he denied the presence of additional Russian troops. Special forces were brought in to Crimea from the mainland, and they managed to suppress potential military resistance without bloodshed. At a time of extreme tension, Putin was technically correct in asserting that force numbers did not exceed the 25,000 allowed by the Russo-Ukrainian Treaty of May 1997, but he was being economical with the truth. The issue raises some very large herme-neutic questions – what is the rational basis for understanding the unfold-ing of Russia's relations with the rest since the end of the Cold War, and in particular how can we explain the recent breakdown not only in the European security system but in commensurate understandings of the processes provoking the breakdown? It does indeed seem that Russia and Western elites live in totally different worlds, divided by different episte-mological understandings of the nature of contemporary reality. The Ukraine crisis crystallised the profound differences between Russian and Atlanticist understanding of the breakdown and its causes. The earlier divergent narratives about the end of the Cold War now became a hermeneutic breakdown and assumed a confrontational military form, reproducing Cold War patterns. Political differences and conflicts over interpretation are hardly surprising, yet here we have fundamental onto-logical differences in understanding the world. The earlier ideological struggle between capitalist democracy and revolutionary socialism was clear, comprehensible and rooted in European modernity. But what is this struggle all about? The post-Cold War crisis of world order is accom-panied by an epistemological crisis unusual in its intensity. Two contrast-ing rationalities and hermeneutical identities are in conflict. Here we will look at US perspectives.

The roots of the epistemological crisis lie in one of the foundational features of American post-war foreign policy thinking, namely German idealism. This is the notion, as the reviewer of Kissinger's biography puts it, 'that reality doesn't exist independently of our perception of that reality'. On this basis, as an intellectual in the 1950s and 1960s, Kissinger helped

---

[2] Peter Baker, 'Pressure Rising as Obama Works to Rein in Russia', *New York Times*, 2 March 2014, www.nytimes.com/2014/03/03/world/europe/pressure-rising-as-obama-wo rks-to-rein-in-russia.html?hp&_r=0, last accessed 30 May 2017.

shape 'our perception of reality, convincing America that there was a missile gap with the Soviets when there was none and urging Washington to confront global communism even in peripheral areas, such as Vietnam'.[3] Cold War ideational legacies continue to shape contemporary US policy towards Russia and are sustained by a whole series of mechanisms. Elite and policy-maker perceptions and attitudes forged in the Cold War years sustain these legacies, and frame the discussions of such crucial issues as NATO enlargement, democracy promotion in the post-Soviet area, and strategic arms talks.[4] Crucially, these 'legacies' have become a relatively permanent feature of US foreign policy *vis-à-vis* Russia, and to that degree are no longer so much legacies as self-regenerating narratives and modes of discourse that preclude a more open-ended understanding of the dynamics and concerns of Russia today. For example, the idea of Greater Europe is interpreted as an attempt to divide the Atlantic system, whereas Russia since Gorbachev's time believes that such a neo-Gaullist strategy would reinvigorate the continent, provide it with independent actorness, and finally heal the divisions of the Cold War. The debate assumed a hermetic and axiological quality, converting dialogue into defiance and confrontation.

The shaping of reality is explicit for American 'neo-cons'.[5] Although the concept of neo-conservatism is imprecise, the term denotes a distinctive stance towards foreign policy. It indicates the moral framing of international policy, the advancement of American values, including democracy, to enhance American security, and an activist US foreign policy couched in terms of American 'leadership' to maintain global order.[6] This exceptionalist policy agenda converged with Clintonian liberal internationalists to create a powerful alliance of liberal interventionists and neo-conservative revisionists. Both movements sought to remake the world in the American image, and for both democracy is the universal foundation for foreign engagement.[7] This gave rise to the trans-democracy analysed earlier. This was the basis for the bipartisan consensus shared by Republican neo-conservatives and Democratic liberal internationalists based on four shared principles: commitment to global 'leadership'; the strengthening of the 'liberal international order'; recognition of the inalienable link between the safety, influence and prosperity of the US

---

[3] Greg Grandin's review of Niall Ferguson, *Kissinger 1923–1968: The Idealist* (London, Allen Lane, 2015), in *Guardian Review*, 17 October 2015, p. 6.

[4] David Parker, *Cold War Ideational Legacies and Contemporary US Foreign Policy towards Russia*, PhD, King's College London, November 2015.

[5] Gary Dorrien, *The Neoconservative Mind: Politics, Culture, and the War of Ideology* (Philadelphia, Temple University Press, 1993).

[6] Paul Craig Roberts, *The Neoconservative Threat to World Order: Washington's Perilous War for Hegemony* (Atlanta, Clarity Press, 2015).

[7] Dorrien, *Imperial Designs*.

and its leadership of the aforementioned 'liberal international order'; and a commitment to spreading democracy.[8]

This bipartisan foreign policy agenda shaped the 'team of rivals' personnel policy of the Obama administrations between 2009 and 2016, where it became increasingly hard to distinguish between liberals and neo-cons. From September 2013 the European and Eurasian desk at the State Department was headed by assistant secretary of state Victoria Nuland. She had been on the staff of Dick Cheney when he was Bush's vice president between 2001 and 2009, and then became one of Hillary Clinton's team. Cheney was the chief architect of the invasion of Iraq in 2003, planning to reshape reality on the ground in the Middle East. Nuland is married to Robert Kagan, a co-founder along with William Kristol in 1997 of the Project for a New American Century (PNAC), a neo-conservative think tank that helped shape a militarist and interventionist US foreign policy for the next decade. Kagan was an enthusiast for the Iraq war and condemned Europe's apparent turn away from militarism towards the exercise of civilian power and normative diplomacy. He defended America's use of hard power, asserting that 'Americans are from Mars, Europeans are from Venus'.[9] He was frustrated that the 'tantalising glimpse of a new kind of international order' at the end of the Cold War gave way to the return of 'international competition among great powers', accompanied by 'the old competition between liberalism and autocracy'.[10] The underlying assumption is that America in some way stands above international law to ensure the continued prevalence of a rule-ordered international system (the rationale of Russian 'regimes' since 1991 in standing above the constitution to manage democracy and developmental goals). The resulting contradiction in the US not only gave rise to the 'double standards' routinely excoriated by Russian leaders, but a bipartisan foreign policy that effectively asserted that the US could act as the arbiter of sovereign legitimacy, which alarmed Russian leaders even more. If a foreign power is considered to have violated 'international order', then it could be overthrown. This was the 'regime change' ideology so feared by the Kremlin. By standing outside of international law the US guarantees its prevalence. This is precisely the tutelary attitude to the constitution and the rule of law practised

---

[8] Dmitry Suslov, 'Hillary Clinton as the Last of the Mohicans, Donald Trump is Only the Beginning', Valdai Discussion Club, 11 August 2016, http://valdaiclub.com/a/highlights/hillary-clinton-as-the-last-of-the-mohicans/, last accessed 30 May 2017.

[9] Robert Kagan, *Of Paradise and Power: America and Europe in the New World Order* (New York, Knopf Doubleday, 2007).

[10] Robert Kagan, *The Return of History and the End of Dreams* (London, Atlantic Books, 2008), pp. 4, 5.

domestically by the Putin system, a paradox that only intensified the conflict between the two. Condemned by Russian leaders as 'double standards', for the US the essence of global leadership is the power to interpret rules for the public good that cannot be constrained by those rules.

This was the formula for America interventionism and universal leadership. Reagan kept the neo-conservatives at arms' length, despatching one of their main ideologues, Paul Wolfowitz, to Indonesia as ambassador. In the Clinton years the liberal interventionists came to predominate, pursuing the policy of NATO enlargement. The Bush administrations saw the neo-conservatives gain unprecedented influence over foreign policy. This was symbolised by the appointment of Wolfowitz as undersecretary of defence for policy. In that capacity, the paper that came to be known as the 'Wolfowitz Doctrine' was produced in early 1992.[11] The document, which provided the foundations for what became known as the Bush Doctrine, was imperial in tone and proclaimed a policy of unilateralism and pre-emptive military interventions to counter threats to American leadership. The core postulate was 'to prevent any hostile power from dominating a region whose resources would, under consolidated control, be sufficient to generate global power'.[12] This is a classic principle of offensive realism, and Trump's challenge to it provoked an intense bipartisan reaction from Republican neo-cons and Democratic liberal internationalists alike.

The final version of what was technically the Defence Planning Guidance for the years 1994–99 argued that '[t]he U.S. must show the leadership necessary to establish and protect a new order that holds the promise of convincing potential competitors that they need not aspire to a greater role or pursue a more aggressive posture to protect their legitimate interests'. This is precisely what Putin would do once Russia's economy had recovered from the depredations of the 1990s, and hence even at this early point the two countries were on a collision course. The leaked version was explicit about the potential threat represented by Russia:

We continue to recognise that collectively the conventional forces of the states formerly comprising the Soviet Union retain the most military potential in all of Eurasia; and we do not dismiss the risks to stability in Europe from a nationalist backlash in Russia or efforts to reincorporate into Russia the newly independent republics of Ukraine, Belarus, and possibly others ... We must, however, be mindful that democratic change in Russia is not irreversible, and that despite its

---

[11] A leaked version was published in the *New York Times* on 7 March 1992.

[12] Paul Wolfowitz, 'Statesmanship in the New Century', in Robert Kagan and William Kristol (eds.), *Present Dangers: Crisis and Opportunity in American Foreign and Defense Policy* (New York and London, Encounter Books, 2000), p. 309.

current travails, Russia will remain the strongest military power in Eurasia and the only power in the world with the capability of destroying the United States.

Russia's critics would argue that this was a prescient analysis, but the final version removed this text with the rather more diplomatic assertion that '[t]he U.S. has a significant stake in promoting democratic consolidation and peaceful relations between Russia, Ukraine and the other republics of the former Soviet Union'.[13]

Obama's foreign policy combined liberal interventionism and neo-con ideas (consolidated above all in a number of influential think tanks and the media), tempered by Obama's cautious instincts and his recognition that America had over-reached itself during the Bush presidency. Obama initially sought to devolve the management of continental affairs to European leaders, prompting concern among East Europeans that the US was becoming disengaged – an 'abandonment' complex which has to be soothed by 'reassurance'. Obama had to deal with the consequences of the financial crisis, managing the retreat from Iraq and Afghanistan, and reforging the American alliance system in the Far East. To Obama's evident chagrin, the Ukraine crisis brought America firmly back into the centre of European security matters. The view emerged that it had been a mistake for America to turn its attention away from Europe, and Obama's alleged *laissez-faire* policy was endlessly condemned by neo-conservatives like William Kristol, Charles Krauthammer and the editorial pages of the *Washington Post* and *Wall Street Journal*.

The combination of ultra-realism and values-based interventionism (in which liberal hawks and neo-conservatives united) sustained an exceptionalist ideology. Obama's practical caution in foreign policy was countered by the articulation of an extraordinary ideology of American leadership. When the Syrian regime apparently crossed Obama's 'red line' prohibiting the use of chemical weapons in August 2013, Moscow worked with Washington to convince Damascus to give up its chemical weapons. Soon after, Putin allowed himself to criticise Obama's ideology, enunciated in his address to the nation on 10 September. In an op-ed piece in the *New York Times*, Putin stressed how Russo-American cooperation had deep roots, fighting on the same side in the Second World War, and called for joint work to resolve the Syrian crisis. Nevertheless, he condemned America's use of force and interventionism:

It is alarming that military intervention in internal affairs in foreign countries has become commonplace for the United States. Is it in America's long-term interest?

---

[13] After significant redrafting, the *Defence Planning Guidance, 1994–99* was officially released on 16 April 1992.

I doubt it. Millions around the world increasingly see America not as a model of democracy but as relying solely on brute force, cobbling coalitions together under the slogan 'you're either with us or against us'. But force has proved ineffective and pointless.[14]

He then listed the various failed interventions, from Afghanistan, Iraq, Libya and Syria, stressing: 'We must stop using the language of force and return to the path of civilized diplomatic and political settlement.' Putin ended by noting that his 'personal relationship with President Obama is marked by growing trust', but he added a passage that he later admitted he had inserted after the main text had been prepared:

> I would rather disagree with the case he [Obama] made on American exception-alism [in his 10 September speech], stating that the United States' policy is 'what makes America different. It's what makes us exceptional'. It is extremely danger-ous to encourage people to see themselves as exceptional, whatever the motiva-tion. There are big countries and small countries, rich and poor, those with long democratic traditions and those still finding their way to democracy. Their poli-cies differ, too. We are all different, but when we ask for the Lord's blessing, we must not forget that God created us equal.[15]

Putin's comments on American politics provoked much scornful com-ment, but reflected his unshakeable belief that Russia was a world power whose voice deserved to be heard, even in Washington.

From a realist perspective, there is no reason for the US and its allies to accord Russia the status that it demands. Stent's study of Russo-American relations in the post-Cold War period examines precisely how the mis-match in perceptions played out in practice, with Russia determined to ignore the enormous asymmetry in power and status, and America trying to find ways to deal with its assertive partner while ensuring its own freedom of action.[16] From the very beginning the US rejected any Russian claim to enjoy any *droit de regard* over the post-Soviet and larger region. The alliance of liberal interventionists and neo-conservatives combined to generate an anti-Russian policy, and it was in this context that personal relations between Obama and Putin, never warm, deteriorated further. Obama staked on Medvedev being returned to the Russian presidency for a second term, and allowed himself to make a series of injudicious comments. He dismissed Putin as someone who 'lived in the past' and on 9 August 2013

---

[14] Vladimir V. Putin, 'A Plea for Caution from Russia', *New York Times*, 12 September 2013.

[15] In response to a question at the Valdai Discussion Club, meeting for the tenth anniversary session in Valdai on 19 September 2013, Putin admitted that he inserted this passage. Personal notes.

[16] Stent, *The Limits of Partnership*.

likened his body language to a 'bored kid in the back of the classroom', a comment that reportedly infuriated Putin.[17]

The Ukraine crisis revealed the complete absence of trust between the two powers. From the American perspective, the problem largely focused on Putin and what was perceived to be his uncooperative if not outright revisionist and dangerous policies. However, in Kissinger's much-quoted words: 'For the West, the demonization of Putin is not a policy; it is an alibi for the absence of one.'[18] In an interview with National Public Radio (NPR) on 30 December 2014 Obama argued that Putin had made a strategic mistake in annexing Crimea, and argued that those who consider Putin a 'genius' had been proved wrong by Russia's economic crisis: 'The big advantage we have with Russia is we've got a dynamic, vital economy, and they don't. They rely on oil. We rely on oil and iPads and movies and you name it.'[19] In an interview with BuzzFeed a couple of months later Obama was asked how he related to Putin:

You know, I don't want to psychoanalyze Mr. Putin. I will say that he has a foot very much in the Soviet past. That's how he came of age. He ran the KGB. Those were his formative experiences. So I think he looks at problems through this Cold War lens, and, as a consequence, I think he's missed some opportunities for Russia to diversify its economy, to strengthen its relationship with its neighbours, to represent something different than the old Soviet-style aggression.[20]

In his State of the Union speech on 20 January 2015 Obama stressed Russia's misfortunes and America's role in creating them:

We are demonstrating the power of American strength and diplomacy. We're upholding the principle that bigger nations can't bully the small – by opposing Russian aggression, supporting Ukraine's democracy, and reassuring our NATO allies. Last year, as we were doing the hard work of imposing sanctions along with our allies, some suggested that Mr. Putin's aggression was a masterful display of strategy and strength. Well, today, it is America that stands strong and united with our allies, while Russia is isolated, with its economy in tatters. That's how America leads – not with bluster, but with persistent, steady resolve.[21]

[17] Steven Lee Myers, 'Putin's Silence on Syria Suggests his Resignation over Intervention', *New York Times*, 28 August 2013, www.nytimes.com/2013/08/29/world/middleeast/put in-on-syria.html?hp&_r=1, last accessed 30 May 2017.

[18] Henry Kissinger, 'To Settle the Ukraine Crisis, Start at the End', *Washington Post*, 5 March 2014.

[19] 'USA Russia: Obama suggests Putin "not so smart"', BBC News, 30 December 2014, www.bbc.co.uk/news/world-us-canada-30629200, last accessed 30 May 2017.

[20] 'Full transcript of BuzzFeed News' interview with President Barack Obama', posted 11 February 2015, www.buzzfeed.com/buzzfeednews/full-transcript-of-buzzfeed-news-int erview-with-president#.yrKEWLLLv, last accessed 30 May 2017.

[21] White House, 'State of the Union Address', 20 January 2015, www.whitehouse.gov/the-press-office/2015/01/20/remarks-president-barack-obama-prepared-delivery-state-unio n-address, last accessed 30 May 2017.

These themes were taken up in the *National Security Strategy* of February 2015, warning that America 'will continue to impose significant costs on Russia through sanctions', and would 'deter Russian aggression'. The document articulated the principles of American exceptionalism, proclaiming the right to intervene anywhere in the world in defence of US interests. In a document that was only twenty-nine pages long, American leadership was mentioned thirty-seven times.[22] The narrative of 'Russian aggression' was later formulated in terms of Russian revisionism, a view embedded at the heart of America's *National Military Strategy* of June 2015. This reflected the uncertainty of the period, finding threats everywhere. Russia, Iran, North Korea and China were identified as 'revisionist' powers and accused of destabilising the global order. The US would counter the 'revisionist powers' that threaten the norms of world order, as well as extremist organisations such as Islamic State, which had the capacity to create armed units.[23] Both strategies were shaped by the view that the rules governing international politics needed to be preserved, accompanied by awareness that the existing mechanisms for America's leadership were weakening. Alexei Fenenko identifies the four key ideas, outlined in the 1991 US *National Security Strategy* and thereafter amplified. First, the end of the Cold War had not achieved the key American goal of dismantling Soviet (Russian) military power, on the model of Germany and Japan after 1945. Second, in the foreseeable future Russia would remain the only country in the world with the technical ability to destroy America's strategic potential. Third, the US needed to justify the presence of its armed forces on the territory of its allies, notably its western European NATO allies as well as Japan and South Korea. And fourth, the US should take the lead in responding to 'non-traditional threats', including transnational terrorism. These principles were later enshrined in the 1995 *National Military Strategy*, which stipulated that the US Department of Defence would take the lead in countering attempts to revise the post-1991 world order.[24] All of this was hardly likely to provide the basis for a productive relationship.

The Ukraine crisis provoked a flood of commentary about the threat posed by Russia. A good summary of these arguments, combining neo-con and liberal hawk positions, was published by the Council on Foreign

---

[22] White House, *National Security Strategy*, February 2015, www.whitehouse.gov/sites/def ault/files/docs/2015_national_security_strategy.pdf, last accessed 30 May 2017.

[23] *The National Military Strategy of the United States of America 2015*, www.jcs.mil/Portals/ 36/Documents/Publications/National_Military_Strategy_2015.pdf, last accessed 9 June 2017.

[24] Alexey Fenenko, 'How the US Military Plans to Neutralize Russia', *Russia Direct*, 9 July 2015, www.russia-direct.org/opinion/how-us-military-plans-neutralize-russia, last accessed 30 May 2017.

Relations in its influential journal, *Foreign Affairs*. Written by Tom Cotton, elected to the Senate in November 2014 and part of the traditionalist Republican wing alongside Mitt Romney and Marco Rubio, the article argued that Russia and America were in a state of 'proxy war', not only in Syria but on a global scale, and that this was a war that the US had to win. Cotton argued that despite having a weak hand, 'Putin is winning' and had been able to break out from international isolation following the Ukraine crisis, with numerous world leaders consulting Russia on matters of global importance. The kernel of the argument ran as follows:

Putin's aggression serves many of his goals, all of which are antithetical to the United States. Most importantly, Putin wants to restore Russia as a global super-power. This is not surprising from a man who once said 'the collapse of the Soviet Union was a major geopolitical disaster of the century'. A concomitant goal is the disruption of the U.S.-led international order of democratic capitalism. Although Putin lacks a viable ideological alternative, he is content to simply undermine the existing order.

Most horrific, Putin sought to 'preserve his grip on power in Russia', and avert the sort of regime changes that had taken place in Georgia, Serbia, Libya and Ukraine. Cotton condemned Obama's alleged softness in standing up to Putin, making the Syrian chemical weapons deal in September 2013, and outlined measures to win the war with Russia:

Little wonder, then, that Putin felt he could spark a proxy war against the United States in Syria with impunity. Obama's appeasement of Putin has only embol-dened him, encouraging him to raise the stakes in Russia's competition with the United States. But Putin doesn't speak the language of diplomacy and concilia-tion; he speaks only the language of strength and force. Thus, only a new policy of across-the-board confrontation can raise the costs for Putin and force him to back down.

The proposals included the imposition of a no-fly zone in Syria, arming Ukraine with offensive weapons, bumping up American forces along NATO's frontline with Russia, the stiffening of economic sanctions, the activation of an 'assertive diplomacy' and the creation of the 'country-at-risk' concept for states where Russia had interests, providing them with military and economic resources to allow them to diversify away from Russia, and the intensification of the struggle in the information field.[25] The article was a call to war, ignoring the dangers and denying the opportunities, and served as the backdrop to the extraordinary bipartisan anti-Russian hysteria in the transition from Obama to Trump.

[25] Tom Cotton, 'Proxy Wars: Russia's Intervention in Syria and What Washington Should Do', *Foreign Affairs*, 24 November 2015, www.foreignaffairs.com/articles/syria/2015-11-24/proxy-wars, last accessed 30 May 2017.

In an extensive interview with Jeffrey Goldberg in *The Atlantic* in spring 2016, Obama sought to shape his legacy as he came to the end of his presidency. I will quote the interview at length, since it provides important insight into the hermeneutic gap between the Russian and American positions. Obama defended an unchanged Historical West, although shifting towards greater burden-sharing, reinforced by liberal internationalist and neo-con hostility to Russia as a hold-out against Western-style democratisation and American hegemony. Nevertheless, his relations with Putin were professional: 'The truth is, actually, Putin, in all of our meetings, is scrupulously polite, very frank. Our meetings are very businesslike. He never keeps me waiting two hours like he does a bunch of these other folks.' He then came to the nub of the matter, and clearly could not envisage a scenario where Russia is treated as an equal. He stressed how important Russia considered its relationship with the US, which was a far greater priority than the US's relationship with Russia:

> He's constantly interested in being seen as our peer and as working with us, because he's not completely stupid. He understands that Russia's overall position in the world is significantly diminished. And the fact that he invades Crimea or is trying to prop up Assad doesn't suddenly make him a player. You don't see him in any of these meetings out there helping to shape the agenda. For that matter, there's not a G20 meeting where the Russians set the agenda around any of the issues that are important.[26]

The condescending and contemptuous tone reflected the broader attitude towards Russia in the post-Cold War era, but more disturbing was the reductive interpretive framework. Obama restrained the more aggressive proposals of his time, such as launching a bombing campaign against the Syrian regime after the chemical weapons attack in August 2013 or providing offensive weapons to the Ukraine armed forces, but this reflected consequentialist prudence rather than empathetic strategy.

Equally disturbing was the simplistic understanding of the rationality of Russian actions. Obama had clearly bought into the views of his advisers who argued that Russia 'invaded' Georgia in 2008, in the words of the interviewer which Obama did not challenge, 'to keep an ex-Soviet republic in Russia's sphere of influence'. Obama did not like Goldberg's suggestion that Putin had been emboldened by the president's moderation, noting that 'Putin went into Georgia on Bush's watch, right smack dab in the middle of us having over 100,000 troops deployed in Iraq'. As discussed earlier, Russian forces entered in response to the Georgian attack

---

[26] Jeffrey Goldberg, 'The Obama Doctrine: The US President Talks through his Hardest Decisions about America's Role in the World', *The Atlantic*, April 2016, www.theatlantic.com/magazine/archive/2016/04/the-obama-doctrine/471525/, last accessed 9 June 2017.

on South Ossetia, but there were wider issues at stake, which Obama gave no indication of understanding. Equally, his analysis of the logic of Russian action in Ukraine is shockingly simplistic: 'Putin acted in Ukraine in response to a client state that was about to slip out of his grasp. And he improvised in a way to hang on to his control there.' Obama went on to make the following crucial points:

He's done the exact same thing in Syria, at enormous cost to the well-being of his own country. And the notion that somehow Russia is in a stronger position now, in Syria or in Ukraine, than they were before they invaded Ukraine or before he had to deploy military forces to Syria is to fundamentally misunderstand the nature of power in foreign affairs or in the world generally. Real power means that you can get what you want without having to exert violence. Russia was much more powerful when Ukraine looked like an independent country but was a kleptocracy that he could pull the strings on.

There were shades of Joseph Nye's idea of 'soft power' here, defined as the ability to achieve national goals without coercion. However, even Nye argued that soft power was essentially a category that only applied to the United States, and he was contemptuous of Russian and Chinese attempts to ape America by devising 'soft power' strategies.[27] Obama was right to the extent that he identified the deleterious consequences of the impasse in which Russia was trapped. Russian interventions in Georgia and Ukraine did expose the fundamental weakness of the Russian position and only exacerbated that weakness, but in conditions of an impasse, Russia's options were severely constrained. It was easy for Obama to condemn Russian actions, but his lack of broader strategic perspective is disturbing.

This is reflected in his further comments on Ukraine. They reveal Obama to be an intelligent and pragmatic politician, but one devoid of an overarching understanding of how America could contribute to the resolution of problems of post-Cold War global disorder. Obama admitted that Moscow had 'escalatory dominance' in a country that was a core Russian interest but not an American one: 'The fact is that Ukraine, which is a non-NATO country, is going to be vulnerable to military domination by Russia no matter what we do.' Asked whether his position on Ukraine was realistic or fatalistic, he responded: 'It's realistic. But this is an example of where we have to be very clear about where our core interests are and what we are willing to go to war for. And at the end of the day, there's always going to be some ambiguity.' He refused to

---

[27] Joseph S. Nye, 'What China and Russia Don't Get About Soft Power', *Foreign Policy*, 29 April 2013, http://foreignpolicy.com/2013/04/29/what-china-and-russia-dont-get-abou t-soft-power/, last accessed 9 June 2017.

endorse the 'crazy Nixon' approach that threatened to scare opponents into submission (which some say was revived by Trump), and which led to devastating bombing campaigns in Cambodia and Laos and yet did not prevent American defeat in Indochina. Asked whether the fear that the American president would get angry would deter Putin from moving into Moldova or some other vulnerable post-Soviet state, Obama responded in measured terms:

There is no evidence in modern American foreign policy that that's how people respond. People respond based in what their imperatives are, and if it's really important to somebody, and it's not that important to us, they know that . . . There are ways to deter, but it requires you to be very clear ahead of time about what is worth going to war for and what is not. Now, if there is somebody in this town that would consider going to war with Russia over Crimea and eastern Ukraine, they should speak up and be very clear about it. The idea that talking tough or engaging in some military action that is tangential to that particular area is somehow going to the decision making of Russia or China is contrary to all the evidence we have seen over the last 50 years.

With such moderate views, one can understand why liberal hawks and neo-cons despaired of Obama. He resolutely refused to buy in to their ambitions to reshape the world in America's image. He stressed that 'diplomacy and technocrats and bureaucrats' were keeping 'America safe and secure', and it was the element of American power that the rest of the world unambiguously appreciated, whereas the deployment of American troops, even when necessary, was always understood in some way as the violation of sovereignty. At the same time, there is something very parochial about Obama's understanding of the world, and this is reflected in his limited understanding of the dynamics of Russian politics and the character of Russian society. A weak and flailing Russia represented a threat, although not of the first rank: 'Unlike China, they have demographic problems, economic structural problems, that would require not only vision but a generation to overcome.' Obama then deployed the classic view that Russian domestic problems provoked external aggression: 'The path that Putin is taking is not going to help them overcome those challenges. But in that environment, the temptation to project military force to show greatness is strong, and that's what Putin's inclination is. So I don't underestimate the dangers there.'[28]

The interview provides a unique insight into the American president's thinking. There is little grandeur or bombast and instead the patient working out of problems. When it comes to Russia, we see a pragmatic

[28] Jeffrey Goldberg, 'The Obama Doctrine: The US President Talks through his Hardest Decisions about America's Role in the World'.

and realist policy, but one devoid of any larger understanding of Russia's strategic position or dilemmas, let alone empathy. While willing to engage with Putin, and conceding that he was not 'completely stupid', Obama was unable to engage in transformational diplomacy, and even transactional relations collapsed on his watch. He was a cautious politician of the best sort, aware of the catastrophic outcomes of earlier rash American interventions, and thus averted even worse outcomes to the Ukrainian and Syrian crises. However, he had no grasp of Russian dilemmas or understanding of larger global shifts, and hence failed to seize Moscow's repeated offers to work together to tackle problems of global disorder.

This paradigm is the foundation of the twenty-five years' crisis. The Cold War ended with the US in a uniquely advantageous position, even though its 'victory' was not quite as crushing as that against its enemies in the Second World War. Nevertheless, American strategy defined by the Wolfowitz Doctrine and other documents focused on the need to sustain military superiority, maintain US security guarantees to its allies, and demonstrate that the US would not be afraid to exercise military power 'in proportion to the nature of the threat'. This entailed a readiness to confront both Russia and China, a strategy that in the end brought these two powers closer together. Nevertheless, Russia was identified as the priority threat, with the 2015 *Military Strategy* stressing that Moscow 'has repeatedly shown disregard for the sovereignty of its neighbours and willingness to use force to achieve its goals'. Although the targeting of Russia as the top threat has deep roots, with the 1994 *Nuclear Posture Review* warning that Russia would be the main adversary as long as it retained nuclear parity with Washington. However, lumping Russia (and China), with the so-called 'rogue states' of Iran and North Korea was something new. It indicated a readiness to contemplate war between the great powers, a view that was made explicit in the 2015 *National Military Strategy* when it talked of the growing danger of war with 'state actors'. The document lamented America's perceived lack of adequate mechanisms to counter other powers in regional conflicts. The response was once again to build up military capacity in Europe and across the world.

The Syrian Gambit

Obama claimed that Russia was no more than a regional power, but the September 2013 joint agreement on the destruction of Syrian chemical weapons rendered the country a global actor. This was to be confirmed two years later when Russia decisively intervened in the Syrian civil war. In his 28 September 2015 speech to the General Assembly, Putin argued that the UN was 'unique in terms of legitimacy, representation and universality', and while noting criticisms and the attempt of the 'one centre of dominance' that tried to reckon without the UN, 'any attempts to undermine the legitimacy of the UN were extremely dangerous'. He warned that that the failure to learn that 'attempts to push for changes in other countries based on ideological preferences ... often lead to tragic consequences':

> The export of revolutions, this time of so-called democratic ones, continues [and it had led to disaster in the Middle East and North Africa]. Instead of bringing about reforms, aggressive intervention harshly destroyed national institutions and lifestyles. Instead of democracy and progress, there is now violence, poverty, social disasters and total disregard for human rights, including even the right to life. To the people who have caused this situation: do you realise what you have done?[29]

Obama and Putin met on the sidelines, with Putin calling for a coordinated policy on Syria, but the meeting only underlined the distance between the two leaders, although they agreed on the threat posed by Islamic State. Both parties spoke of the need for a coalition to fight against the common enemy, but they had a very different understanding of what this entailed. A coalition from the American perspective would comprise countries ready to accept American leadership and strategy, whereas Putin sought to recreate something along the lines of the anti-Hitler coalition, an alliance of equals.

On 30 September Putin dramatically raised the stakes by launching a bombing campaign in Syria from its airbase in Latakia, accompanied later by cruise missiles from its Caspian Sea flotilla. The intervention had a number of goals.[30] First, to ensure the survival of the regime (although not necessarily Assad himself), which Lavrov later admitted had been within weeks of falling, as he put it, to terrorists.[31] Second, given the continuing low level insurgency in Russia's predominantly Muslim North Caucasus, it made sense to fight the terrorists 'over there' rather than back home. Up to 4,000 people from Russia and some 5,000 from other former Soviet republics joined the insurgency in Syria.[32] Russia's forward strategy entailed the danger of blowback, radicalising the domestic insurgency

---

[29] '70-ya sessiya General'noi Assemblei OON', 28 September 2015, http://kremlin.ru/eve nts/president/news/50385, last accessed 9 June 2017.

[30] For an assessment, see Roy Allison, 'Russia and Syria: Explaining Alignment with a Regime in Crisis', *International Affairs*, Vol. 89, No. 4, 2013, pp. 795–823.

[31] 'Foreign Minister Sergey Lavrov's Remarks and Answers at a News Conference on the Results of Russian Diplomacy in 2017', RF Ministry of Foreign Affairs, www.mid.ru/en/ vistupleniya_ministra/-/asset_publisher/MCZ7HQuMdqBY/content/id/2599609, last accessed 9 June 2017, last accessed 30 May 2017.

[32] 'Putin: Russia Inflicts Major Damage on Terrorists in Syria, It Helps Start Talks', *Sputnik*, 23 February 2017.

and provoking the intervention of foreign jihad forces. Third, the goal was to support a regime that provided Russia with a strategic platform in the region, including military bases. The collapse of the regime would have deprived Russia of its main Arab ally in the region. Fourth, to defend the principle enunciated two days earlier at the UN, namely that incumbent regimes should not be overthrown by outside forces. Fifth, to challenge not only US unilateral behaviour, but also what was considered the absence of a coherent Western strategy in Syria, aiming to defeat Islamic State while at the same time destroying the only serious force capable of achieving that goal, namely the Syrian government and its allies. And sixth, the larger strategic objective was to reinforce Russia's claim to be a global rather than a regional power, as Obama had earlier labelled it. The intervention was designed to break out of the diplomatic isolation imposed after the Ukrainian events of 2014, and ultimately to compel the West to establish more equitable forms of political and military cooperation. The goal was to establish a framework for changes in world order that would secure Russia's interests, including its special status in post-Soviet space. In the event, these goals were achieved to a remarkable extent, above all the survival of the Assad regime and the reassertion of Russia's global presence. In his last speech as president to the UN in September 2016, Obama accused Russia of trying to recover 'lost glory' through the means of military power, although he conceded that 'for most of human history, power has not been unipolar. The end of the Cold War may have led too many to forget this truth.'[33] It was not a truth that Russia would let the US forget. Nevertheless, Russia risked getting bogged down in a protracted war that in the end would only reinforce its isolation. As Russia discovered in Afghanistan and the US in Vietnam, it is easier to go in than come out.[34]

For the hard-liners in Moscow, the Syrian campaign testified that 'Russia is preparing to restore its status as a world power'. Russia was now prepared to act against American interests, and thus its foreign policy should rely on military power as Russia 'restored its presence where we have political, economic and military-strategic interests'.[35] The tactical goals were to push back the insurgency from the environs of Damascus, relieve the siege of Aleppo, and demonstrate the

---

[33] 'Address by President Obama to the 71st Session of the United National General Assembly', 20 September 2016, www.whitehouse.gov/the-press-office/2016/09/20/addr ess-president-obama-71st-session-united-nations-general-assembly, last accessed 30 May 2017.

[34] Vladimir Frolov, 'Voiti v Siriyu legko, vyiti slozhno', *Vedomosti*, 29 September 2016, p. 6.

[35] Leonid Ivashov, the president of the Academy of Geopolitical Problems (and a former senior official in the Russian Ministry of Defence), in *Kommersant-Vlast'*, 17 October 2016, p. 8.

insubstantiality of the so-called 'moderate opposition'. Although Moscow was well aware that there could be no return to the pre-war situation, regime collapse in its view would precipitate a mass slaughter of Alawis and allies that would make the other killings of the five-year war pale into insignificance. The EU failed to articulate a coherent view of the Syrian conflict, even though it was dealing with a flood of refugees that predated the Russian intervention. A meeting of EU foreign ministers in Luxembourg on 12 October 2015 insisted that the Russian attacks 'must cease immediately', and made the protection of civilians an international priority.[36] Moscow insisted that it was hitting Islamic State and its affiliates; NATO and the US argued that the strikes were hitting the 'moderate' anti-Assad opposition groups even harder; while Moscow claimed that military supplies to the 'moderate' opposition were in fact reinforcing radical groups.[37]

Putin's decision to enter the Syrian conflict was one of the most high-risk actions he had ever undertaken. On the one side, his meeting with Obama and the attempts to regularise the situation in Ukraine clearly signalled that the Kremlin was looking for ways to temper the conflict with the West. This did not mean a retreat from his fundamental positions. Tsygankov expresses very well what was at stake:

Putin's long-standing objective has been to establish Russia as a nation that acts in accordance with formal and informal norms of traditional great power politics and is recognised as a major state by the outside world. The norms of traditional power politics include a general agreement on major threats to the international system, multilateral diplomacy to solve disputes, and respect for both sovereignty and major powers' spheres of influence. Putin firmly believes that the West has violated these norms by breaking all existing rules and principles.[38]

Russian politicians endlessly listed the cases where these norms were breached, beginning with the wars in former Yugoslavia, in which traditional patterns of great power politics were repudiated, and with it multilateral diplomacy and respect for the sovereignty of states. Putin and Lavrov signalled that Assad's departure was not excluded, but this would have to be part of a wider settlement. Putin is a legitimist, opposing

---

[36] 'EU Urges Russia to Quit', *Guardian*, 13 October 2015, p. 17.

[37] For critical analyses, see Seymour M. Hersh, 'Military to Military', *London Review of Books*, Vol. 38, No. 1, 7 January 2016, pp. 11–14, www.lrb.co.uk/v38/n01/seymour-m-hersh/military-to-military, last accessed 30 May 2017; and Gordon Hahn, 'American Misadventures and Russian Gains', *Russian and Eurasian Politics*, 15 February 2017, https://gordonhahn.com/2017/02/15/american-misadventures-and-russian-gains-obamas-muslim-brotherhood-strategy-general-flynns-russia-play-and-trumps-debacle/, last accessed 30 May 2017.

[38] Andrei Tsygankov, 'The Kremlin's Syria Gamble is Risky, but could have a big Payoff', 3 October 2015, www.russia-direct.org/opinion/kremlins-syria-gamble-risky-could-have-big-payoff, last accessed 30 May 2017.

the violent overthrow of leaders who in one way or another offended the dominant powers, but the argument that Putin intervened in Syria as part of his aversion to forced regime change is mistaken. Myers exaggerates when he argues that 'at the heart of the airstrikes is Mr. Putin's defense of the principle that the state is all powerful and should be defended against the hordes, especially those encouraged from abroad. It is a warning about Russia as much as Syria.'[39] Russia sought a cooperative resolution, but not as a junior partner to states which Putin held responsible for provoking the Syrian disaster in the first place. As far as he was concerned, it made no sense to pursue two mutually incompatible goals, the defeat of Islamic State and Assad's overthrow. This incoherent policy only confirmed Putin's very low opinion of the competence and intelligence of Western leaders.

Russia created an information centre in Baghdad with Syria, Iraq and Iran, and invited others to join.[40] This coalition was Shia-based, but Sunni Egypt and Jordan, as well as Israel, were not unsympathetic, while the Gulf States, Saudi Arabia and Turkey were more critical of Russian policy. Concerned that in the restricted air space over Syria some sort of collision could take place, in late September 2015 Shoigu requested that the US secretary of defence, Ashton Carter, re-establish military contacts in order to 'de-conflict' operations in Syria.[41] The two countries fundamentally disagreed over the fate of Assad. While Obama called for his overthrow, his administration began to contemplate the possibility of Assad participating in some sort of transitional regime. For Putin, Assad was the cornerstone of the immediate struggle against Islamic State, but in the longer term he accepted some sort of transitional government. The US strategy envisaged fighting against Islamic State and Assad simultaneously, hoping that some 'moderate' forces would be able to fill the ensuing vacuum in case of victory. The experience of Iraq and Libya suggested that chaos and civil conflict would be the more likely outcome, as Putin never tired of stressing. In his UN General Assembly speech he noted that only the Syrian government and Kurdish forces were fighting Islamic State.

The risks soon became manifest. On 31 October 2015 a Russian civilian airliner carrying tourists from Sharm el Sheikh was downed by a bomb placed on board, with the loss of all 224 lives. On 24 November

[39] Steven Lee Myers, 'In Putin's Syria Intervention, Fear of a Weak Government Hand', *New York Times*, 4 October 2015, www.nytimes.com/2015/10/04/world/europe/in-putins-syria-intervention-fear-of-a-weak-government-hand.html?_r=0, last accessed 30 May 2017.
[40] Fyodor Lukyanov, 'Porozn' protiv zla', 29 September 2015, www.rg.ru/2015/09/30/lukjanov.html, last accessed 9 June 2017.
[41] Bryan Bender, 'The Hotline to Moscow goes Cold', 2 October 2015, www.politico.com/story/2015/10/white-house-moscow-hotline-214398, last accessed 30 May 2017.

2015 a Turkish F-16 fighter jet shot down a Russian Sukhoi SU-24 M fighter, which was striking Turkmen insurgents close to the southern tip of Hatay province on the Turkish-Syrian border. This was the first time that a NATO member had shot down a Russian plane since 1952. The pilot was killed in his parachute by the Turkmen fighters, while the surviving co-pilot insisted that no warning had been given. The Turkmen militants were led by a Turkish ultranationalist called Alparslan Çelik, a son of the former mayor of the Keban municipality in Turkey's Elazig province. The incident precipitated the worst crisis in Russo-Turkish relations in a generation. Erdoğan had come to power at the head of the AK Party in 2003 and served as prime minister until 2014, when he became president and in 2017 turned Turkey into a presidential republic. Relations with Putin had become increasingly warm, overturning centuries of hostility. The strategic ambitions of the two countries converged: '[B]oth hoped to carve out a larger role for themselves in the global order and were becoming increasingly frustrated with what they saw as the West's refusal to give them a seat at the table.'[42] Both countries were outsiders to the dominant European order, although they feared becoming united in an alliance of the outcasts. Turkey remained an ambivalent member of NATO, refusing US access to its bases during the Iraq war of 2003. The country also started membership negotiations with the EU. Foreign minister Ahmet Davutoğlu pursued a 'zero problems' policy with its neighbours, a policy that spectacularly failed as Turkey came into conflict with practically all of its partners. Relations with Israel spoiled as a result of the Gaza flotilla raid in May 2010. Turkey did not join the sanctions against Russia, allowing the country to become a conduit for enhanced trading opportunities, raising annual bilateral trade to $30 billion. In 2014 some 4.4 million Russian tourists visited Turkey, taking advantage of visa-free travel and the friendly relations between the two countries. Above all, Turkey gets much of its gas from Russia. Turkey was a long-standing NATO member with aspirations to join the EU, but Russia and Turkey shared a critical stance on US foreign policy, and opposed the prioritisation of human rights in interstate relations.

However, when it came to Syria, the two sides disagreed fundamentally. Moscow argued that Assad should be part of a negotiated solution and that his precipitate overthrow would unleash the sort of state collapse and sectarian war unleashed by Western intervention in Iraq and Libya; whereas Ankara sought to replace Assad and his Alawite minority regime

---

[42] Jeffrey Mankoff, 'Russia and Turkey's Rapprochement: Don't Expect an Equal Partnership', *Foreign Affairs*, 20 July 2016, www.foreignaffairs.com/articles/turkey/2016-07-20/russia-and-turkeys-rapprochement, last accessed 30 May 2017.

by a Sunni majority one. Putin and Erdoğan were authoritative rulers who enjoyed warm relations, but Erdoğan had a long record of turning against his former allies, notably in the case of the modernising Islamist Fethullah Gülen, a cleric who had been Erdoğan's ally until 2013, when he was forced into exile in the US. Assad himself had once been a close family friend. The downing of the plane provoked Putin's fury, and he imposed a range of sanctions on tourism, agriculture, construction, and shelved plans to build the Turkish Stream gas pipeline to Europe while work on the Akkuyu nuclear plant by Rosatom was suspended. Russia also announced the deployment of S-400 air-defence missile systems to Syria, from where they could hit targets well inside Turkey. Russia also intensified its bombing campaign against insurgent groups allied with Turkey in the Syrian border region. Russia also increased support for the Kurdish Democratic Union Party (PYD) in Syria, which Turkey considered part of the Kurdistan Workers' Party (PKK), the group with which the government had restarted its war in 2015. A week after the incident, on the sidelines of the Paris climate change talks, Putin asserted that he had 'every reason to think that the decision to shoot down our plane was dictated by the desire to protect the oil supply lines to Turkish territory, right to the ports where it is loaded onto tankers'. Russian officials went further and claimed that Erdoğan and his family were personally involved in the illegal oil trade with Islamic State.[43]

Finding himself isolated, from June 2016 Erdoğan sought reconciliation with Israel and Russia, apologising for the death of the pilot. The failed coup of 15 July 2016 exposed the tensions in a country trapped between Kemalist secularism, traditionally safeguarded by the military, and various forms of Islamism. The role of Gülen in the coup is unclear, although he was held responsible, provoking a mass purge of alleged Gülenists. Relations were restored with Russia, and most of the latter's sanctions lifted. The assassination of the Russian ambassador to Turkey, Andrei Karlov, in December 2016 did not derail the restored relationship, and the two worked together to broker a ceasefire in Syria. Russia and Turkey are great powers in a Europe that has failed to create the institutions to incorporate their cultural, historical and civilisational diversity into a unity of the Greater Europe type. The continent returned to the competitive multipolar order of the nineteenth century exacerbated by the normative competition of the twenty-first.

By 2016 Syrian forces encircled East Aleppo, and the regime prepared to destroy the insurgent forces with Russian assistance. Some 275,000

---

[43] Paulo Gorjão, 'Diplomatic Tensions between Ankara and Moscow as a Window of Opportunity', IPRIS Viewpoints, No. 190, 4 December 2015.

civilians, including 100,000 children, were also trapped. The US still supported the 'moderate opposition', even though it was often hard to distinguish them from Islamic State and the Fath al-Sham Front (Levant Conquest Front, the al-Qaeda affiliate formerly known as the Al-Nusrah Front). In two laboriously negotiated deals of February and September 2016 the US committed itself to separating the 'moderate rebels' from the jihadis, but it failed to do so. The ceasefire plan between Kerry and Lavrov agreed on 9 September 2016 broke down amidst acrimony and mutual accusations. The Pentagon was hostile to the agreement with Russia and threatened to disobey the presidential order to share intelligence with Russia. Stephen F. Cohen identified a covert struggle between the 'party of war' led by defence secretary Carter and Hillary Clinton, and a 'party of peace' led by Kerry.[44] It is widely believed that the peace deal was deliberately sabotaged, allegedly by defence secretary Carter, by the US bombing of Syrian government forces at Deir Ezzor on 17 September 2016, killing about 100 Syrian soldiers and allowing Islamic State fighters to gain the strategic heights above the airport. The attack appeared to be part of the broader US policy to destroy Syrian government positions east of Palmyra. Matters came to a head with the destruction of a UN aid convoy bringing much-needed supplies into Aleppo on 19 September, the seventh day of the ceasefire. At an emergency meeting of the UNSC on 25 September, Russia was accused of 'barbarism' by Samantha Power, and the two powers engaged in confrontational public diplomacy.[45] The UN report released on 21 December was less clear about who was responsible.[46] Some American politicians (including Clinton) called for a no-fly zone, but this entailed the interception and shooting down of Syrian and Russian planes, threatening an escalation with global consequences. Russia was in no mood to back down.[47] Events gained a dangerous momentum with the potential to turn into a nuclear confrontation between the two powers.[48]

---

[44] Stephen F. Cohen, Interview on the John Batchelor Show, 2 August 2016, http://john batchelorshow.com/schedules/tuesday-2-august-2016, last accessed 30 May 2017.

[45] Richard Gowan, 'Russian Perfidy at the UN', *The American Interest*, 29 September 2016, www.the-american-interest.com/2016/09/29/russian-perfidy-at-the-un/, last accessed 30 May 2017.

[46] Michelle Nichols, 'UN Enquiry says Air Strike hit Syria Aid Convoy in September', Reuters, 21 December 2016, www.reuters.com/article/us-mideast-crisis-syria-convoy-i dUSKBN14A2H3, last accessed 30 May 2017.

[47] For the military options, including specification of the planes that would be involved in a Syrian war, see Dave Majumdar, 'Why the United States Should Exercise Restraint before Launching a New War in Syria', *The National Interest*, 3 October 2016, http://nationalinter est.org/feature/why-the-united-states-should-exercise-restraint-before-17919, last accessed 30 May 2017.

[48] Robert Parry, 'Do We Really Want Nuclear War with Russia', Consortium News, 3 October 2016, https://consortiumnews.com/2016/10/03/do-we-really-want-nuclear-wa r-with-russia/, last accessed 30 May 2017.

The US ended bilateral relations with Russia over Syria on 3 October 2016, encouraging those who believed in a military solution to the conflict. Hawks called for more aggressive measures, including heavier sanctions, the supply of man-portable air-defence systems (Manpads), and a no-fly zone. Russia at this time announced that its Khmeimim air base would become a permanent facility, and deployed the S-300V4 system to defend it and Syrian air space in general. If there was to be a no-fly zone, it would be a Russian one. Russia's decision to pull out of the plutonium agreement on 5 October was accompanied by a list of demands that can only be called an ultimatum to Washington. To the Kremlin, Western policy in Syria appeared nihilistic, demanding Assad's overthrow and blocking any Russian-brokered peace. Moscow simply could not understand why it would be in the West's interests to see the secular Syrian government fall. The ensuing power vacuum would in all likelihood end with Islamic State's black flag flying over Damascus. The poisonous relations between the two countries permeated the US presidential election in autumn 2016.

Russian air power and Iranian irregulars helped Syrian forces regain control of Aleppo, and in December 2016 worked with Turkey and Iran to broker a ceasefire. The UNSC on 31 December unanimously supported the Russo-Turkish ceasefire plan, and the two countries co-chaired a peace conference in Kazakhstan. More broadly, the defeat of Islamic State would not resolve the problems which had given rise to it in the first place. It was a symptom of the larger crisis of state integration and national development in the region. On this, the positions of the US and Russia did not substantively differ, providing scope for cooperation, which under Trump took place on the ground. Nevertheless, 'the new highly asymmetrical relationship between the two powers leaves almost no room for mutual respect'.[49] Overall, Russia's Syrian campaign consistently defied expectations. Russia did not get bogged down in an Afghan-style quagmire, and registered some notable successes, above all what it considered the liberation of Aleppo and Palmyra. Russia had asserted itself as a great power, with the military and diplomatic resources to match. Putin had proved his point: the unipolar moment was over.

Between Hegemony and Nationalism

The assertion by Republican candidate Mitt Romney in the 2012 campaign that Russia is 'without question our No. 1 geopolitical foe' sounded

---

[49] Dmitri Trenin, 'The Prospect of a Superpower War in Syria is Hardly Far-Fetched', *Financial Times*, 6 October 2016, www.ft.com/content/7500631e-8af5-11e6-8cb7-e7ad a1d123b1, last accessed 9 June 2017.

ridiculous, but by 2016 it had become part of the 'new normal'. Brzezinski habitually reveals the raw sinews of geopolitical contestation embedded in the relationship. He led the way in demonising Putin, being the first on 3 March 2014 to compare the Crimean events to Hitler's occupation of the Sudetenland in 1938 and the final occupation of Czechoslovakia in early 1939,[50] followed the next day by Hillary Clinton.[51] The comparison was endorsed, not surprisingly, on 5 March 2014 by senators John McCain and Marc Rubio. McCain went further, condemning the Obama administration for its misguided attempts to work with Russia: 'The whole administration deserves blame, everybody, for the weakness and total misperception of the nature of Vladimir Putin. And pushing the reset button is certainly a graphic illustration of that.'[52] This sentiment fed into American policy-making during the Ukraine crisis and in Syria, inhibiting the potential for pragmatic relations. It was precisely this postulate that was challenged by the Republican presidential candidate.

In his various interventions at the St Petersburg International Economic Forum (SPIEF) in June 2016, Putin refused to use the term 'Cold War' to describe the stand-off between Russia and the West. He stressed the absence of ideological rivalry between the two systems and looked to deepen economic ties with countries such as Italy, Germany and even the US, whose business leaders attended the forum in greater number than in earlier years. Despite the geopolitical tensions, Russia increased its total investments in US Treasury bonds from $72 billion in 2015 to $90.9 billion in 2016. The 26 per cent increase placed Russia sixteenth, with China in top place, holding $1.15 trillion of securities, followed by Japan and Ireland.[53] With Trump advocating a more isolationist America focused on its own problems, Putin repeated his statement that Trump was a 'vivid' (*yarkii*) person, while Trump complimented Putin on his leadership qualities.[54]

---

[50] Zbigniew Brzezinski, 'After Putin's Aggression in Ukraine, the West must be Ready to Respond', *Washington Post*, 3 March 2014.

[51] Timothy Stanley, 'Hillary, Putin's no Hitler', 6 March 2014, where he refers to Godwin's law: 'The longer a debate rages, the greater the likelihood that someone will compare someone else to Hitler', http://edition.cnn.com/2014/03/05/opinion/stanley-hillary-clinton-hitler/, last accessed 30 May 2017.

[52] Ed O'Keefe, 'McCain, Rubio agree with Clinton's Putin-Hitler comparison', *Washington Post*, 5 March 2014

[53] 'Russia Has Bought US Treasury Bonds Worth 91 Billion Dollars', Lenta.ru, 16 August 2016.

[54] Tyler Pager, 'Putin Repeats Praise of Trump: He's a "Bright" Person', *Politico*, 17 June 2016, www.politico.com/story/2016/06/putin-praises-trump-224485, last accessed 30 May 2017.

Trump was an outsider to the political establishment, having never served in an elected office before his unexpected victory in November 2016, but his populist insurgency was grounded in his long experience as a maverick business tycoon. His unorthodox views raised hopes in Moscow that he would bring some new ideas to the table, although Russian elites were well aware that he was unstable in his views and unpredictable in his behaviour. His Democratic opponent, Clinton, represented policy continuity and intensified hostility towards Russia. By contrast, Trump expressed the view that 'NATO is obsolete and it's extremely expensive for the United States, disproportionately so', and 'it should be readjusted to deal with terrorism'.[55] He later warned that he would only assist European nations during a Russian invasion if they first 'fulfilled their obligations to us'. He also noted that the US had 'to fix our own mess before trying to alter the behaviour of other nations': 'I don't think we have the right to lecture.' He also insisted that 'America first' was a 'brand-new, modern term', and did not signal isolationism of the sort advocated by Charles Lindbergh's America First Committee before the US entered the Second World War.[56] Above all, candidate Trump adopted a radical position:

We desire to live peacefully and in friendship with Russia … We have serious differences … But we are not bound to be adversaries. We should seek common ground based on shared interests. Russia, for instance, has also seen the horror of Islamic terrorism. I believe an easing of tensions and improved relations with Russia – from a position of strength – are possible. Common sense says this cycle of hostility must end. Some say the Russians won't be reasonable. I intend to find out. If we can't make a good deal for America, then we will quickly walk from the table.[57]

Trump's neo-isolationist strategy downplayed the promotion of American values through democracy promotion, and placed less emphasis on multilateral institutions.[58] New thinking was in the air, raising hopes in Moscow for some sort of rapprochement.

Russia took centre stage in the campaign. The alleged break-in by Russian hackers of the emails of Clinton campaign manager John

---

[55] Interview on ABC's 'This Week', 27 March 2016, www.realclearpolitics.com/video/20 16/03/27/trump_europe_is_not_safe_lots_of_the_free_world_has_become_weak.html, last accessed 30 May 2017.

[56] David E. Sanger and Maggie Haberman, 'Donald Trump Sets Conditions for Defending NATO Allies against Attack', *New York Times*, 20 July 2016.

[57] 'Transcript: Donald Trump's Foreign Policy Speech', *New York Times*, 27 April 2016, www.nytimes.com/2016/04/28/us/politics/transcript-trump-foreign-policy.html?_r=0, last accessed 30 May 2017.

[58] For example, Shawn Donnan and Demetri Sevastopulo, 'US Looks to Bypass WTO Disputes System', *Financial Times*, 27 February 2017, p. 6.

Podesta (the founder of the Centre for American Progress) revealed the contents of her speeches to Wall Street bankers and the financing of the Clinton Foundation. The second batch uploaded to WikiLeaks from the Democratic National Committee's server exposed how the Democratic establishment had been biased against Bernie Sanders in the Democratic primaries in favour of Clinton. Convincing evidence of a Russian cyber-attack was missing.[59] The Department of Homeland Security and the Federal Bureau of Investigation (FBI) issued a threadbare report on the matter on 6 January 2017. A large part of the document was devoted to the programming of RT in 2012, and lacked elementary information about the Internet Protocols addresses (IPs) or other signatures of the Advanced Persistent Threat (APT) 29 (which began in summer 2015) and APT 28 (from spring 2016) hacks of Democrat emails, and accused the least likely Russian security bodies (the GRU (Main Intelligence Directorate of the General Staff of the Russian Armed Forces) and the FSB) of being responsible.[60] Excessive reliance was placed on assessments of the 'cyber-security complex', notably CrowdStrike, which came up with the names of Cozy Bear (the FSB) and Fancy Bear (the GRU), when in fact no groups as such existed – these were fictional personifications of the APTs.[61] Julian Assange, the editor-in-chief of WikiLeaks, vigorously denied that Russia was the source of the two batches of material published on his site.[62] The leaks exposed misconduct by Clinton and the Democrats, and were thus not 'fake news', but in the end attention focused less on the substance than on how the material entered the public domain. The expulsion of thirty-five Russian diplomats on 29 December 2016 as punishment for Russia's alleged interference in the US election campaign was reminiscent of the worst periods of the Cold War. Putin's refusal to reciprocate by expelling the

---

[59] I am sceptical, but the key point is the extraordinary level of rhetorical violence. While the Trump administration may have been prone to advancing 'alternative facts' (in Kellyanne Conway's famous formulation), the defenders of traditional Atlanticism were equally prone to make up 'facts' when necessary, asserting apodictic opinions and unverified claims about Russia.

[60] *Background to 'Assessing Russian Activities and Intentions in Recent US Elections': The Analytic Process and Cyber Incident Attribution*, 6 January 2017, www.dni.gov/files/documents/ICA_2017_01.pdf, last accessed 30 May 2017. For a critique, see Ronald Deibert, 'The DHS/FBI Report on Russian Hacking was a Predictable Failure', *Just Security*, 4 January 2017, www.justsecurity.org/35989/dhsfbi-report-russian-hacking-predictable-failure/, last accessed 30 May 2017.

[61] There is a vast literature on this, but for a good analysis of the 'cybersecurity complex', see Yasha Levine, 'From Russia, with Panic', *The Baffler*, No. 34, 2017, https://thebaffler.com/salvos/from-russia-with-panic-levine, last accessed 30 May 2017.

[62] 'Assange: Russian Government not the Source of WikiLeaks Emails', 3 January 2017, www.foxnews.com/politics/2017/01/03/assange-russian-government-not-source-wikileaks-emails.html, last accessed 30 May 2017.

equivalent number of US diplomats made Obama look petty and vindictive. Trump tweeted: 'Let us move on to bigger and better things'.

Instead, politicians across-the-board lined up to denounce Putin and to present Russia as a hostile state, with constructive engagement denounced as weakness and appeasement. The Clinton campaign sought to pin the blame for losing the election on Russia, while Republicans used Kremlin-bashing as a way of disciplining Trump and bringing him back into the fold of Atlanticist orthodoxy. The national security establishment used allegations of Russian interference in the US election campaign to impede Trump's attempt to normalise relations with Russia.[63] Although Russia's challenge to American global leadership was nothing like as systemic as during the Cold War, anti-Russian rhetoric exceeded earlier levels.[64] The 'golden showers' report published on BuzzFeed on 10 January 2017 sought to demonstrate that Russia had somehow gained a hold on Trump during his visit to Moscow in 2013. Prepared by a former British security official, Christopher Steele, the report hit a new a low in its puerile collection of unsubstantiated allegations.[65]

Trump's unexpected victory is a paradigmatic case of the role that contingency and personality plays in international affairs. Trump represented a populist version of the 'America first' tradition, reviving Patrick Buchanan's critique of George H. W. Bush's vision of an American-centred new world order. Buchanan later endorsed Russia's critique of Western 'exceptionalism' and its claims to have won the Cold War. He warned that 'this will inevitably result in war, as more and more nations resist America's moral imperialism'.[66] This is a tradition that adopts a narrower definition of American interests, and is reluctant to intervene in world affairs except in defence of these narrow interests. Obama remained a firm globalist, 'which puts the emphasis on the world system that runs out of Washington – a modern version of an empire – rather than

[63] Katrina van den Heuvel, 'Neo-McCarthyite Furore around Russia is Counterproductive', *Washington Post*, 21 February 2017.

[64] Dmitry Suslov, 'The US Elections and the Cold War 2.0: Implications and Prospects for Russia', Valdai Discussion Club, 9 September 2016, http://valdaiclub.com/news/the-us-ele ctions-and-the-cold-war-2-0-implications-and-prospects-for-russia/, last accessed 9 June 2017.

[65] Unable to travel to Moscow, Steele paid Russian informants for the material. 'US Presidential Election: Republican Candidate Donald Trump's Activities in Russia and Compromising Relationship with the Kremlin', BuzzFeed, 10 January 2017, www.docu mentcloud.org/documents/3259984-Trump-Intelligence-Allegations.html, last accessed 30 May 2017.

[66] Patrick J. Buchanan, 'The Mind of Mr. Putin', 2 October 2015, http://buchanan.org/bl og/the-mind-of-mr-putin-124130, last accessed 30 May 2017.

on the US itself.[67] Obama's presidency nevertheless moderated US hegemony, encouraging its allies in Europe and the Middle East to take more responsibility for their security. By contrast, Trump sought to reshape the US alliance system and America's place in the world. As Robert English notes, Trump sought Russian cooperation on global issues, recognised that Washington bore some responsibility for the deterioration in relations, and acknowledged 'the right of all nations to put their own interests first' and that the US does 'not seek to impose our way of life on anyone'.[68]

Trump's insurgency questioned America's commitment as self-proclaimed guardian of the liberal international order, and in effect sought to return to off-shore balancing, an approach long advocated by American realists. Mearsheimer and Walt describe the consequences of America's ill-considered interventions, which had plunged large parts of the world into chaos, and argued that these 'costly debacles' were 'the natural consequences of the misguided grand strategy of liberal hegemony' pursued by both the Democrats and Republicans. Based on the logic of 'the indispensable nation', this approach 'holds that the United States must use its power not only to solve global problems but also to promote a world order based on international institutions, representative governments, open markets, and respect for human rights'. In short, 'liberal hegemony is a revisionist grand strategy', intended not merely to uphold the balance of power but to promote democracy and human rights.[69] Instead, US policy in their view should focus on checking the emergence of regional hegemons and intervene only when necessary. The argument leads to a critique of the whole trend of US policy after 1989:

In Europe, once the Soviet Union collapsed, the region no longer had a dominant power. The United States should have steadily reduced its military presence, cultivated amicable relations with Russia, and turned European security over to the Europeans. Instead, it expanded NATO and ignored Russian interests, helping spark the conflict over Ukraine and driving Moscow closer to China.[70]

For neo-conservatives and liberal internationalists alike, Trump's victory represented the end of the US as the 'indispensable nation'. Kagan

[67] Dmitri Trenin, 'National Interest, the Same Language of Beijing, Washington and Moscow', Moscow Carnegie Centre, 29 December 2016, http://carnegie.ru/2016/12/2 9/national-interest-same-language-of-beijing-washington-and-moscow-pub-67631, last accessed 30 May 2017.

[68] Robert David English, 'Russia, Trump, and a New Detente', Foreign Affairs, 10 March 2017, www.foreignaffairs.com/articles/russian-federation/2017-03-10/russia-trump-an d-new-d-tente, last accessed 30 May 2017.

[69] John J. Mearsheimer and Stephen M. Walt, 'The Case for Offshore Balancing', Foreign Affairs, Vol. 95, Vol. 4, July–August 2016, p. 71.

[70] Mearsheimer and Walt, 'The Case for Offshore Balancing', p. 76.

stressed US 'responsibility for global order', noting how Europe took for granted the American willingness to act in its defence and in support of the open economic order, and forgot 'how abnormally unselfish American behaviour has been since the second world war'. The US, according to Kagan, was 'no longer in the reassurance business. For decades an abnormal US foreign policy has aimed at denying Russia and China spheres of interest.' This made sense, in his view, when defending an order that prevented a breakdown like that of the first half of the twentieth century, but a narrow reading of US interests did not require it. He argued that almost every American intervention over the last seventy years had been to defend some principle of global order, rendering them 'wars of choice'; but for a more 'normal' US policy, it did not matter 'who exercises hegemony in east Asia and in eastern and central Europe'.[71] Robin Niblett, the director of Chatham House, agrees, arguing that the US 'provided the security umbrella under which the liberal international system has flourished'. Already under Obama European allies were encouraged to take greater responsibility for their own security, but with a more inward-looking America and transactional foreign policy, this assumed a 'mercenary' twist as Trump would protect 'only those countries that pay, so that it can focus on making itself great again at home'.[72] Coming hard on the heels of the Brexit vote in the UK, other commentators were less ambiguous and talked simply of 'the end of the Anglo-American order'.[73] Kagan went further, and called on the new US administration to confront 'the two great revisionist powers, Russia and China': 'The further accommodation of Russia can only embolden Vladimir Putin, and the tough talk with China will likely lead Beijing to test the new administration's resolve militarily.' For Kagan, 'China and Russia are classic revisionist powers', seeking to restore 'the hegemonic dominance they once enjoyed in their respective regions'.[74] As we have seen, this is a greatly simplified representation, and all the more dangerous for that.

---

[71] Robert Kagan, 'An End to the Indispensable Nation', *Financial Times*, 21 November 2016, p. 13. For his broader analysis, see Robert Kagan, 'The Twilight of the Liberal World Order', Brookings, 24 January 2017, www.brookings.edu/research/the-twilight-of-the-liberal-world-order/, last accessed 30 May 2017.

[72] Robin Niblett, 'Liberalism in Retreat: The Demise of a Dream', *Foreign Affairs*, Vol. 96, No. 1, January–February 2017, p. 20.

[73] Ian Buruma, 'The End of the Anglo-American Order', *The New York Times Magazine*, 29 November 2016, www.nytimes.com/2016/11/29/magazine/the-end-of-the-anglo-ameri can-order.html?_r=1, last accessed 30 May 2017.

[74] Robert Kagan, 'Backing into World War III', *Foreign Policy*, 6 February 2017, http://for eignpolicy.com/2017/02/06/backing-into-world-war-iii-russia-china-trump-obama/, last accessed 9 June 2017.

Russia had long chafed at the American struggle to deprive it of a 'sphere of interest' in the name of the American-dominated open global order. Russian statists argued that this order was not so open if it meant that Russia's access was dependent on the country's renunciation not only of great power interests but also of defined independent strategic concerns. The neo-revisionist position, as outlined earlier, asserts that the rules-based order is a patrimony of all of humanity and should be located at the level of international society and not within a specific power system. While American interventions may have been benign in intent (and that is highly questionable), they ultimately served to maintain American national interests and to reinforce its hegemonic position.[75] In the post-Cold War years the neo-conservative and liberal interventionist positions effectively fused, although the rhetoric differed, in defence of liberal order and American power. Obama's attempt to transfer greater responsibility for regional security to its allies and to forge agreements with adversaries through diplomacy signalled a new realism in American policy that recognised the limits of American power.[76] Even before Trump's election, this politics of 'retreat' and the underlying logic of a shift towards 'off-shore balancing' was the subject of withering critique.[77] The 'bipartisan' foreign policy consensus in defence of liberal hegemony and interventionism remained in place, but was challenged from the other flank by the emergence of Trump's brand of conservative neo-isolationism and overt nationalism. Not surprisingly, it was attacked with equal ferocity by the Democrat liberal interventionists and Republican neo-conservative hegemonists. The nationalist shift did, however, open up the possibility of a more pluralistic international system. As Niblett recognises, the liberal international economic order could evolve into a 'less ambitious project ... that encompasses states with diverse domestic political systems'.[78]

Moscow welcomed the conciliatory tweets from Trump, although harsh strictures continued to emanate from Congress, and his administration was hardly pro-Russian. The appointment of Rex Tillerson as secretary of state was a bold move. Tillerson had joined Exxon Mobil in 1975, and following successes in the Middle East and Southeast Asia, in the late 1990s he saved the $17 billion Sakhalin I project, which in 2005 started producing millions of barrels of oil. He became chief executive in 2006, and thereafter Exxon Mobil forged strong ties with Rosneft and its head, Igor Sechin. In 2011 they

---

[75] This is a classic postulate of offensive realism.
[76] This comes out in Obama's interview with Goldberg in *The Atlantic*, April 2016.
[77] Robert J. Lieber, *Retreat and Its Consequences: American Foreign Policy and the Problem of World Order* (Cambridge, Cambridge University Press, 2016).
[78] Niblett, 'Liberalism in Retreat: The Demise of a Dream', p. 17.

signed a multibillion dollar deal to drill Russia's vast Arctic, shale and deep-water fields, which in 2014 led to the discovery of a vast oil field in the Kara Sea. The project was shortly afterwards halted as sanctions were imposed, much to Tillerson's displeasure. Putin awarded Tillerson the 'Order of Friendship' in 2013. Exxon Mobil represented a type of parallel quasi-state in the US, forging relations with foreign leaders that were not always aligned with official US policy. He had cut a deal with the Kurdish Regional Government that undermined the central government in Baghdad. On the other hand, he had ended Exxon Mobil's long history of financing right-wing groups that denied anthropomorphic climate change.[79] In the event, the storm of criticism of Trump's putative links with Russia and that of some of his nominated officials forced the resignation of Michael Flynn on 13 February after just twenty-four days in his post as national security adviser. This limited Trump's scope for action when it came to Russia. Flynn had planned to work with Russia against what he considered the greater enemy, Islamic terrorism, but his downfall – at the hands, some thought, of the US security establishment – revealed the deep hostility towards Russia. Flynn's replacement, lieutenant general Herbert McMaster, was strongly supportive of NATO and repeatedly talked of the need for the advanced containment of Russia in the Baltic region, Ukraine and in cyber-space, views shared by the defence secretary, James Mattis and vice president Mike Pence. The American alliance system in Europe and Asia (to contain Russia and China) would be preserved and strengthened.

The Trump administration signalled a tougher line against China. The strategy appeared to be to peel Russia away from its alignment with China (and Iran) as part of a 'big deal' that would offer Russia a path back to the West. However, the idea of 'doing a deal' was as insubstantial as the reset, since both failed to address Russia's underlying insecurities. These will only be allayed by membership of some sort of overarching security and political community, and even then, as Gaullist France demonstrates, identity issues are not so easily resolved. Nevertheless, Trump's accession appeared to offer an opportunity to recalibrate relations. Trump's abandonment of the Trans-Pacific Partnership (TPP) as part of his broader critique of regional trade blocs signalled a broader reassessment of US leadership in the APR. In response, China moved quickly to assert its own vision of an integrated Eurasia that excluded the US but encompassed Russia. As Niblett notes: 'We may be on the brink of a Eurasian century,

---

[79] The Editorial Board, 'Flawed Choices for the State Department', *New York Times*, 12 December 2016, www.nytimes.com/2016/12/12/opinion/flawed-choices-for-the-state-d epartment.html?_r=0, last accessed 30 May 2017.

rather than a Pacific century.'[80] Moscow now found itself in the unusual position of potentially being courted by both Atlantic and Asian powers. This renewed triangular politics, reminiscent of the Kissinger years, is anachronistic. As we have seen, Russia's position (along with China's) is anti-hegemonic, decrying the existence of blocs and calling for all states to interact in a sovereign manner and to subordinate themselves to international society. Trump's election signalled the weakening of Cold War-style bloc politics, and to that extent was welcomed by Russia and China. He was clear that America's relationship with NATO would change and there would have to be greater burden-sharing with European partners. The priority would be America's security and needs, and the concerns of a globalist Europe still mired in the old Atlantic model would come second. These issues were far from new, since the rise of Asia obviously raised questions about the future of the transatlantic relationship.[81] A rethinking of American strategic priorities was long overdue.

The post-Cold War attempt to maintain the 'unipolar' moment and blunt the emergence of a more pluralistic international system meant that a dynamic of hostility with Russia became constitutive of the liberal international order, thus denying its drive towards universality and repudiating its essential liberalism and pluralism. In the event, the insurgent Trump soon discovered how hard it would be to overcome the anti-Russian hostility that had become constitutive of the new Atlanticism. He could take heart from Franklin Roosevelt's no less controversial re-establishment of relations with the Soviet Union in 1933, which established a platform for joint efforts in the Second World War. The discursive shift from 'leadership' to 'greatness' potentially allowed the restoration of normal diplomatic intercourse. Trump clearly sought a rapprochement with Russia, but he was trapped by the inertia of Cold War institutions and thinking. By now, Russia too had abandoned hope of joining a transformed Greater West, and major steps had been taken towards the creation of Greater Eurasia. Nevertheless, alarmed by the emergence of 'Kissinger's worst nightmare', a Russo-Chinese alignment, Trump sought to drive a wedge between the two by reversing the anti-Putin animus of the previous administration and favouring Russia while making demands on China. Russia had always balanced its deepening ties with China by ensuring a diversity of good relations with other Asian states, notably with Japan, South Korea, India and Vietnam, but Russia was in no mood to renege on the nascent

---

[80] Robin Niblett, 'Liberalism in Retreat', 13 December 2016, www.chathamhouse.org/expert/comment/liberalism-retreat, last accessed 30 May 2017.

[81] Luis Simón, 'Europe, the Rise of Asia and the Future of the Transatlantic Relationship', *International Affairs*, Vol. 91, No. 5, 2015, pp. 969–89.

politics of trust with China. To do so would mean irreparable damage to its reputation as a partner on which other states could rely. The same logic also applies to relations with Iran, where Russian neutrality in any future attack would be essential.

The Russo-Chinese strategic alignment had gone too far to allow for a repetition of Kissingerian divide and rule diplomacy. The relationship was a stabilising factor in international relations, and although both states remained independent players in the international system, they were allied in the anti-hegemonic bloc and neither would turn on the other. For Putin, the term 'strategic cooperation' was no longer adequate, and instead he noted that both sides now talking of 'comprehensive partnership and strategic collaboration. "Comprehensive" means we work virtually on all major avenues; "strategic" means that we attach enormous inter-governmental importance to this work.'[82] The wedge strategy assumes that Russia's alignment with China and other Asian states is not inherently valuable but instrumental and used to bargain with the West. In practice, Russia's neo-revisionist anti-hegemonic stance represents an epochal shift, predicated on the Historical West's inability to become a Greater West. The repeated failure to establish a stable long-term relationship provoked a historical shift in Russia's identity and foreign policy. Incremental improvements in relations would be welcome (including the lifting of sanctions), but it is hard to see what the US could offer Russia in any putative 'big deal'. The Russo-US relationship will remain at best transactional, and at worst openly confrontational.

The American 'deep state' reasserted itself, and the fifth post-Cold War reset ended before it had begun. In keeping with his promise to 'make America great again', Trump proposed a $54 billion increase in US defence spending, which was 80 per cent of Russia's total defence spending for 2016, while signalling his intention of expanding the $1 trillion modernisation of US nuclear weapons capabilities launched by Obama. Trump's initial instinct to improve relations with Russia was never going to be at the price of American military and economic supremacy. The anti-Russian fervour only legitimated 'the kind of nationalist assertiveness that, in normal times, liberals try to tamp down'.[83] In his 16 February 2017 news conference Trump defended his policy, arguing '[i]f we have a good relationship with

---

[82] 'Interview to the Xinhua News Agency of China', 23 June 2016, http://en.kremlin.ru/e vents/president/news/52204, last accessed 9 June 2017.

[83] Walter Russell Mead, 'Manchurian Candidate? Trump isn't Sounding Like a Russian Mole', *The American Interest*, 24 February 2017, www.the-american-interest.com/2017/ 02/24/trump-isnt-sounding-like-a-russian-mole/, last accessed 30 May 2017.

Russia, believe me, that's a good thing, not a bad thing'.[84] In conditions of rampant Russophobia, even small moves by Trump to improve relations would be seen as appeasement, if not some form of collusive relationship with the Kremlin. The one redeeming feature of a Trump presidency had been its promise of repairing relations with Russia and working together to resolve issues of mutual concern. Instead, Trump was forced to prove his toughness on Russia, reducing the scope for deal-making and heightening the risk of a miscalculation leading to war.

---

[84] 'Full Transcript and Video: Trump News Conference', *New York Times*, 16 February 2017, www.nytimes.com/2017/02/16/us/politics/donald-trump-press-conference-transcript.html?_r=0, last accessed 30 May 2017.

9   The EU, Europe and Russia

The cold peace was characterised by a fundamental tension between continental and Atlanticist conceptions of European order. In December 1989 Gorbachev came to Malta with radical ideas about transcending the logic of conflict between East and West. Instead of the creation of a new model of relations, a negative transcendence took place. A power shift was registered, in which Russia was discounted as a great power. This reflected the state of affairs at the time, with the Soviet Union disintegrating and Russia entering a decade of weakness. The Atlantic alliance system emerged as the supreme power on the European continent and geopolitical and systemic pluralism were denied. Soviet concerns and interests were discounted, as were those of the newly formed Russian Federation. Long before Putin assumed the presidency, relations between Russia and the Atlantic system were at best uneasy. Putin's early years were marked by a renewed attempt, in the framework of the new realism, to negotiate some sort of improved framework for relations with the Historical West. Instead, the enlargement agenda was accelerated and the transformative impulse suppressed. A radicalised wider Europe agenda was implemented that in the end destroyed whatever remained of the strategic partnership between Russia and the EU. Putin's Munich speech in 2007 revealed how tired Putin had become of Russia's position as perpetual *demandeur*, and he began to assert Russia's claims more forcefully. Nevertheless, Russia has not renounced its aspiration for some sort of Greater European arrangement.

The EU and the Idea of Europe

The EU is a child of the Cold War but it is far more than an instrument of the Cold War. Early attempts at European integration were supported by the US, and in particular by the militantly anti-communist John Foster Dulles, secretary of state in the Eisenhower years from 1953 to 1959, and by his brother, Allen Dulles, the long-term head of the CIA between 1953 and 1961.[1] The latter in particular encouraged European unity to create a bulwark against the Soviet Union. De Gaulle favoured continental integration as a way of resisting US power, but for the US any limit that the future EU could impose on America was outweighed by Europe's enhanced capacity to constrain Soviet influence. Even with the end of the Cold War, the US policy of containing and marginalising potential rival powers continued, with soft containment trapping Russia in its strategic impasse, until cooperation with a re-emergent China opened up new strategic options.[2] As for the EU, '[t]he fall of communism liberated Europeans from dependence on American power. But hopes that they would discover an independent political vocation of their own were soon disappointed.'[3]

Despite claiming a post-modern style, where the traditional competitive struggle of great powers gives way to a post-Westphalian community of post-sovereign nations built on free trade, a commitment to liberal normative values and elements of social solidarity, the EU assumed some of the characteristics of a great power. The resulting tension provoked Russian accusations of 'double standards', where post-modern rhetoric was contradicted by classical expansionist practices.[4] Internally the post-modern element predominated, but in external relations a more traditional logic operated. Whether this represented the 'return of geopolitics' is a moot point, but undoubtedly the struggle over space and territory returned with a vengeance.[5] The EU exercised a benevolent form of normative hegemony over its neighbours, radiating 'a liberal ideology claiming universal validity, despite this ideology's European origins'.[6] Normative power in this context is also a form of hegemony.[7] More than that, the thrust of the EU neighbourhood policy 'reflects imperialism as the Union seeks and enjoys the monopoly on what those norms entail and actively aims at exporting them in an attempt to provide internal legitimacy in the absence of a Westphalian identity construction'.[8] This

---

[1] For a critique of the latter, see Tim Weiner, *Legacy of Ashes: The History of the Central Intelligence Agency* (New York, Doubleday, 2007).

[2] Peter J. Katzenstein, *A World of Regions: Asia and Europe in the American Imperium* (Cornell and London, Cornell University Press, 2005).

[3] David Marquand, *The End of the West: The Once and Future Europe* (Princeton, Princeton University Press, 2011), p. 48.

[4] James Headley, 'Challenging the EU's Claims to Moral Authority: Russian Talk of "Double Standards"', *Asia Europe Journal*, Vol. 13, No. 3, 2015, pp. 297–307.

[5] See Klinke, 'Postmodern Geopolitics?'

[6] Julian Pänke, 'The Fallout of the EU's Normative Imperialism in the Eastern Neighbourhood', *Problems of Post-Communism*, Vol. 62, 2015, p. 352.

[7] Thomas Diez, 'Normative Power as Hegemony', *Cooperation and Conflict*, Vol. 48, No. 2, 2013, pp. 194–210.

[8] Pänke, 'The Fallout of the EU's Normative Imperialism', p. 352.

economic-region began to replicate the bloc politics with which it had been associated during the Cold War. The problem was exacerbated by the anti-Russian rhetoric of some of the former communist member states. 'European-ness' became a measure of achievement, rendering Eurasia synonymous with barbarism. This logic undermined the potential for traditional forms of inter-state diplomacy based on current realities rather than the degree to which the target state measures up to externally regulated standards. This didactic approach meant that the EU was negligent of the power consequences of its own actions, believing that benign intentions negated traditional categories of power. Rather than transcending the logic of conflict, the EU became an instrument for its perpetuation.

The EU's relations with Russia were problematic from the beginning, and became more so with the passage of time. As Sergei Prozorov has demonstrated, the relationship was built not on the basis of sovereign equality but on the tutelary principle of teacher and pupil.[9] This was evident in the way that the EU's Common Strategy on Russia was devised in 1999. Despite some early contacts with Russian officials, this 'was nevertheless very much a unilateral exercise'. There was not much that was 'common', 'in the sense that they are the result of mutual consultations between two partners', and instead the 'common' referred to was the position of the Member States.[10] This applied equally to the PCA, signed in 1994, but which only came into force on 17 December 1997, as well as the Interim Agreement on trade-related matters signed in 1995: '[B]oth proved to be inadequate bilateral instruments for the purposes of governing the relations between the two sides.'[11] Moscow was receptive to the argument that an enlarged EU was the cornerstone of stability in Europe, but dissenting voices were there from the start. For example, the former USSR ambassador to the European Community, Vladimir Shemyatenkov, argued that 'despite all the sweeteners of a *partnership*, it [EU enlargement] means the actual exclusion of Russia (and the Russians) from the zone of peace, stability and prosperity'.[12]

To this day 'the legal framework for the relationship [between the EU and Russia] remains, in some sense, unresolved'.[13] This culminated in

---

[9] Sergei Prozorov, *Understanding Conflict between Russia and the EU: The Limits of Integration*, paperback edn (Basingstoke, Palgrave Macmillan, 2016).

[10] Marc Maresceau, 'EU Enlargement and EU Common Strategies on Russia and Ukraine: An Ambiguous yet Unavoidable Connection', in Christophe Hillion (ed.), *EU Enlargement: A Legal Approach* (Oxford and Portland, Hart Publishing, 2004), p. 183.

[11] Maresceau, 'EU Enlargement', p. 184.

[12] Cited in Maresceau, 'EU Enlargement', p. 184.

[13] Maxine David, 'EU-Russia Relations: Effects of the 2014 Ukraine Crisis', *Russian Analytical Digest*, No. 158, December 2014, p. 5.

the exclusionary logic that kept Russia out of negotiations of the AA with Ukraine, even though it would have a profound effect on bilateral relations between Russia and Ukraine.[14] EU enlargement to Eastern Europe changed the quality of the political relationship with Russia.[15] Instead of achieving a Europe 'free of new dividing lines', enlargement renewed the division of Europe while restoring classical 'imperial' tropes of power relations between core and periphery.[16] As noted, the trans-democratic claim that security can be advanced by promoting liberal democracy and integration into European institutions became divisive when it was perceived to take the form of aspirations for 'regime change' and 'colour revolutions'. The idea of 'external governance' by definition denigrates the autonomy and political subjectivity of the target country by assuming a process of norm and regulatory transfer, rather than negotiation between equals accompanied by elements of 'convergence'.[17] The realist critique of the EU is certainly far from new, but the Ukraine crisis questioned the EU's survival as a transformative institution.[18] Critics of the EU had long argued that the post-national imperative undermined the sovereignty of states and rendered them incapable of resisting incorporation into the American-dominated Atlantic system.[19]

While the EU in its liberal aspirations is a benign and progressive phenomenon, it is only one part of the Atlantic walnut. The other is NATO, while overarching the two is American 'leadership'. The EU may well be post-territorial, but the announcement in April 2007 that NATO planned to build a BMD system in Central Europe was a harsh reminder that Europe remains part of a spatialised and militarised world

---

[14] Rilka Dragneva and Kataryna Wolczuk, 'The EU-Ukraine Association Agreement and the Challenges of Inter-Regionalism', *Review of Central and East European Law*, Vol. 39, Nos. 3–4, 2014, pp. 213–44.

[15] Simone Tholens and Raffaella A. Del Sarto, 'Partnership or Power Projection?: The EU and its "Neighbourhood"', openDemocracy, 18 November 2014, www.open democracy.net/can-europe-make-it/simone-tholens-raffaella-adel-sarto/partnership-or-power-projection-eu-and-its-', last accessed 9 June 2017.

[16] Richard Sakwa, 'The Death of Europe? Continental Fates after Ukraine', *International Affairs*, Vol. 91, No. 3, May 2015, pp. 553–79.

[17] For discussion of 'external governance', see Sandra Lavenex, 'EU External Governance in "Wider Europe"', *Journal of European Public Policy*, Vol. 11, No. 4, 2004, pp. 680–700; Sandra Lavenex and Frank Schimmelfennig, 'EU Rules beyond EU Borders: Theorizing External Governance in European Politics', *Journal of European Public Policy*, Vol. 16, No. 6, 2009, pp. 791–812.

[18] For example, Adrian Hyde-Price, '"Normative" Power Europe: A Realist Critique', *Journal of European Public Policy*, Vol. 13, No. 2, 2006, pp. 217–34; Michelle Pace, 'The Construction of EU Normative Power', *Journal of Common Market Studies*, Vol. 45, No. 5, 2007, pp. 1041–64.

[19] John Laughland, *The Tainted Source: The Undemocratic Origins of the European Idea* (London, Sphere, 1998); Thierry Baudet, *The Significance of Borders: Why Representative Government and the Rule of Law Require Nation States* (Leiden, Brill, 2012).

order. The EU was trapped between the under-development of its CSDP and the over-development of security ties with its Atlantic partners. America's deployment of missile defence systems in Europe raises some fundamental questions about European security where a major actor stands outside these processes. The EU's norms, while pre-eminently technocratic, have become politicised while lacking an overarching normative commitment to the idea of a plural and united Europe. The absence of a continental vision means that when these norms encountered a resistant other, in this case Russia, the norms themselves became geopolitical, vitiating their benign and transformative character. Cocooned within the Atlantic system, the EU failed to develop an autonomous and transformative foreign and security policy, and instead amplified Atlanticist rather than continental concerns.

The Maastricht Treaty came into effect in February 1992 and brought external affairs into the purview of the EU, mandating a CFSP. Despite this, foreign and security policy is not a community competence, and thus member states retain their autonomy. The disarray in the EU and tensions between members states was in full view at the time of the invasion of Iraq in 2003, which was condemned by the 'old Europe' of France and Germany but enthusiastically endorsed by the 'new Europe' in the East. In response, the Lisbon Treaty of 2009 sought to streamline the management of foreign policy. It created a permanent European Council presidency and the post of High Representative at the head of a new European External Action Service (EEAS), who would also be a Vice President of the European Commission. The EEAS under its inaugural head, Catherine Ashton, sought to 'coordinate' EU foreign policy, as mandated by its remit, and did not 'lead' in the way that a traditional national foreign minister of a major power would. The brokering of a peace deal between Serbia and Kosovo ranks as her greatest achievement.[20] The EEAS had limited resources and instruments at its disposal, and the traditional 'expectations gap' between what the EU promised and delivered was not overcome. In 2014 the EEAS had only one full-time and one part-time staff member working on Ukrainian issues. Earlier, it did not seem to matter that the EU did not have a foreign policy; its very existence was foreign policy enough. On assuming the post of commissar of foreign affairs in the first Bolshevik government in late 1917, Leon Trotsky announced that he would 'issue a few revolutionary decrees and shut up shop'; so it seemed that it was enough for the EU to declare its existence as proof of the transformative power of normative ideas and values. Trotsky's policy of 'no war, no peace'

---

[20] Florian Bieber, 'The Serbia-Kosovo Agreements: An EU Success Story?', *Review of Central and East European Law*, Vol. 40, Nos. 3–4, 2015, pp. 285–319.

soon succumbed to the harsh realities of power politics as Germany imposed the draconian Brest-Litovsk peace, and the EU now faced a similarly harsh reality shock as its 'ring of friends' became an arc of fire.

Apart from trade and aid policy, the EU is a 'derived power', as Jan Techau puts it, since the EU's diplomatic capacity is largely sourced from that of its ally, the US, 'which has the military power to back up its diplomatic efforts'.[21] The EU is also an 'occasional power', since only rarely do the concerns of the member states coincide to give EU institutions the mandate to speak on their behalf. The EU's successful brokering efforts in normalising relations between Serbia and Kosovo, the coordinated response to Russian actions in Ukraine, and its effective participation in the Iran nuclear talks are examples of successful coordination, but the lack of common interests between member states impedes the development of a more coordinated EU foreign policy. The predominance of Atlanticist positions allowed little room for Euro-Atlantic diversity, and reinforced the EU's strategic marginalisation. As one study puts it, '[t]he irrelevance of the EU to shape or influence its European neighbourhood was fully apparent throughout 2014, marking a continuation of the downward trajectory of the EU's influence which has become the characteristic of the past half-decade in the region'.[22]

The hermetic and comprehensive character of the Atlantic community is at odds with a vision of a plural Europe within pan-European structures. The tension has been evident since at least the creation of the first institutions that became the EU. The smaller Europe model is so designated both because of its relatively circumscribed territorial vision, based on Western Europe, as well as the limits placed on a distinctive security and defence identity. The Atlantic representation of Europe's destiny was challenged by Gaullists and others, who called for a more independent European security and political identity. For some this was to focus on the EU alone, as it developed a more ramified foreign and security policy. For traditional Gaullists this was too limiting, and their vision encompassed some sort of continental structure uniting the whole continent from Lisbon to Vladivostok. In Strasbourg on 23 November 1959 De Gaulle delivered his famous Europe 'from the Atlantic to the Urals' speech, arguing that 'the whole of Europe' would 'decide the destiny of the world'. For de Gaulle, Europe should act as the third pole between the

---

[21] Jan Techau, 'Strategic Options for Europe, the Occasional Power', Carnegie Europe, 18 December 2015, http://carnegieeurope.eu/2015/12/18/strategic-options-for-europe-occ asional-power/in9e, last accessed 30 May 2017.

[22] Ana E. Juncos and Richard Whitman, 'Europe as a Regional Actor: Neighbourhood Lost?', *The JCMS Annual Review of the European Union in 2014*, Vol. 53, No. S1, September 2015, p. 200.

US and the Soviet Union. Thirty years later Gorbachev delivered his common European home speech in the same city. As described, this is what Russia today calls 'Greater Europe', the idea that Europe should manage its own affairs within a long-term vision.[23] This idea has been advanced by various politicians across the continent, and should not be seen simply as Russia undermining the existing Atlantic and European communities. This is in sharp contrast to the wider Europe agenda, which in the absence of reconciliation, inevitably fosters conflict.

Realist critics argue that ultimately a values-based foreign policy becomes an exercise in organised hypocrisy. The values themselves become an instrument in the realist struggle for power, thus eroding the legitimacy of the values themselves. This certainly came to be Putin's view, and his critique is one that has a long pedigree in the study of international politics. Carr was one of the first to understand that legitimacy has to be tied to purpose and the realities of power. Raymond Geuss subjected the whole idea of normative power to excoriating critique.[24] Bull noted of Martin Wight that he 'saw the Grotian approach to international morality, for example, as founded upon the recognition that the moral problems of foreign policy are complex, as against the view of the Kantians that these problems are simple, and the view of the Machiavellians that they are non-existent'.[25] More broadly, the whole notion of Kantian ethics in foreign policy has been attacked. This is not to suggest that values have no part to play in shaping foreign policy. On the contrary, a foreign policy driven only by immediate concerns of power-enhancement will not only lack a moral compass but will also lack a basis on which to assess what a country's interests really are. My argument endorses Kissinger's view that the most effective foreign policy is one that combines the principles of power and legitimacy. An excess of values occludes understanding of the security concerns of others. This is especially important in the case of Russia, located in a far from benign security environment.

I have argued that Russia's logic of transformation is pitted against the Atlantic community's logic of enlargement, but there have been attempts to reconcile the two. The current legal basis for cooperation between Russia and the EU is the PCA, on whose basis the Common European Economic Space was launched at the St Petersburg summit in May 2003 to cover four areas of common concern: economy and environment; freedom, security

[23] A point made by Mark Mazower, *Dark Continent* (London, Vintage, 2000).

[24] Raymond Geuss, *Philosophy and Real Politics* (Princeton and Oxford, Princeton University Press, 2008).

[25] Cited in Aleksandar Jankovski, 'Russia and the United States: On Irritants, Friction, and International Order or What We Can Learn from Hedley Bull', *International Politics*, Vol. 53, No. 6, 2016, pp. 730–1.

and justice; external security; and research and education. The Moscow summit in May 2005 outlined a series of 'road maps' for their implementation. The document incorporated the Russian notion of a Greater Europe:

> The EU and Russia recognize that processes of regional cooperation and integration in which they participate and which are based on the sovereign decisions of States, play an important role in strengthening security and stability. They agree to actively promote them in a mutually beneficial manner, through close result-oriented EU-Russia collaboration and dialogue, thereby contributing effectively to creating a greater Europe without dividing lines and based on common values.[26]

As the ten-year PCA expired, negotiations for a new Russia–EU Basic Agreement were launched at the Khanty-Mansi summit in 2008 to provide, according to the EU, a more comprehensive framework for Russo-EU relations, and 'to include substantive, legally binding commitments in all areas of the partnership', whereas the Russian side favoured a more general statement of principles. The negotiations had not gone very far before being suspended in 2014. The Partnership for Modernisation was agreed by the Rostov summit in July 2010, reinforcing dialogue in the context of the common spaces, and represented an attempt to provide a new dynamism to the stalled programme. In the end this all came to naught, and in 2014 targeted sanctions were imposed restricting access to capital markets, defence, dual-use goods, and sensitive technologies (including in the energy sector). The Permanent Partnership Council at the level of the heads of the respective foreign services had long fallen into desuetude, last meeting in November 2011. Vladimir Chizhov, Russia's permanent representative to the EU, noted the wide range of accumulating problems, which had been apparent long before the Ukraine crisis. He was one of those who argued that 'the return to "business as usual" would be both unrealistic and useless'.[27] A new model of relations is required.

Lavrov repeatedly referred to the concept of Greater Europe, arguing in January 2014 that Moscow's work on creating 'a common economic and humanitarian space stretching from Lisbon to Vladivostok in the future' correlated with the appeals of the EU leadership 'for a common market and free trade zone in this space'.[28] In his address to the UN General

---

[26] 'Road Map for the Common Space of External Security'. For this and other documents and progress reports, see http://eeas.europa.eu/russia/about/index_en.htm, last accessed 30 May 2017.

[27] Andrei Zolotov interview with Vladimir Chizhov, 'Russia-EU Relations: Still Waiting for a New Shift in Momentum', *Russia Direct*, 6 June 2016, www.russia-direct.org/qa/russia-eu-relations-still-waiting-new-shift-momentum, last accessed 30 May 2017.

[28] RF Ministry of Foreign Affairs, 'Speech by the Russian Foreign Minister Sergey Lavrov', Moscow, 21 January 2014, http://archive.mid.ru//brp_4.nsf/0/9ECCD0C0F39435 F344257C6A003247B2, last accessed 9 June 2017.

Assembly on 28 September 2015 Putin stressed that a resolution of the Donbas question would allow Ukraine to 'develop as a civilised state, and a vital link in creating a common space of security and economic cooperation, both in Europe and Eurasia'.[29] Putin was even more explicit in an article for a Greek paper ahead of his visit in May 2016. He noted that 'Russia proceeds from the need to establish dialogue with the European Union in the spirit of equality and genuine partnership on a variety of issues ranging from visa liberalization to the formation of an energy alliance', but he noted that 'European colleagues' were not yet ready to pursue 'such a mutually beneficial and promising path'. Progress could only be made if 'the deficient approach of one-sided relationships' was abandoned. Relations had come to a crossroads and there was only one way forward:

I am convinced we should draw appropriate conclusions from the events in Ukraine and proceed to establishing, in the vast space stretching between the Atlantic and the Pacific oceans, a zone of economic and humanitarian cooperation based on the architecture of equal and indivisible security. Harmonizing European and Eurasian integration processes would be an important step in this direction.[30]

The 'normative paradox' emerges when the EU does not apply to its neighbours the values and practices that it exercises within its own borders or proclaims in dialogue with the other.[31] Condemned as 'double standards' by Moscow, the paradox is certainly not limited to the EU. Russia has not discovered a consistent practice to implement its proclaimed sovereignty and equality in relations with its neighbours.[32] Casier questions the dichotomy between norms and interests, and notes that the norm-driven inputs into EU foreign policy are not necessarily reflected in actual foreign policy behaviour of the EU, and suggests that the normative agenda in Eastern Europe serves instrumental purposes.[33] In other words, the view of Russia as a non-normative or *Realpolitik* actor is challenged. Equally, the EU's engagement with Russia has become less normative as it has tried to find new ways to establish a constructive

[29] 'Vladimir Putin, speech to the 70th session of the UN General Assembly', 28 September 2015, http://kremlin.ru/events/president/news/50385, last accessed 9 June 2017.

[30] Vladimir Putin, 'Russia and Greece: Cooperation for Peace and Prosperity', *Kathimerini*, 26 May 2016, reproduced at http://en.kremlin.ru/events/president/news/51997, last accessed 9 June 2017.

[31] Tom Casier, 'The EU-Russia Strategic Partnership: Challenging the Normative Argument', *Europe-Asia Studies*, Vol. 65, No. 7, September 2013, pp. 1377–95.

[32] As described by James Sherr, *Hard Diplomacy and Soft Coercion: Russia's Influence Abroad* (London, Royal Institute of International Affairs, 2013).

[33] Casier, 'The EU-Russia Strategic Partnership'.

relationship.[34] Russia's refusal to accept normative hierarchy in relations with the EU (and indeed with the Atlantic community as a whole) has been the source of much of the tension. Equality is an enduring theme of official speeches, strategy documents and partnership statements.[35] The Partnership for Modernisation agreement, for example, stressed the 'equality of partners and the mutual respect of interests'.[36] The representation of Europe as a normative power establishes a hierarchy in which others inevitably become the objects of transformation or suspicion. If neighbours prove resistant to the EU's self-defined benign strictures, then the full apparatus of 'othering' is unleashed, generating a cycle of mutual recriminations – of which relations between Russia and the EU are a classic example.[37] The issue is not that Russia repudiates either the norms of the EU or the ultimately benign nature of the Atlantic security system, but no way has been found to ensure Russia's institutional association in these systems with the autonomy and status that would satisfy its elites. The result is an epochal breakdown in relations.

The Battle for Europe

Even before the cold peace gave way to renewed confrontation, the EU and Russia struggled for influence across the post-Soviet space: 'Russia increasingly positioned itself as a counterforce to the EU's approaches to their "common neighbourhood".' Russia advanced alternative models of economic modernisation and societal development to those of the EU.[38] Dmitry Suslov argues that '[f]or the first time in their relations, Russia and the EU must now formulate a model of interaction that focuses not on the strategic goal of building a common space. A new model presumes that Moscow and Brussels de facto belong to different political and economic communities.'[39] The wider Europe model assumed a single space based on the gradual convergence, and ultimate integration, of all other entities into an EU-centred European community focused on

---

[34] Casier, 'The EU-Russia Strategic Partnership', p. 1379.

[35] Examples are given in Casier, 'The EU-Russia Strategic Partnership', p. 1381.

[36] 'Joint Statement on the Partnership for Modernisation', EU-Russia Summit, Rostov-on-Don, 31 May – 1 June 2010.

[37] Thomas Diez, 'Constructing the Self and Changing Others: Reconsidering "Normative Power Europe"', *Millennium*, Vol. 33, No. 3, 2005, pp. 613–36.

[38] Tuomas Forsberg and Hiski Haukkala, *The European Union and Russia* (London, Palgrave, 2016), p. 204.

[39] Dmitry Suslov, *Without a 'Common Space': A New Agenda for Russia–EU Relations*, Moscow, Valdai Paper No. 49, June 2016, p. 3, http://valdaiclub.com/a/valdai-papers/valdai-paper-49-without-a-common-space-a-new-agenda-for-russia-eu-relations/, last accessed 9 June 2017.

Brussels.[40] EU elites divided between those still wanting to bring Russia into that process, and Atlanticist hard-liners who considered the attempt futile and sought to strengthen neo-containment to constrain the perceived danger from the east. The Yukos affair from 2003, whereby the country's most successful oil company was effectively expropriated and its leader, Mikhail Khdorkovsky, jailed, undermined those who sought rapprochement with Russia.[41] Moscow, however, had moved beyond any EU-centric model, and sought to create an equal partnership based on equivalence between the two poles of Europe, the EU and the EEU.[42] Elements of the old agenda linger on, above all for visa-free travel, energy dialogue, and non-discrimination against ethnic Russians in the EU, but talk of partnership is long gone. The idea of a 'common economic, human and security space stretching from Lisbon to Vladivostok', which Russia and the EU proclaimed since the late 1980s, 'is losing political relevance and becoming increasingly infeasible with each passing day'.[43] Greater Europe remains official policy, but Russia developed its Greater Eurasia Project to consolidate the heartland, while Greater Asia rail and other networks stretched from Shanghai to Shannon. The idea of pan-continental unity became one more of Europe's shattered dreams.

Since the financial crisis of 2008, the EU has been buffeted by various crises.[44] There is a growing consensus that while the EU in its traditional form may be doomed, some form of 'deeper Europe' will emerge.[45] Over Ukraine, the EU's ill-prepared advance into what was a contested neighbourhood provoked the gravest international crisis of our era, but left the EU sidelined as the great powers took over. The EU appeared bereft of actor autonomy and policy instruments, prompting calls for greater foreign policy coordination. Lavrov repeatedly expressed surprise at how little autonomy Europe really enjoyed when it came to the big decisions about the fate of the continent. He recalled the statement by Biden that the American leadership had cajoled Europe into imposing sanctions on

---

[40] In the parlance of Soviet nationality politics, there was to be a gradual *sblizhenie* (coming closer) of all European states, but not necessarily their *sliyanie* (merger).

[41] Richard Sakwa, *Putin and the Oligarch: The Khodorkovsky–Yukos Affair* (London, I. B. Tauris; New York, Palgrave Macmillan, 2014).

[42] Suslov, *Without a 'Common Space'*, p. 3.

[43] Suslov, *Without a 'Common Space'*, p. 4.

[44] See the Special Issue edited by Randall Hansen, 'Europe's Crisis: Background, Dimensions, Solutions', *West European Politics*, Vol. 37, No. 6, November 2014.

[45] The argument advanced by Jan Zielonka (although he does not use the term 'deeper Europe'), *Is the EU Doomed?* (Cambridge: Polity Press, 2014). For an erudite study of contemporary problems of European integration, see Nathaniel Copsey, *Rethinking the European Union* (London, Palgrave Macmillan, 2015).

Russia, even though the EU had initially been opposed.[46] Lavrov noted 'that we for some previous years over-estimated the independence of the European Union and even big European countries. So, it's geopolitics.'[47] At the same time, he called for the 'integration of integrations' between the EU and the EEU to create a Greater Europe.[48]

The appointment of the Italian foreign minister, Federica Mogherini, to head the EEAS as high representative and vice president (HRVP) of the European Commission at the EU summit on 6 September 2014 provided an opportunity for a rethink. This was balanced by the appointment of Tusk, the former Polish prime minister, to replace Herman van Rompuy as head of the European Council, and in March 2017 he was re-appointed for a second two-and-a-half-year term (despite the opposition of the Polish government). Tusk adopted a hawkish approach: 'For Putin, and Russia today, the EU is a problem. And we have to understand, and I think we are close to this moment, that Russia is not our strategic partner. Russia is our strategic problem.'[49] In an interview with European media in March 2015 he insisted that 'Putin's policy is to have enemies and be in conflict', and he warned that any attempt to weaken the sanctions regime would 'risk a crisis with the White House'.[50] It was clear where Tusk's loyalties lay. He called himself 'an incurably pro-American European who is fanatically devoted to trans-Atlantic cooperation'. In January 2017 he sent a letter to member states warning that the Trump administration was a danger to the Union, alongside Russia and radical Islam: 'With the new administration seeming to put into question the last 70 years of American foreign policy', America now had to be considered not a friend of the EU but a 'threat'.[51] As a perceptive analysis puts it, 'How was it that the foreign relations of the EU's

[46] Joseph Biden's comments were made at the John F. Kennedy Jr. Forum at Harvard University's Institute of Politics on 2 October 2014, in which he noted the EU's reluctance to move from individual to sectoral sanctions: 'It was America's leadership and the president of the United States insisting, oft times almost having to embarrass Europe to stand up and take economic hits to impose costs', that got them to agree. *RT Question More*, 3 October 2014, http://rt.com/usa/193044-us-embarrass-eu-sanctions/, last accessed 30 May 2017.

[47] Lavrov's interview with France 24', 16 December 2014. Lavrov condemned the 'bloc discipline' in the Atlantic community, which he argued was 'stricter than the discipline that existed within the Warsaw Treaty Organisation', 'Russia's Lavrov gives interview to state TV', 25 December 2014, ministry transcript of 30 December 2014.

[48] 'Russian Foreign Minister: We are not Interested in Alienation or Confrontation between Russia, West', Interfax, 29 December 2014.

[49] Foy, 'Donald Tusk'.

[50] Ian Traynor, 'Donald Tusk: Putin's Policy Is to Have Enemies and Be in Conflict', *Guardian*, 15 March 2015, www.theguardian.com/world/2015/mar/15/donald-tusk-putins-policy-enemies-conflict-european-council-sanctions-russia, last accessed 30 May 2017.

[51] Michael Crowley, 'The Man Who Wants to Unmake the West', *Politico*, March–April 2017, www.politico.com/magazine/story/2017/03/trump-steve-bannon-destroy-eu-european-union-214889, last accessed 30 May 2017.

twenty-eight sovereign members, and the peace of Europe, were allowed to become hostage to the geopolitical ambitions of Poland?'[52]

Russia's 2016 *Foreign Policy Concept* no longer describes the EU as a 'strategic partner', and instead notes that the EU 'remains an important trade-economic and foreign policy partner' (paragraph 63). Lavrov was scathing, arguing that

the current crisis in relations with the EU is the result of a persistent reluctance of partners to build dialogue on the basis of true partnership ... Russia has repeatedly expressed readiness to cooperate with the EU on a broad range of issues – from abolition of short-term visas to rapprochement in the energy sphere ... A short-sighted line towards seizing geopolitical space has prevailed. The culmination of such a course was a coup d'état in Ukraine backed by a number of EU countries.

He reiterated a point that has become standard in Russian thinking – the EU's negligible independent weight in the management of global affairs:

It seems that we somehow overestimated the independent role of the Europeans on the global arena ... It appears that the Ukrainian crisis highlighted a high degree of the EU dependence on the political and economic influence of Washington. We would like to deal with a strong EU that would build relations with partners on the international arena judging first of all from its own interests and not making solidarity with players outside the region a top priority.[53]

The Chinese shared Lavrov's sentiments. For them, 'close cooperation between the EU and the US is a sign of Europe's subordination to America's politics and goals'.[54] Lavrov argued Russia was part of a rapidly changing world, with new centres of growth and influence emerging, notably in the APR, but '[a]t the same time, we have been witnessing such an unusual phenomenon as the transformation of Europe into a region that is projecting outwards not the traditional well-being, but instability'.[55] The continent was facing the worst refugee crisis since 1945. In 2015 alone some 1.8 million asylum-seekers entered the EU fleeing war and poverty in the Middle East and North Africa. In desperation, in March 2016 the EU signed a deal with Ankara whereby Turkey

[52] Matthew Dal Santo, 'Russia, Europe's Scapegoat for All Seasons', *The Nation*, 18 March 2016, www.thenation.com/article/russia-europes-scapegoat-for-all-seasons/, last accessed 9 June 2017.

[53] 'FM: Russian Foreign Policy Rests on Multi-vector Nature and Self-sufficiency', *TASS*, 25 May 2016, http://tass.ru/en/politics/877924, last accessed 30 May 2017.

[54] Marcin Kaczmarski, *An Essential Partner in the Background: Europe in China's Policy During the Rule of Xi Jinping*, Warsaw, Centre for Eastern Studies, OSW Studies No. 56, April 2016, p. 11.

[55] '"Europe is Turning into a Region That Projects Instability Outwards" – Russian FM', 2 June 2016, www.rt.com/news/345186-europe-instability-lavrov-refugee/, last accessed 30 May 2017.

would take back refugees seeking asylum in return for a €3 billion assistance package, visa-free travel and an acceleration of the membership negotiations. Lavrov's view that the EU was no longer just a danger to itself but projected instability represented a significant radicalisation of the Russian critique.

José Manuel Barroso's successor as president of the European Commission, Jean-Claude Juncker, was a realist of the old school, a staunch federalist and supporter of deeper European integration. He had also, as prime minister of Luxembourg, been well-disposed towards Russia. In a speech in Passau on 8 October 2015 Juncker noted: 'We must make efforts towards a practical relationship with Russia. It's not sexy but that must be the case, we can't go on like this.'[56] Soon after the G20 summit in Antalya in November 2015, Juncker wrote to Putin suggesting closer trade ties between the EU and the EEU as part of the attempt to re-engage. He stressed the importance of good relations between the EU and Russia, 'which to my regret have not been able to develop over the past year'.[57] This came soon after the Paris killings of 13 November at a time when it made sense to unite in the fight against Islamic State and to forge a peace deal in Syria. EU hard-liners objected to the initiative, led by the Lithuanian foreign minister Linas Linkevicius. He noted that the letter did not refer to the sanctions or Russia's actions in Ukraine.[58] Russo-EU relations became hostage to developments in Ukraine and the historical grievances of East European elites. Despite criticism, Juncker attended SPIEF in June 2016, the first visit by such a senior EU official since Crimea's transfer. Officials in Berlin considered lifting travel restrictions on Russian legislators and reducing the period to three months in which sanctions last before requiring renewal. Already on 31 May Steinmeier argued that the 'all or nothing' approach to force Russia's compliance with the Minsk agreement was not working. He warned that sanctions were not an end in themselves but 'should lead to a political solution'.[59]

Mogherini sought to adapt EU foreign policy to the new conditions. On assuming office on 1 November 2014, she reorganised the EEAS and

[56] 'Speech of President Juncker in Passau, Germany', 8 October 2015, www.denederland segrondwet.nl/9353000/1/j9vvihlf299q0sr/vjy3fgc69kvc?ctx=vhyzn0sukawp&start_tab0=40, last accessed 30 May 2017.

[57] Andrius Sytas, 'Exclusive: EU's Juncker Dangles Trade Ties with Russia-Led Bloc to Putin', Reuters, 19 November 2015, http://uk.reuters.com/article/uk-eu-russia-trade-kr emlin-exclusive-idUKKCN0T82O920151119, last accessed 30 May 2017.

[58] Andrius Sytas, 'EU's Juncker Dangles Trade Ties with Russia-led Bloc to Putin', Reuters, 19 November 2015, http://uk.reuters.com/article/2015/11/19/uk-eu-russia-tra de-kremlin-exclusive-idUKKCN0T82O920151119, last accessed 9 June 2017.

[59] Howard Amos, 'EU Unity Crumbles as Russia Sanctions Extension Debate Rages', International Business Times, 2 June 2016, www.ibtimes.com/eu-unity-crumbles-russia-s anctions-extension-debate-rages-2376693, last accessed 30 May 2017.

moved it into the Berlaymont building to be closer to the European Commission. The EEAS was remoulded and the Ukrainian desk significantly bolstered, with up to eight staff members assigned. Mogherini launched a review of EaP as well as the *European Security Strategy*, originally formulated by Javier Solana over a decade earlier. This was accompanied by a discussion about the degree to which the EU needed to think more 'geopolitically', although it was not clear how this was to be defined. If it meant a realist engagement with the world as it is rather than the trans-democratic anticipation of a reality to be born, then traditional forms of diplomacy and bargaining could be restored. However, if it meant more explicit contestation for influence over the neighbourhood, then this would only intensify conflict. Mogherini's 'issues paper' of 19 January 2015 outlined ideas for stabilising the relationship.[60] The paper provoked a storm of protest against the purported return to 'business as usual' in Russo-EU relations. The paper focused largely on institutional aspects of the relationship, including resumption of formal dialogue, trilateral talks on a DCFTA, and recognition of the EEU, elements of what could have become a 'grand bargain'. Critics argued that the fundamental problem was Russia's view of itself as a great power, which inevitably required a 'sphere of influence' and hence limited sovereignty for its neighbours, hence there was no basis for dialogue, let alone negotiation.[61] This arguably represents a fundamental misreading of the Russian position, which sought to create pan-European structures precisely to avoid a return to spheres of influence.

This did not mean that the EU did not adjust its policies. The fourth EaP summit in Riga on 21 and 22 May 2015 outlined the principles of 'differentiation and inclusivity'. In the wake of the catastrophic events attending the previous summit in Vilnius, this was a sombre occasion. Poroshenko reiterated Ukrainian aspirations to join the EU, while the foreign minister, Pavlo Klimkin, sought an explicit commitment about Ukraine's eligibility for membership. The Ukrainian demands were rejected, reflecting the broader tension between EaP's ambitious aspirations for the transformation of the region and its refusal to extend the accession agenda to these countries. Juncker was dismissive, arguing that Ukraine's accession to the EU was out of the question because 'they are

---

[60] 'Issues Paper on Relations with Russia' EU Foreign Affairs Council, 19 January 2015, http://blogs.ft.com/brusselsblog/files/2015/01/Russia.pdf, last accessed 30 May 2017. It was published in the *Financial Times* on 15 January 2015.
[61] Kadri Liik, 'The Real Problem with Mogherini's Russia Paper', European Council on Foreign Relations, 20 January 2015, www.ecfr.eu/article/commentary_the_real_proble m_with_mogherinis_russia_paper402, last accessed 30 May 2017.

not ready [and] we are not ready'.[62] The Joint Declaration affirmed 'the sovereign right of each partner freely to choose the level of ambition and the goals to which it aspires in its relations with the European Union', accompanied by a new emphasis on 'differentiated relations between the EU and its six sovereign, independent partners'.[63] At the same time, the European Commission reviewed the ENP's 'assumptions', 'scope', and 'instruments'. The review was prompted by the ENP's inability to 'offer adequate responses to ... recent developments in [the neighbourhood and] to the changing aspirations of our partners. Therefore, the EU's own interests have not been fully served either.' The review asserted that the Russian-Georgian War and the Ukraine crisis 'have been caused by an increasingly assertive Russian foreign policy, which has also resulted in exacerbating divisions between Russia and the EU'. As a result, the challenges facing the EU's neighbourhood policy 'cannot be adequately addressed without taking into account, or in some cases cooperating with the neighbours of the neighbours'. Although the EU would not repudiate its values, it was 'essential to consult partners on their interests, ambitions for this partnership [while] the EU needs to define more clearly its own aims and interests, while promoting the values on which it is based'.[64] A review of the academic literature on the ENP came to much the same conclusion, noting that it failed to take into account local needs and conditions.[65]

The pragmatic approach was reflected in the modified ENP announced on 18 November 2015, representing a retreat from the expansive agenda enunciated in earlier versions. The new ENP was more transactional than its precursor, and scaled back the ambition to reshape the EU's neighbours in its own image.[66] The catastrophic failure of the Arab Spring and the Ukraine crisis delivered a powerful salutary shock, and forced a shift to a more differentiated and less lofty approach. This was not a shift to

---

[62] Alastair MacDonald and Adrian Croft, 'EU Defies Russian "Bully" but Disappoints ex-Soviets', Reuters, 22 May 2015, http://in.reuters.com/article/ukraine-crisis-eu-idINKB N0O62E320150521, last accessed 30 May 2017.

[63] *Joint Declaration of the Eastern Partnership Summit*, Riga, 21–22 May 2015, www.consi lium.europa.eu/en/meetings/international-summit/2015/05/21-22/, last accessed 30 May 2017.

[64] European Commission, High Representative of the European Union for Foreign Affairs and Security Policy, 'Joint Consultation Paper: Towards a New European Neighbourhood Policy', JOIN (2015) 6 final, Brussels, 4 April 2015, http://ec.europa.eu/enlargement/nei ghbourhood/consultation/consultation.pdf, last accessed 30 May 2017.

[65] Hrant Kostanyan (ed.), *Assessing European Neighbourhood Policy: Perspectives from the Literature* (Brussels, CEPS, and London, Rowman and Littlefield, 2017), p. 70.

[66] European Commission press release, 'Review of the European Neighbourhood Policy (ENP): Stronger Partnerships for a Stronger Neighbourhood', 18 November 2015, http://europa.eu/rapid/press-release_IP-15-6121_en.htm, last accessed 30 May 2017.

lower normative standards but a belated understanding that the historical problems of development and political integration that had been resolved in the European context could not be exported as a pre-digested package to countries with very different levels of development and historical experiences. Enlargement as a foreign policy tool outside the Western Balkans was essentially shelved by the Commission announcement in July 2014 that there would be no more accessions before 2019. In March 2016 Juncker argued that Ukraine would not join the EU or NATO for another twenty to twenty-five years.[67] The announcement sought to allay concerns in advance of the 6 April referendum in the Netherlands on ratifying the AA with Ukraine. In the event, on a turnout of 32 per cent, 66 per cent voted against, a decisive victory for the 'no' camp that reflected not only the traditionally strong Eurosceptic tradition in the country but also a realignment of left and right in defence of a revived sovereignty agenda and against the EU's alleged degeneration into a subaltern element of the Atlantic community.

The various challenges facing the EU, including Trump's anti-EU sentiments, provoked the stirrings of what has been called a revived 'Gaullist moment' for Europe, 'where strategic autonomy and independence should be the guiding principle in foreign and security issues'.[68] The EU foreign ministers' summit on 14 March 2016 outlined five principles for relations with Russia: first, the full implementation of the Minsk Accords; second, the strengthening of relations with all neighbours; third, increasing the resilience of the EU, in particular in the sphere of energy security, cyber-threats and strategic communications; fourth, selective engagement with Russia on foreign policy issues, notably Iran, North Korea, the regulation of the crisis in the Middle East and in particular Syria, migration, terrorism and climate change; and fifth, support for Russian civil society and people-to-people contacts.[69] The aim was to establish a new *modus operandi* for Russo-EU relations, but the lack of ambition was striking.

These priorities were evident in revisions to the *European Security Strategy*. Adopted in the more benign environment of 2003, the document argued that '[l]arge-scale aggression against any Member State is

---

[67] 'Ukraine Will Not Join EU, NATO for Another 20–25 Years, Juncker Says', *DPA International*, 3 March 2016, www.dpa-international.com/news/top_stories/ukraine-wil l-not-join-eu-natofor-another-20-25-years-juncker-says-a-48506292.html, last accessed 9 June 2017.

[68] Jean-Yves Haine, 'A New Gaullist Moment? European Bandwagoning and International Polarity', *International Affairs*, Vol. 91, No. 5, 2015, p. 991.

[69] As reported by Mogherini, 'Glavy MID ES prinyali pyat' printsipov postroeniya otnosheniya s Rossiei', RIA Novosti, 14 March 2016, http://ria.ru/politics/20160314/13897382 98.html, last accessed 9 June 2017.

now improbable'. The *Strategy* recognised that '[e]ven in an era of globalisation, geography is still important. It is in the European interest that countries on our borders are well-governed', as well as stressing that '[i]t is not in our interest that enlargement should create new dividing lines in Europe'. Russia was listed several times as a partner in resolving the various security challenges facing the continent.[70] Ideas for revising the document after the Caucasus crisis were aired in the European Council's 11 December 2008 report on the implementation of the *European Security Strategy*.[71] In the end, the Council feared that a full review would provoke disagreements, especially over Russia, so revisions were limited to the addition of materials on new security challenges such as cyber-security, energy security and climate change.[72] The revised *EU Global Strategy*, adopted by the European Council on 28 June 2016, could hardly be more different. The language of partnership had disappeared, and instead a stern and didactic tone predominated:

The sovereignty, independence and territorial integrity of states, the inviolability of borders and the peaceful settlement of disputes are key elements of the European security order. These principles apply to all states, both within and beyond the EU's borders.

Serbia would no doubt have its own views on the issue, having effectively lost Kosovo, but the next paragraph made it clear what the document had in mind:

However, peace and stability are no longer a given. Russia's violation of international law and the destabilisation of Ukraine, on top of protracted conflicts in the wider Black Sea region, have challenged the European security order at its core. The EU will stand united in upholding international law, democracy, human rights, cooperation and each country's right to choose its future freely.

The next paragraph was unyielding in its evocation of the principles underlying the post-Cold War European security order, but gave no hint of understanding why Russia had for so long been uncomfortable with that order:

[70] *A Secure Europe in a Better World: European Security Strategy*, Brussels, 12 December 2003, www.consilium.europa.eu/uedocs/cmsUpload/78367.pdf, last accessed 9 June 2017.

[71] 'Report of the Implementation of the European Security Strategy: Providing Security in a Changing World', www.satcen.europa.eu/key_documents/report%20on%20the%20implementation%20of%20the%20ess.pdf, last accessed 30 May 2017.

[72] Nadezhda Arbatova, 'The EU's New Security Strategy', Valdai Discussion Club, 8 July 2016, http://valdaiclub.com/news/the-eu-new-security-strategy/, last accessed 30 May 2017.

Managing the relationship with Russia represents a key strategic challenge. A consistent and united approach must remain the cornerstone of EU policy towards Russia. Substantial changes in relations between the EU and Russia are premised upon full respect for international law and the principles underpinning the European security order, including the Helsinki Final Act and the Paris Charter. We will not recognise Russia's illegal annexation of Crimea nor accept the destabilisation of eastern Ukraine. We will strengthen the EU, enhance the resilience of our eastern neighbours, and uphold their right to determine freely their approach towards the EU. At the same time, the EU and Russia are interdependent. We will therefore engage Russia to discuss disagreements and cooperate if and when our interests overlap.

The *European Union Global Strategy* promised continued cooperation on a limited range of foreign policy issues, including 'selective engagement' on such matters as climate, the Arctic, maritime security, education, research and cross-border cooperation. Engagement would also include 'deeper societal ties through facilitated travel for students, civil society and business'.[73] The *Strategy* declared that '[p]rincipled pragmatism will guide our external action in the years ahead'.[74] There was less emphasis on the ENP, and instead the focus was on fostering the 'resilience' of neighbouring states accompanied by the assertion of the EU's 'strategic autonomy'. Deeper partnership with NATO was repeatedly mentioned, with the EDA to coordinate military planning between the two. The defence component of European integration was to be developed through the more rational use of military capabilities. The *Strategy* fundamentally repudiated Gaullist pan-continental aspirations, and instead it was clear that the EU would focus on its 'wider Europe' agenda of consolidating a sphere of influence in its neighbourhood. There was no recognition that the breakdown of the European security order in 2014 may have had broader causes other than Russia's apparently irrational flouting of the post-Cold War foundations of European order. The involution of Greater Europe aspirations was evident.

EU-Russian relations were at rock bottom. The high level of economic interactions, above all in energy, did not result in any meaningful positive political interdependence. The relationship remained at the transactional level, despite repeated attempts to achieve 'partnership and cooperation', 'common spaces', and a 'partnership for modernisation'. Instead, mutual recriminations predominated. As Bordachev notes, '[t]he partnership that for 20 years was regarded as something

---

[73] European Union, *Shared Vision: Common Action: A Stronger Europe. A Global Strategy for the European Union's Foreign and Security Policy*, June 2016, p. 33, http://europa.eu/glob alstrategy/en, last accessed 30 May 2017.
[74] European Union, *Shared Vision*, p. 8.

stable and economically grounded has crumbled under the impact of Ukraine-related contradictions'. In his view, the order that emerged after 1989 'suited just one side, the West', identified in Europe with the EU, '[b]ut it was unsuitable for the other side, Russia'. The EU accused Russia of democratic backsliding, whereas Russian commentators argued that 'the irreversible degradation of this order in the security sphere began in 1999, when EU countries and the US bombed Yugoslavia out of existence'. Even the deal over transit to the Russian exclave of Kaliningrad in 2002 exposed the 'degradation' of the relationship, 'when the EU refused to grant an insignificant concession on Kaliningrad transit to a country it called its "true strategic partner"'.[75] Prospects for Russo-EU relations depend on understanding where the relationship went wrong. Early hopes for strategic partnership have now given way to a deep alienation on both sides, leaving open only the option, at best, of pragmatic transactional relations for the foreseeable future. From the EU's perspective, Russia had been a poor pupil, and its stubborn insistence on playing by its own set of rules and not those of the EU means that relations will remain superficial. Educational and other links will continue, but there is little immediate prospect for visa-free travel or any other deepening of relations. There had long been a debate in the EU about whether to prioritise Moscow or Kiev, but after 2014 the die was cast firmly in favour of Ukraine. The fact that such a futile choice was even posed reflects the lack of a strategic perspective and the absence of some sort of overarching structure of continental reconciliation and integration in the post-Cold War years.

Brexit and the election of Trump created a new strategic environment for Russo-EU relations. Obama had already signalled that Europe needed to take greater responsibility for its security and the management of regional affairs, but after the change of administration in Washington the EU returned to plans to create a military headquarters, and sought to 'strengthen the relevance' of the EU's rapid-reaction forces, known as battle-groups. At that time the EU's CSDP was running seventeen military and civilian missions, including a naval force protecting ships from Somali pirates. EU defence plans gained in ambition, but still fell far short of creating a separate army. The idea was championed by Juncker in March 2015 as a means of raising the EU's standing in global affairs,

---

[75] Timofei Bordachev, 'Some Important Questions and Points Regarding Russia's EU Strategy', Valdai Club Foundation, 15 March 2016, http://valdaiclub.com/opinion/high lights/questions-and-points-regarding-russia-eu-strategy/, last accessed 30 May 2017.

not least *vis-à-vis* Russia.[76] NATO was resolutely opposed to the EU going it alone in defence matters, but with the British on the way out and hostile noises from the White House, the idea gained support. On the other side, the key problem 'was Russia's growing exasperation with being the junior partner in its relations with the West, and being forced to accept diktats coming from that direction'.[77] Status issues were central to the deterioration in Russo-EU relations, notably Russia's refusal to accept tutelage from the EU, and the Ukraine breakdown was undoubtedly the 'culmination of a long-term crisis in EU-Russia relations'. The EU positioned itself at the centre of a unipolar pan-European order, a claim that was contested by Russia. In the end, 'the EU offers and demands ... things that Putin's Russia does not think it needs or wants'.[78] In the larger context, Igor Ivanov argues that Europe and Russia have little chance of reconciliation: 'The paths of Europe and Russia are seriously diverging and will remain so for a long time ... probably for decades to come.' He stressed that Russia would not become the eastern flank of a 'failed greater Europe'. It was time to forget 'these beautiful plans', and instead Russia's destiny was now to become the leader of a greater Eurasia stretching from Belarus to the Chinese border.[79]

Dependence and Disruption

Once again Europe became a battleground. Russia was suspected of fomenting divisions by exploiting bilateral relationships and supporting populist movements. The sanctions imposed in 2014 were subsequently extended several times for six-month periods. In response, Moscow sought to exploit divisions to break the unanimity required for their extension, as well as to stimulate alternative policies that would help Russia break out of its strategic isolation. Moscow's policy was prompted in part by the breakdown of diplomacy as well as by simplified views of the EU as an international actor. By now, the Kremlin had come to see the EU as little more than an American puppet ready to betray its own principles when it was to the advantage of the Atlantic security system. The key lesson of the Ukraine crisis for Moscow was that the EU seemed incapable of defending its own normative principles, and thus it made sense to undermine the EU's

---

[76] Jennifer Rankin 'EU Scales Back Plans for Military HQ as it Unveils Crisis Response Blueprint', *Guardian*, 14 November 2016, www.theguardian.com/world/2016/nov/14/eu-scales-back-plans-for-military-hq-as-it-unveils-crisis-response-blueprint, last accessed 30 May 2017.

[77] Haukkala, 'From Cooperative to Contested Europe?', p. 31.

[78] Haukkala, 'From Cooperative to Contested Europe?', p. 31.

[79] Cited in Emmott, 'Risk of Nuclear War in Europe Growing'.

coherence to ensure a diversity of views as the member states exercised their traditional foreign policy prerogatives. In practice, Moscow's policy acted as little more than an irritant, and further alienated European elites and reinforced attempts to improve the Union's crisis management capacities and its 'resilience' in the face of the Russian challenge.

Russia and the EU are economically interdependent, but this has not been translated into the establishment of a shared political community. Trade rose steadily to 2014. The value of EU exports to Russia in 2009 totalled €65.7 billion, but by 2013 had almost doubled to €119.8 billion, accounting for 6.9 per cent of total EU exports. Over the same period the value of EU imports from Russia rose from €119.6 billion to reach €206.1 billion, representing 12.3 per cent of its total imports. The EU remains the single largest market for Russia, with energy comprising some 85 per cent of all EU imports from Russia, whereas vehicles and equipment make up some 65 per cent of Russian imports from the EU. With sanctions and Russia's pivot to the East, the EU's share in Russian trade fell from 53 per cent in 2013 to 46.5 per cent in early 2017. Energy represents a large proportion of this. In 2013 oil and natural gas comprised 68 per cent of Russia's total export revenues, and provided around 35 per cent of its budgetary income. Despite the bumpy political relationship, the volume of Russian gas imported to the EU rose by 17 per cent since 2005. In 2016, 34 per cent of EU gas imports came from Russia, and it is anticipated that Russia will remain the main supplier until 2035.[80] Having risen steadily until 2010, the EU's demand for natural gas is now decreasing, falling back to 1995 levels by 2014. The EU's consumption of oil has also fallen by 17 per cent since 2005, but the EU-28 still imports 83 per cent of its oil consumption. Russia is the leading oil supplier to the EU, covering 29 per cent of imports, with some 75 per cent of its exports going to the EU.[81] Overall, Russia remains the main supplier of fossil fuels to the EU, in 2013 providing 34 per cent of the oil, 41 per cent of natural gas, and 28 per cent of the coal imported by the Union.[82] Germany and Italy import the largest volumes of Russian gas, but Russia is the sole supplier to five states (Bulgaria, Estonia, Finland, Latvia and Slovakia).

[80] Elena Mazneva and Anna Shiryaevskaya, 'Putin's Russia Seen Dominating European Gas for Two Decades', Bloomberg, 1 March 2017, www.bloomberg.com/news/articles/2017-03-01/putin-s-russia-seen-dominating-european-energy-for-two-decades, last accessed 30 May 2017.

[81] Andrey Mochan, 'Worst Friends, Best Enemies: Trade between the EU and Russia', Carnegie Moscow Centre, 20 June 2016, http://carnegie.ru/commentary/2016/06/20/worst-friends-best-enemies-trade-between-eu-and-russia/j25r, last accessed 30 May 2017.

[82] Marco Siddi, 'The EU's Energy Union: A Sustainable Path to Energy Security?', *The International Spectator*, Vol. 51, No. 1, 2016, p. 133.

The EU's Third Energy Package of September 2009 sought to create a more competitive gas and supply market by separating production from transport and ensuring third-party access to pipelines. The Third Energy Package was a series of legislative acts designed to reduce monopolies in the energy market, including a provision which prohibits gas producers from owning primary gas pipelines. As far as Russia was concerned, this was an 'anti-Gazprom' law, since it was the most affected by the legislation. Although Russian energy policy is often characterised as 'geopolitical' and the EU's as market-based, they both indulge in a good share of both; and Russia responded to the Third Energy Package largely through legal and technocratic instruments typical of the market approach.[83] The Ukraine crisis intensified calls for a common EU energy policy in the context of what was considered Russia's 'hybrid warfare'. This describes, as mentioned, the multiple forms of pressure one country can exert against another and reflects the intensified 'securitisation' of inter-state relations. The term was used by Matthew Bryza, the former US ambassador to Azerbaijan, when he argued that 'energy is a weapon in Moscow's "hybrid" war against Ukraine, along with covert invasion, military advisors and mercenaries, and information warfare'.[84] The strategic purpose was clear when the idea of an energy union was mooted in April 2014 by Tusk, at the time Polish prime minister, when he stressed the need to remove 'Russia's energy stranglehold' on Europe.[85] In February 2015 an Energy Union was announced that would build a network of connector pipelines to create an integrated European energy market, with states cooperating to increase their energy security and decarbonise their economies.

If the EU perceived itself to be at market risk, Russia had long been worried by transit risks. This in particular concerned Ukraine, through which half of Russian gas deliveries to Europe passed. Since the 1990s there had been endless controversies over deliveries across the country and to the Ukrainian market. Shutdowns in 2006 and 2009 caused irreparable reputational damage to Russia, irrespective of the specific rights or wrongs of its case. Understandably, Russia intensified efforts to bypass Ukraine as a transit country. Already it had built two parallel lines of Nord Stream from Vyborg on the Gulf of Finland to Greifswald in Germany, with the second coming on stream a year after the first in

[83] Tatiana Romanova, 'Is Russian Energy Policy towards the EU Only About Geopolitics? The Case of the Third Liberalisation Package', *Geopolitics*, Vol. 21, No. 4, October–December 2016, pp. 857–79.

[84] Matthew J. Bryza, 'Disarm Russia's Gas Weapon', 20 June 2014, www.atlanticcouncil.org/blogs/new-atlanticist/disarm-russia-s-gas-weapon-call-russia-s-bluff-and-stem-ukraine-s-corruption, last accessed 9 June 2017.

[85] Donald Tusk, 'A United Europe Can End Russia's Energy Stranglehold', *Financial Times*, 21 April 2014.

October 2012. On the other side, by early 2014 Russia had just about everything in place to build South Stream, the 2,446 km-long pipeline under the Black Sea to Bulgaria and then up through the Balkans to Hungary and the Austrian hub at Baumgarten. The project had been launched in 2007 as an alternative to the EU's planned Nabucco pipeline intended to bring Azerbaijani gas to Europe via Turkey. Nabucco fell by the wayside, but the EU sought to block South Stream, arguing that it infringed Third Energy Package competition and access rules and in the end it too was abandoned in December 2014. The alternative Turkish Stream was planned to take gas under the Black Sea to Turkey and then on to Europe. The immediate focus for Russia was building two new lines of Nord Stream, for which a consortium was formed with German companies, even though the project faced enormous criticism.

Germany had long exercised a pragmatic yet transformative policy *vis-à-vis* the Soviet Union and its continuer-state, Russia. The policy of 'change through rapprochement' (*Wandel durch Annäherung*) was the keystone of *Ostpolitik* and later of détente as a whole. The policy was devised in large part by the Social Democrat Egon Bahr, the policy adviser to Willy Brandt when he was mayor of Berlin and later when elected chancellor in 1969. Bahr understood that in the nuclear age transformative diplomacy would be less risky and probably more effective than confrontation. Bahr sought, as we would now put it, transformation through engagement to create a European peace order.[86] In the post-Cold War era Germany built on its earlier energy partnership and cooperation over the unification of the country to develop a 'special relationship' with Russia. Strong personal relations between Russian and German leaders endured up to the time Merkel came to power in November 2005. She explicitly warned that she would not engage in any variation of this so-called 'bathhouse diplomacy', although she met frequently with Putin. Relations with Moscow cooled and the pragmatic relationship was increasingly devoid of substance.

The 'Weimar Triangle' initiative of 2008 sought to enhance trust between Polish, German and French leaders.[87] In the wake of Medvedev's plans of

---

[86] Bahr's ideas and a discussion can be found in 'Statements and Discussion', *GHI Bulletin, Supplement*, No. 1, 2003, pp. 137–67, www.ghi-dc.org/publications/ghi-bulletin/bulletin-su pplements/bulletin-supplement-1-2004.html?L=0, last accessed 9 June 2017. On the 'European peace order', see Rachèle Raus, 'Egon Bahr and the Concept of a "European Peace Order" (1963–1970)', Centre Virtuel de la Connaissance sur l'Europe (CVCE), 16 May 2013; www.cvce.eu/content/publication/2006/6/6/72b54117-68d2-450a-92aa-8ca668 c75d6d/publishable_en.pdf, last accessed 9 June 2017.

[87] Stefan Meister, *A New Start for Russian–EU Security Policy: The Weimar Triangle, Russia and the EU's Eastern Neighbourhood*, Brandenburg, Genshagener Paper, No. 7, July 2011, www.robert-schuman.eu/en/doc/actualites/genshagener-papiere-2011-7-eng.pdf, last accessed 9 June 2017.

June 2008 for a EST, the Meseberg Memorandum of 4 and 5 June 2010, signed by Merkel and Medvedev, proposed an EU-Russia Political and Security Committee, to be co-chaired by Ashton and Lavrov, for the exchange of views and to establish the ground rules for civil and crisis management operations. The EU and Russia were to cooperate to resolve the Transnistria question. Meseberg potentially offered a path for the pan-European management of European problems, and it is precisely for this reason that the initiative was not endorsed by the EU, fearing that it would allow Russia to shape decision-making on European security. In Deauville in October 2010 France, Germany and Russia met in trilateral format to push forward the Meseberg agenda of establishing a new framework for security cooperation. These initiatives ran into the Libyan sands the following year. The Meseberg process by definition threatened American primacy in the Atlantic security community. Vladimir Socor, reflecting classic fears about the 'Gaullist heresy', notes that '[t]he German initiative seems to offer Russia a ticket to decision-making on European security, in return for co-operating on Transnistria, and before actually delivering results there or in any other conflicts. This ticket is a cheap one for Russia to enter the EU's decision-making sanctuary.'[88] With Putin's return to the Kremlin in 2012, attempts to modify the European security architecture to satisfy Russia's concerns were dropped. The strategic impasse was confirmed, and an important opportunity to redress the asymmetry in the post-Cold War European security order was missed.

Rather than seeking to achieve change through engagement, the American critique of Meseberg represented a policy of engagement only after change. The exclusionary dynamic effectively meant that change was no longer part of an organic dialogical process but instead became mechanical. In EU parlance, this type of conditionality represents a 'something for something' policy, where the rewards were typically real, whereas the American policy demanded change for less than certain rewards. In this context, the Ukraine crisis provoked a profound debate in Germany. There was a struggle for its soul between the Atlanticists who sought to end the 'special relationship', and those who argued that at a time of intensified conflict Germany was called upon once again to act as the 'honest broker' in the Bismarckian style. Germany had taken the lead in building the economic component of Greater Europe by creating a ramified network of economic links. By 2014 some 6,200 German companies had significant activities in Russia, creating genuine interdependence. Not surprisingly,

---

[88] Vladimir Socor, 'Meseberg Process: Germany Testing EU-Russia Security Co-operation Potential', Jamestown Foundation, *Eurasian Daily Monitor*, Vol. 7, Issue, 22, October 2010.

business groups were the most opposed to sanctions, yet soon conformed to the new reality and accepted the predominance of politics over economics. The Social Democratic foreign minister in Merkel's coalition government, Steinmeier, revived elements of the old policy, arguing that Europe could not develop without Russia or in opposition to Russia. However, this was balanced by Germany's view of itself as the defender of 'Europe whole and free', the modern manifestation of the *europäische Friedensordnung* devised by the Congress of Vienna, and this tempered the scope for pragmatic deal-making.

Despite the deterioration in relations and Germany's lead in devising the sanctions policy, Merkel ensured continued dialogue with Moscow, although Germany's insistence that Russia fulfil its obligations under the Minsk-2 agreement was not matched by commensurate pressure on Kiev. Germany remained Moscow's chief interlocutor and strains of the old *Ostpolitik* remained.[89] As Steinmeier put it, although German officials are convinced that the country's security is 'inextricably linked to that of the United States', most of them had 'opposed the invasion of Iraq [in 2003], because they saw it as a war of choice that had dubious legitimacy and the clear potential to spark further conflict'.[90] Germany's history, he argued, had destroyed any belief in national exceptionalism, and instead the country now chose law over power whenever possible, and defended the international order created by the US and Europe after the Second World War. Although committed to the normative order of international society and a key member of the post-war hegemony, Germany practised what can be called 'normal diplomacy', and this suggests that it could become an ally in defending the autonomy of international society from hegemonic power. The idea of 'Russia against the rest' from this perspective simplifies matters, since many in the West were also concerned about the liberal hegemony's overweening ambitions and lapses from its own proclaimed standards. Although not a subaltern power, there is a significant constituency in Germany who share the concerns of the subalterns.

Gabor Steingart argues that '[e]very mistake starts with a mistake in thinking'.[91] The mistake in this case is to assume that Russia's neo-revisionism repudiated the normative foundations of European order. The problem for Russia, as argued earlier, was the absence of a continental

---

[89] Marco Siddi, 'German Foreign Policy towards Russia in the Aftermath of the Ukraine Crisis: A New *Ostpolitik?*', *Europe-Asia Studies*, Vol. 68, No. 4, June 2016, pp. 665–77.

[90] Frank-Walter Steinmeier, 'Germany's New Global Role: Berlin Steps Up', *Foreign Affairs*, Vol. 95, No. 4, July–August 2016, p. 109.

[91] Gabor Steingart, 'The West on the Wrong Path', *Handelsblatt*, 8 August 2014, www.handelsblatt.com/meinung/kommentare/essay-in-englisch-the-west-on-the-wrong-path/10308406.html, last accessed 30 May 2017.

framework for that order to be institutionalised. In 2014 Russia committed revisionist acts in Ukraine, of the sort that it had long condemned the Western powers for, but this did not mean that Russia was out to destroy the whole system of European security. This was recognised by a number of EU states and by a vocal constituency within Germany, providing an opening for a return to 'engagement' with Russia. There remained a deep well of popular sentiment that refused to endorse the new orthodoxy, and as in the rest of Europe, it was challenged from the left and the right as well as those who remained loyal to the *Ostpolitik* tradition. The left-wing Die Linke party became the largest opposition grouping in the Bundestag and was relentless in its criticism of Merkel's Ukraine policy. Their sympathy towards Russia, as is customary nowadays, provoked the criticism that they were acting as Putin's 'fifth column'. The 'Alternative für Deutschland' (AfD), established in February 2013, equally made no secret of its sympathy. It won 4.7 per cent in the 2013 federal elections, narrowly missing the 5 per cent threshold to enter parliament, and in the May 2014 European Parliament elections it gained 7.1 per cent of the vote, giving it seven out of Germany's ninety-six seats. A number of right-wing conspiracy theorists, such as Ken Jebsen, defended Putin's policies in Ukraine.[92]

The Kremlin's policy of resistance after 2012 included support for antisystemic forces across the EU. Russia was promiscuous in its choices, ranging from radical leftist groups such as Syriza in Greece and Podemos in Spain, as well as far right movements such as the Front National in France and the Northern League in Italy. The Front National received a €9.4 million loan from a Russian bank in 2014, and in 2016 sought another loan to fight the 2017 presidential election. The strategy was considered a pragmatic way of influencing European developments, rather than a new version of the Soviet Union's support for ideological allies. As one commentator notes, 'Moscow's alleged meddling in Europe resembles the political meddling Washington has long allowed itself in Ukraine and other such nations, as well as in Russia itself'.[93] However, the Soviet policy at least had the virtue of political consistency, whereas the new policy smacked of opportunism. This was the counterpart of the populism inherent in some of the organisations themselves. The ideological element was not entirely absent. As noted, in his Valdai speech in September 2013 Putin lambasted Europe for the betrayal of the values on which it was ostensibly based. A policy of 'divide and rule' inevitably acquires eclectic features. Although alleged Russian influence was greatly exaggerated, the UK considered itself

---

[92] Andreas Kindsvater, 'The Chill in German-Russian Relations Won't Lead to a New Cold War', *Russia Direct*, 8 December 2014, www.russia-direct.org/chill-german-russian-rela tions-wont-lead-new-cold-war, last accessed 30 May 2017.

[93] Patrick Lawrence, 'The Perils of Russophobia', *The Nation*, 29 December 2016.

a particular target. The Kremlin remained neutral, but Russian media commentary favoured a 'yes' vote for Scottish independence in the referendum of 18 September 2014, and a 'no' vote in the Brexit referendum of 23 June 2016. Both potentially set a precedent for the break-up of a European nation state and for the secession of an EU member. Members of the United Kingdom Independence Party (UKIP) regularly appeared on Russia media. The party's quondam leader, Nigel Farage, praised Putin as a 'superb orator' and said he played 'the Syria thing' brilliantly.[94]

Despite the elements of opportunism, there was a deeper alignment of views with certain European states. On 2 October 2016 Viktor Orbán staged a referendum on the EU's right to set quotas for the mandatory resettlement of refugees in Hungary. Although an overwhelming majority (98.3 per cent) voted 'no' to Brussels, the referendum was declared invalid since turnout was only 43.3 per cent, below the 50 per cent threshold. There was little support for Hungary leaving the EU, but the vote was 'a signal to Europe that he [Orbán] is focused on the nation state, a Europe of nations, a Europe independent of America and a Europe open to Russia in the spirit of Greater Europe'.[95] Russia's defence of the sovereignty of the nation state was a key part of its attractiveness to populists in Europe, but its continued commitment to the secondary institutions of international society imposes limits on its support for untrammelled sovereignty. Nevertheless, Russia's endorsement of European populists, even though relatively limited, had damaging reputational consequences. It whipped up fears not only of Russian interference in domestic electoral politics, but also concerns that Russia was trying to undermine European democracy as a whole. By aligning with a motley crew of anti-immigration right wingers, Russia was in danger of alienating mainstream political forces, and thus rendering itself peripheral to the key questions facing the continent.

---

[94] Péter Kréko, 'Europe's Dismay Grows over Brexit after British Referendum', Newsweek. com, 11 March 2016, http://europe.newsweek.com/europes-dismay-grows-over-threat-brexit-after-british-referendum-326686, last accessed 30 May 2017.

[95] Gabor Stier, 'Viktor Orban: De Gaulle's Hungarian Successor', Valdai Club, 14 October 2016, http://valdaiclub.com/a/highlights/viktor-orban-de-gaulle-hungarian-successor/, last accessed 30 May 2017.

10   Towards a Post-Western World

As Russia was increasingly isolated in the West, Eurasian integration and closer partnerships with countries in the East offered compensation and confirmed that Russia had alternatives. Balancing strategies are predicted by realist theories, and as Waltz notes, 'American behaviour over the past century in Central America provides little evidence of self-restraint in the absence of countervailing power'. In that context, '[c]ontemplating the history of the United States and measuring its capabilities, other countries may well wish for ways to fend off its benign ministrations'.[1] The emergence of an anti-hegemonic alignment sought precisely to defend its members from 'benign ministrations', but above all it represented the emergence of a different model of world order. With the end of the cold peace, Russian foreign policy

carried out a painful but revitalizing renewal of relations with the West, rejecting a model of relations that it had found dissatisfying for two decades, began the struggle to establish new rules of the game with the US and EU and, finally, completed a long-needed pivot to Asia, thereby establishing a more balanced system of foreign political and economic ties and creating a new pole of development and security in Eurasia ... Global trends and the early results of those efforts make it illogical for Russia to return to a Western-centric, and essentially Eurocentric policy.[2]

Russia's 'pivot to the East' was officially proclaimed in Putin's state of the nation speech of 12 December 2012, although it reflected trends that had been apparent for some time. These included the need to develop Siberia and the Russian Far East, the new opportunities for increased trade, above all in agricultural goods, in the APR, and the growing political and security convergence with some leading states in the region. Russia became part of an increasingly dense network that represented the embryo of a post-Western world order. In the framework of my model of a two-level international system, the establishment of a parallel world order questioned the hegemonic ambitions of the US-led liberal order,

---

[1] Waltz, 'Structural Realism', p. 29.   [2] Suslov, *Without a 'Common Space'*, p. 4.

but it did not challenge the principles institutionalised by international society. The goal was multipolarity and pluralist international relations. An alternative project of world order appeared to be in the making, increasingly by-passing the Historical West. The dilemma for the Kremlin was whether Russia was jumping from the frying pan into the fire: swapping a subordinate relationship with the Atlantic community with some sort of subaltern status to China. Putin was right to assert that when it came to China, 'the level, nature and confidence of our relations have probably reached an unprecedented level in their entire history', but the same had once been said of Russo-German relations.[3] Overall, '[t]he international equilibrium [was] broken; theory leads one to expect its restoration'.[4] The theory of structural realism in this case appears correct.

Beyond the West

In his speech to the Munich Security Conference on 18 February 2017, Lavrov argued that '[t]he historic era that could be called the post-Cold War order has come to an end'. The period's main characteristic had been 'the complete failure of the Cold War institutions to adapt to new realities', as 'NATO remained a Cold War institution' and the 'liberal world order . . . was pre-programmed for crisis'. The world was now faced by the challenge of 'building a democratic and fair world order, a post-West world order, if you will, in which each country develops its own sovereignty within the framework of international law'.[5] The project of transforming the Historical West gave way to the development of the post-West.

The 'West' as a concept is largely a device of the Cold War. It came to represent a political community that stretched far beyond the physical constraints of the Atlantic seaboard to encompass a range of countries allied against the Soviet Union. It included not only the Commonwealth countries of Canada, Australia and New Zealand, but also Japan, Thailand and others aligned with the US and its allies. With the end of the Cold War, the West became an anachronistic concept, since it now lacked a common purpose and a distinctive global ideology.[6] For some

---

[3] Vladimir Putin, 'Plenary Session of the 19th St Petersburg International Economic Forum', 19 June 2015, http://en.kremlin.ru/events/president/news/49733, last accessed 30 May 2017.

[4] Waltz, 'Structural Realism', p. 30.

[5] 'Foreign Minister Sergey Lavrov's Address and Answers to Questions at the 53rd Munich Security Conference', 18 February 2017, www.mid.ru/en/vistupleniya_ministra/-/asset_publisher/MCZ7HQuMdqBY/content/id/2648249, last accessed 9 June 2017.

[6] Owen Harries, 'The Collapse of "The West"', *Foreign Affairs*, Vol. 72, No. 4, 1993, pp. 41–53.

this was to be welcomed, while for others it was a matter of concern, but for all it was clear that historic patterns of global interactions were giving way to a more dynamic multi-centred model.[7] The industrialisation of many countries in the global South, above all China, reduced the relative dominance of the West, allowing talk of 'the rise of the rest'.[8] The problem became one of integrating the new with the old. The West as a framework for world order endured, with the US, NATO and the EU at its core. NATO enlargement, accompanied as we have seen by ineffective mechanisms to mitigate Russia's concerns, preserved the geopolitical identity of the Atlantic security system and the Historic West. Russia's gambit had been to create a Greater West, which would have expanded Western hegemony to encompass Russia and by implication the whole of post-Soviet Eurasia, therefore obviating the forced choice of those caught in the middle. With Russia's intermediation from within the expanded West, the Asian powers could also have been brought into this expanded order, which could have become truly global. Instead, in the post-Cold War era the West assumed an unexpectedly immutable quality and became an enduring power system in international relations. The liberal international order appeared set to become generalised as coterminous with the international system in its entirety.

It is precisely this presumed universalism that was challenged by both Russia and China. Just as Russia denied its imputed status as a defeated power, so 'the East' as a whole sought to escape from its historic subaltern status.[9] From Gorbachev to Putin, Russia rejected the domination of the international system by a single power. This was not just a realist move to create a balancing coalition, but a more complex attempt to maintain a two-level international system, with the Grotian intermediary institutions such as the UN at the top, and a pluralist multipolarity at the second level. The defence of pluralism was not simply a realist response to Western hegemony, but the normative defence of an alternative model of international order, and as a consequence the advancement of a different sort of international relations. The combination of realism and normativity characterised Russia's neo-revisionism as a whole. Russia had been one of the first to advance this anti-hegemonic strategy, based on its traditional

[7] Christopher S. Browning and Marko Lehti (eds.), *The Struggle for the West: A Divided and Contested Legacy* (London and New York, Routledge, 2010).

[8] Alice H. Amsden, *The Rise of 'the Rest': Challenges to the West from Late-Industrializing Economies* (New York, Oxford University Press, 2003). See also Fareed Zakaria, *The Post-American World: The Rise of the Rest* (London, Penguin, 2011) and Vladimir Popov and Piotr Dutkiewicz (eds.), *Mapping a New World Order: The Rest beyond the West* (Cheltenham, Edward Elgar, 2017).

[9] Ayşe Zarakol, *After Defeat: How the East Learned to Live with the West* (Cambridge, Cambridge University Press, 2011).

foreign policy orientations and ideational preferences, but as 'the East' gained in material strength and autonomous political identity, the 'correlation of forces' (as Soviet jargon once put it) tilted in its favour. Russia had been ahead of the curve, but it now became part of the anti-hegemonic wave. Just as Russian foreign policy was not consistently revisionist but neo-revisionist, so it was not anti-Western, but post-Western.

The 'West' has traditionally represented a civilisational complex, and thus comfortably embraces many countries that are geographically far from the West, notably Japan. In the mid-1990s Christopher Coker warned of the 'twilight of the west', having in mind not Western civilisation as such, whose decline had long ago been anticipated by Oswald Spengler and Arnold Toynbee, but the Atlantic community as the political and cultural foundation of NATO. Coker meticulously describes how the idea of an 'Atlantic community' had to be constructed in the post-war years, and did not enjoy the automatic allegiance of its members, in particular in Europe. It was ultimately the Soviet threat that kept the alliance together, although it was challenged by alternative projects, above all the Gaullist vision of an independent Europe responsible for its own security that at its most expansive included the Soviet Union and at its most exclusive would be able to manage its affairs without the US. By the end of the Cold War, moreover, the countries making up the alliance were undergoing major demographic changes that turned them into multicultural societies, with diverse orientations that weakened the traditional focus on Atlantic security. On this basis, Coker was pessimistic about the future of the community.[10] Instead, the Atlantic community survived and expanded and became a global power. There were even suggestions that Japan should join NATO.[11]

The term 'beyond the West' can be applied in two senses. The first is the idea that the concept of West has narrowed to the Atlantic community and its allies. With the disintegration of the eastern 'second world' at the end of the Cold War, the ideas of the West became universalised and thus lost their specificity as the ideational framework for one bloc alone. Instead, globalisation and the universal human rights agenda took their place. The West as a specific civilisational construct dissolved into a broader globalised community. In the second sense, beyond the West means the creation of an alternative to Western hegemony. Paradoxically, as this non-West develops, the original meaning of the West would be restored to regain its former legitimating function as a specific community

---

[10] Christopher Coker, *Twilight of the West* (Boulder, Westview Press, 1997).
[11] On 2 May 2016, in a meeting with Shinzo Abe, Merkel apparently suggested Japanese membership, https://sputniknews.com/world/201605021038965568-merkel-abe-nato-membership/, last accessed 30 May 2017.

based on a distinct set of values and institutions. In this multi-order world, the West would once again become one of the poles, while the post-Western constellation becomes another. The world would thus be split between two political and economic camps, with strategic rivalry between the US and allies on the one side, and Russia, China and their allies on the other. The confrontation between the two orders will impose hierarchy within the blocs, and the danger emerges of 'the marginalization of Russia and the EU such that they transform into junior partners to China and the US respectively. That reality is already near at hand for the European Union. The same could happen to Russia if it does not carry out structural reforms to its economy and administration.'[12]

The debate over whether America is rising or falling is an essential feature of its pre-eminence, and the various perspectives on this question shape the challenge to America's global leadership. Anti-hegemonic powers tend to exaggerate the extent of US decline to suggest that history is on their side and to reinforce their status, but this is only part of the story.[13] Russia's neo-revisionism seeks to temper the practical application of moral universalism in what are perceived to be arbitrary and punitive ways, while ensuring that the instruments of global governance reflect universal concerns. The divergence between Russia and Western ideas of global governance was noted by Putin in his biennial meeting with ambassadors in June 2016, when he observed that the clash represented the 'confrontation between different visions of how to build global governance mechanisms in the twenty-first century'.[14] The question reduced to who would make the rules, for what purpose, and serving which vision of the future. In other words, the struggle is for legitimacy as well as hegemony. The defence of legitimate alternatives became part of the struggle to institutionalise pluralism at the global level. Western sanctions accelerated the trend to find ways to weaken the dollar, such as pricing oil in gold instead of dollars, but this did not entail withdrawal from global economic integration. State-denying globalisation was to be replaced by a new model of international economic integration. China helped Russia to withstand the sanctions, while the BRICS countries created alternatives to Western-dominated international institutions. The new integration model challenged Western monism and created a more pluralistic international system. As a Valdai report put it, '[t]he Atlantic community is a unique example of value unification. By contrast, non-western states are

---

[12] Suslov, *Without a 'Common Space'*, p. 6.

[13] See Bruce Jones, *Still Ours to Lead: America, Rising Powers, and the Tension between Rivalry and Restraint* (Washington, Brookings Institution Press, 2014).

[14] 'Soveshchanie poslov i postoyannykh predstavitelei Rossiiskoi Federatsii', 30 June 2016, http://kremlin.ru/events/president/transcripts/52298, last accessed 9 June 2017.

together in stressing the importance of diversity, insisting that no uniform emblems of a "modern state and society" are either desirable or possible. This is an approach more in tune with the conditions of a multipolar world.'[15]

Russia's neo-revisionism does not challenge the principles of liberal internationalism, but its striving for parity of esteem and diplomatic equality inevitably brought it into contradiction with the security order centred on the US. American global dualism allows it to pursue traditional geopolitical goals of great power maximisation (the nineteenth-century model) while claiming to be serving the dispassionate interests of the liberal international order (the claimed post-Westphalian globalised twenty-first-century system).[16] American dualism – a power system combined with a liberal values order – inevitably generated double standards as the two operative systems combined and clashed in often arbitrary ways. This is nothing new. Hegemonic powers always couch their global goals in the language of a civilising mission, and apply selectively the international law that they impose on others.[17] From an offensive realist perspective, the goal for the US is to impede the rise of the others, or to use their language, to prevent the rise of an alternative regional hegemon. Already in 1992 the Wolfowitz Doctrine, discussed earlier, declared that the goal of foreign policy should be 'to prevent any hostile power from dominating a region whose resources would, under consolidated control, be sufficient to generate global power'. Mearsheimer elaborates on the options for the US, arguing that China's rise cannot be peaceful.[18] The US was distracted by wars in Afghanistan and Iraq and became even more indebted to China, but Obama's 'pivot to Asia' signalled a return to the containment agenda, including the strengthening of its network of military bases in East Asia. For Obama, Russia was an annoying sideshow and a distraction from his main priorities, which were financial stabilisation, domestic reform and China. Trump's accession signalled that the containment of China would become the central plank of US foreign policy within a restored triangular politics, including potentially an attempt to create a 'balancing coalition' with Russia.

Institutionalising the Non-West

The attractive power of the West is countered by a newly magnetised force in the East. Threatened by Western sanctions and containment, Russia

---

[15] *War and Peace in the 21st Century*, Valdai Discussion Club Report, p. 5.
[16] Perry Anderson, *American Foreign Policy and Its Thinkers* (London, Verso, 2014).
[17] Carr, *The Twenty Years' Crisis*; Geuss, *Philosophy and Real Politics*.
[18] Mearsheimer, *Tragedy of Great Power Politics*, pp. 360–411.

finds succour in the East, as it has done rhetorically so many times in the past.[19] This time there is a substantive institutional underpinning to the shift. The reorientation will not be immediate and neither will it be complete, but it will be significant and will provide both a complement and in part an alternative to Russia's Western ties. It also entails major challenges to Russia's ability to maintain foreign policy autonomy. The developing alignment with China is only part of a growing 'Greater Asia' power system. Russia and the EEU were in danger of being squeezed between Greater Asia and the new Atlanticism. The threat is mitigated by consciously non-hegemonic behaviour, or as Xi Jinping put it, a new model of great power relations. Russia and China worked to avoid the emergence of new contested zones in Central Asia of the type that had been created in Europe – both powers tried to avoid Kyrgyzstan or Uzbekistan becoming a new Ukraine. At the same time, Russia devoted greater resources to the development of its own sparsely populated eastern territory. The Russian Far East has a population of only 6.2 million, compared to China's 130 million in neighbouring regions. The shift will have fundamental consequences on the country's self-identification for generations to come, just as the building of St Petersburg did three centuries ago.

The Shanghai Five came together in 1996, but with the accession of Uzbekistan the Shanghai Cooperation Organisation (SCO) was established on 15 June 2001 as a regional cooperative association comprising China, Kazakhstan, Kyrgyzstan, Russia, Tajikistan and Uzbekistan. Afghanistan, Belarus, Iran and Mongolia are observer states. At Russia's insistence, the SCO summit in Ufa (the capital of the Republic of Bashkortostan), on 10 July 2015 invited India and Pakistan to join, and they became full members at the Astana summit in 2017. Four of the world's nine nuclear powers are now members. The SCO initially focused on fighting terrorism and extremism, as well as fostering cooperation in education, energy, transport and communications. The SCO currently works on three main areas: regional security, economy and culture. The Ufa summit stressed the growing role of the SCO in improving cooperation in the financial sphere and project financing, accompanied by plans to establish an SCO development bank and a special drawing account. There were also plans for the SCO to facilitate the resolution of international problems. SCO's development strategy until 2025 was adopted along with the *Ufa Declaration*. Point 6 declared that the 'peaceful coexistence of nations is impossible without universal, scrupulous and consistent application of the generally recognised

---

[19] Natasha Kuhrt, *Russian Policy towards China and Japan: The El'tsin and Putin Periods* (London, Routledge, 2011); Paradorn Rangsimaporn, *Russia as an Aspiring Great Power in East Asia: Perceptions and Policies from Yeltsin to Putin* (Basingstoke, Palgrave Macmillan, 2009).

principles and rules of international law'. Point 21 celebrated the twentieth anniversary of the WTO, reaffirming 'support for working together to strengthen an open, transparent, non-discriminatory, and rules-based multilateral system as embodied in the WTO'.[20]

In 1996, Primakov presented a plan to bring together the RIC countries of Russia, India and China to foster multipolarity.[21] In November 2001 Jim O'Neil, a leading economist at Goldman Sachs, published a research paper in which he added Brazil to the earlier RIC to make BRIC, the acronym which lasted until South Africa formally joined the group in December 2010 to make BRICS.[22] O'Neil was writing from an emerging markets perspective, and assessed the countries in terms of their potential as investment opportunities and the strength of their stock markets. Putin took up the Primakov challenge, and in June 2006 the group was formally established, and the first formal session was a gathering of BRIC finance ministers in New York in September 2006. Putin then hosted the first BRIC summit in Yekaterinburg in June 2009, and since then BRICS summits have been held annually. Today the BRICS encompass 30 per cent of the earth's landmass, 43 per cent of global population, 46 per cent of the global labour force, and with 30 per cent of global GDP surpasses the EU or the US as the single largest community of its kind in the world. By 2014 the BRICS countries held 40 per cent of global foreign exchange reserves, 31 per cent belonging to China alone. The BRICS' share of global trade rose from 7 per cent in 2001 to 17 per cent in 2015, and by 2040 it is estimated that it will account for a greater share of global GDP than the original G7 combined.[23]

BRICS is a loose association of countries that share certain interests, but it is not a formal alliance or even an organisation.[24] Nevertheless, the depth of normative congruence is often under-estimated, focused on

[20] VII BRICS Summit, *Ufa Declaration*, 9 July 2015, www.brics.utoronto.ca/docs/150709-ufa-declaration_en.html, last accessed 30 May 2017.
[21] For an Indian account, see Rakesh Krishnan Simha, 'Primakov: The Man who Created Multipolar World and BRICS', *Russia and India Report*, 27 June 2015, https://in.rbth.com/blogs/2015/06/27/primakov_the_man_who_created_multipolarity_43919, last accessed 9 June 2017.
[22] Jim O'Neil, *Building Better Global Economic BRICs*, Goldman Sachs Global Economics Paper No. 66, New York, November 2001, www.goldmansachs.com/our-thinking/archive/archive-pdfs/build-better-brics.pdf, last accessed 30 May 2017. The idea was further developed in a paper by Dominic Wilson and Roopa Purushothaman, *Dreaming with the BRICs: The Path to 2050*, Goldman Sachs Global Economics Paper No. 99, New York, October 2003, http://avikdgreat.tripod.com/InterestingReads/BRIC_GoldmanSachs.pdf, last accessed 30 May 2017.
[23] Shashi Tharoor, 'BRICS and their Soft Power', *Rising Powers in Global Governance: Opinion*, 20 December 2016, http://risingpowersproject.com/brics-soft-power/, last accessed 30 May 2017.
[24] Kwang Ho Chun, *The BRICs Superpower Challenge* (Farnham, Ashgate, 2013).

creating a more plural, and thereby in their view, a more legitimate international system.[25] This includes support for reform of the UNSC to ensure greater representation from the global South. The association is not so much South-South, but represents a powerful East-South bloc to rival the hegemony of the North. The body brings together both developed and developing countries, and has, for example, a coordinated strategy in the WTO to create a fairer order concerning agricultural policies. Developing countries have long sought the liberalisation of the international economic order, complaining that agricultural subsidies in the US and the EU distort the market to the detriment of third world producers. BRICS has also taken the lead in coordinating discussions over climate change, although it maintains a low profile in security questions. The initiative 'reflected more the perceived inability of the global economic order in satisfying their respective interests and needs, than the strength of common BRICS views'.[26]

The BRICS created parallel structures, including a shift away from dependence on the Western financial system.[27] The gridlock in IMF and World Bank reform puts 'multilateralism at risk'.[28] IMF reform in particular has been an arduous process. The G20 Seoul Summit in 2010 reallocated voting rights to reflect the new global economic realities, but ratification was held up by the US Congress and only came into effect in January 2016. The cumulative quota for emerging and developing countries (EMDCs) rose by 2.1 per cent from 36.6 to 38.7 per cent. BRICS and EMDCs continued to press for further substantive quota formula review.[29] The failure adequately to reform the Bretton Woods financial institutions prompted the development of an alternative financial architecture. Russia and China increasingly settle energy trades in roubles and yuan. The South Africa BRICS summit in 2013 agreed to create a New Development Bank (NDB), which was formally launched at the Fortaleza summit in Brazil in June 2014. The NDB is headquartered in Shanghai and became operative in 2016, headed by the Indian economist Kundapur Kamath. The NDB finances infrastructure projects and

[25] Oliver Stuenkel, *The BRICS and the Future of Global Order* (London and Lanham, Lexington Books, 2015).
[26] Andrea E. Goldstein, 'China's G20 Presidency: Coming at the Wrong Moment', in Alessia Amighini (ed.), *China Dream: Still Coming True?* (Milan, Italian Institute for International Political Studies (ISPI), 2016), p. 87.
[27] Marin Katusa, *The Colder War: How the Global Energy Trade Slipped from America's Grasp* (London, John Wiley and Sons, 2014).
[28] Jakob Vestergaard and Robert H. Wade, 'Still in the Woods: Gridlock in the IMF and the World Bank Puts Multilateralism at Risk', *Global Policy*, Vol. 6, No. 1, February 2015, pp. 1–12.
[29] RISS Report, *The IMF Quota Formula Review: Opportunities for BRICS and Developing World* (Moscow, Russian Institute for Strategic Studies, August 2016).

plans to switch from the US dollar to a basket of currencies. Threats to remove Russia from SWIFT accelerated the establishment of the Mir bank payment system, a domestic version of Visa and MasterCard, accompanied by moves to create alternatives to the Bank for International Settlements and the IMF. A Contingent Reserve Arrangement was launched at the seventh summit in Ufa on 8 and 9 July 2015 to provide a financial safety net in the event of a financial shock or crisis in the balance of payments of a member state. It provides an outlet for China's foreign currency reserves as an alternative to US government bonds. This reflects China's economic predominance, representing over 60 per cent of aggregate BRICS GDP.

In this way the 'non-West' began to develop a parallel set of financial structures. Given the disparate nature of the countries involved, this was accompanied by the incorporation of China's earlier 'peaceful rise' rhetoric to become the leitmotif of the group as a whole, stressing that BRICS was not directed against anyone but would be beneficial for all. This was accompanied by the argument that, unlike the Western 'teachers of humanity', the BRICS did not try to force its solutions on other countries. Instead, as argued by Vadim Lukov, Russia's ambassador-at-large, BRICS had four strategic goals: 'First, each BRICS member wants to pursue an independent policy line on the world stage; second, we all want a reform of the global financial system, reforming the IMF in the first instance; third, we want to strengthen the role of the UN and the primacy of law in international relations; and fourth, we want to use the factor of complementarity of our economies to speed up these economies' development.'[30] China and India are the only BRICS countries that have registered consistent growth over the last three decades. India's population (1.25 billion) is second only to China's (1.4 billion), but its economy is five times smaller. Despite its size, India lacks a permanent seat in the UNSC and is a relative pygmy in world affairs.[31] China needs BRICS neither for trade nor security reasons, but stresses that it provides a framework for cooperation that increases stability in the international system. The Goa summit of 15 and 16 October 2016 revealed divisions, with China refusing to support an Indian motion condemning alleged Pakistani terrorism, but the Goa Declaration condemned 'unilateral military interventions and economic sanctions in violation of international law and universally recognised norms

[30] Dmitry Babich, 'BRICS Summit in Ufa', *The BRICS Post*, 8 July 2015, http://thebrics post.com/brics-summit-in-ufa-yoga-for-putin-finance-for-crimea-stability-for-the-worl d/, last accessed 9 June 2017.

[31] Sanjaya Baru, 'India and China in a multipolar world', *The Hindu*, 11 May 2015, www.the hindu.com/opinion/lead/sanjaya-baru-writes-india-and-china-in-a-multipolar-world/arti cle7190817.ece, last accessed 30 May 2017.

of international relations'. It was dedicated to 'building responsive, inclusive and collective solutions'.[32] The grouping amplifies the weight of the member states in the international system and creates a discursive space for an alternative model of international relations.

Opening the combined BRICS and SCO meeting on 9 July 2015 in Ufa with the leaders of the other EEU states in attendance, Putin noted: 'For us this [the Eurasian landmass] isn't a chessboard, it's not a geopolitical playing field – this is our home, and all of us together want our home to be calm and affluent, and for it not to be a place of extremism or for attempts to protect one's interests at the expense of others'. This was an explicit rebuke to Brzezinski's conceptualisation of Eurasia as the field for a renewed Great Game.[33] Putin went on to argue that the two organisations as well as the EEU '[i]n many ways share similar traditional values, common laws of morality, truth and justice'. He then went on to outline what was in effect the programme of the non-West:

We are united in the sense that the aims that have been set can only be achieved by acting collectively, on the basis of genuine partnership, trust, equal rights, respect and acknowledgement of each other's interests. We call for the drawing-up of coordinated responses to global challenges, for the affirmation of just foundations for contacts between states, with the UN playing a key role, based on international law, the principles of indivisibility, security and peoples freely determining their own destiny.[34]

The combined meeting was unprecedented, bringing together a good part of humanity, including the leaders of fifteen states from various continents. Although there were clear differences in emphasis, overall the meeting symbolised the emergence of a powerful new voice in global affairs. The post-Western world was becoming a reality.

China Dreaming

On 29 November 2012, just days after being elected leader, Xi Jinping outlined his 'Chinese dream'. The idea was popularised as part of Chinese socialist thought to represent a strategic vision promising the modernisation of China by 2049, the hundredth anniversary of the establishment of the People's Republic of China (PRC). The concept

---

[32] 'Goa Declaration at 8th BRICS Summit', 16 October 2016, www.mea.gov.in/bilateral-documents.htm?dtl/27491/Goa+Declaration+at+8th+BRICS+Summit, last accessed 9 June 2017.

[33] Brzezinski, *Grand Chessboard*.

[34] 'Putin says Eurasia's Not a Chessboard, It's Our Home', Interfax, 9 July 2015, http://russialist.org/interfax-putin-says-eurasias-not-a-chessboard-its-our-home/, last accessed 30 May 2017.

encompasses not only a set of national ideas but also the role of the individual in Chinese modernity.[35] For Xi the term meant 'the great rejuvenation of Chinese society', but as leader he eschewed the democratising political reforms that had long been sought by more liberal academics and policymakers, and instead pursued a policy based on the tightening of discipline, an anti-corruption campaign, and the strengthening of his personal leadership. He proved an ideal interlocutor for Putin. The breakdown in relations with the Atlantic system accelerated developments that had already been in train, stimulating a growing entente between Russia and China based on 'mutual empathy and geopolitical convergence based on overlapping worldviews and a joint resentment of US global dominance'.[36] Russia sought to harness China's pre-eminence to achieve developmental and geopolitical goals that were considered to be of mutual interest, and it is for this reason that China in turn exercised self-restraint *vis-à-vis* Russia.[37] The relationship was not an alliance but an *alignment*, a long-term engagement in which the two parties expect mutual support, and work together on the assumption that they share common interests and policy concerns. The relationship is increasingly broad-based and institutionalised.[38] The foundation is a narrowing in the identity gap between the two powers and a common commitment to changing the rules of international relations, although not of international society.[39]

A structural change in world politics had long been in the making, with a relative shift in the balance not only of power but also of aspirations. Neither Russia nor China sought a revolution in the structure of international affairs, but they converged on the neo-revisionist agenda of escaping their perceived subaltern status to create genuine multipolarity. As Ikenberry puts it, 'the struggle over international order today is not about fundamental principles. China and other emerging great powers do not

---

[35] See Alessia Amighini (ed.), *China Dream: Still Coming True?* (Milan, Italian Institute for International Political Studies (ISPI), 2016).

[36] Trenin, *Should We Fear Russia?*, p. 66, uses the word 'entente' to describe the relationship, but argues that there would be no 'geopolitical merger' between the two.

[37] Marcin Kaczmarski, 'The Asymmetric Partnership? Russia's Turn to China', *International Politics*, Vol. 53, No. 3, 2016, pp. 415–34. For an extended version, see Marcin Kaczmarski, *Russia-China Relations in the Post-Crisis International Order* (London and New York, Routledge, 2015).

[38] Thomas Ambrosio, 'The Architecture of Alignment: The Russia-China Relationship and International Agreements', *Europe-Asia Studies*, Vol. 69, No. 1, January 2017, pp. 110–56; Alexander Korolev, 'The Strategic Alignment between Russia and China: Myths and Reality', *The Asan Forum*, 30 April 2015, www.theasanforum.org/the-strategic-alignment-between-russia-and-china-myths-and-reality/, last accessed 30 May 2017.

[39] Cf. Gilbert Rozman, *The Sino-Russian Challenge to the World Order* (Stanford, Stanford University Press, 2014), p. 275 and *passim*.

want to contest the basic rules and principles of the international order; they wish to gain more authority and leadership within it.'[40] Although 'China is not a status quo power [ready] to preserve and emplace the US-led order, it is not yet a revolutionary power discontented with and willing to undermine the existing order'. It not only lacked the resources but also 'has not articulated distinctive values to underwrite the world order'.[41] China's neo-revisionism was distinctive, since it could potentially become part of a bipolar 'G2' condominium with the US, but at the same time China has not entirely lost the 'third world' instincts of the G77, the UN grouping of developing nations. As one commentary puts it, 'China is a disruptive power but not a revolutionary one', a sentiment it shares with Russia.[42]

The re-emergence of China is one of the major events of our era. In 1990 China provided less than 2 per cent of global GDP, but by 2016 it was 15 per cent (almost ten times Russia's share). It spent $215 billion on defence, some four times as much as Russia, and its foreign reserves totalled more than $3 trillion, eight times Russia's. The EU remained China's largest trade partner, but trade with the US in 2016 reached $558 billion, creating a relationship of mutual dependency. China's ascent has been far from smooth, and declining growth rates, environmental disasters, gender imbalances, an aging population and unresolved political contradictions will undoubtedly tarnish the dream. Nevertheless, in late 2016 China in PPP terms became the world's largest economy, and today its military spending is second only to that of the US. Its various infrastructure initiatives in the framework of the Belt and Road Initiative assert a Chinese presence from its western provinces to Rotterdam. This is a powerful reminder of the pre-eminence enjoyed by China for over a thousand years as the old Silk Road transported its fine goods and culture across the Eurasian landmass.

Chinese engagement in Central Asia raises some fundamental geopolitical challenges, since the region is traditionally a focus of Russian security concerns. The nineteenth-century Great Game saw Britain and Russia locked into a chimerical struggle in Central Eurasia, but China has been careful not to threaten Russian national interests in the region. It has focused mostly on economic cooperation while embracing Russia as a geopolitical partner. The two countries face similar modernisation dilemmas, notably

---

[40] G. John Ikenberry, 'The Future of the Liberal World Order', *Foreign Affairs*, Vol. 90, No. 3, May–June 2011, p. 57.

[41] Suisheng Zhao, 'China as a Rising Power Versus the US-led World Order', *Rising Powers Quarterly*, Vol. 1, No. 1, 2016, p. 14.

[42] Evan A. Feigenbaum, 'China and the World: Dealing with a Reluctant Power', *Foreign Affairs*, Vol. 96, No. 1, January–February 2017, p. 33.

'whether China will succeed in developing its own model or have to fully embrace the Western liberal order'. As with Russia, China's standing in international affairs 'will be highly dependent on Xi Jinping's ability to balance China's revisionist demands – which, according to the China Dream, are simply requests for recognition of its natural and historical position as a great power – with the inevitable reaction and containment they provoke'.[43] Like Russia, China's demands are not revisionist but represent an assertion of status within the existing system, and are thus neo-revisionist. The old Soviet and Maoist revolutionary dream of over-throwing the capitalist world order is long gone. The issue then became the terms on which they would join the globalising liberal international order. Dissatisfied with the mix of coercion and consent on offer, the two have now constituted themselves as the core of the post-Western order, while remaining committed to the overarching institutions of international society. The struggle now is for pluralism in the international system – a multi-order world whose international relations would reflect substantive multipolarity.

The Russo-Chinese relationship is one of the most important in the world, and although all such relationships are fraught with tensions involving status and advantage, in recent years it has moved beyond the prag-matic towards something approaching a genuine alignment based on common concerns and interests. This falls short of a formal alliance, which would limit the options of both sides and run the risk of alienating others, but it is more than normal relations between two great powers. Lavrov insisted that Russia was pursuing a 'multi-vector' foreign policy as outlined in the *Foreign Policy Concept* of February 2013, and thus 'relations with China are not of an opportunistic nature and not directed against anyone'.[44] The Arab Spring alarmed the leaders of both countries, since each in different ways faces potentially disruptive domestic political mobi-lisation. From 2012 a popular movement emerged in Hong Kong demand-ing genuine universal suffrage, while the regime was challenged by the bout of contentious politics sparked by the flawed parliamentary election in December 2011 and the anti-corruption demonstrations in 2017. It was not so much a case of two authoritarian countries finding common cause but of two regimes aware of their different vulnerabilities seeking to protect what they perceived to be fragile domestic peace and order. These were 'stability regimes', which in the case of Russia was reminiscent of the late

---

[43] Paolo Magri, 'Introduction', in Alessia Amighini (ed.), *China Dream: Still Coming True?* (Milan, Italian Institute for International Political Studies (ISPI), 2016), p. 8.

[44] 'Foreign Minister Sergey Lavrov's Interview with Rossiya Segodnya News Agency', 9 December 2014, Russian Ministry of Foreign Affairs, www.rusemb.org.uk/foreign policy/2820, last accessed 30 May 2017. See also coverage and modified translations in 'Lavrov's Big Interview'.

Soviet system when mobilisation had declined and the goal became regime preservation and the (failed) search for a new developmental model. In both countries '[t]he regime tries to defuse disputes between citizens and the state by using the techniques characteristic of stability maintenance – mediation, compensation, intimidation – to pre-empt an explosive confrontation'.[45]

Following the establishment of diplomatic relations in 1949 the countries endured a stormy relationship, moving from the friendship of the two great communist powers in the 1950s to the rupture of relations and the seven-month undeclared war along the disputed Ussuri River border at the height of the Sino-Soviet split in 1969. This allowed Kissinger to engineer an American rapprochement with China, symbolised by Richard Nixon's triumphal visit in February 1972. Following Mao Zedong's death in 1976, China embarked on reforms that propelled the country's dramatic rise. China became deeply embedded in the world economy and enjoyed a symbiotic relationship with the US, effectively bankrolling its deficit through the purchase of US Treasury bonds. The fundamental question is whether this made China part of the Historical West in political terms. If so, then it would have no reason to challenge the established order, and its relationship with Russia would remain contingent and little more than an 'axis of convenience'.[46] In practice, while China certainly was wary of jeopardising its relationship with the West, it shared with Russia the desire to create a more pluralistic world order. Unlike Russia, China never aspired to be part of a reformulated 'Greater West', and thus had greater clarity about its long-term strategic objectives. Sceptics argue that 'China and Russia flex their muscles not because they are powerful but because they are weak . . . it is domestic insecurity that is breeding belligerence', with the natural corollary that the US needed to restore the power of the 'big stick' by building up its armed forces.[47] Earlier I argued that this 'diversionary' argument is far too simplistic. Nevertheless, whether derived from strength or weakness, Russia and China converged on aspirations to create a world order beyond the West. If the response was limited to intensified containment, then this would become anti-West. Joint military exercises, favourable

---

[45] Chaohua Wang, '"I'm a Petitioner – Open Fire"', *London Review of Books*, 5 November 2015, p. 16.

[46] Bobo Lo, *Axis of Convenience: Moscow, Beijing and the New Geopolitics* (London, Blackwell for RIIA; Washington, Brookings Institution Press, 2008); Bobo Lo, *The Illusion of Convergence: Russia, China, and the BRICS*, Paris, IFRI, Russie.Nei.Visions No. 92, March 2016.

[47] Robert D. Kaplan, 'Eurasia's Coming Anarchy: The Risks of Chinese and Russian Weakness', *Foreign Affairs*, Vol. 92, No. 2, March–April 2016, pp. 33, 39.

shifts in public opinion and suspicion of American intentions, means that the current alignment could become an alliance.[48]

The normalisation of relations with Russia in the late 1980s was followed by the establishment of a strategic partnership in the 1990s, culminating in the signing of the Treaty of Good-Neighbourliness and Friendly Cooperation in July 2001, which committed both countries not to enter 'any alliance or be party to any bloc ... which compromises the sovereignty, security and territorial integrity of the other contracting party'.[49] The final unresolved border issues were settled by the 2004 Complementary Agreement, whereby Russia ceded several territories and islets, including the whole of Tarabarov Island in the Amur River, to China. Lavrov noted 'our relations have reached a new level – a comprehensive, equitable and trustful partnership and strategic interaction', allowing relations between the two countries to become 'the best in their entire history'. He went on to explain the basis for such good relations:

The reason for such successful development is rooted in the fact that it is based on the mutual consideration of interests, mutual respect, equality, and non-interference in internal affairs. These are – in every sense – mutually beneficial relations, in which there are no seniors and juniors, leaders and followers. The course of Russian-Chinese relations takes into account the core interests of the two nations and we have no plans to change it.[50]

Russia's resentment at its apparent tutelary relationship with the Atlantic powers was evident here, and found a more congenial model of international politics with China.

This congeniality was reinforced by Xi's leadership. Xi's assertive style was in the Putin mould, and the two went on to establish a strong personal bond, meeting more frequently than the leaders of any other major state. Xi assumed power soon after secretary of state Hillary Clinton argued that the US stood at a 'pivot point'. As its various wars in Afghanistan and the Middle East wound down, '[o]ne of the most important tasks of American statecraft over the next decade will therefore be to lock in a substantially increased investment – diplomatic, economic strategic, and otherwise – in the Asia-Pacific region'.[51] Shortly afterwards, she announced the New Silk Road initiative in a speech in July 2011 in

---

[48] Korolev, 'The Strategic Alignment'.

[49] See www.fmprc.gov.cn/mfa_eng/wjdt_665385/2649_665393/t15771.shtml, last accessed 30 May 2017.

[50] 'Foreign Minister Sergey Lavrov's Interview with Rossiya Segodnya News Agency', 9 December 2014.

[51] Hillary Clinton, 'America's Pacific Century', *Foreign Policy Magazine*, 11 October 2011, http://foreignpolicy.com/2011/10/11/americas-pacific-century/, last accessed 9 June 2017.

Chennai, which notably excluded China and Russia from her vision of a liberal and pluralistic trading region in Central and South Asia.[52] In her landmark 'pivot to Asia' speech in October 2011, she defined China's rise as an emerging threat and outlined a comprehensive strategic response, including reinforcing traditional security alliances, broadening trade and investment as well as multilateral partnerships, expanding the military presence in new arenas, and advancing democracy and human rights.[53] China's dramatic rise shattered the equilibrium, requiring a 'resetting of the balance' by the US and its allies, including a reinforcement of the alliance with Japan and South Korea and establishment of the US-led TPP.[54] After many years of negotiation, the TPP, bringing together twelve Asia-Pacific countries including the US and Canada but excluding China, was signed in November 2015.[55] Soft containment assumed harder forms. The announcement in July 2016 on the deployment of the US ballistic Terminal High-Altitude Area Defence (THAAD) defence system in South Korea threatened to derail the much improved relations between Seoul and Beijing, just as BMD deployment in Europe had done between Moscow and Washington. THAAD deployment, however, took place in a very different strategic environment, since North Korea had demonstrable nuclear ambitions and, unlike Iran, had test-fired strategic missiles. China nevertheless considered the deployment part of a broader effort to encircle China in the Asia-Pacific.[56] The concern is not so much with the interceptor missiles but the radar system, which in forward-based mode has a range of 2,000 km.[57] The commonality in threat perception and responses in Beijing and Moscow is striking.

This was reflected in deepening economic relations. In May 2015 the two countries pledged to increase the volume of bilateral trade up to $200 billion by 2020, which required an average increase of over 13 per cent year-on-year to achieve the goal. In conditions of recession this proved

---

[52] US Department of State, 'Remarks on India and the United States: A Vision for the 21st Century', Chennai, India, 20 July 2011, www.state.gov/secretary/20092013clinton/rm/2011/07/168840.htm, last accessed 9 June 2017.

[53] Hillary Clinton, 'America's Pacific Century'.

[54] Wang Wen and Jia Jinjing, 'Silk Road Economic Development: Vision and Path', in Alessia Amighini (ed.), *China Dream: Still Coming True?* (Milan, Italian Institute for International Political Studies (ISPI), 2016), pp. 102–3.

[55] China had been invited at an early stage to join the negotiations, but refused.

[56] Paul Haenle and Anne Sherman, 'The Real Answer to China's THAAD Dilemma', *The Diplomat*, 12 September 2016, http://thediplomat.com/2016/09/the-real-answer-to-chinas-thaad-dilemma/, last accessed 30 May 2017.

[57] For South Korean perspectives and analysis, see Tong Zhao, 'China and South Korea's Path to Consensus on THAAD', Carnegie-Tsinghua, 13 October 2016, http://carnegietsinghua.org/2016/10/13/china-and-south-korea-s-path-to-consensus-on-thaad-pub-64856, last accessed 30 May 2017.

hopelessly unrealistic, although the economic relationship developed rapidly.[58] On the eve of the crisis in 2013 Sino-Russian bilateral trade peaked at $88.8 billion, but with the financial and economic crisis it came to only $61.4 billion in 2015, far below the $100 billion target for that year. As the EU's share in Russian trade fell, by 2015 China overtook Germany to become Russia's largest trading partner.[59] With the Russian economy in the doldrums, trade volumes actually decreased, falling by 28.6 per cent in 2015.[60] Trade turnover started to rise again in 2017. By 2016, cumulative Chinese investment in Russia reached $33 billion, making it one of the largest foreign investors, although the total invested in 2015 came to only $560 million, less than 0.5 per cent of China's foreign investments, and in early 2016 Chinese foreign direct investment stock in Russia amounted to only $3.4 billion – as Chinese corporations adopted a wait-and-see attitude so as not to fall foul of US and EU sanctions.[61] In 2015 China lent $18 billion to Russian businesses, a total second only to that provided by Cyprus (representing mostly recycled Russian money). Chinese investment in the Russian Far East remained low, with the Chinese complaining about the obstacles imposed by the Russian bureaucracy, outdated legislation and the lack of entrepreneurial initiative.[62] Empirical data demonstrate just how far Russia's 'pivot' to the East has advanced, but the major difficulty was 'the enormous inertia that persists in Russia, a kind of "European curse" – a habit of measuring itself against how things are in the West'.[63] Even the view that the entente between Russia and China is designed to serve as a counter-weight to the West is itself a Western construct, since most serious Chinese and Russian commentators argue that it helps resolve mutual common challenges and averts a potential confrontation in Central Asia.[64]

[58] For a sceptical view, see Ian Bond, *Russia and China: Partners of Choice and Necessity?* (London, Centre for European Reform, December 2016).

[59] Timofei Bordachev, 'Russia's Pivot to the East and Comprehensive Eurasian Partnership', Valdai Discussion Club, 31 August 2016, http://valdaiclub.com/a/high lights/russia-pivot-to-the-east-and-comprehensive/, last accessed 30 May 2017.

[60] Alexander Gabuev, 'Russia and China: Little Brother or Big Sister?', Carnegie Moscow Centre, 5 July 2016, http://carnegie.ru/publications/?fa=64006, last accessed 9 June 2017.

[61] Eurasian Development Bank, *EAEU and Eurasia: Monitoring and Analysis of Direct Investments 2016* (St Petersburg, Centre for Integration Studies, Report 41, 2016), pp. 7–8.

[62] Rensselaer Lee and Artyom Lukin, *Russia's Far East: New Dynamics in Asia Pacific and Beyond* (Boulder, Lynne Rienner, 2016).

[63] Bordachev, 'Russia's Pivot to the East'.

[64] Timofei Bordachev, 'The Great Win-Win Game', *Russia in Global Affairs*, No. 4, October–December 2016, pp. 106–15; Vitaly Vorobyov, 'Interconnecting Strategies', *Russia in Global Affairs*, No. 4, October–December 2016, pp. 116–23.

In the energy sphere, following various disputes, the EU looked to diversify supplies, while Russia sought to diversify markets away from Europe. If in the third quarter of 2011 Germany and Holland consumed around 30 per cent of all exported Russian oil, by the third quarter of 2014 that share had fallen to 22 per cent. Over the same period, China's share in Russia's oil exports rose from 9 to 14 per cent, and combined exports to Japan and Korea doubled to 10 per cent. The trend accelerated following the imposition of sanctions. In June 2013 Rosneft signed a deal with the state-owned China National Petroleum Corporation (CNPC), worth some $270 billion under which Russia was expected to supply 360.3 million tons of crude to China. On 21 May 2014, after ten years of negotiations, Gazprom finally signed a major gas supply contract with CNPC. The plan was for Gazprom to supply CNPC with 38bcm of natural gas per year for thirty years, although there was flexibility in terms of delivery volumes allowed by the 'take or pay' clause. The sticking point over the years had been the price, and the precise terms remain secret. The agreement committed the parties to build a new pipeline from Eastern Siberia to North-East China, the so-called 'Eastern route'. The new 'Power of Siberia' pipeline was to be co-funded, with Gazprom investing some $55 billion and CNPC $22 billion.[65] The gas deal was only one of some forty agreements signed at that time, accompanied by a statement criticising EU and US interference in the affairs of other states and the imposition of sanctions.[66] Russia had always been keener to build a pipeline through Altai, the 'Western route', to provide an alternative market for Russia's main gas-producing fields in Western Siberia, but the project has been repeatedly delayed.

Despite the sanctions, CNPC bought a stake in the enormous Yamal LNG plant along with Total and Russian companies. On 15 March 2016 a $1.1 billion deal was agreed between Yamal LNG and the Silk Road Fund, a $30 billion special-purpose vehicle, giving the fund a 9.9 per cent stake in the project. In December 2015 Sinopec bought a stake in Russia's Sibur energy company. Thus the two countries rapidly developed a pipeline and supply network, the sinews of geopolitics in the twenty-first century. This does not mean that there were not points of tension. As pragmatic realists, the two countries engaged in protracted battles over pricing and routes, and the economic downturn in the two countries from 2014 delayed the implementation of some of the more ambitious plans. Further deals were inked during Putin's visit to China in September

[65] The Eurasian Geopolitical Forum, *EGF Gazprom Monitor*, Issue 36, May 2014, p. 2.
[66] Donald N. Jensen, 'Russia Goes East', *Institute of Modern Russia*, 23 June 2014, https://imrussia.org/en/analysis/world/762-russia-goes-east, last accessed 9 June 2017.

2015, prompting the head of Rosneft, Igor Sechin, to suggest that the energy deals between his company and Chinese partners would be worth over half a trillion dollars over the next twenty years. In October 2015 Russia once again overtook Saudi Arabia to become China's biggest supplier of crude oil, at almost one million barrels per day (a tenth of Russia's output), a growth of 30 per cent year-on-year.[67]

Russia's travails strengthened China's hand in energy negotiations, but on the major political questions a degree of policy alignment was clear. China abstained in the American-sponsored UN motion condemning the secession of Crimea on 27 March 2014. With the Russian economy hitting the rocks as the oil price plummeted, the Chinese foreign minister, Wang Yi, on 21 December 2014 noted: 'We believe that Russia has opportunities and knowledge to overcome the current problems in the economy. The Chinese-Russian relations of strategic partnership are at a high level, we are always supporting and helping our friend. If the Russian side needs it, we shall offer all possible support we may have.'[68] As the respected Canadian analyst Patrick Armstrong commented: 'Why is China doing this? Self-interest: if Washington can bring Russia down, China knows it's next on the list.'[69] Nonetheless, the Chinese leadership was wary of going too far, and tempered its support in ways that would not alienate the Atlantic powers. China had its own concerns about separatism, having long faced an insurgency in the Muslim Xinjiang region, hence it did not endorse Crimea's annexation. However, the degree to which China went in signalling its support for Russia was surprising. Chinese state banks extended credit lines to a number of Russian lenders, and the timing of the major gas deal of 2014 signalled Chinese support for an embattled Russia, even if CNPC drove a hard bargain, and ultimately China did not become as big an alternative source of financing as Russia had hoped. Although China condemned the sanctions, it was careful not to fall foul of them, constraining financial flows and investment. This was compounded by the profound lack of detailed knowledge about each other's business culture and regulatory frameworks, reinforcing investor fears about entering alien markets. Russia acted in a defensive and reactive manner, whereas China talked of the 'strategic opportunity' to increase its global influence.

[67] 'Russia Becomes China's Top Crude Supplier', 21 October 2015, www.rt.com/business/ 319283-china-russia-oil-supplies/, last accessed 30 May 2017.

[68] 'Russia Will Be Able to Overcome Economic Problems – Chinese Foreign Minister', *TASS*, 21 December 2014, http://itar-tass.com/en/economy/768328, last accessed 30 May 2017.

[69] Patrick Armstrong, 'New NWO', *Russian Federation Sitrep*, 8 January 2015.

China remains committed to international integration and has become a pillar of the global market system. In November 2015 the IMF admitted the renminbi as part of what now became its basket of five reserve currencies. The move rewarded China's efforts to liberalise its financial markets and ease restrictions on capital flows, although its per capita income was barely a quarter of its peers in the group, who were all mature liberal democracies with fully convertible currencies and open capital markets.[70] The renminbi is used to settle a quarter of China's trade, but in August 2015 it accounted for only 2.79 per cent of global payments in value terms, although it was on an upward trend whereas the yen's share was only 2.76 per cent and declining.[71] China has not only overtaken the US as the world's leading trading nation, but China is the leading trade partner for 123 countries compared to sixty-four for the US. The global predominance of the dollar is challenged, with 15 per cent of global trade now conducted in renminbi. China's achievement puts Russia's rather lame performance in perspective, and aspirations to turn Moscow into a major global financial centre remain a pipe dream.

Sino-American relations are foundational for both, and there are many instances where the two co-operated, as evidenced by the November 2014 statement on climate change. Nevertheless, there is clearly a long-term deterioration in relations. China's moves to assert its assumed territorial rights aroused the concerns of its neighbours. There were a number of long-running disputes, including with Japan over the Diaoyo/Senkaku islands, with Vietnam over the Spratly Islands, and with the Philippines over the maritime claims embodied in China's 'nine-dash line' in the South China Sea. China claimed some 80 per cent, including the islands, rocks and reefs – and potentially rich mineral resources. The building of long landing strips on artificially elevated islands alarmed Washington and its allies in the region. What was a dream for some was a nightmare for others.[72] China's assertion of sovereignty rights within the 'nine-dash' region was censured by the International Court of Arbitration in July 2016 in an action brought by the Philippines, but the judgment was angrily dismissed by China. Deng Xiaoping's 'hide and bide' strategy now gave way to the reassertion of China's perceived rights. In response, the US deployed naval vessels to enforce the openness of the seas (although

---

[70] Shawn Donnan and James Kynge, 'Boost for China as it Joins IMF Elite', *Financial Times*, 1 December 2015, p. 1.

[71] James Kynge, 'Pivotal Moment for the Redback and China, *Financial Times*, 30 November 2015, special report, 'The Future of the Renminbi', p. 1.

[72] See Axel Berkofsky, 'Chinese Foreign and Security Policies: Dream at Home, Nightmare Abroad?', in Alessia Amighini (ed.), *China Dream: Still Coming True?* (Milan, Italian Institute for International Political Studies (ISPI), 2016), pp. 65–79.

there had been no disruptions), much to China's displeasure. China perceived the US as intent on impeding its global rise. American attempts to block Western participation in the China-sponsored AIIB was particularly provocative, and in the end futile. Even the staunch US ally, the UK, in March 2015 agreed to work with the bank, followed by a number of other European countries and even the World Bank. China made an initial contribution of $50 billion, and contributions by other participants soon reached the target of $100 billion, two-thirds that of the IMF's Asian Development Bank.

The Russo-China relationship is marred by some long-standing problems. The Chinese had never forgotten or forgiven Russia's acquisition of great swathes of Chinese territory in the nineteenth century, at the time of China's 'century of humiliation'. Fu Ying describes the vicissitudes but argues that Russia and China have now forged a 'strategic partnership'. While aware of fears that that the two countries could forge an anti-Western 'axis', she stresses that the two countries have 'established a high level of political trust and will continue to work in concert on all fronts'.[73] She analysed the vulnerabilities of the relationship, describing how China had gained its understanding of alliances from its painful historical experience. Each successive Chinese regime had signed an alliance treaty with Russia, but none had been able to protect or advance vital Chinese national interests. Nevertheless, today China's relationship with Russia stood out from the seventy-two partner relationships the country had forged across the world. In 2008 the forty-year negotiations on demarcating the 4,300-kilometre border were finally completed, and 'equality and mutual respect' fostered 'a high degree of political confidence'.[74] There were differences, with Russia traditionally oriented to Europe while China focused on Asia, and the change in the relative balance of power provided some discomfort in Moscow, prompting talk of 'the China threat'.[75] Nevertheless, on Ukraine and Syria the two countries achieved a high level of understanding, and while upholding the territorial integrity of Ukraine, Fu quotes Xi to the effect that the crisis is 'not coming from nowhere'.[76]

The two countries, in Trenin's words, have created 'a new type of major power relationship' based on the formula 'China and Russia will

---

[73] Fu Ying, *Are China and Russia Axis or Partners?* (Beijing, 2016), p. 2, is an extended version of Fu Ying's article 'How China Sees Russia: Beijing and Moscow are Close, but Not Allies', *Foreign Affairs*, Vol. 95, No. 1, January–February 2016, pp. 96–105. The longer version has more details of Russia's successive betrayals of China, but at the same time was more positive about the potential of the relationship.

[74] Fu, *Are China and Russia Axis or Partners?*, p.14.

[75] Fu, 'How China Sees Russia', p. 99.   [76] Fu, 'How China Sees Russia', p. 100.

never go against each other, but they do not have to follow each other'. The new regional order was based on the principle that no single power would dominate Eurasia, and instead in the new multilateral order each country would take into account the interests of the other. The new model was based on '[h]armony in place of balance, diversity in place of homogeneity, and consensus in place of one-country leadership'.[77] Overall, Fu stressed that strong relations between Russia and China did not represent a challenge to the US or the US-led world order, although both countries 'called for the international system to become more just'.[78] Russia was increasingly perceived in China as a country that resists 'international hegemony', and amidst warming cultural appreciation between the two countries, there is no doubt that they remain 'independent strategic actors' but the relationship represents a fundamental realignment in international politics.[79]

Greater Eurasia and the World

National identity reformation in China and Russia has converged, but the gap is unlikely to narrow further. Rozman argues that China's thinking is based 'on a world bifurcated between East and West', whereas Russia is driven by 'a desire for Eurasianism as a third important civilisation'.[80] This is true, but what the Chinese call the 'Shanghai spirit' of cooperation and creating win-win situations helps ensure that irreducible differences are treated in a dialogical rather than absolutist manner. This is certainly the case with the various belts and roads.

China's 21st Century SREB initiative was outlined by Xi at the Nazarbaev University during his visit to Kazakhstan on 7 September 2013 and in October, on a visit to Jakarta, he outlined how SREB would develop maritime regional infrastructure and trade with the Association of East Asian Nations (ASEAN) countries. This bloc has traditionally defended the sovereignty of its member states, although in recent years there have been moves towards greater intergovernmental solidarity. SREB is an ambitious attempt to promote regional cooperation, economic integration and communication and transport networks. The accompanying maritime belt was to be supported by upgrades to ports and transport

---

[77] Dmitri Trenin, 'New Triangular Diplomacy Emerges Amid Changing Global Landscape', Carnegie Moscow Center, 22 February 2017, http://carnegie.ru/2017/02/2 2/new-triangular-diplomacy-emerges-amid-changing-global-political-landscape-pub-6 8115, last accessed 30 May 2017.

[78] Fu, 'How China Sees Russia', p. 105.

[79] The quotations are from Matthieu Duchâtel, 'China and Russia: Towards an Alliance Treaty?', European Council on Foreign Relations, October 2016, p. 4.

[80] Rozman, *Sino-Russian Challenge*, p. 270.

hubs. The Chinese-led AIIB and the NDB provide resources for building road, rail, sea, air and pipeline infrastructure. On 28 March 2015 China officially announced that the two projects would be known collectively as the 'One Belt, One Road' strategy, a grandiose plan to link Asia, Eurasia and Africa with transport and infrastructure.[81]

The deepening spirit of camaraderie was evident when Xi visited Moscow on 9 May 2015 to celebrate the seventieth anniversary of the end of the Second World War in Europe, an event boycotted by most Western leaders. Xi and first lady Peng Liyuan were given pride of place at the Red Square victory parade. The momentous Joint Statement signed the previous day agreed on 'cooperation and conjugation', as Alexander Lukin puts it, between the EEU and SREB.[82] The plan to unify the two projects was the beginning of a long convergence process. On 8 May thirty-two agreements were signed, including two economic framework declarations and measures granting Russian companies access to Chinese finance. Russia gained access to the $40 billion Silk Road Construction Fund for agricultural and other projects, while China gained a potentially lucrative and reliable transport corridor to Europe. With the establishment of the EEU there are only two customs posts between Beijing and Brussels (on the Sino-Kyrgyzstan border, and the Belarus-Polish border). The bulk of the agreements were no longer resource-based but featured plans to intensify finance, banking and investment ties, as well as to develop R&D, high tech, transport and infrastructure partnerships. Plans included the joint development of a heavy lift helicopter, joint exploitation of the Glonass and BeiDou satellite navigation systems, and cooperation with the giant Chinese company Huawei in telecommunications and shipbuilding (with the Russian United Shipbuilding Corporation). The ultimate, though remote, goal was the establishment of a 'common economic space'.

There were clear synergies between the two countries, with Russia strong in basic science, military and dual-use technologies, while China had an impressive record in infrastructure development, transport and civilian technologies.[83] A few months later, in September 2015, Putin stood next to Xi in Beijing in the military parade to celebrate the

---

[81] Alexander Cooley, *New Silk Route or Developmental Cul-de-Sac?*, PONARS Eurasian Policy Memo No. 372, July 2015.

[82] Alexander Lukin, *Shanghai Cooperation Organization: Looking for a New Role*, Valdai Papers, Special Issue (Valdai Discussion Club, 2015), p. 2, http://valdaiclub.com/a/val dai-papers/valdai_paper_special_issue_shanghai_cooperation_organization_looking_ for_a_new_role/, last accessed 9 June 2017.

[83] Larisa Smirnova, 'The Real Meaning of Xi Jinping's Visit to Moscow', *Russia Direct*, 15 May 2015, www.russia-direct.org/analysis/real-meaning-xi-jinpings-visit-moscow, last accessed 30 May 2017.

seventieth anniversary of China's victory in the Second World War. These forms of solidarity may be largely symbolic, but they generated a deepening climate of trust between the two countries. In June 2016 Putin completed his fifteenth visit to China, where the two sides agreed to develop a wide-bodied long-haul plane, a heavy helicopter, and to coordinate their space programmes. There was constant close interaction between the Russian and Chinese leaderships on the whole gamut of developmental and international issues. Nonetheless, there were some major pitfalls. Chinese attempts to turn the SCO into a multilateral economic cooperation body were blocked by its other members, including Russia, and SREB represented in part an alternative strategy. These countries were concerned about China's economic dominance, and preferred to rely on traditional forms of post-Soviet cooperation. Russia fought to keep the SCO a political and security organisation and not an instrument for economic integration. The CSTO is Russia's favoured instrument for regional security cooperation, and in October 2016 it adopted its *Collective Security Strategy 2025*, outlining anti-terrorism and peacekeeping activities. Another problem is the capacity of the EEU to act as an effective partner to OBOR. While China invested billions into the development of the Belt, the early years of the EEU were troubled. There was a certain conceptual incompatibility between the two. The EEU is a classic territorially based regional integration project, with unified tariffs and deepening labour, capital and, ultimately, fiscal integration. OBOR, on the other hand, is all about flexibility and network connectivity.

On 19 and 20 May 2016 Putin hosted the ASEAN-Russia summit, which discussed ways of deepening economic cooperation. At that time Russo-ASEAN trade was lamentably low, comprising less than 1 per cent of the group's total trade. Russia lacked significant sea trade logistics or a Pacific merchant fleet. Russia was particularly concerned to draw Japan and the ASEAN countries into the development of Siberia and the Russian Far East. There was even talk of establishing an ASEAN-EEU free trade area, building on the existing free trade area between the EEU and Vietnam, agreed in May 2015. At the same time, India was forging closer partnerships with Asia-Pacific as well Eurasian countries as a whole. The Chinese-sponsored Regional Comprehensive Economic Partnership (RCEP) was boosted by Trump's cancellation of TPP, comprising ASEAN and the states with which it has free trade agreements, including India, Japan, South Korea, Australia and New Zealand, but not the US. Russia had kept aloof from these projects, but at the ASEAN meeting intimated that it would join RCEP. At that summit Russia sought to find ways to coordinate the two nascent mega-regional communities: the Greater Eurasia emerging from closer cooperation between the EEU and SREB, backed by the SCO; and Asia's RCEP. The goal was to ensure coordination between the four major integration structures – the EEU, SCO, BRI and ASEAN. Suslov argues that '[t]he mega community will no doubt have every chance of becoming the backbone of the world order in the 21st century'.[84]

Russia's economic weakness undermined these aspirations, and too often it appeared that its Asia-Pacific strategy remained secondary to its broader global and Atlantic agendas. Russia's 'pivot to the East' is both substantive and real, but Russia's Asia-Pacific strategy remains inconsistent. The meeting of the Eastern Economic Forum in Vladivostok in September 2016 demonstrated Russia's commitment to developing its Far Eastern territories and of integrating into the larger Asian economy, yet it ignored the East Asia Summit (EAS) held in Laos just three days later. Putin had attended its inaugural summit in Kuala Lumpur in 2005, and Russia became a full member in 2011. The EAS had ambitions to become Asia's OSCE, but Putin's failure to participate in subsequent summits (in contrast to Obama's regular attendance) suggested a lack of commitment to the region's security dialogue.[85] In general, international society in the APR is typically described as pluralist, with weak institutionalisation and persistent rivalries, as opposed to the more 'solidarist' version in Europe. The pluralist environment was more in keeping with Russia's normative inclinations, but Russia often found itself marginalised in the more anarchic international environment.

The emergence of a potentially powerful new global constellation, bringing together Russia and China as well as other allies such as India, was a vivid manifestation of a nascent multi-order world. Ideational and geopolitical pluralism was back on the political agenda. Russian elites considered the strategic convergence of the three Eurasian projects – the SCO, EEU and the BRI – as one of the country's priorities.[86] The coordination plans 'brought Russia's relations with China to a new level, laying the groundwork for the continued expansion of trade and economic relations and the economic development in Central Eurasia, as well as for the gradual emergence of a new political and economic community of Greater Eurasia'. Closer ties with China in conditions of the

---

[84] Dmitry Suslov, 'A Pivot towards Asia, Integration and Mega-Regions', Valdai Discussion Club, 9 June 2016, http://valdaiclub.com/news/a-pivot-towards-asia-integration-and-mega-regions-balancing-russia-s-apr-policy/, last accessed 30 May 2017.

[85] Alexander Gabuev, 'The Wrong Forum: Russian Engagement in the Asia-Pacific', Carnegie Moscow Centre, 15 September 2016, http://carnegie.ru/commentary/2016/09/15/wrong-forum-russian-engagement-in-asia-pacific/j5ha, last accessed 30 May 2017.

[86] Sergey Luzyanin, Vladimir Matveev and Larisa Smirnova, Shanghai Cooperation Organisation: Model 2014–15, Russian International Affairs Council, Working Paper No. 21, 2015, pp. 4, 12–13.

'systemic rift in Russia-US relations since 2014' demonstrated 'the absurdity of the US claims that Russia is being isolated'. Above all:

It reflects an understanding by both Moscow and Beijing that in the years to come the US containment policy towards the two countries, along with attempts to draw them into a Washington-centred world order, will be gaining momentum, making Russian-Chinese rapprochement a necessity in terms of improving the odds for the non-Western world of winning in the ongoing struggle for defining what the future world order will look like.[87]

An enlarged SCO would become, in Lukin's words, 'an emerging corner-stone of the multipolar world in the making, a platform offering a Eurasian alternative to Western Europe'.[88] He goes on to list the precise features of that alternative: non-interference in the domestic affairs of other states; maintaining the central role of the UN and the Security Council; creating a more just system of international governance, taking into account the interests of the non-Western world while not disbanding the current system; and respecting differences in values, and refraining from imposing one's values as universal ones.[89]

At the same time, Russia complemented its Sino-Centric Asia policy with a broader strategy of engagement with ASEAN. However, few conflicts are as deeply entrenched as that between Russia and Japan. The dispute over the four Kurile Islands (labelled the Northern Territories by Japan), seized by the Soviet Union in the dying days of the Second World War, prevented the two countries from signing a post-war peace treaty and poisoned relations between the two countries. Under the leadership of Shinzo Abe, Japan reinforced its alignment with the Historical West. Under US pressure, Japan joined the sanctions regime, but sought to soften them as far as possible. The Japanese administration was riled by the visit by senior Russian officials, including Medvedev, to the disputed islands in August 2015.[90] Fearing a resurgent China, Japan reinforced its long-standing security and other ties with the US, but it also looked to transform its relationship with Russia. Economic ties remain under-developed, and are marked by suspicion on both sides. The deepening energy relationship was criticised as forcing Japan into a position of 'dependence' on Russia.[91] On 6 May 2016 Putin hosted Abe in Sochi, and at the long-awaited summit in Japan on 15 and 16 December 2016 the two leaders agreed to implement a 'special economic regime' for the Kurile Islands and plans were outlined for

---

[87] Suslov, 'Pivot towards Asia'.   [88] Lukin, *Shanghai Cooperation Organization*, p. 6.
[89] Lukin, *Shanghai Cooperation Organization*, p. 6.
[90] Justin McCurry, 'Japan puts Putin visit on hold, citing territory dispute and Syria strikes' *Guardian*, 16 October 2015, p. 24.
[91] Interview with senior Japanese foreign ministry official, Tokyo, August 2015.

a visa-free regime for citizens of Russia's Sakhalin region and Japan's Hokkaido prefecture. Although there was no breakthrough, the meetings signalled a new level of engagement between the two countries. The inaugural Eastern Economic Forum in 2015 focused investment attention on Russia's Far East, while the second in September 2016 saw a significant Japanese presence. Abe suggested that Vladivostok should become Russia's gateway to Asia, as well as the entry point for investment in the Russian Far East region. In 2015 some $15.35 billion was invested in the region, and even more in 2016.[92]

The various 'turns to the East' reflected the centre of economic gravity moving to the APR, but Russia struggled to bolster its great power status and find a developmental model for its Far Eastern regions.[93] The residual Soviet legacy of economic autarchy obstructed the flow of foreign investment. The major projects – the East Siberia-Pacific Ocean (ESPO) pipeline, Kozmino port and oil terminal, the Vostochny space centre, building the infrastructure for the Asia-Pacific Economic Cooperation (APEC) forum in Vladivostok in 2012 – were largely financed from its own resources, although the Power of Siberia gas pipeline was built with Chinese support. The EEU-BRI partnership drew on classic global governance models to develop regional international institutions and a body of community law that would ultimately reduce the scope of national sovereignty. As America turned towards economic nationalism, China emerged as the defender of globalisation and a rules-based international order. Out of the alphabet soup of acronyms and institutions, a pattern began to emerge. At SPIEF 2016 Putin outlined grandiose plans for 'Greater Eurasia'. Instead of the much-vaunted but stillborn Greater Europe, Putin announced the beginning of talks 'on the formation of comprehensive trade and economic partnership in Eurasia with the participation of the European Union states and China. I expect that this will be one of the first steps towards the formation of a major Eurasian partnership.' He noted that '[d]espite all the well-known problems in our relations', the EU remained Russia's 'key trade and economic partner'. He thus invited Europeans to join the project for the Eurasian partnership, and he welcomed the initiative by Nazarbaev to hold consultations between the EEU and the EU.[94] Contrary to those who argue that Putin sought to weaken the EU and to exacerbate its internal

[92] Gleb Fedorov, 'With a Pragmatic Asia Strategy, Russia Shifts Focus Away from China', Russia beyond the Headlines, 20 December 2016.

[93] Viktor Larin, 'Asia-Pacific Region or Greater Eurasia?', Valdai Club, 12 December 2016, http://valdaiclub.com/a/highlights/asia-pacific-region-or-greater-eurasia/, last accessed 30 May 2017.

[94] 'Plenary session of St Petersburg International Economic Forum', 17 June 2016, op. cit.

divisions, the ambitious plan for a trading bloc from the Pacific to the Atlantic sought to make the EU a full partner, with the support of the Chinese leadership. Russia would not have to choose between Europe and Asia, and Eurasia in between would unite the two.

The conjugation of the core organisations from 2016 gained the moniker of the Greater Eurasia Project (GEP). Putin mentioned GEP in his 1 December 2016 annual address to parliament, stressing the need to create a 'multilevel integration model in Eurasia'. As Diesen puts it, 'Russia's geoeconomic strategy for a "Greater Eurasia" aims to utilise economic connectivity to remove Russia from the periphery of Europe and Asia, and reposition it at the heart of an integrated Eurasia'.[95] The development of substantive multipolarity has profound geopolitical ramifications. The GEP was more than a way of compensating for failures in the West but represented what many in Moscow considered a long-delayed rebalancing of policy. At the same time, Russia was the main proponent of the creation of a parallel set of global institutions, and this helps explain the ferocity of the onslaught against the country. Russia worked to create a Greater Eurasian community, encompassing its partners in the EEU as well as China, India and Iran and ASEAN to create 'a major Euro-Asian political and economic arc, one which spans from Belarus all the way to the border with Australia'.[96] The goal was not to repudiate globalisation or the institutions of international society, but to render them less West-centric. In that aim Russia found allies in Asia, and indeed, within many Western countries. Oliver Stuenkel argues that the Ufa Declaration and associated documents signalled an important step towards the creation of a post-Western world.[97] Western sanctions forced Russia to redouble its efforts to engage with Greater Asia, while China sees Eurasia as an essential part not only of its economic but also its political future. With 'Sino-Russian relations … closer than they have been at any time in the past fifty years, giving them the chance to reshape the global order to their liking', Kissinger's worst nightmare is coming to pass.[98] The creation of systemic alternatives is not intended to be anti-Western but to act as models for a more inclusive and plural international system. Non-Western alternatives exist and are taking increasingly structured forms.

---

[95] Glenn Diesen, *Russia's Geoeconomic Strategy for a Greater Eurasia* (London, Routledge, 2017), p. 1.

[96] Suslov, 'Pivot towards Asia'.

[97] Oliver Stuenkel, 'The Ufa Declaration: An Analysis', 9 July 2015, www.postwesternworld.com/2015/07/09/the-declaration-analysis/, last accessed 30 May 2017.

[98] Mathew Burrows and Robert A. Manning, *Kissinger's Nightmare: How an Inverted US-China-Russia May Be a Game-Changer*, Moscow, Valdai Paper No. 33, November 2015, p. 3.

11 The New Globalism and the Politics of Resistance

The financial and other crises buffeting the Western world after 2008 revived the orthodox Soviet belief in the inevitable decline of the West. As the Valdai Club 2015 briefing materials put it: 'The world is standing at a parting of the ways: will the internal problems of the leading countries and the growing strength of the non-Western centres bring us to a revolutionary explosion or will changes be slow and systematic?' The dominance of the West was acknowledged, but two trends undermined the status quo: '[T]he relative decline of America's allies, from the EU to Japan; and the narrowing of the gap between them and BRICS countries in terms of influence on global processes'. The document generously conceded that a 'revolutionary demolition of the western-centric global order' was not inevitable, and there was 'still scope for orderly reform', but for Russia, 'interdependence is turning into a source of pressure and vulnerability'.[1] The response was to insulate Russia from external pressure by creating an alternative framework of international governance while reinforcing traditional instruments of diplomacy and great power behaviour. The presentiment of Western decline was exaggerated, yet profound shifts in the balance of global power are happening. Russia was accused of trying to accelerate the West's decline by undermining the Western democratic order through various forms of asymmetrical attacks.[2] Russia and the West entered a *danse macabre*, in which each anticipated the demise of the other.

The Global Impasse

After the rupture of 2014 there could be no going back to 'business as usual'. The deep well of mistrust between the Atlantic community and Russia meant that although there could be occasional cooperation, there was no foundation for a sustainable relationship based on trust. European

---

[1] *War and Peace in the 21st Century*, Valdai Discussion Club Report, p. 2.
[2] Fareed Zakaria, 'Vladimir Putin Wants a New World Order: Why Would Donald Trump Help Him?', *Washington Post*, 15 December 2016.

security was once again militarised. In that context, for both sides, 'business as usual' would mean returning to a condition that provoked the crisis in the first place. The Cold War may have long ended, but the institutions and ideas that sustained it lived on, in the end reproducing a conflict that mimicked elements of the original. Two contrasting narratives shaped public debate. For the Atlantic powers, Russia had been offered participation in a stable rules-based system but for reasons of its own (above all, the alleged emergence a self-serving kleptocratic regime) had chosen isolation. Russia argued that it had been trapped in a strategic impasse where membership of the Historical West would have entailed the repudiation of elements of its identity and status, and where every independent move was stymied (soft containment). Ultimately, Russia's security and interests had been threatened by the enlargement of Cold War institutions and their associated ideational apparatus. If these institutions had been nested in some form of reconciliation, then their enlargement would have been acceptable to Russia. The idea of Greater Europe was perceived as an attempt to drive a wedge between the two wings of the Atlantic alliance; whereas for Russia, it promised precisely to provide a framework for reconciliation and pluralism.

Atlanticism consolidated and advanced to Russia's borders. The formula of Europe 'whole and free' was appropriated to become a project of the Atlantic system, and not a common endeavour of all Europeans. The Gaullist vision of European continentalism was lost. Enlargement rather than transformation became the order of the day. This meant that the European security order curved back in on itself. Enlargement generated increased resistance from Russia but also changed the nature of the bodies that enlarged. Neither the EU nor NATO after 1989 had originally been hostile towards Russia, but benign intentions were subverted by the primacy of an enlarging rather than a transcending agenda. The former Soviet bloc countries, and even some former Soviet states, only too eagerly sought to associate themselves with the enlargement dynamic, but in so doing they re-incorporated the old Cold War 'captive nations' rhetoric into the Atlantic community. The 'hedging' strategy against Russia hastened Russia's transformation into a state that apparently needed hedging against.

This became the new 'normal'. The present confrontation is wide-ranging, and increasingly deeply rooted. Russia and the US consider themselves 'exceptional' and their foreign policies are imbued with messianic elements, but neither is seriously bent on territorial acquisition or wars of conquest. The US is certainly concerned to maintain its hegemonic status, but this is embedded in liberal internationalist institutions and tempered by commitment to universal values. As long as these values serve US interests – and they mostly do – then the US is a satisfied power, and the revisionism of Bush junior and the project for unchallengeable American primacy (while certainly not entirely overcome) was modified by Obama and recast by Trump. Trenin rightly argues that the confrontation between the US and Russia is here to stay, and that the US sanctions will last for a long time. The broader context is a new period of global turbulence:

> The quarter-century-long Pax America – a period when no one seriously contested American dominance – ended in the mid-2010s. Analysis of this phenomenon has previously focused on the word 'Americana', alluding to American hegemony and a unipolar world. However, there is also the other element, the 'pax', meaning generally cordial relations among all major world players. This time of peace and tranquillity has come to an end and key world players – the United States, China and Russia – have entered a new phase of rivalry.[3]

Most commentators would not recognise the Pax Americana as an era of cordiality, but Trenin is right to note the onset of an extended period of contestation. In response, he argues that the US changed its global strategy: 'From an emphasis on universalism (the stimulation of globalisation, the promotion of democratic values in the world), Washington is moving to strengthen the position of the enlarged West [the Historical West in the parlance of this book] and actively deter countries that challenge the United States.'[4]

On the other side, the intensifying alignment between Russia and China represented far more than a banal 'pivot to Asia' or a response to Russia's alienation from the West. Russia and China had long been dissatisfied with the structures of international governance, considering that they had not been treated as equals in that system. Russian leaders from Gorbachev to Putin argued that Russia had voluntarily ended the Cold War and transformed the domestic order, and considered that the country by right deserved to be integrated as an equal in the top table of international leadership, irrespective of its economic and military weight. China's route to neo-revisionism was rather more tortured, although also based on the view that its equality was merited by its history and size. Both sought to adapt the Western developmental model to modernise their societies, although China rather more adroitly mostly avoided alienating

---

[3] Dmitri Trenin, 'Managing Risks in the Russia-United States Conflict', Carnegie Moscow Center, 30 May 2016, http://carnegie.ru/commentary/2016/05/30/managing-risks-in-rus sia-united-states-conflict/j0eg, last accessed 30 May 2017.

[4] Dmitri Trenin, 'Why the Standoff between the US and Russia is Here to Stay', *Russia Beyond the Headlines* (from *RBK Daily*), 25 May 2016, http://rbth.com/opinion/2016/05/25/why-the-standoff-between-the-us-and-russia-is-here-to-stay_597219, last accessed 30 May 2017.

its Western interlocutors. Neither was ready to repudiate the horizontal ties with the West, but both had come to the conclusion that it would be in their interests to strengthen the links between each other in the context of the vertical commitment to international society. The deepening institutionalisation of non-Western regional and global associations meant that Russia achieved more in a decade with China than in a quarter-century with the EU and the Historical West. There was no strategic impasse in the East, and instead wide horizons for development and cooperation.

In his *Grand Chessboard*, Brzezinzki, the leading exponent of American exceptionalism, argued that 'the tectonic shift in world affairs' had for the first time rendered a 'non-Eurasian power ... not only as a key arbiter of Eurasian power relations but also as the world's paramount power'. The disintegration of the Soviet Union made the US 'the sole and, indeed, the first truly global power'.[5] The 'three grand imperatives of imperial geostrategy' were 'to prevent collusion and maintain security dependence among the vassals, to keep tributaries pliant and protected, and to keep the barbarians from coming together'.[6] The three goals began to unravel, but remained the implicit imperatives of US foreign policy. Brzezinski later argued that '[a]s its era of global dominance ends, the United States needs to take the lead in realigning the global power architecture'. He identified five 'basic verities' of the coming 'new global alignment'. First, the US remained 'the world's politically, economically, and militarily most powerful entity but, given complex geopolitical shifts in regional balances, it is no longer the globally imperial power. But neither is any other major power.' The second verity was that 'Russia is experiencing the latest convulsive phase of its imperial devolution', if it acted wisely it could become 'a leading European nation-state', but it was currently needlessly alienating its neighbours. Third, China was rising, but for the time being did not pose an outright challenge to America. Fourth, 'Europe is not now and is not likely to become a global power', but remained a useful ally of the US. Fifth, the 'violent political awakening amongst post-colonial Muslims' unified 'large numbers of Muslims against the outside world'. These five verities, in his view, meant that the US 'must take the lead in realigning the global power architecture in such a way that the violence ... can be contained without destroying the global order'.[7] Most tributaries remained pliant, but the rise of anti-hegemonic regional alignments of the subalterns, including BRICS, the

---

[5] Brzezinski, *Grand Chessboard*, p. xiii.   [6] Brzezinski, *Grand Chessboard*, p. 40.
[7] Zbigniew Brzezinski. 'Towards a Global Realignment', *The American Interest*, Vol. 11, No. 6, 17 April 2016, www.the-american-interest.com/2016/04/17/toward-a-global-realign ment/, last accessed 30 May 2017.

SCO and the entente between Russia and China, meant that the 'barbarians' were coming together.

Adopting a counter-intuitive position, William Wohlforth argues that this could, paradoxically, help to moderate tension between the US-led West and others. He notes some 'convergence in expectations' of power, since when 'sides see their relative power in roughly similar terms, bargaining is smoother'. The US and its allies had learned 'about the limits of their power in recent years, causing an across the board moderation of the heady expectations that met the new millennium'. Equally, exaggerated ideas about the BRICS and other associations critical of the US-led global order, 'a narrative closely connected to the idea of the rapid return of a true multipolar system with roughly equal states at the top', had also 'suffered setbacks'. The BRICS countries found themselves in the doldrums, while expectations about China's ability to act as a global superpower had been over-estimated. The EU had been considered the heart of an 'expanding liberal order', but it is now in deep crisis. In short, a new equilibrium was emerging, in which the US would remain pre-eminent but China and Russia would assert their interests along with a range of other actors, and in the long-term 'it is hard to make the case that underlying trends clearly favour either the liberal west or the non-liberal major powers'. Only the rise of India could change the balance. The background conditions suggest a 'live-and-let-live equilibrium between the US-led west and the rest'.[8] This is a sensible corrective to exaggerated views about changes in the global balance of power, while at the same time recognising the genuine shifts.

Seventy years after the end of the Second World War, the Trump presidency signalled a 'rethinking [of] the role that the international order should play in US grand strategy'. Mazarr warns that attempts to restore the unified US-dominated system by 'confronting the rule breakers and aggressively promoting liberal values' could be counter-productive: '[I]n trying to hold the old order together, Washington could end up accelerating the dissolution.' Instead, in his view the US must learn to 'lead the more diversified, pluralistic system that is now materializing'.[9] It is not clear why the US should 'lead' the new system, but the article signalled recognition that the international system had indeed become more plural. There remained a tension between two representations of the post-war liberal order. 'One is a narrow, cautious view of the UN and

[8] William Wohlforth, 'Live-and-Let-Live Equilibrium: Best Option for the 21st Century World', Valdai Discussion Club, 16 August 2016, http://valdaiclub.com/a/highlights/live-and-let-live-equilibrium-best-option/, last accessed 9 June 2017.

[9] Michael J. Mazarr, 'The Once and Future Order: What Comes after Hegemony?', *Foreign Affairs*, Vol. 96, No. 1, January–February 2017, p. 25.

the core international financial institutions as guardians of sovereign equality, territorial inviolability, and a limited degree of free trade.' The other 'is a more ambitious agenda: protecting human rights, fostering democratic political systems, promoting free-market economic reforms, and encouraging good governance'.[10] Mazarr notes that China and Russia had become the 'two most important dissenters', and although they had divergent views and ambitions, their 'broad complaints had much in common':

Both countries feel disenfranchised by a US-dominated system that imposes strict conditions on their participation and, they believe, menaces their regimes by promoting democracy. And both countries have called for fundamental reforms to make the order less imperial and more pluralistic.[11]

This was Russia's position from the very beginning. Russia and China allied in defence of the autonomy of the international society represented by the UN and other instruments of global governance. This did not mean that either sought to undermine the liberal world order, but only its hegemonic practices. This is the essence of their neo-revisionist position, which is reformist rather than revolutionary. As Mazarr notes, their grievances and ambitions could be accommodated by 'a more flexible, pluralistic approach to institutions, rules, and norms'.[12] It would entail the repudiation of the traditional postwar US grand strategy, which assumed that the 'unitary US-led order reflected universal values, was easy to join, and exercised a gravitational pull on other countries'. The old Cold War playbook, in which democracies were rallied and norm-breakers were punished, would only create a new generation of embittered outcasts.[13] Instead, a more pluralistic international system would allow states to solve their historical problems at their own pace, and to adapt to the exigencies of international society in their own way. The US-led liberal world order would remain an important pole, but the repudiation of transformative ambitions would provide space for engagement with global problems of development and inclusion. However, practices are perhaps the hardest to change, and neo-revisionism ran into a rock of hegemonic consolidation. Russia looked for a way out of its strategic impasse, but for that a new model of world order was required. In the absence of such a transformation, the dialectic of resistance and confrontation would intensify.

---

[10] Mazarr, 'Once and Future Order', p. 26.
[11] Mazarr, 'Once and Future Order', p. 27.
[12] Mazarr, 'Once and Future Order', p. 28.
[13] Mazarr, 'Once and Future Order', p. 29.

Asymmetrical Communication

Russia became one of the most contested issues in the 2016 US presidential election. Moscow was accused of trying to influence the outcome, and even of undermining American democracy as a whole. 'Russophobia' was pushed to new levels, but even the term was painted as an instrument in the Kremlin's manipulative strategies. Russophobia was defined as 'another stage of Russia's communications with the Kremlin's opponents, both foreign and domestic'. The goal, as in the nineteenth century, was to neutralise the West's criticism of Russian expansionism.[14] Nevertheless, the extraordinary level of hostility was real. Although the evidence of the Kremlin's involvement in the cyberattacks is not conclusive, it would be in keeping with Russia's challenge to US global hegemony. As Tsygankov notes, Russia has 'developed multiple tools for projecting Russia's power and ideas into the Western information space'. These tools included the establishment of the Russia Today (later RT) TV station, and various programmes to 'navigate the global cyber space and deflect Western criticisms'. But as Tsygankov argues:

Moscow sees itself responding to the information war launched against it by the West in order [to] install a friendly regime in Russia, as it did in Yugoslavia, Iraq, Georgia, Ukraine and Libya. Russia's assertiveness is not the method of launching a new Cold War on the West, let alone destroying its domestic institutions. The Kremlin's fight is one for greater recognition of Russia's values and interests, especially in Europe and Eurasia.

If the West's dismissal of Russia's power concerns and the demonisation of Putin continued, then Russia could well shift into a Cold War mode against the West, which would be a 'self-fulfilling prophecy coming true'.[15]

The use of Cold War language such as 'informational warfare' to describe the distorted communications between Russia and the West is a measure of the degree to which engagement and dialogue have broken down. If diplomacy is defined as an institution for communication, then the forced use of alternative forms is an indication of the catastrophic decline in the practice of diplomacy during the cold peace, and even more so afterwards. US representatives at the UN used language that would not have been contemplated even in the

---

[14] Jolanta Darczewska and Piotr Żochowski, *Russophobia in the Kremlin's Strategy: A Weapon of Mass Destruction*, Warsaw, Centre for Eastern Studies, OSW Point of View No. 56, October 2015, p. 5.
[15] Andrei Tsygankov, 'How Cyber Power Fits into Russia's Current Foreign Policy', *Russia Direct*, 3 October 2016, www.russia-direct.org/opinion/how-cyber-power-fits-russias-cu rrent-foreign-policy, last accessed 30 May 2017.

tensest periods of the Cold War.[16] Diplomacy is based on respect for the political subjectivity of the other, even when there are profound disagreements. Indeed, the whole point of diplomacy is to manage difference, and to find a way of achieving optimal outcomes in those conditions.[17] The contemporary decline of diplomacy reflects the didactic character of the liberal international order, which presumes that Russia is somehow an illegitimate interlocutor, and therefore its views can be discounted. Radical liberals hold precisely this position, dismissing the Kremlin's foreign policy as little more than tactical manoeuvring to maintain the power of regime. This axiological stance was countered by Moscow's support for various anti-establishment and insurgent movements in the West, which in turn intensified axiological escalation. Only in the East were the traditional niceties of diplomacy and restraint from interfering in the internal affairs of states retained.

The informational war was accompanied by complaints about the declining standards of journalism and the revival of McCarthyism.[18] Non-mainstream views on Russia and its activities were condemned as 'Kremlin propaganda' and 'fake news'. This had a chilling effect on the quality of public debate, with those advancing what had become 'dissident' views condemned as 'Putin apologists', 'Moscow stooges' or 'agents of Russian influence'. In its report on *Britain's Useful Idiots*, the Henry Jackson Society noted that European populists from both left and right sought to establish connections with Putin's Russia, the former in defence of 'traditional values', and the latter out of traditional admiration for Russia and 'in part out of ideological folly: they see anybody who opposes Western imperialism as a strategic bedfellow'. Recommendations included pointing out 'pro-Russia connections of individuals and parties across the political spectrum', and legislation across Europe should be amended or adopted 'that forces politicians to declare all media appearances they make, whether they receive money for them or not'.[19] A flood of reports in the US sought to expose the way that '[t]he Kremlin uses these Trojan horses to destabilize European politics so efficiently, that even Russia's limited might could

---

[16] The US permanent representatives under Obama, Susan Rice (2009–13) and Samantha Power (2013–16), used egregiously offensive language about Russia, accompanied by walk-outs and boycotts, a tradition that was continued by Trump's representative, Nikki Haley.

[17] For a classic and still pertinent study, see Henry Kissinger, *Diplomacy* (New York, Simon and Schuster, 1995).

[18] Robert Parry, 'New York Times and the New McCarthyism', *Consortium News*, 7 September 2016, https://consortiumnews.com/2016/09/07/new-york-times-and-the-new-mccarthyism/, last accessed 30 May 2017.

[19] Andrew Foxall, *Britain's Useful Idiots: Britain's Left, Right and Russia* (London, Henry Jackson Society, October 2016), p. 2.

become a decisive factor in matters of European and international security', and urged Western governments to fund civil society groups and the media 'to shed light on the Kremlin's dark networks'.[20] The Kremlin's alleged subversive tactics were described in the report *The Kremlin Playbook*.[21]

Alleged Russian hacking and other forms of interference against Western agencies and states were interpreted as forms of 'asymmetrical communication'. It is always hard to identify the source of a hack, although this does not prevent accusations being made. It was not clear what Moscow had to gain in 2016, other than discrediting the assumed victory of Clinton, whom they considered a dangerous warmonger. It was clear that Russia had much to lose, including further reputational damage. A sophisticated interpretation of Russian behaviour suggests that it is a form of communication. With the country trapped in a strategic impasse, and with the West apparently deaf to normal forms of communication (the discursive block mentioned earlier), then such actions represented a rather crude way of trying to get the US and its allies back to the negotiating table. In his UN speech on 28 September 2015 Putin had talked of creating a new 'anti-Hitler coalition' to fight Islamic State, but the West's failure to take Russia seriously was jolted when Palmyra was liberated a few months later: 'Basically, Russia forced the West to engage with it in Syria and used that to begin to escape from the isolation it had entered into in 2014 with the Ukraine crisis.'[22] This appears to be the only 'rational' response for Russia where dialogue about crucial security issues, such as Ukraine and Syria, is blocked. By 'inserting itself into developing situations, Russia forces its inclusion in the debate around the resolution of those situations'.[23] This may help explain the extraordinary list of demands in October 2016 when Russia announced that it was pulling out of the plutonium-destruction agreement. As we have seen, the conditions set for Russia rejoining the treaty 'amounted to not much less than the return of Alaska', including the US scaling back its military presence in the states that had joined NATO to the levels of 1 September 2000, the repeal of the Magnitsky Act and the Ukraine

[20] Radosław Sikorski, Foreword to Atlantic Council, *The Kremlin's Trojan Horses* (Washington, November 2016), p. 1.

[21] Center for Strategic and International Studies, *The Kremlin Playbook: Understanding Russian Influence in Central and Eastern Europe* (Washington, CSIS, October 2016).

[22] Alexander Baunov, 'Hitting Rock Bottom: US-Russian Relations Plunge Again', Carnegie Moscow Centre, 11 October 2016, http://carnegie.ru/commentary/?f a=64816, last accessed 30 May 2017.

[23] Eugene Scherbakov, 'The Weird Logic behind Russia's Alleged Hacking', *The National Interest*, 6 October 2016, http://nationalinterest.org/feature/the-weird-logic-behind-rus sias-alleged-hacking-17963, last accessed 30 May 2017.

Freedom Support Act, to lift all anti-Russian sanctions and for the US to compensate Russia for the damage inflicted on its economy, including the damage caused by Russia's counter-sanctions.[24] If this was part of Russia's communications strategy, then it would have been well-advised to change its media consultants.[25]

Russia under-estimated the depth of US resistance to sharing strategic initiatives with what it considered a subaltern actor. In other words, these forms of 'asymmetrical communication' – if that indeed is how such actions can be understood – were at best ineffective, and at worst damaging. In turn, the Western military-ideational complex went on the offensive. The media image of Russia has been intensely negative, with Russia's alleged autocratic system presented as the 'dark double' and mirror image of the American system. David Foglesong describes how American opinion leaders have cast Russia in this role since the late nineteenth century, variously describing it as a lost land striving to become like America, or the embodiment of evil.[26] The binary picture is maintained by suppressing elements of Russian politics that do not fit into this frame, and by exaggerating the negative features in Russia while reinforcing America's perception of itself as a beacon of freedom with the exclusive right to global leadership.[27] This is the mirror image of the way that the Russian state-run television stations present the West.

The Atlantic allies increased funding to beat off Russian 'informational warfare', considered to be an asymmetrical response to the Western victory in the Cold War and Russia's failure to adapt to its reduced status. The US greatly increased the budget of the Broadcasting Board of Governors (BBG), the parent company of the classic Cold War media agencies Voice of America and Radio Free Europe/Radio Liberty, as well as Radio Free Asia and the Office of Cuba Broadcasting (Radio and TV Martí). The BBG budget in 2016 was $758 million, its German equivalent Deutsche Welle received €294 million, while the BBC gained an extra £289 million over four years from the British security and defence budget to boost its World Service output on top of the annual budget of

---

[24] Baunov, 'Hitting Rock Bottom'.
[25] This in the end was the advice of Angus Roxburgh, who worked for a time as a Kremlin adviser on press relations. Nevertheless, he argues 'the advent of a new Cold War was probably due as much to American insensitivity as it was to Putin's stridency in pursuing his legitimate goal of restoring Russian pride and status, *The Strongman: Vladimir Putin and the Struggle for Russia* (London, I. B. Tauris, 2011), p. 321.
[26] David S. Foglesong, *The American Mission and the 'Evil Empire': The Crusade for a 'Free Russia' since 1881* (Cambridge, Cambridge University Press, 2007).
[27] Andrei P. Tsygankov, 'The Dark Double: The American Media Perception of Russia as a Neo-Soviet Autocracy, 2008–2014', *Politics*, Vol. 37, No. 1, 2016, pp. 19–35.

£245 million. By comparison, RT received $260 a year for its global TV broadcasting.

In response to Russia's alleged covert political interference, NATO established what it called a 'Strategic Communications Command' (Stratcom) in Riga as part of a 'soft power' strategy combining public affairs and psychological operations. In March 2015 Mogherini created a similar body under the EEAS, the East StratCom Task Force, a rapid-response team designed to 'address Russia's ongoing disinformation campaigns' whose goal was to 'weaken and destabilise the West by exploiting existing divisions or creating artificial new ones'.[28] The fiscal 2017 House and Senate bills in the US planned to create a powerful new security services committee to counter alleged Russian propaganda and destabilisation in the US and abroad. The agency was without geographic limit and would 'counter active measures by the Russian Federation to exert covert influence over peoples and governments' by 'exposing false-hoods, agents of influence, corruption, human rights abuses, terrorism and assassinations carried out by the security services or political elites of the Russian Federation or their proxies'.[29] Freedom of speech came under pressure as alternative perspectives were condemned as 'Russian propaganda' and 'fake news'. In a rare moment of sanity, a year-long investigation into possible interference in German politics found no proof of a Russian-sponsored disinformation campaign against the government.[30]

The vast networks of sponsored think tanks also swung into action, producing a stream of reports exposing Russia's nefarious activities and its 'Trojan horses'. The report *Winning the Information War*, produced by the Centre for European Policy Analysis (CEPA) in Washington, DC, warned that '[t]he Russian government uses disinformation, incitement to violence and hate speech to destroy trust, sap morale, degrade the information space, erode public discourse and increase partisanship'.[31] In this model, the West is presented as supine and open, while the monstrous Russian bear has almost supernatural powers to shape opinions,

---

[28] ISPI, 'Means, Goals and Consequences of the Pro-Kremlin Disinformation Campaign', 19 January 2017, www.ispionline.it/en/pubblicazione/means-goals-and-consequences-p ro-kremlin-disinformation-campaign-16216, last accessed 30 May 2017.

[29] Spencer Ackerman and Julian Borger, 'US Move to Counter Russian Subversion', *Guardian*, 1 December 2016, p. 22.

[30] Esther King, 'German Intelligence Finds No Evidence of Russian Meddling', Politico. eu, 7 February 2017, drawing on a report in *Süddeutsche Zeitung*, www.politico.eu/article/ german-intelligence-finds-no-evidence-of-russian-meddling/, last accessed 30 May 2017.

[31] Edward Lucas and Peter Pomeranzev, *Winning the Information War: Techniques and Counter-strategies to Russian Propaganda in Central and Eastern Europe* (Washington, Centre for European Policy Analysis, August 2016), p. ii.

win elections and in general destabilise a vulnerable and innocent West. This hermetic discourse has long been prevalent in security circles in NATO's eastern members, but this militarised discursive model was now generalised to the Atlantic community as a whole. Not to be outdone, on 23 November 2016 the European Parliament passed a resolution calling on the EU to 'respond to information warfare by Russia', targeting in particular Sputnik and RT as the most dangerous 'tools' of 'hostile propaganda'.[32] The resort to administrative measures to stifle criticism by putatively pluralistic democracies undermined the democracies themselves, and was no less damaging than Cold War McCarthyism.

The securitised and asymmetrical communicative sphere reflects the hermeneutical problem mentioned earlier and one that endured throughout the cold peace years, namely the incommensurate understanding of global processes. Thomas Graham argues that the US and Russia 'understand terrorism in profoundly different ways'. For the US, the al-Qaeda attack on 9/11 is the defining moment, interpreted not only as an attack on domestic territory but also as an attack on American values, 'ultimately aimed at destroying the United States as a functioning democratic society'. For Russia, terrorism is defined as the struggle to maintain territorial integrity, epitomised in the Chechen conflicts in which North Caucasian groups attacked Moscow and other cities and sought to seize a piece of national territory to create a separate state. Although Obama did not use the 'freedom agenda' in the way Bush did, he remained committed to 'the advance of democratic principles as essential to long-term success in counterterrorism' (a facet of the trans-democracy discussed earlier). For Russia, the struggle against terrorism relies on the harsh suppression of terrorists and those who threaten domestic order and stability.[33] Framed in this way, the terrorist threat justified the aggrandisement of presidential power.[34]

Russia's *Information Security Doctrine* of 5 December 2016 superseded a similar document issued in September 2000. The emphasis now was on the security of the state rather than the individual to enhance national information sovereignty. It described the perceived threats to Russia's national interests and security in the information sphere, and outlined ways of combating them. The focus was on countering propaganda and the

[32] "'At War With Russia": EU Parliament Approves Resolution to Counter Russian Media "Propaganda"', RT.com, 23 November 2016, www.rt.com/news/367922-eu-resolution-russian-media/, last accessed 30 May 2017.

[33] Thomas Graham, 'Can Russia and the United States Cooperate in Syria?', *Rethinking Russia Digest*, 26 September–9 October 2016, pp. 23–6, quotations at p. 24.

[34] Thomas F. Remington, 'Putin, Parliament, and Presidential Exploitation of the Terrorist Threat', *The Journal of Legislative Studies*, Vol. 15, Nos. 2–3, 2009, pp. 219–38.

recruitment efforts of terrorist organisations, as well as the struggle against cybercrime and cyber-espionage. The document noted Russia's dependence on foreign information technologies, which rendered Russia dependent on 'the geopolitical interests of foreign countries'. The document called for the establishment of 'a national system for managing the Russian segment of the internet' (known as Ru.net), raising fears that the hitherto remarkably free Russian cyber-sphere would be subject to increased regulation along Chinese lines. In fact, Russia planned to learn from Chinese experience on how to manage information spaces.[35] Already in 1995 SORM (System for Operative Investigative Activities) allowed the FSB to monitor telephone and internet communications, and regulations have been regularly tightened since then as part of the struggle against 'extremism'. In 2016 legislation required all internet service providers (ISPs) to store personal data on drives physically located on Russian territory, thus effectively blocking foreign internet services. The law (sponsored by Irina Yarovaya) forced mobile operators to store user data for six months, and to make it available to intelligence agencies without any special judicial procedure. The *Doctrine* warned that one of the main threats to Russia was 'the increase in opportunities that a series of foreign countries has to influence Russia's information infrastructure for military purposes', and talked of the expanded use of 'informational-psychological influences' by foreign intelligence services 'intended to destabilise' various regions of the world, including Russia. The *Doctrine* noted the discriminatory measures against Russian media abroad, and warned against the increased informational activity, targeting in particular 'young Russians, with the goal of undermining traditional Russian spiritual and moral values'. The *Doctrine* called for these threats to be neutralised, above all the 'informational-psychological activities aimed at disrupting the historical foundations and patriotic traditions associated with the defence of the motherland'.[36] In short, the *Doctrine* basically sought to detach Russia from the global web while developing a national system of internet management.

The New Globalism

At the Davos World Economic Forum (WEF) on 17 January 2017, Xi Jinping led a large delegation. His landmark speech argued that China

---

[35] Andrei Soldatov, 'Q & A: Russia, China Swapping Cybersecurity, Censorship Tips', RFE/RL, *Russia Report*, 4 December 2016. Andrei Soldatov (with Irina Borogan) is the author of *Red Web: The Struggle between Russia's Digital Dictators and New Online Revolutionaries* (New York, Public Affairs, 2015).

[36] *Doktrina informatsionnoi bezopasnosti Rossiiskoi Federatsii*, 5 December 2016, http://static.kremlin.ru/media/acts/files/0001201612060002.pdf, last accessed 9 June 2017.

could take the lead in globalisation, usurping America's role as the defender of free trade: 'Pursuing protectionism is like locking oneself in a dark room', he said. 'Wind and rain may be kept outside, but so is light and air.'[37] In other words, globalisation (or in more neutral parlance, international economic and societal integration), was no longer the unique property of the Atlantic system but a universal public good, which China was ready to defend. Xi also argued that the December 2015 Paris climate deal should not be derailed, in a warning shot against any attempt by the Trump administration to weaken its provisions.[38] In a wide-ranging programmatic speech at the UN in Geneva the next day, he called for a 'new model' of relations with the US, condemned 'trade protectionism and isolationism', and insisted that 'big countries should treat small countries as equals instead of acting as a hegemon imposing their will on others'. He called for multilateral action on climate change, terrorism, nuclear disarmament and other issues facing humanity, and promised that 'we will build a circle of friends across the whole world':

We will strive to build a new model of major country relations with the United States, a comprehensive strategic partnership of coordination with Russia, a partnership for peace, growth, reform and among different civilizations and a partnership of unity and cooperation with BRICS countries.[39]

China had long tried to avoid taking responsibility for managing global affairs, but Xi's ascension to the Chinese leadership marked a shift that rapidly gathered pace.[40] The WEF founder, Klaus Schwab, noted that Xi's presence was 'a sign of the shift from a unipolar world dominated by the US to a more multipolar system'.[41] In a speech in December 2016 the Chinese foreign minister, Wang Yi, mentioned 'global governance' nine times, not challenging the US geopolitically but calling for a thorough reform of the instruments of economic governance in the crucial spheres

---

[37] Larry Elliott and Graeme Wearden, 'China Can Take Lead on Globalisation as US Retreats under Trump, Says Xi', *Guardian*, 18 January 2017, p. 18.
[38] Tom Phillips, 'Paris Climate Deal Must Not Be Derailed, Says Xi', *Guardian*, 20 January 2017, p. 25.
[39] 'President Xi Speech to Davis in Full', 17 January 2017, www.weforum.org/agenda/20 17/01/full-text-of-xi-jinping-keynote-at-the-world-economic-forum, last accessed 30 May 2017; Tom Miles and Stephanie Nebehay, 'Xi Portrays China as Global Leader as Trump Era Looms', Reuters, 18 January 2017, http://uk.reuters.com/article/uk-china-usa-idUKKBN1522OO, last accessed 30 May 2017.
[40] The debates are perceptively analysed by Alexander Lomanov, 'Kitai: rastushchee ponimanie global'noi roli i otvetstvennosti', in V. V. Mikheev and V. G. Shvydko (eds.), *Transtikhookeanskaya bezopasnost': ierarkhiya sily i otvetstvennosti* (Moscow, IMEMO RAN, 2016), pp. 48–81.
[41] Elliott and Wearden, 'China Can Take Lead'.

of finance, trade and investment, energy, and development.[42] This was no longer the bipolar globalism of the post-war years, or the unipolar system of the first post-Cold War quarter-century, but a plural world in which international society (the institutions of global political and economic governance) were reclaimed as the patrimony of humanity. The Chinese were reshaping globalism for the common good.

This allowed Russia to break out from its post-Cold War strategic impasse and its stalemated historical situation. Russia's strategy of resistance was ultimately volitional rather than emanating from substantive empirical shifts in material realities. The lesson Putin drew from Gorbachev's and Yeltsin's relations with the Historical West was 'never to be weak, and never to appear weak: "the weak get beaten"'.[43] The anti-hegemonic strategy reflected a particular understanding of the international system, and was motivated by ideas and perceptions of Russia's appropriate status rather than a substantive material base. The dead end of the cold peace gave way to something new. This was not a 'new Cold War' (although in Europe and in US relations elements of this were restored), but a novel historical situation in which Russia looked to be a constitutive member of an alternative global order. It had failed to transform the Historical West into a Greater West, and the creation of a Greater Europe looked further away than ever, but Greater Eurasia developed rapidly. For the first time since the fall of communism the idea of a 'new world order' really was on the horizon, in the sense of the emergence of a transformative alternative world order. The hitherto subaltern powers found their voice and institutionalised a set of relations autonomous from the Atlantic system. They now had the resources to challenge the hegemonic 'liberal international order'. The goal was not to destroy the latter but to generate plural international relations at the horizontal level, while strengthening the autonomy of international society on the vertical axis. New transnational configurations emerged driven by economic growth and the erosion of traditional geopolitical alignments. This gave rise in Eurasia to what Kent E. Calder calls 'the new continentalism'.[44] This was not a Jowitt-style 'new world disorder', but the opposite: the emergence of an anti-hegemonic bloc that created a more plural and balanced world system.

[42] Xie Tao, 'Assessing the China Challenge for Trump's Presidency', Carnegie-Tsinghua, 18 January 2017, http://carnegieendowment.org/2017/01/18/assessing-china-challenge-for-trump-s-presidency-pub-67690, last accessed 30 May 2017.
[43] Trenin, *Should We Fear Russia?*, p. 27.
[44] Kent E. Calder, *The New Continentalism: Energy and Twenty-first Century Eurasian Geopolitics* (London and New Haven, Yale University Press, 2012).

Graham Allison describes the tension between an established power and a rising challenger as the 'Thucydides Trap'. Of the fifteen cases since 1500, eleven resulted in military conflict.[45] This occurs when the aggregate power of the challenger approaches that of the incumbent dominant power, the crossover point, typically but not always sparking tension and war. International relations theory calls this a 'power transition'. From the 1890s Germany was the challenger to Britain, in the end provoking the First World War. The end of the Soviet Union was one of these periods, and the international system transitioned from a bipolar structure into a unipolar mode dominated by the US. The shift at the time was a peaceful one, in large part because of Gorbachev's endeavours, but provoked tensions that have not yet been resolved. The main challenger today is obviously China, although there is considerable debate whether it really is approaching the threshold crossover point, but the danger of a Sino-American war is real.[46] Although palpably lacking the material resources, Russia nevertheless is also a challenger power. Russia refused to accept a subaltern status in the post-Cold War era, and pursued its vision of itself as a great power with Gaullist tenacity. This ideational consistency is rooted in Russia's identity politics, but also reflects the embedded institutional and elite structures inherited from the Soviet Union.

Russia is resigned to the fact that sanctions and counter-sanctions will become the norm. The Cold War bipolar system will not be restored, but neither will a new 'concert of powers' take its place because of the great variety of actors with different ways of exerting influence. The new system will be a 'dialectical combination of competition and interdependence'.[47] The old 'Historic West' (the US and its allies) is now balanced by 'Greater Eurasia' led by Russia and China, with other countries (notably Iran and Turkey) aligning selectively with either or both. The Atlantic system at the core of the Historic West came under unprecedented strain as a result of Brexit and Trump's election, exacerbating long-term trends towards a gradual loosening of Atlantic ties. On the other side, Greater Eurasia gradually assumed more delineated and institutionalised forms, although there were clear limits to the depth of integration processes. Greater Eurasia remains a general orientation with sufficient flexibility and economic potential to attract participants, but not so exclusive as to generate bloc discipline. Much rests on the fate of the Chinese economy. Comparisons are drawn

---

[45] Graham Allison, 'Avoiding Thucydides' Trap', *Financial Times*, 22 August 2012.

[46] Christopher Coker, *The Improbable War: China, the United States and the Logic of Great Power Conflict* (London, Hurst, 2014).

[47] Fyodor Lukyanov, 'The Goal is to Streamline Chaos and Rationalize Diversity', Valdai Discussion Club, 20 January 2016, http://valdaiclub.com/news/the-goal-is-to-streamline-chaos-and-rationalize-diversity/, last accessed 30 May 2017.

between the perceived threat from Japan in the 1980s, before the country entered a long period of stagnation.[48] There is the possibility that the same fate could befall China accompanied by scepticism that China will be able to translate its allegedly faltering economic strength into a consistent great power status.[49] At the global level, the BRICS was the most structured of the international groupings, but others, represented mostly in the G20, also contributed to shape debates about development and regional alignments. Russia now ranks itself among 'the rest', although it does not foreclose the option of becoming part of 'the West' if the strategic limitations of the cold peace period can be overcome and the West can be transformed to become something greater.

A disparate but nevertheless strengthening tide of anti-hegemonic arrangements and organisations began to emerge. This was nothing like as formalised or intense as its counterpart during the Cold War, since Russia lacked the attractive power, ideological conviction or economic resources of the USSR. It made no sense for countries wilfully to antagonise the Atlantic powers, with whom they were tied by so many trade and political relations. Nevertheless, the dangers of unipolarism were clear, accompanied by wars of choice. The creeping universalisation of American law and practices of universal jurisdiction represented a new type of power that threatened the sovereignty of states everywhere. In response, counter-hegemonic movements gained vitality and dynamism. The editors of the inaugural issue of *Rising Power Quarterly* note that global transformations were accompanied by

the rise of various actors that bring with themselves not only a re-ordering in the hierarchical structure of world politics, but more importantly a redistribution of the roles played by these actors positioned in different levels of this hierarchical structure. It is no longer only the great powers that set the rules of the governing system, but rather rising, emerging and middle powers started to have significant shares in the process of rebuilding the global architecture.[50]

In all of this, Russia was in the vanguard. Its attempts to join a transformed West had ended in failure, and instead the institutions and practices of the Historical West were reinforced. In response, Russia became one of the most active proponents of the creation of a non-West.

[48] Michael R. Auslin, *The End of the Asian Century: War, Stagnation, and the Risks to the World's Most Dynamic Region* (New Haven, Yale University Press, 2017).

[49] Stephen G. Brooks and William C. Wohlforth, 'The Once and Future Superpower', *Foreign Affairs*, Vol. 95, No. 3, 2016, pp. 91–104.

[50] Emel Parlar Dal and Ali Murat Kurşun, 'Foreword: The Launch of Rising Powers Quarterly', *Rising Powers Quarterly*, Vol. 1, No. 1, 2016, p. 7.

Conclusion

As he contemplated events at the end of 2016, Putin could draw a certain degree of satisfaction from the way that the tide of history appeared to be turning in his favour.[1] The election of an 'America first' president committed to transactional dealings meant that the values-based imperative, which Putin had always considered hypocritical and the grounds for double standards, would give way to a type of engagement in which Russia's concerns and interests would at last be recognised. Trump evidently would seek to peel Russia away from the nascent anti-hegemonic bloc, creating more room for Putin to manoeuvre, always a central concern. However, given his commitment to 'loyalty', it was highly unlikely that Putin would repudiate the intensified relationship with China. Russia remained neutral in the British referendum on EU membership, but the vote in favour of Brexit, alongside the continuing crisis of the euro and the refugee and migration pressures, meant that the EU would be preoccupied with its own problems and would have little time to continue its push into what Russia considered a region of 'privileged interests'. No official Russian document or speech ever spoke in favour of breaking-up the EU, but the rising tide of sovereignty-minded 'populists' of left and right across the continent inevitably found an ideological ally in Moscow. Russian attempts to reach a negotiated settlement in Syria had been rebuffed, in anticipation of Assad's swift fall, but now with Russian and Iranian support the regime in Damascus had stabilised, and was even able to recapture Aleppo in December 2016. Even Obama had changed his tune. In early 2014 he described Russia as a 'regional power' acting out of 'weakness', and later that year argued that 'Russia doesn't make anything. Immigrants aren't rushing to Moscow in search of opportunity', but he now called it a 'military superpower' with 'influence around the world'. He went on to note that 'in order for us to solve many big problems around the world, it is

[1] Cf. Sergei Karaganov, '2016 – A Victory of Conservative Realism', *Russia in Global Affairs*, 13 February 2017, http://eng.globalaffairs.ru/number/2016–A-Victory-of-Conservative-Realism-18585, last accessed 9 June 2017.

in our interest to work with Russia and obtain their cooperation'.[2] On top
of it all, Putin topped the Forbes power list, although Trump was named
Time's person of the year.

Russia was far from isolated, and instead had achieved one of Putin's –
and that of all previous Russian and Soviet leaders – key goals, namely, to
be reckoned with in the management of global affairs. Under Gorbachev
the basis shifted away from communist ideology to a new type of liberal
and humanitarian engagement outlined in the NPT. The aspiration in the
end was not just to put an end to what was increasingly perceived as a
futile and pointless Cold War, but to transcend the logic on which the
Cold War was fought – the endless realist quest for power and status. For
Gorbachev and his successors this meant a renewed orientation towards
the institutions of international society, notably the UN and the whole
framework of global humanitarian governance along with a commitment
to democracy and civil and human rights. It emphatically did not mean an
automatic alignment with the American-sponsored Atlantic system. In
Russian eyes, it meant an end of conflict with that system, but then both
would enter the post-Cold War order as cooperative partners equally
oriented to an international society that ultimately was bigger than both
of them. This was one reason why Article 15.4 of Russia's new constitution of December 1993 stated that '[g]enerally recognised principles and
norms of international law and the international treaties of the Russian
Federation are a constituent part of its legal system'. In other words,
Russian sovereignty was tempered by international norms. It was in this
framework that the Russian leadership sought to adapt not to Western
values and governance norms, but to what were considered universal
values and global norms. Russia's post-communist transformational project was not Westernisation but what in Gorbachevian parlance was
termed 'universal human values'.

In the event, the disintegration of the Soviet Union and the chaotic
Russia that emerged prompted Western talk of victory. In the early post-
Cold War years the institutions and states comprising the Atlantic system
adopted a benign view of Russia, and sought to assist its economic and
political development while securing its nuclear arsenal. However,
instead of the vaunted post-Cold War transformation of the international
system, the Kremlin perceived only an enlargement agenda of the existing
Atlantic order. The late Soviet and then the Russian leadership had
assumed that the world would become more plural (later advanced by

[2] The first comment in a speech delivered in the Netherlands on 25 March 2014, the second
in an interview with *The Economist* on 2 August 2014, and the third in a speech in Berlin on
17 November 2016, https://patrickarmstrong.ca/2016/11/21/obama-changes-his-mind-o
n-russia/, last accessed 30 May 2017.

Primakov and his successors through the formula of multipolarity), but instead a monist system was consolidated. Instead of the end of communism opening up debate about different types of political community and alternative ways of embedding market relations into the societal nexus, discourse became remarkably impoverished and monological. Globalisation and end of history narratives only reasserted the apparent victory of the 'liberal international order', instead of enriching the debate over varieties of capitalism and new ways of achieving the material and spiritual enrichment of communities globally through empowerment and equality.

An epistemological gap opened up between the Atlantic community and Russia, which in the end precipitated a breakdown of the European security order, a crisis with global implications. While official Russia was committed to the values of the Atlantic system, as evidenced in a continuing commitment to the OSCE, these were considered shared values rather than specifically 'Western'. In this spirit Russia joined the CoE, and endeavoured to develop equal relations with the EU. Putin in his early years was even willing to contemplate some sort of membership of NATO. However, the Atlantic system is more than just a community of values (despite much talk of its post-modern and post-sovereign character); it is also a hegemonic power system with American leadership at its core. By definition, Russia could only join this system as a subordinate and not an equal. The invitation to join was genuine and sincere, and, as far as the radical liberals in Russia are concerned, it would have provided a unique opportunity for Russia to transform itself into a working liberal democracy. But even other liberals, notably Kozyrev, found the terms of membership unacceptable. For ideational and sociological reasons, Russia could not join as a subaltern.[3] Competing visions of national identity shape Russian foreign policy, which its leaders ignore at their peril.[4] On one thing there was agreement: Russia could not trade its historic identity and great power status for membership of the Atlantic community. In sociological terms, only one of the four great epistemic-interest group communities in Russia, the liberals – and even this faction contained a strong strain of traditional statist thinking – were ready to accept this version of the post-Cold War settlement. The other three – the conservative-*siloviki*, the neo-traditionalists, and the Eurasianists – were agreed on nothing except that Russia was a great power and a geopolitical

---

[3] Morozov is right to note that much of Russia's model of modernity is European, but this was always considered not so much a borrowing as a common endeavour to create 'Europe', Morozov, *Russia's Postcolonial Identity*.
[4] Hopf, *Social Construction of Foreign Policy*.

and civilisational alternative to the West, although to various degrees they recognised the superiority of international society.

The competing narratives about the end of the Cold War are thus grounded in a profound interpretive gulf about the character of the international system. From this perspective, it is irrelevant whether the intentions of the Atlantic system were benign or malign – the issue was not the terms of its expansion, but the qualitative transformation of relations as a whole. In practical terms this may not have been so difficult. All it would have required is the creation of some substantive bridging institutions between Russia and the Atlantic community. In the security sphere a strengthened OSCE would have been a start, possibly along with the creation of a European security council. In political terms, some sort of pan-European commission encompassing Russia, the EU, Turkey and all the former Soviet states would have provided a platform for reconciliation and development, and started the process of Greater European integration. This would have required a reinvigorated continental vision of the Gaullist sort. The fundamental dynamic would no longer have been expansion but the transformation of the pan-European political community.[5] Instead, the positions hardened and the gulf between Russia and the Historical West widened. The Western powers were exasperated that their benign intentions could be construed as expansive in the aggressive sense; and Russia was increasingly frustrated by the Atlantic system's inexorable advance that seemed not only to negate Russia's concerns about changes in the power balance in its neighbourhood, but to delegitimise the language in which these concerns could be expressed. In the cold peace years there remained the residual belief that some way would be found of reconciling these differences, although the frustrations expressed by Putin in Munich in 2007 found their counterpart in the no less anguished discourse of Western leaders at Russia's apparent self-isolation and obtuse refusal to join one of the most successful alliances in history. In the end, as Kissinger notes, Putin convinced himself that the US was a structural rival: '[B]y "structural" I mean that he may very well believe that America defines its basic interest as weakening Russia.'[6] The sentiment worked the other way as well, and Russia became defined as a structural enemy.

Aspirations for greater European integration failed to find substantive institutional form. Instead, competing integration projects emerged that inevitably came into confrontation along the tradition line of fracture in 'frontline Europe'. On the one side the EU and its wider Europe project

---

[5] Cf. Andrew Linklater, *Transformation of Political Community: Ethical Foundations of the Post-Westphalian Era* (Cambridge, Polity, 1998).
[6] Goldberg, 'World Chaos and World Order'.

advanced to the East, even though accession for the post-Soviet states was not on the agenda, while on the other side the post-Soviet legacy integration projects gave way to more ambitious plans for Eurasian integration. The intensification of Eurasian integration plans reflected the stalemate in Russo-EU relations. The extension of the EU's wider Europe posed no immediate security or economic threat to Russia, but the absence of some sort of overarching mode of reconciliation meant that it was increasingly perceived as part of the unmediated enlargement of the Atlantic community, especially when accompanied by trans-democratic norm promotion strategies. The constructivist argument that if you identify someone as an enemy, in due course they will become one, works both ways. The notion of 'Russian aggression' was reinforced by the Ukraine crisis but had deep roots in the structure of post-Cold War international relations. Russia's frustration at what it perceived to be its strategic impasse provoked a constant rhetoric of resistance and challenge, which was inevitably seen by the Atlantic community as the rumblings of an angry and potentially dangerous adversary. The negative transcendence of the Cold War reinforced Russia's sense of having been boxed into a corner after 1989, whereas it considered itself a partner in the new system of international politics. This in turn gave rise to the narrative of Western persecution, 'Russophobia' and humiliation, reinforcing traditional narratives about the fundamental incompatibility between Russia and the West.

The 2014 events marked the culmination of processes that had been in train since the beginning of the post-Cold War era. The frustration and exasperations boiled over into open conflict in Ukraine. The year represented the end of illusions, and although characterised as a new Cold War by some, European developments were only part of a broader realignment in global politics. For Russia, the hitherto foundational principle of integration into a transformed Western community accompanied by the creation of some sort of Greater Europe from Lisbon to Vladivostok was over, at least for this generation. Russia remained a central trade and political interlocutor of the Atlantic system, but a new dynamic emerged based on an understanding that the Historical West would not be transformed into a Greater West, with Russia a core constitutive member. Instead, the long slow-burning shift towards the East was accelerated. The idea of Greater Eurasia with Russia at its centre was given institutional form within the framework of the EEU, but also included a number of other forms of integration and alignments that sustained the Greater Eurasian Partnership with Asian and other partners. The BRI provided economic muscle, working with the EEU and BRICS, complemented by Greater Asia aspirations, with the SCO at its heart. The deepening alignment meant that the earlier focus on relations with Germany and the US gave way to a new focus on relations with China.[7]

Attempts to integrate into the US-led order had failed, and alternative strategies were now pursued. Stuck in an impasse and subject to soft containment strategies, Russia and its allies began to push back and laid the foundations for a post-Western world order. Russia could work with the Historical West, but the window had closed on it joining. Russia was now ready to use hard power to defend its positions, 'first, to stop NATO's expansion into territories that Russia considers vital to its own security, thereby averting the large-scale war that expansion would inevitably have brought; and second, to forestall yet another illegitimate Western effort to bring about regime change, this time in Syria (where Russia has demonstrated both military might and diplomatic prowess)'.[8]

On this basis, despite the hesitancies and contradictions, Russia's assertion of an independent position in international affairs is justifiable, in the sense of being both reasonable and rational. The defence of the autonomy of international society and the creation of an anti-hegemonic alignment have the potential finally to create the transformative 'new world order' announced at the end of the Cold War. This ambition finds strong support not only in Russia, China and other countries ready to align with them, but also in many Western countries.

The renewed confrontation between Russia and the West is not a replay of the Cold War, although many of its institutional and ideational features, particularly in Europe, have been revived. Competition between the Atlantic community and Russia has become entrenched as the 'new normal', while the rudiments of an anti-hegemonic alignment has formed in the East. Profound shifts in global politics are taking place, reshaping the international system. In this context, it is more urgent than ever to understand the logic and dynamics of Russian foreign policy. International relations today are more perilous than at any time since 1989. The original Cold War was a regional confrontation with global implications, while the present confrontation is a global process with regional implications. New ways of managing conflict between what are emerging as two clearly delineated blocs are required, otherwise there is a real danger of an accidental slide into war. No 'new world order' has been formed, but the reshaping of the international system offers opportunities to resolve the unfinished agenda of 1989.

---

[7] Dmitri Trenin, 'Russia-China Entente Must Move Past Rhetoric', *Global Times*, 8 September 2016, www.globaltimes.cn/content/1005412.shtml, last accessed 30 May 2017.

[8] Sergei Karaganov, 'Mutual Assured Deterrence', Project Syndicate, 17 February 2017, www.project-syndicate.org/commentary/russia-role-in-new-world-order-by-sergei-karaganov-2017-02, last accessed 9 June 2017.

Select Bibliography

A Twenty-first Century Concert of Powers: Promoting Great Power Multilateralism for the Post-Atlantic Era, The 21st Century Concert Study Group, Peace Research Institute Frankfurt, 2014.

Abu-Lughod, Janet L., *Before European Hegemony: The World System AD 1250–1350* (New York, Oxford University Press, 1991).

Acharya, Amitav, *The End of American World Order* (Cambridge, Polity, 2014).

'Global International Relations (IR) and Regional Worlds: A New Agenda for International Studies', *International Studies Quarterly*, Vol. 58, No. 4, 2014, pp. 647–59.

'Advancing Global IR: Challenges, Contentions, and Contributions', *International Studies Review*, Vol. 18, No. 1, 2016, pp. 4–15.

Adomeit, Hannes, 'Germany's Russia Policy: From Sanctions to Nord Stream 2?', Transatlantic Academy 2015–16 Paper Series, No. 3, March 2016, www .transatlanticacademy.org/publications/germany%E2%80%99s-russia-pol icy-sanctions-nord-stream-2, last accessed 30 May 2017.

Afanas'ev, Yurii N. (ed.), *Inogo ne dano* (Moscow, Progress, 1988).

Aleksashenko, Sergey, *Evaluating Western Sanctions on Russia* (Washington, Atlantic Council, December 2016).

Alexander, Andrew, *America and the Imperialism of Ignorance: US Foreign Policy since 1945* (London, Biteback, 2012).

Allison, Roy, 'Russia Resurgent? Moscow's Campaign to "Coerce Georgia to Peace"', *International Affairs*, Vol. 84, No. 6, November 2008, pp. 1145–71.

'Russia and Syria: Explaining Alignment with a Regime in Crisis', *International Affairs*, Vol. 89, No. 4, 2013, pp. 795–823.

Russia, the West, and Military Intervention (Oxford, Oxford University Press, 2013).

'Russian "Deniable" Intervention in Ukraine: How and Why Russia Broke the Rules', *International Affairs*, Vol. 90, No. 6, 2014, pp. 1255–97.

Ambrosio, Thomas, *Challenging America's Global Preeminence: Russia's Quest for Multipolarity* (Farnham, Ashgate, 2005).

'The Architecture of Alignment: The Russia-China Relationship and International Agreements', *Europe-Asia Studies*, Vol. 69, No. 1, January 2017, pp. 110–56.

Amighini, Alessia (ed.), *China Dream: Still Coming True?* (Milan, Italian Institute for International Political Studies (ISPI), 2016).

Amsden, Alice H., *The Rise of 'the Rest': Challenges to the West from Late-Industrializing Economies* (New York, Oxford University Press, 2003).

Anderson, Perry, 'Two Revolutions: Rough Notes', *New Left Review*, No. 61, January–February 2010, pp. 59–96.

American Foreign Policy and Its Thinkers (London, Verso, 2014).

Arrighi, Giovanni, *The Long Twentieth Century: Money, Power and the Origins of Our Time* (London, Verso, 2009).

Ashford, Emma, 'Not-So-Smart Sanctions', *Foreign Affairs*, Vol. 95, No. 1, January–February 2016, pp. 114–23.

Atlantic Council, *The Kremlin's Trojan Horses* (Washington, November 2016).

Auslin, Michael R., *The End of the Asian Century: War, Stagnation, and the Risks to the World's Most Dynamic Region* (New Haven, Yale University Press, 2017).

Averre, Derek and Lance Davies, 'Russia, Humanitarian Intervention and the Responsibility to Protect: The Case of Syria', *International Affairs*, Vol. 91, No. 4, 2015, pp. 813–34.

Bacevich, Andrew J., *The Imperial Tense: Prospects and Problems of American Empire* (Lanham, Rowman and Littlefield, 2003).

Bacon, Edwin and Bettina Renz with Julian Cooper, *Securitising Russia: The Domestic Politics of Putin* (Manchester, Manchester University Press, 2006).

Baudet, Thierry, *The Significance of Borders: Why Representative Government and the Rule of Law Require Nation States* (Leiden, Brill, 2012).

Beckman, Peter R. and Paul. W. Crumlish, *The Nuclear Predicament: Nuclear Weapons in the Twenty-First Century*, 3rd edn (London, Pearson, 1999).

Belopolsky, Helen, *Russia and the Challengers: Russian Alignment with China, Iran and Iraq in the Unipolar Era* (Basingstoke, Palgrave Macmillan, 2009).

Bickerton, Christopher, *European Integration: From Nation States to Member States* (Oxford, Oxford University Press, 2012).

Bieber, Florian, 'The Serbia-Kosovo Agreements: An EU Success Story?', *Review of Central and East European Law*, Vol. 40, Nos. 3–4, 2015, pp. 285–319.

Bisley, Nick, *The End of the Cold War and the Causes of the Soviet Collapse* (Basingstoke, Palgrave, 2004).

Great Powers in the Changing International Order (Boulder, Lynne Rienner, 2012).

Black, J. L., *Russia Faces NATO Expansion: Bearing Gifts or Bearing Arms?* (Lanham, Rowman and Littlefield, 2000).

Vladimir Putin and the New World Order (Lanham, Rowman and Littlefield, 2004).

The Return of the Cold War: Ukraine, the West and Russia (London, Routledge, 2016).

Bordachev, Timofei, 'The Great Win-Win Game', *Russia in Global Affairs*, No. 4, October–December 2016, pp. 106–15.

Breedlove, Philip M., 'NATO's Next Act: How to Handle Russia and Other Threats', *Foreign Affairs*, Vol. 95, No. 4, July–August 2016, pp. 96–105.

Brooks, Stephen G. and William C. Wohlforth, *World Out of Balance: International Relations and the Challenge of American Primacy* (Princeton and Oxford, Princeton University Press, 2008).

America Abroad: The United States' Global Role in the 21st Century (New York, Oxford University Press, 2016).

'The Once and Future Superpower', *Foreign Affairs*, Vol. 95, No. 3, 2016, pp. 91–104.

Brown, Archie, *The Gorbachev Factor* (Oxford, Oxford University Press, 1996).

'Gorbachev, Lenin, and the Break with Leninism', *Demokratizatsiya*, Vol. 15, No. 2, 2007, pp. 230–44.

Browning, Christopher, 'Reassessing Putin's Project: Reflections on IR Theory and the West', *Problems of Post-Communism*, Vol. 55, No. 5, September–October 2008, pp. 3–13.

Brzezinski, Zbigniew, 'The Premature Partnership', *Foreign Affairs*, Vol. 73, No. 2, March–April 1994, pp. 67–82.

The Grand Chessboard: American Primacy and its Geostrategic Imperatives (New York, Basic Books, 1997).

Bugajski, Janusz, *Cold Peace: Russia's New Imperialism* (Westport, Greenwood Press, 2004).

Bull, Hedley, *The Anarchical Society: A Study of Order in World Politics* (Oxford, Oxford University Press, 1995[1977]).

Bull, Hedley and Adam Watson, *The Expansion of International Society* (Oxford, Oxford University Press, 1984).

Burrows, Mathew and Robert A. Manning, *Kissinger's Nightmare: How an Inverted US-China-Russia May be a Game-Changer* (Moscow, Valdai Paper No. 33, November 2015).

Buzan, Barry, *An Introduction to the English School of International Relations* (Cambridge, Polity, 2014).

'The "Standard of Civilisation" as an English School Concept', *Millennium*, Vol. 42, No. 3, 2014, pp. 576–94.

Buzan, Barry and Ole Waever, *Regions and Powers: The Structure of International Security* (Cambridge, Cambridge University Press, 2003).

Calder, Kent E., *The New Continentalism: Energy and Twenty-first Century Eurasian Geopolitics* (London and New Haven, Yale University Press, 2012).

Calleo, David P., *Rethinking Europe's Future* (Princeton, Princeton University Press, 2003).

Follies of Power: America's Unipolar Fantasy (Cambridge, Cambridge University Press, 2009).

Carr, E. H., *The Twenty Years' Crisis, 1919–1939: An Introduction to the Study of International Relations*, Reissued with a New Introduction and additional material by Michael Cox (London, Palgrave, 2001[1939]).

Casier, Tom, 'The EU-Russia Strategic Partnership: Challenging the Normative Argument', *Europe-Asia Studies*, Vol. 65, No. 7, September 2013, pp. 1377–95.

Center for Strategic and International Studies, *The Kremlin Playbook: Understanding Russian Influence in Central and Eastern Europe* (Washington, CSIS, October 2016).

Cerny, Philip G., 'The Limits of Global Governance: Transnational Neopluralism in a Complex World', in Rafaelle Marchetti (ed.), *Partnerships in International Policymaking: Civil Society and Public Institutions in European and Global Affairs* (Basingstoke and New York, Palgrave Macmillan, 2016), pp. 31–47.

Chandra, Amresh, 'Strategic Triangle among Russia, India and China: Challenges and Prospects', *Journal of Peace Studies*, Vol. 17, No. 2-3, April–September 2010, pp. 40–60.

Charap, Sam and Timothy Colton, *Everyone Loses: The Ukraine Crisis and the Ruinous Contest for Post-Soviet Eurasia* (London, Routledge/Adelphi, 2016).

Chebankova, Elena, 'Contemporary Russian Conservatism', *Post-Soviet Affairs*, Vol. 32, No. 1, 2016, pp. 28–54.

Clark, Christopher, *The Sleepwalkers: How Europe Went to War in 1914* (London, Penguin, 2013).

Clinton, Hillary, 'America's Pacific Century', *Foreign Policy*, 11 October 2011, http://foreignpolicy.com/2011/10/11/americas-pacific-century/, last accessed 9 June 2017.

Hard Choices: A Memoir (New York, Simon and Schuster, 2014).

Clunan, Anne L., *The Social Construction of Russia's Resurgence: Aspirations, Identity, and Security Interests* (Baltimore, Johns Hopkins University Press, 2009).

Cockburn, Patrick, *Chaos and Caliphate: Jihadis and the West in the Struggle for the Middle East* (New York and London, OR Books, 2016).

Cohen, Stephen F., *Failed Crusade: America and the Tragedy of Post-Communist Russia* (New York, W. W. Norton, 2000).

Soviet Fates and Lost Alternatives: From Stalinism to the New Cold War (New York, Columbia University Press, 2009).

Why Cold War Again? How America Lost Post-Soviet Russia (London and New York, I. B. Tauris, 2017).

Coker, Christopher, *Twilight of the West* (Boulder, Westview Press, 1997).

The Improbable War: China, the United States and the Logic of Great Power Conflict (London, Hurst, 2014).

Colas, Alejandro and Richard Saull, *The War on Terrorism and the American 'Empire' after the Cold War* (London, Routledge, 2005).

Connolly, Richard, 'The Empire Strikes Back: Economic Statecraft and the Securitisation of Political Economy in Russia', *Europe-Asia Studies*, Vol. 68, No. 4, June 2016, pp. 750–73.

'Hard Times? Defence Spending and the Russian Economy', *Russian Analytical Digest*, No. 196, 23 December 2016, pp. 2–5.

'Russia Economic Power', in Natasha Kuhrt and Valentina Feklyunina (eds.), *Assessing Russia's Power: A Report* (King's College London and Newcastle University, 2017), pp. 21–4.

Connolly, Richard and Cecilie Sendstad, *Russia's Role as an Arms Exporter* (London, Chatham House Research Paper, March 2017).

Conradi, Peter, *Who Lost Russia? How the World Entered a New Cold War* (London, Oneworld, 2017).

Cooper, Robert, *The Postmodern State and the World Order* (London, Demos, 1996).

The Breaking of Nations: Order and Chaos in the Twenty-first Century (New York, Atlantic Monthly Press, 2003).

Copsey, Nathaniel, *Rethinking the European Union* (London, Palgrave Macmillan, 2015).

Copsey, Nathaniel and Karolina Pomorska, 'The Influence of Newer Member States in the European Union: The Case of Poland and the Eastern Partnership', *Europe-Asia Studies*, Vol. 66, No. 3, May 2014, pp. 421–43.

Cottey, Andrew, *Security in 21st Century Europe*, 2nd edn (Basingstoke, Palgrave Macmillan, 2013).

Cox, Robert W., 'Social Forces, States and World Orders: Beyond International Relations Theory', *Millennium: Journal of International Studies*, Vol. 10, No. 2, 1981, pp. 126–55.

Cunliffe, Philip, 'The Doctrine of the "Responsibility to Protect" as a Practice of Political Exceptionalism', *European Journal of International Relations*, Vol. 23, No. 2, 2017, pp. 466–86.

Darczewska, Jolanta and Piotr Żochowski, *Russophobia in the Kremlin's Strategy: A Weapon of Mass Destruction*, Warsaw, Centre for Eastern Studies, OSW Point of View No. 56, October 2015.

David, Maxine, 'EU-Russia Relations: Effects of the 2014 Ukraine Crisis', *Russian Analytical Digest*, No. 158, December 2014, pp. 5–8.

Dawisha, Karen, 'Is Russia's Foreign Policy That of a Corporatist-Kleptocratic Regime?', *Post-Soviet Affairs*, Vol. 27, No. 4, 2011, pp. 331–65.

Putin's Kleptocracy: Who Owns Russia? (New York, Simon and Schuster, 2014).

DeHaas, Marcel, *Russian Security Policy under Putin* (London, Routledge, 2010).

Deyermond, Ruth, 'The Uses of Sovereignty in Twenty-first Century Russian Foreign Policy', *Europe-Asia Studies*, Vol. 68, No. 6, 2016, pp. 957–84.

Diesen, Glenn, *EU and NATO Relations with Russia: After the Collapse of the Soviet Union* (Aldershot, Ashgate, 2015).

Russia's Geoeconomic Strategy for a Greater Eurasia (London, Routledge, 2017).

Diez, Thomas, 'Constructing the Self and Changing Others: Reconsidering "Normative Power Europe"', *Millennium: Journal of International Studies*, Vol. 33, No. 3, 2005, pp. 613–36.

'Normative Power as Hegemony', *Cooperation and Conflict*, Vol. 48, No. 2, 2013, pp. 194–210.

Dorrien, Gary, *The Neoconservative Mind: Politics, Culture, and the War of Ideology* (Philadelphia, Temple University Press, 1993).

Imperial Designs: Neoconservatism and the New Pax Americana (London and New York, Routledge, 2004).

Dower, John W., *Embracing Defeat: Japan in the Wake of World War II* (New York, Norton, 2000).

Doyle, Michael W., *Ways of War and Peace: Realism, Liberalism and Socialism* (New York, W. W. Norton, 1997).

Liberal Peace: Selected Essays (London, Routledge, 2012).

Dragneva, Rilka and Kataryna Wolczuk (eds.), *Eurasian Economic Integration: Law, Policy and Politics* (Cheltenham, Edward Elgar, 2013).

'The EU-Ukraine Association Agreement and the Challenges of Inter-Regionalism', *Review of Central and East European Law*, Vol. 39, Nos. 3–4, 2014, pp. 213–44.

Ukraine between the EU and Russia: The Integration Challenge (London, Palgrave Macmillan, 2015).

Dugin, Aleksandr, *Novaya formula Putina: osnovy eticheskoi politiki* (Moscow, Algoritm, 2014).

Dunne, Tim and Christian Reut-Smith (eds.), *The Globalization of International Society* (Oxford, Oxford University Press, 2017).

Dutkiewicz, Piotr and Richard Sakwa (eds.), *Eurasian Integration: The View from Within* (London and New York, Routledge, 2015).

Ellman, Michael and Vladimir Kontorovich (eds.), *The Destruction of the Soviet Economic System: An Insiders' History* (New York, M. E. Sharpe, 1998).

Emel, Parlar Dal, and Ali Murat Kurşun, 'Foreword: The Launch of Rising Powers Quarterly', *Rising Powers Quarterly*, Vol. 1, No. 1, 2016, pp. 7–11.

Engström, Maria, 'Contemporary Russian Messianism and New Russian Foreign Policy', *Contemporary Security Policy*, Vol. 35, No. 3, 2014, pp. 356–79.

European Union, *Shared Vision: Common Action: A Stronger Europe: A Global Strategy for the European Union's Foreign and Security Policy*, June 2016, http://europa.eu/globalstrategy/en, last accessed 30 May 2017.

Evangelista, Matthew, *Unarmed Forces: The Transnational Movement to End the Cold War* (Cornell, Cornell University Press, 2002).

Falk, Richard, *The Declining World Order: America's Imperial Geopolitics* (London, Routledge, 2004).

Feigenbaum, Evan A., 'China and the World: Dealing with a Reluctant Power', *Foreign Affairs*, Vol. 96, No. 1, January–February 2017, pp. 33–40.

Feklyunina, Valentina, 'Soft Power and Identity: Russia, Ukraine and the "Russian World(s)"', *European Journal of International Relations*, Vol. 22, No. 4, 2016, pp. 773–96.

Ferguson, Niall, *Kissinger 1923–1968: The Idealist* (London, Allen Lane, 2015).

Flockhart, Trine, 'The Coming Multi-Order World', *Contemporary Security Policy*, Vol. 37, No. 1, 2016, pp. 3–30.

Foglesong, David S., *The American Mission and the 'Evil Empire': The Crusade for a 'Free Russia' Since 1881* (Cambridge, Cambridge University Press, 2007).

Forsberg, Tuomas and Hiski Haukkala, *The European Union and Russia* (London, Palgrave, 2016).

Forsberg, Tuomas and Graeme Herd, 'Russia and NATO: From Windows of Opportunities to Closed Doors', *Journal of Contemporary European Studies*, Vol. 23, No. 1, pp. 41–57.

Foucault, Michel, 'Polemics, Politics and Problematizations', interview with Paul Rabinow in May 1984, in Paul Rabinow (ed.), *Essential Works of Foucault*, Vol. 1, Ethics (New York, The New Press, 1998).

Foxall, Andrew, *Britain's Useful Idiots: Britain's Left, Right and Russia* (London, Henry Jackson Society, October 2016).

Fukuyama, Francis, 'The End of History', *The National Interest*, No. 16, Summer 1989, pp. 3–17.

The End of History and the Last Man (New York, Free Press, 1992).

Furman, Ekaterina and Alexander Libman, 'Europeanisation and the Eurasian Economic Union', in Piotr Dutkiewicz and Richard Sakwa (eds.), *Eurasian*

Integration: The View from Within (London and New York, Routledge, 2015), pp. 173–192.

Fu Ying, *Are China and Russia Axis or Partners?* (Beijing, 2016).

'How China Sees Russia: Beijing and Moscow are Close, but Not Allies', *Foreign Affairs*, Vol. 95, No. 1, January–February 2016, pp. 96–105.

Garten, Jeffrey E., *A Cold Peace: America, Japan, Germany, and the Struggle for Supremacy* (New York, The Twentieth Century Fund/Times Books, 1992).

Garthoff, Raymond L. *The Great Transition: American-Soviet Relations and the End of the Cold War* (Washington, Brookings Institution Press, 1994).

Gates, Robert, *Duty: Memoirs of a Secretary at War* (London, W. H. Allen, 2014).

Geis, Anna, '"The Concert of Democracies": Why Some States are More Equal than Others', *International Politics*, Vol. 50, No. 2, 2013, pp. 257–77.

Gerasimov, Valerii, 'Tsennost' nauki i predvidenii', *Voenno-promyshlennyi kur'er*, No. 8, 27 February 2013, http://vpk-news.ru/articles/14632, last accessed 30 May 2017.

'Mir na granyakh voiny', *Voenno-promyshlennyi kur'er*, No. 10, 15 March 2017, http://vpk-news.ru/articles/35591, last accessed 9 June 2017.

Geuss, Raymond, *Philosophy and Real Politics* (Princeton and Oxford, Princeton University Press, 2008).

Gilpin, Robert, *War and Change in World Politics* (Cambridge, Cambridge University Press, 1981).

'The Theory of Hegemonic War', *Journal of Interdisciplinary History*, Vol. 18, No. 4, 1988, pp. 591–613.

Goldgeier, James M., 'NATO Expansion: Anatomy of a Decision', *Washington Quarterly*, Vol. 21, No. 1, Winter 1998, pp. 85–102.

Not Whether but When: The US Decision to Enlarge NATO (Washington, Brookings, 1999).

Goldgeier, James M. and Michael McFaul, *Power and Purpose: US Policy toward Russia after the Cold War* (Washington, Brookings Institution, 2003).

Gong, Gerrit W., *The Standard of 'Civilization' in International Society* (Oxford, Clarendon Press, 1984).

Gooding, John, 'Gorbachev and Democracy', *Soviet Studies*, Vol. 42, No. 2, 1990, pp. 195–231.

Gorbachev, M. S., *Perestroika: New Thinking for Our Country and the World* (London, Collins, 1987).

Gorbachev, Mikhail and Daisaku Ikeda, *Moral Lessons of the Twentieth Century: Gorbachev and Ikeda on Buddhism and Communism* (London, I. B. Tauris, 2005).

Gorlizki, Yoram and Oleg Khlevniuk, *Cold Peace: Stalin and the Soviet Ruling Circle, 1945–1953* (New York, Oxford University Press, 2004).

Grachev, Andrei, *Gorbachev's Gamble: Soviet Foreign Policy and the End of the Cold War* (Cambridge, Polity, 2008).

Gramsci, Antonio, *Selections from the Prison Notebooks*, edited and translated by Quintin Hoare and Geoffrey Nowell Smith (London, Lawrence and Wishart, 1971).

Grant, Thomas D., *Aggression against Ukraine: Territory, Responsibility, and International Law* (New York, Palgrave Macmillan, 2015).

Gromyko, Alexei, 'Smaller or Greater Europe?', *Revista di Studi Politici Internazionali*, Vol. 81, Issue 324, October–December 2014, pp. 517–26.

'Russia, the US, and Smaller Europe (the EU): Competition for Leadership in a Polycentric World', Institute of Europe, Russian Academy of Sciences, Working Paper, No. 14, 2015. The Russian version is published as Aleksei Gromyko, 'Rossiya, SShA, Malaya Evropa (ES): Konkurentsiya za liderstvo v mire politsentrichnosti', *Sovremennaya Evropa*, No. 4, 2015, pp. 5–14.

Gromyko, Alexei A. and V. P. Fëdorova (eds.), *Bol'shaya Evropa: Idei, real'nost', perspektivy* (Moscow, Ves' mir, 2014).

Haas, Richard, 'The Unraveling: How to Respond to a Disordered World', *Foreign Affairs*, Vol. 93, No. 6, November–December 2014, pp. 70–9.

Haine, Jean-Yves, 'A New Gaullist Moment? European Bandwagoning and International Polarity', *International Affairs*, Vol. 91, No. 5, 2015, pp. 991–1008.

Hansen, Randall (ed.), Special Issue, 'Europe's Crisis: Background, Dimensions, Solutions', *West European Politics*, Vol. 37, No. 6, November 2014.

Hardt, Michael and Antonio Negri, *Empire* (Cambridge, Harvard University Press, 2001).

Multitude: War and Democracy in the Age of Empire (London, Penguin, 2005).

Harries, Owen, 'The Collapse of "The West"', *Foreign Affairs*, Vol. 72, No. 4, 1993, pp. 41–53.

Harvey, David, *The New Imperialism* (Oxford, Oxford University Press, 2005).

Hast, Susanna, *Spheres of Influence in International Relations: History, Theory and Politics* (Farnham, Ashgate, 2014).

Haukkala, Hiski, 'A Norm-Maker or a Norm-Taker? The Changing Normative Parameters of Russia's Place in Europe', in Ted Hopf (ed.), *Russia's European Choice* (Basingstoke, Palgrave Macmillan, 2008), pp. 35–56.

'Russian Reactions to the European Neighbourhood Policy', *Problems of Post-Communism*, Vol. 55, No. 5, September–October 2008, pp. 40–8.

'The European Union as a Regional Normative Hegemon: The Case of European Neighbourhood Policy', *Europe-Asia Studies*, Vol. 60, No. 9, November 2008, pp. 1601–22.

'Lost in Translation? Why the EU has Failed to Influence Russia's Development', *Europe-Asia Studies*, Vol. 61, No. 10, December 2009, pp. 1757–75.

The EU-Russia Strategic Partnership: The Limits of Post-Sovereignty in International Relations (London and New York, Routledge, 2010).

'From Cooperative to Contested Europe? The Conflict in Ukraine as a Culmination of a Long-Term Crisis in EU-Russia Relations', *Journal of Contemporary European Studies*, Vol. 23, No. 1, 2015, pp. 25–40.

Hazzard, Shirley, *Defeat of an Ideal: Self-Destruction of the United Nations* (London, Macmillan, 1973).

Headley, James, 'Is Russia Out of Step with European Norms? Assessing Russia's Relationship to European Identity, Values and Norms through the Issue of Self Determination', *Europe-Asia Studies*, Vol. 64, No. 3, 2012, pp. 427–47.

'Challenging the EU's Claims to Moral Authority: Russian Talk of "Double Standards"', *Asia Europe Journal*, Vol. 13, No. 3, 2015, pp. 297–307.

Hill, Fiona and Clifford Gaddy, *Mr. Putin: Operative in the Kremlin*, new and expanded edn (Washington, Brookings Institution Press, 2015).

Hill, William H., *Russia, the Near Abroad and the West: Lessons from the Moldova-Transdniestria Conflict* (Washington, Woodrow Wilson Center Press and Baltimore, The Johns Hopkins University Press, 2012).

Hobson, John M., *The Eurocentric Conception of World Politics: Western International Theory, 1760–2010* (Cambridge, Cambridge University Press, 2012).

Hopf, Ted, *Social Construction of Foreign Policy: Identities and Foreign Policies, Moscow, 1955 and 1999* (Cornell, NY, Cornell University Press, 2002).

(ed.), *Russia's European Choice* (Basingstoke, Palgrave Macmillan, 2008).

Horvath, Robert, *Putin's 'Preventative Counter-Revolution': Post-Soviet Authoritarianism and the Spectre of Velvet Revolution* (London and New York, Routledge, 2013).

Howard, R. T., *France's Secret Wars with Britain and America, 1945–2016* (London, Biteback, 2016).

Hufbauer, Gary Clyde and Jeffrey J. Schott, *Economic Sanctions Reconsidered*, 3rd revised edn (Washington, Peterson Institute, 2009).

Hughes, James, 'Russia and the Secession of Kosovo: Power, Norms and the Failure of Multilateralism', *Europe-Asia Studies*, Vol. 65, No. 5, 2013, pp. 992–1016.

Huntington, Samuel P., 'The Clash of Civilizations?', *Foreign Affairs*, Vol. 72, No. 3, Summer 1993, pp. 23–49.

The Clash of Civilizations and the Remaking of World Order (New York, Simon and Schuster, 1996).

Hurrell, Andrew, 'Hegemony, Liberalism and Global Order: What Space for Would-be Great Powers?', *International Affairs*, Vol. 82, No. 1, 2006, pp. 1–19.

On Global Order: Power, Values, and the Constitution of International Society (Oxford, Oxford University Press, 2007).

Hyde-Price, Adrian, '"Normative" Power Europe: A Realist Critique', *Journal of European Public Policy*, Vol. 13, No. 2, 2006, pp. 217–34.

Ikenberry, G. John, *Liberal Order and Imperial Ambition: Essays on American Power and International Order* (Cambridge, Polity, 2004).

'The Future of the Liberal World Order', *Foreign Affairs*, Vol. 90, No. 3, May–June 2011, pp. 56–68.

Liberal Leviathan: The Origins, Crisis, and Transformation of the American World Order (Princeton, Princeton University Press, 2011).

Jankovski, Aleksandar, 'Russia and the United States: On Irritants, Friction, and International Order or What We Can Learn from Hedley Bull', *International Politics*, Vol. 53, No. 6, 2016, pp. 727–51.

Jervis, Robert, *Perception and Misperception in International Politics* (Princeton, Princeton University Press, 1976).

Johnson, Chalmers, *Blowback: The Costs and Consequences of American Empire* (London, Sphere, 2002).

The Sorrows of Empire: Militarism, Secrecy, and the End of the Republic (London, Verso, 2004).

Jones, Bruce, *Still Ours to Lead: America, Rising Powers, and the Tension between Rivalry and Restraint* (Washington, Brookings Institution Press, 2014).

Jowitt, Ken, *New World Disorder: The Leninist Extinction* (Berkeley, University of California Press, 1992).

Juncos, Ana E. and Richard Whitman, 'Europe as a Regional Actor: Neighbourhood Lost?', *The JCMS Annual Review of the European Union in 2014* 53, September 2015, pp. 200–15.

Kaczmarski, Marcin, *Russia-China Relations in the Post-Crisis International Order* (London and New York, Routledge, 2015).

An Essential Partner in the Background: Europe in China's Policy During the Rule of Xi Jinping, Warsaw, Centre for Eastern Studies, OSW Studies No. 56, April 2016.

'The Asymmetric Partnership? Russia's Turn to China', *International Politics*, Vol. 53, No. 3, 2016, pp. 415–34.

Kagan, Robert, *Of Paradise and Power: America and Europe in the New World Order* (New York, Knopf Doubleday, 2007).

The Return of History and the End of Dreams (London, Atlantic Books, 2008).

Kagan, Robert and William Kristol (eds.), *Present Dangers: Crisis and Opportunity in American Foreign and Defense Policy* (New York and London, Encounter Books, 2000).

Kailitz, Steffen and Andreas Umland, 'Why Fascists Took Over the Reichstag but Have Not Captured the Kremlin: A Comparison of Weimar Germany and Post-Soviet Russia', *Nationalities Papers*, Vol. 45, No. 2, 2017, pp. 206–21.

Kalb, Marvin, *Imperial Gamble: Putin, Ukraine, and the New Cold War* (Washington, Brookings Institution Press, 2015).

Kant, Immanuel, 'Perpetual Peace: A Philosophical Sketch', in *Kant: Political Writings*, edited by Hans Reiss, 2nd enlarged edn (Cambridge, Cambridge University Press, 1991), pp. 93–130.

Kaplan, Robert D., 'Eurasia's Coming Anarchy: The Risks of Chinese and Russian Weakness', *Foreign Affairs*, Vol. 92, No. 2, March–April 2016, pp. 33–41.

'Missiles in Europe: Back to the Future?', *Russia in Global Affairs*, July–August 2016, http://eng.globalaffairs.ru/pubcol/Missiles-in-Europe-Back-to-the-Future-18267, last accessed 30 May 2017.

Karaganov, Sergei and Igor Yurgens (eds.), *Rossiya vs Evropa: Protivostoyane ili Soyuz* (Moscow, Astrel', 2009).

Kasparov, Garry with Mig Greengard, *Winter is Coming: Why Vladimir Putin and the Enemies of the Free World Must be Stopped* (London, Atlantic Books, 2015).

Katzenstein, Peter J., *A World of Regions: Asia and Europe in the American Imperium* (Cornell and London, Cornell University Press, 2005).

Katusa, Marin, *The Colder War: How the Global Energy Trade Slipped from America's Grasp* (London, John Wiley and Sons, 2014).

Kennedy, Paul, *The Rise and Fall of the Great Powers: Economic Change and Military Conflict from 1500 and 2000* (London, Unwin Hyman, 1988).

Keohane, Robert, *After Hegemony: Cooperation and Discord in the World* (Princeton, Princeton University Press, 1984).

Kiely, Ray, *Empire in the Age of Globalisation: US Hegemony and Neo-Liberal Disorder* (London, Pluto Press, 2005).

King, Charles, *The Black Sea: A History* (Oxford, Oxford University Press, 2004).

Kissinger, Henry, *Diplomacy* (New York, Simon and Schuster, 1995).

World Order: Reflections on the Character of Nations and the Course of History (London, Allen Lane, 2014).

Klein, Margarete, *Russia's Military: On the Rise?*, Washington, Transatlantic Academy, 2015–16 Paper Series, No. 2.

Klinke, Ian, 'Postmodern Geopolitics? The European Union Eyes Russia', *Europe-Asia Studies*, Vol. 64, No. 5, 2012, pp. 929–47.

Kokoshin, Andrei, *Real'nyi suverenitet v sovremennoi miropoliticheskoi sistemy*, 3rd edn (Moscow, Evropa, 2006).

Kolstø, Pål, 'Crimea vs. Donbas: How Putin Won Russian Nationalist Support – and Lost it Again', *Slavic Review*, Vol. 75, No. 3, Fall 2016, pp. 702–25.

Kolstø, Pål and Helge Blakkisrud (eds.), *The New Russian Nationalism: Imperialism, Ethnicity and Authoritarianism 2000–2015* (Edinburgh, Edinburgh University Press, 2016).

Korolev, Alexander, 'Russia's Reorientation to Asia: Causes and Strategic Implications', *Pacific Affairs*, Vol. 89, No. 1, March 2016, pp. 53–73.

Kostanyan, Hrant (ed.), *Assessing European Neighbourhood Policy: Perspectives from the Literature* (Brussels, CEPS, and London, Rowman and Littlefield, 2017).

Kozhanov, Nikolay, *Russia and the Syrian Conflict: Moscow's Domestic, Regional and Strategic Interests* (Berlin and London, Gerlach Press, 2016).

Kozyrev, Andrei, 'Partnership or Cold Peace?', *Foreign Policy*, No. 99, Summer 1995, pp. 3–14.

Kramer, Mark, 'The Myth of a No-NATO-Enlargement Pledge to Russia', *Washington Quarterly*, Vol. 32, No. 2, 2009, pp. 39–61.

Kremenyuk, Viktor, *Uroki kholodnoi voiny* (Moscow, Aspekt Press, 2015).

Krickovic, Andrej, 'Catalyzing Conflict: The Internal Dimension of the Security Dilemma', *Journal of Global Security Studies*, Vol. 1, No. 2, May 2016, pp. 111–26.

Krickovic, Andrej and Maxim Bratersky, 'Benevolent Hegemon, Neighbourhood Bully, or Regional Security Provider? Russia's Efforts to Promote Regional Integration after the 2013–2014 Ukraine Crisis', *Eurasian Geography and Economics*, Vol. 57, No. 2, 2016, pp. 180–202.

Krickovic, Andrej and Yuval Weber, 'How Can Russia Contribute to our Understanding of Change in World Politics?', paper delivered to the ISA conference, Baltimore, 25 February 2017.

Kristensen, Hans M., Matthew McKinzie and Theodore A. Postol, 'How US Nuclear Force Modernization is Undermining Strategic Stability: The Burst-Height Compensating Super-Fuze', *Bulletin of the Atomic Scientists*, 1 March 2017, http://thebulletin.org/how-us-nuclear-force-modernization-undermin ing-strategic-stability-burst-height-compensating-super10578, last accessed 30 May 2017.

Kubálková, Vendulka and A. A. Cruickshank, *Thinking about Soviet 'New Thinking'* (Berkeley, University of California Press, 1989).

Kühn, Ulrich, and Anna Péczeli, 'Russia, NATO, and the INF Treaty', *Strategic Studies Quarterly*, Spring 2017, pp. 66–99.

Kuhrt, Natasha, *Russian Policy towards China and Japan: The El'tsin and Putin Periods* (London, Routledge, 2011).

Kupchan, Charles A., *No One's World: The West, The Rising Rest, and the Coming Global Turn* (New York, Oxford University Press, 2012).

Kuus, Merje, *Geopolitics Reframed: Security and Identity in Europe's Eastern Enlargement* (Basingstoke, Palgrave Macmillan, 2007).

Kwang Ho Chun, *The BRICs Superpower Challenge* (Farnham, Ashgate, 2013).

Lane, David and Vsevolod Samokhvalov (eds.), 'Eurasia in a Global Context', *special issue of European Politics and Society*, Vol. 17, No. S1, 2016.

Lanxin Xiang, 'China and the International "Liberal" (Western) Order', in T. Flockhart et al. (eds.), *Liberal Order in a Post-Western World* (Washington, Transatlantic Academy, May 2014), pp. 107–120.

'The Peak Moment for China-Russia Ties', *Russia in Global Affairs*, No. 3, July–Sept. 2016, pp. 152–6.

Larson, Deborah Welch and Alexei Shevchenko, 'Shortcut to Greatness: The New Thinking and the Revolution in Soviet Foreign Policy', *International Organization*, Vol. 57, No. 1, 2003, pp. 77–109.

Laruelle, Marlene, *Russian Eurasianism: An Ideology of Empire*, translated by Mischa Gabowitsch (Washington, Woodrow Wilson Center Press; Baltimore, The Johns Hopkins University Press, 2008).

Russian Nationalism and the National Reassertion of Russia (London, Routledge, 2009).

The 'Russian World': Russia's Soft Power and Geopolitical Imagination (Washington, Center on Global Interests, May 2015).

'The Three Colors of Novorossiya, or the Russian Nationalist Mythmaking of the Ukrainian Crisis', *Post-Soviet Affairs*, Vol. 32, No. 1, 2015, pp. 55–74.

Laughland, John, *The Tainted Source: The Undemocratic Origins of the European Idea* (London, Sphere, 1998).

Lavenex, Sandra, 'EU External Governance in "Wider Europe"', *Journal of European Public Policy*, Vol. 11, No. 4, 2004, pp. 680–700.

Lavenex, Sandra and Frank Schimmelfennig, 'EU Rules beyond EU Borders: Theorizing External Governance in European Politics', *Journal of European Public Policy*, Vol. 16, No. 6, 2009, pp. 791–812.

Lebow, Richard Ned and Janice Gross Stein, *We All Lost the Cold War* (Princeton, Princeton University Press, 1995).

Ledeneva, Alena V., *Can Russia Modernise? Sistema, Power Networks and Informal Governance* (Cambridge, Cambridge University Press, 2013).

Lee, Rensselaer and Artyom Lukin, *Russia's Far East: New Dynamics in Asia Pacific and Beyond* (Boulder, Lynne Rienner, 2016).

Legvold, Robert, *Return to Cold War* (Cambridge, Polity, 2016).

Leichtova, Magda, *Misunderstanding Russia: Russian Foreign Policy and the West* (Farnham, Ashgate, 2014).

Lieber, Robert J., *Retreat and Its Consequences: American Foreign Policy and the Problem of World Order* (Cambridge, Cambridge University Press, 2016).

Lieber, Keir A. and Daryl G. Press, 'The Rise of U.S. Nuclear Primacy', *Foreign Affairs*, Vol. 85, No. 2, March–April 2006, pp. 42–54.

Light, Margot, *The Soviet Theory of International Politics* (Brighton, Wheatsheaf, 1987).

Linklater, Andrew, *Transformation of Political Community: Ethical Foundations of the Post-Westphalian Era* (Cambridge, Polity, 1998).

Linklater, Andrew and Hidemi Suganami, *The English School of International Relations: A Contemporary Reassessment* (New York, Cambridge University Press, 2006).

Lo, Bobo, *Axis of Convenience: Moscow, Beijing and the New Geopolitics* (London, Blackwell for RIIA; Washington, Brookings Institution Press, 2008).

Russia and the New World Disorder (Washington, Brookings, 2015).

The Illusion of Convergence: Russia, China, and the BRICS, Paris, IFRI, Russie. Nei.Visions No. 92, March 2016.

Lomanov, Alexander, 'Kitai: rastushchee ponimanie global'noi roli i otvetstvennosti', in V. V. Mikheev and V. G. Shvydko (eds.), *Transtikhookeanskaya bezopasnost': ierarkhiya sily i otvetstvennosti* (Moscow, IMEMO RAN, 2016), pp. 48–81.

Lucas, Edward, *The New Cold War: How the Kremlin Menaces both Russia and the West* (London, Bloomsbury, 2008).

Deception: Spies, Lies and How Russia Dupes the West (London, Bloomsbury, 2013).

Lucas, Edward and Peter Pomeranzev, *Winning the Information War: Techniques and Counter-Strategies to Russia Propaganda in Central and Eastern Europe*, a report by CEPA's Information Warfare Project in partnership with the Legatum Institute (Washington, Centre for European Policy Analysis, 2016).

Mackinder, Halford J., 'The Geographical Pivot of History', *The Geographical Journal*, Vol. 170, No. 4, 1904, pp. 421–44.

Maier, Charles S., *Among Empires: American Ascendancy and Its Predecessors* (Cambridge, Harvard University Press, 2006).

Mälksoo, Lauri, *Russian Approaches to International Law* (Oxford, Oxford University Press, 2015).

Mann, Michael, *Incoherent Empire* (London, Verso, 2005).

Mansfield, E. D. and Jack Snyder, *Electing to Fight: Why Emerging Democracies go to War* (Cambridge, Cambridge University Press, 2005).

Maresceau, Marc, 'EU Enlargement and EU Common Strategies on Russia and Ukraine: An Ambiguous Yet Unavoidable Connection', in Christophe Hillion (ed.), *EU Enlargement: A Legal Approach* (Oxford and Portland, Hart Publishing, 2004), pp. 181–219.

Markus, Stanislav, *Property, Predation, and Protection: Piranha Capitalism in Russia and Ukraine* (Cambridge, Cambridge University Press, 2015).

Marquand, David, *The End of the West: The Once and Future Europe* (Princeton, Princeton University Press, 2011).

Marsh, Christopher and Nikolas K. Gvosdev, *Russian Foreign Policy: Interests, Vectors and Sectors* (New York, CQ Press, 2013).

Matlock, Jack F., *Autopsy on an Empire: The American Ambassador's Account of the Collapse of the Soviet Union* (New York, Random House, 1995).

Reagan and Gorbachev: How the Cold War Ended (New York, Random House, 2004).

Super-Power Illusions: How Myths and False Ideologies Led America Astray – and How to Return to Reality (New Haven and London, Yale University Press, 2010).

Mazarr, Michael J., 'The Once and Future Order: What Comes after Hegemony?', *Foreign Affairs*, Vol. 96, No. 1, January–February 2017, pp. 25–32.

Mazower, Mark, *Dark Continent* (London, Vintage, 2000).

MccGwire, Michael, 'NATO Expansion: "A Policy Error of Historic Importance"', *Review of International Studies*, Vol. 24, No. 1, 1998, pp. 23–42; reprinted in *International Affairs*, Vol. 84, No. 6, November 2008, pp. 1282–301.

Mead, Walter Russell, 'The Return of Geopolitics: The Revenge of the Revisionist Powers', *Foreign Affairs*, Vol. 93, No. 3, May–June 2014, pp. 69–79.

'Washington and Brussels: Rethinking Relations with Moscow?', in Aldo Ferrari (ed.), *Putin's Russia: Really Back?* (Milan, Ledi Publishing for ISPI, 2016), pp. 37–54.

Mearsheimer, John, 'The False Promise of International Institutions', *International Security*, Vol. 19, No. 3, 1994/5, pp. 5–49.

The Tragedy of Great Power Politics, updated edn (New York, W. W. Norton, 2014[2001]).

'Why the Ukraine Crisis is the West's Fault: The Liberal Delusions that Provoked Putin', *Foreign Affairs*, Vol. 93, No. 5, September–October 2014, pp. 77–89.

Mearsheimer, John J. and Stephen M. Walt, 'The Case for Offshore Balancing', *Foreign Affairs*, Vol. 95, Vol. 4, July–August 2016, pp. 70–83.

Minxin Pei, *China's Crony Capitalism: The Dynamics of Regime Decay* (Cambridge, Harvard University Press, 2016).

Monaghan, Andrew, *A 'New Cold War'? Abusing History, Misunderstanding Russia* (London, Chatham House Research Paper, May 2015).

Morgenthau, Hans J., *Politics among Nations: The Struggle for Power and Peace*, 7th edn (New York, McGraw-Hill, 2005).

Morozov, Viatcheslav, 'Subaltern Empire? Towards a Postcolonial Approach to Russian Foreign Policy', *Problems of Post-Communism*, Vol. 60, No. 6, November–December 2013, pp. 16–28.

Russia's Postcolonial Identity: A Subaltern Empire in a Eurocentric World (London, Palgrave Macmillan, 2015).

Mosse, George L., *The Fascist Revolution: Towards a General Theory of Fascism* (New York, Howard Fertig, 2000).

Müllerson, Rein, *Regime Change: From Democratic Peace Theories to Forcible Regime Change* (Leiden, Martinus Nijhoff, 2013).

Myers, Steven Lee, *The New Tsar: The Rise and Reign of Vladimir Putin* (London, Simon and Schuster, 2015).

Neumann, Iver B., 'Russia as a Great Power, 1815–2007', *Journal of International Relations and Development*, Vol. 11, 2008, pp. 128–51.

'Entry into International Society Reconceptualised: The Case of Russia', *Review of International Studies*, Vol. 37, No. 2, 2011, pp. 463–84.

Russia and the Idea of Europe: A Study in Identity and International Relations (London, Routledge, 2016).

Niblett, Robin, 'Liberalism in Retreat: The Demise of a Dream', *Foreign Affairs*, Vol. 96, No. 1, January–February 2017, pp. 17–24.

Nye, Joseph S., *Bound to Lead: The Changing Nature of American Power* (New York, Basic Books, 1991).

Is the American Century Over? (Cambridge, Polity, 2015).

Oliker, Olga, 'Putinism, Populism and the Defence of Liberal Democracy', *Survival*, Vol. 59, No. 1, 2017, pp. 7–24.

Østbø, Jardar, *The New Third Rome: Readings of a Russian Nationalist Myth* (Stuttgart, Ibidem-Verlag, 2016).

Pace, Michelle, 'The Construction of EU Normative Power', *Journal of Common Market Studies*, Vol. 45, No. 5, 2007, pp. 1041–64.

Panarin, Alexander, *Revansh istorii: Rossiiskaya strategicheskaya initsiava v XXI veke* (Moscow, 1998). An English version was published as *The Revenge of History: Russian Strategic Initiative in the Twenty-first Century* (Moscow, Logos, 1998).

Pänke, Julian, 'The Fallout of the EU's Normative Imperialism in the Eastern Neighbourhood', *Problems of Post-Communism*, Vol. 62, 2015, pp. 350–63.

Parker, David, *Cold War Ideational Legacies and Contemporary US Foreign Policy towards Russia*, submitted for PhD, King's College London, November 2015.

Perry, William, *My Journey at the Nuclear Brink* (Stanford, Stanford Security Studies, 2015).

Pipes, Richard, *Alexander Yakovlev: The Man who Saved Russia from Communism* (DeKalb, Northern Illinois University Press, 2015).

Pivovarov, Yurii S., 'Mezhdu kazachestvom i knutom: K stoletiyu russkoi konstitutsii i russkogo parlamenta', *Polis*, No. 2, 2006, pp. 5–26.

Russkaya politika v ee istoricheskom i kul'turnom otnosheniyakh (Moscow, Rosspen, 2006).

'Russkaya vlast' i publichnaya politika: Zametki istorika o prichinakh neudachi demokraticheskogo tranzita', *Polis*, No. 1, 2006, pp. 12–32.

Pivovarov, Yurii S. and A. I. Fursov, 'Russkaya sistema i reformy', *Pro et Contra*, Vol. 4, No. 4, Autumn 1999, pp. 176–97.

Plokhy, Serhii, *The Last Empire: The Final Days of the Soviet Union* (New York, Oneworld Publications, 2014).

Popov, Vladimir and Piotr Dutkiewicz (eds.), *Mapping a New World Order: The Rest beyond the West* (Cheltenham, Edward Elgar, 2017).

Pouliot, Vincent, *International Security in Practice: The Politics of NATO-Russia Diplomacy* (Cambridge, Cambridge University Press, 2010).

Primakov, E. M., *Mysli vslukh* (Moscow, Rossiiskaya gazeta, 2011).

Vyzovy i alternativy mnogopolyarnogo mira: role Rossii (Moscow, MGU, 2014).

Mir bez Rossii: k chemu privedet politicheskaya utopiya (Moscow, Tsentrpoligraf, 2016).

Vstrechi na perekrestakh (Moscow, Tsentrpoligraf, 2016).

Prozorov, Sergei, *Understanding Conflict between Russia and the EU: The Limits of Integration*, paperback edn (Basingstoke, Palgrave Macmillan, 2016).

Putin, Vladimir, *First Person: An Astonishingly Frank Self-portrait by Russia's President Vladimir Putin*, with Nataliya Gevorkyan, Natalya Timakova, and Andrei Kolesnikov, translated by Catherine A. Fitzpatrick (London, Hutchinson, 2000).

Rangsimaporn, Paradorn, *Russia as an Aspiring Great Power in East Asia: Perceptions and Policies from Yeltsin to Putin* (Basingstoke, Palgrave Macmillan, 2009).

Reddaway, Peter and Dmitri Glinski, *The Tragedy of Russia's Reforms: Market Bolshevism against Democracy* (Washington, The United States Institute of Peace Press, 2001).

Remington, Thomas F., 'Putin, Parliament, and Presidential Exploitation of the Terrorist Threat', *The Journal of Legislative Studies*, Vol. 15, Nos. 2-3, 2009, pp. 219–38.

Renz, Bettina and Hanna Smith, *Russia and Hybrid Warfare: Going beyond the Label*, Helsinki, Aleksanteri Papers No. 1, 2016.

Russia's Military Revival (Cambridge, Polity, 2017).

Rhodes, Richard, *Arsenals of Folly: The Making of the Nuclear Arms Race* (London, Simon and Schuster, 2009).

Roberts, Paul Craig, *The Neoconservative Threat to World Order: Washington's Perilous War for Hegemony* (Atlanta, Clarity Press, 2015).

Robinson, Neil, *Ideology and the Collapse of the Soviet System: A Critical History of the Soviet Ideological Discourse* (Aldershot, Edward Elgar, 1995).

Rodt, Annemarie Peen and Stefan Wolff (eds.), *Self-Determination after Kosovo* (London, Routledge, 2015).

Romanova, Tatiana, 'Sanctions and the Future of EU-Russian Economic Relations', *Europe-Asia Studies*, Vol. 68, No. 4, June 2016, pp. 774–96.

'Is Russian Energy Policy towards the EU Only About Geopolitics? The Case of the Third Liberalisation Package', *Geopolitics*, Vol. 21, No. 4, October–December 2016, 2016, pp. 857–79.

Rosato, Sebastian, 'The Flawed Logic of Democratic Peace Theory', *American Political Science Review*, Vol. 97, No. 4, November 2003, pp. 585–602.

Rosenberg, Justin, 'Globalization Theory: A Post-Mortem', *International Politics*, Vol. 42, No. 1, March 2005, pp. 2–74.

The Follies of Globalisation Theory: Polemical Essays (London, Verso Books, 2001).

Rossbach, Stefan, *Gnostic Wars: The Cold War in the Context of a History of Western Spirituality* (Edinburgh, Edinburgh University Press, 1999).

Roxburgh, Angus, *The Strongman: Vladimir Putin and the Struggle for Russia* (London, I. B. Tauris, 2011).

Rozman, Gilbert, *The Sino-Russian Challenge to the World Order* (Stanford, Stanford University Press, 2014).

Rubenstein, Joshua, *The Last Days of Stalin* (London and New Haven, Yale University Press, 2016).

Rutzen, Douglas 'Civil Society under Assault', *Journal of Democracy*, Vol. 26, No. 4, 2015, pp. 28–39.

Sakwa, Richard, 'The Regime System in Russia', *Contemporary Politics*, Vol. 3, No. 1, 1997, pp. 7–25.

'Konets epokhi revolyutsii: antirevolyutsionnye revolyutsii 1989–1991 godov' ('The End of the Age of Revolutions: The Anti-revolutions of 1989–1991'), *Politicheskie Issledovaniya – Polis* (Moscow, in Russian), No. 5, 1998, pp. 23–38.

'The Age of Paradox: The Anti-revolutionary Revolutions of 1989–91', in Moira Donald and Tim Rees (eds.), *Reinterpreting Revolution in Twentieth-century Europe* (London, Macmillan, 2001), pp. 159–76.

'"New Cold War" or Twenty Years' Crisis?: Russia and International Politics', *International Affairs*, Vol. 84, No. 2, March 2008, pp. 241–67.

Putin: Russia's Choice, fully revised and updated 2nd edn (London and New York, Routledge, 2008).

'The Dual State in Russia', *Post-Soviet Affairs*, Vol. 26, No. 3, July–September 2010, pp. 185–206.

The Crisis of Russian Democracy: The Dual State, Factionalism and the Medvedev Succession (Cambridge, Cambridge University Press, 2011).

'Russia and Europe: Whose Society?', special issue, Ioannis Stivachtis and Mark Webber (eds.), 'Europe After Enlargement', *The Journal of European Integration*, Vol. 33, No. 2, March 2011, pp. 197–214.

'Conspiracy Narratives as a Mode of Engagement in International Politics: The Case of the 2008 Russo-Georgian War', *Russian Review*, Vol. 71, October 2012, pp. 2–30.

'The Cold Peace: Russo-Western Relations as a Mimetic Cold War', *Cambridge Review of International Affairs*, Vol. 26, No. 1, 2013, pp. 203–24.

Putin and the Oligarch: The Khodorkovsky–Yukos Affair (London, I. B. Tauris; New York, Palgrave Macmillan, 2014).

Putin Redux: Power and Contradiction in Contemporary Russia (London and New York, Routledge, 2014).

'Dualism at Home and Abroad: Russian Foreign Policy Neo-Revisionism and Bicontinentalism', in David Cadier and Margot Light (eds.), *Russia's Foreign Policy* (London, Palgrave Macmillan, 2015), pp. 65–79.

'The Death of Europe? Continental Fates after Ukraine', *International Affairs*, Vol. 91, No. 3, May 2015, pp. 553–79.

The New Atlanticism, Valdai Paper No. 17 (Moscow, Valdai Club, May 2015), www.scribd.com/doc/266515275/The-New-Atlanticism, last accessed 30 May 2017, reprinted as 'The New Atlanticism', *Russia in Global Affairs*, special issue, July–September 2015, pp. 99–109, http://eng.globalaffairs.ru/number/The-New-Atlanticism-17695, last accessed 30 May 2017.

Frontline Ukraine: Crisis in the Borderlands, paperback edn with a new Afterword (London and New York, I. B. Tauris, 2016).

'The Rise of Leninism: The Death of Political Pluralism in the Post-revolutionary Bolshevik Party', in Tony Brenton (ed.), *Historically Inevitable?*

Turning Points of the Russian Revolution (London, Profile Books, 2016), pp. 262–83.

Sarotte, Mary Elise, *1989: The Struggle to Create Post-Cold War Europe* (Princeton, Princeton University Press, 2009).

'Perpetuating US Pre-eminence: The 1990 deals to "Bribe the Soviets Out" and Move NATO In', *International Security*, Vol. 35, No. 1, 2010, pp. 110–37.

'A Broken Promise? What the West Really Told Moscow About NATO Expansion', *Foreign Affairs*, Vol. 93, No. 5, September–October 2014, pp. 90–7.

Sauer, Sten, 'The False Promise of Continental Concert: Russia, the West and the Necessary Balance of Power', *International Affairs*, Vol. 91, No. 3, 2015, pp. 539–52.

Sauer, Tom, 'The Origins of the Ukraine Crisis and the Need for Collective Security between Russia and the West', *Global Policy*, published online, October 2016, http://onlinelibrary.wiley.com/doi/10.1111/1758-5899.12374/full, last accessed 9 June 2017.

Schoen, Douglas E. with Evan Roth Smith, *Putin's Master Plan: To Destroy Europe, Divide NATO, and Restore Russian Power and Global Influence* (New York, Encounter, 2016).

Sergunin, Alexander, *Explaining Russian Foreign Policy Behavior: Theory and Practice* (Stuttgart, Ibidem-Verlag, 2016).

Service, Robert, *The End of the Cold War* (London, Pan, 2016).

Sherr, James, *Hard Diplomacy and Soft Coercion: Russia's Influence Abroad* (London, Royal Institute of International Affairs, 2013).

Shifrinson, Joshua R., 'The Malta Summit and US-Soviet Relations: Testing the Waters Amidst Stormy Seas. New Insights from American Archives', www.wilsoncenter.org/publication/the-malta-summit-and-us-soviet-relations-testing-the-waters-amidst-stormy-seas, last accessed 30 May 2017.

'Put it in Writing: How the West Broke its Promise to Moscow', *Foreign Affairs*, 29 October 2014, www.foreignaffairs.com/articles/142310/joshua-r-itzkowitz-shifrinson/put-it-in-writing, last accessed 30 May 2017.

'Deal or No Deal? The End of the Cold War and US Offer to Limit NATO Expansion', *International Security*, Vol. 40, No. 4, 2016, pp. 7–44.

Shirreff, Richard, *2017 War with Russia: An Urgent Warning from Senior Military Command* (London, Coronet, 2016).

Siddi, Marco, 'German Foreign Policy towards Russia in the Aftermath of the Ukraine Crisis: A New *Ostpolitik*?', *Europe-Asia Studies*, Vol. 68, No. 4, June 2016, pp. 665–77.

'The EU's Energy Union: A Sustainable Path to Energy Security?', *The International Spectator*, Vol. 51, No. 1, 2016, pp. 131–44.

Silvius, Ray, *Culture, Political Economy and Civilisation in a Multipolar World Order* (London, Routledge, 2017).

Simón, Luis, 'Europe, the Rise of Asia and the Future of the Transatlantic Relationship', *International Affairs*, Vol. 91, No. 5, 2015, pp. 969–89.

Slaughter, Anne-Marie, *A New World Order* (Princeton, Princeton University Press, 2005).

Slobodchikoff, Michael O., *Building Hegemonic Order Russia's Way: Order, Stability, and Predictability in the Post-Soviet Space* (Lanham, Lexington Books, 2014).

Smith, Martin A., 'Russia and Multipolarity since the End of the Cold War', *East European Politics*, Vol. 29, No. 1, 2013, pp. 36–51.

Snetkov, Aglaya, *Russia's Security Policy under Putin: A Critical Perspective* (London, Routledge, 2015).

Snyder, Jack with Edward D. Mansfield, 'Turbulent Transitions: Why Emerging Democracies go to War', in Jack Snyder, *Power and Progress: International Politics in Transition* (London, Routledge, 2012), pp. 125–43.

Soldatov, Andrei with Irina Borogan, *Red Web: The Struggle between Russia's Digital Dictators and New Online Revolutionaries* (New York, Public Affairs, 2015).

Sperling, James and Mark Webber, 'NATO and the Ukraine Crisis: Collective Securitisation', *European Journal of International Security*, Vol. 2, No. 1, 2016, pp. 19–46.

Spykman, Nicholas J., *The Geography of the Peace* (New York, Harcourt and Brace, 1942).

Stahl, Bernhard, Robin Lucke and Anne Felfeli, 'Comeback of the Transatlantic Security Community? Comparative Securitisation in the Crimea Crisis', *East European Politics*, Vol. 32, No. 4, 2016, pp. 525–46.

Steinmeier, Frank-Walter, 'Germany's New Global Role: Berlin Steps Up', *Foreign Affairs*, Vol. 95, No. 4, July–August 2016, pp. 106–13.

Stent, Angela E., *The Limits of Partnership: US–Russian Relations in the Twenty-first Century* (Princeton, Princeton University Press, 2014).

Stoner, Kathryn and Michael McFaul, 'Who Lost Russia (This Time)? Vladimir Putin', *The Washington Quarterly*, Vol. 38, No. 2, Summer 2015, pp. 167–87.

Strange, Susan, *The Retreat of the State: The Diffusion of Power in the World Economy* (Cambridge, Cambridge University Press, 1996).

Stuenkel, Oliver, *The BRICS and the Future of Global Order* (London and Lanham, Lexington Books, 2015).

Post-Western World: How Emerging Powers are Remaking Global Order (Cambridge, Polity, 2016).

Sultanov, Bulat, 'Kazakhstan and Eurasian Integration', in Piotr Dutkiewicz and Richard Sakwa (eds.), *Eurasian Integration: The View from Within* (London and New York, Routledge, 2015), pp. 97–110.

Suisheng Zhao, 'China as a Rising Power Versus the US-led World Order', *Rising Powers Quarterly*, Vol. 1, No. 1, 2016, pp. 13–21.

Suslov, Dmitry, *Without a 'Common Space': A New Agenda for Russia–EU Relations*, Moscow, Valdai Paper No. 49, June 2016, http://valdaiclub.com/a/valdai-papers/valdai-paper-49-without-a-common-space-a-new-agenda-for-russia-eu-relations/, last accessed 9 June 2017.

Talbott, Strobe, *The Russia Hand: A Memoir of Presidential Diplomacy* (New York, Random House, 2003).

Teper, Yuri, 'Official Russian Identity Discourse in Light of the Annexation of Crimea: National or Imperial?', *Post-Soviet Affairs*, Vol. 32, No. 4, 2015, pp. 378–96.

Thakur, Ramesh, *Governance for a World without World Government*, Valdai Paper No. 35, November 2015, http://valdaiclub.com/a/valdai-papers/governance-for-a-world-without-world-government/, last accessed 30 May 2017.

Thorun, Christian, *Explaining Change in Russian Foreign Policy: The Role of Ideas in Post-Soviet Russia's Conduct towards the West* (Basingstoke, Palgrave Macmillan, 2009).

Toal, Gerard, *Near Abroad: Putin, the West and the Contest over Ukraine and the Caucasus* (Oxford, Oxford University Press, 2017).

Tolstrup, Jakob, *Russia vs. the EU: The Competition for Influence in Post-Soviet States* (Boulder, First Forum Press, 2014).

Trenin, Dmitri, *Should We Fear Russia?* (Cambridge, Polity, 2016).

Trenin, Dmitri, and Bobo Lo, *The Landscape of Russian Foreign Policy Decision-Making* (Moscow, Moscow Carnegie Centre, 2005).

Tsygankov, Andrei P., *Russia's Foreign Policy: Change and Continuity in National Identity*, 2nd edn (Lanham, Rowman and Littlefield, 2010).

Russia and the West from Alexander to Putin: Honor in International Relations (Cambridge, Cambridge University Press, 2012).

The Strong State in Russia: Development and Crisis (Oxford, Oxford University Press, 2014).

'Vladimir Putin's Last Stand: The Sources of Russia's Ukraine Policy', *Post-Soviet Affairs*, Vol. 31, No. 4, 2015, pp. 279–303.

'Crafting the State-Civilization', *Problems of Post-Communism*, Vol. 63, No. 3, 2016, pp. 146–58.

'The Dark Double: The American Media Perception of Russia as a Neo-Soviet Autocracy, 2008–2014', *Politics*, Vol. 37, No. 1, 2016, pp. 19–35.

Urban, Mark, *The Edge: Is the Military Dominance of the West Coming to an End?* (Boston, Little, Brown, 2015).

Van Herpen, Marcel H., *Putin's Wars: The Rise of Russia's New Imperialism* (Lanham, Rowman and Littlefield, 2014).

Vestergaard, Jakob and Robert H. Wade, 'Still in the Woods: Gridlock in the IMF and the World Bank Puts Multilateralism at Risk', *Global Policy*, Vol. 6, No. 1, February 2015, pp. 1–12.

Vorobyov, Vitaly, 'Interconnecting Strategies', *Russia in Global Affairs*, No. 4, October–December 2016, pp. 116–23.

Wallerstein, Immanuel, *World-System Analysis: An Introduction* (Durham, Duke University Press, 2004).

Waltz, Kenneth N., *Theory of International Politics* (New York, Random House, 1979).

'Structural Realism after the Cold War', *International Security*, Vol. 25, No. 1, Summer 2000, pp. 5–41.

Watson, Adam, *The Evolution of International Society: A Comparative International Analysis*, reissue with a new introduction by Barry Buzan and Richard Little (London, Routledge, 1992).

Weaver, Carol, *The Politics of the Black Sea Region: EU Neighbourhood, Conflict Zone or Future Security Community?* (Basingstoke, Ashgate, 2013).

Weiner, Tim, *Legacy of Ashes: The History of the Central Intelligence Agency* (New York, Doubleday, 2007).

Wendt, Alexander, *Social Theory of International Politics* (Cambridge, Cambridge University Press, 1999).

Westad, Odd Arne, *The Global Cold War: Third World Interventions and the Making of Our Times* (Cambridge, Cambridge University Press, 2005).

White, Stephen and Valentina Feklyunina, *Identities and Foreign Policies in Russia, Ukraine and Belarus: The Other Europes* (London, Palgrave Macmillan, 2014).

Wilson, Andrew, *Ukraine Crisis: What It Means for the West* (London and New Haven, Yale University Press, 2014).

Wohlforth, William, 'Realism and the End of the Cold War', *International Security*, Vol. 19, No. 3, 1994/5, pp. 91–129.

(ed.), *Cold War Endgame: Oral History, Analysis, Debates* (Philadelphia, University of Pennsylvania Press, 2003).

The Return of Realpolitik: Stability vs. Change in the US-Led World Order, Moscow, Valdai Discussion Club, Valdai Paper No. 11, February 2015.

Wood, Elizabeth A., William E. Pomeranz, E. Wayne Merry and Maxim Trudolyubov, *Roots of Russia's War in Ukraine* (Washington, Woodrow Wilson Center Press with Columbia University Press, 2015).

Zakaria, Fareed, *The Post-American World: The Rise of the Rest* (London, Penguin, 2011).

Zarakol, Ayşe, *After Defeat: How the East Learned to Live with the West* (Cambridge, Cambridge University Press, 2011).

Zhurchenko, Tatiana, *Borderlands into Bordered Lands: Geopolitics of Identity in Post-Soviet Ukraine* (Stuttgart, Ibidem-Verlag, 2010).

Zielonka, Jan, *Is the EU Doomed?* (Cambridge, Polity Press, 2014).

Zygar, Mikhail, *All the Kremlin's Men: Inside the Court of Vladimir Putin* (New York, Public Affairs, 2016).

Index